SI SI

SI

SI SI

SI

SI

SI

SI

SI

Niele Toroni

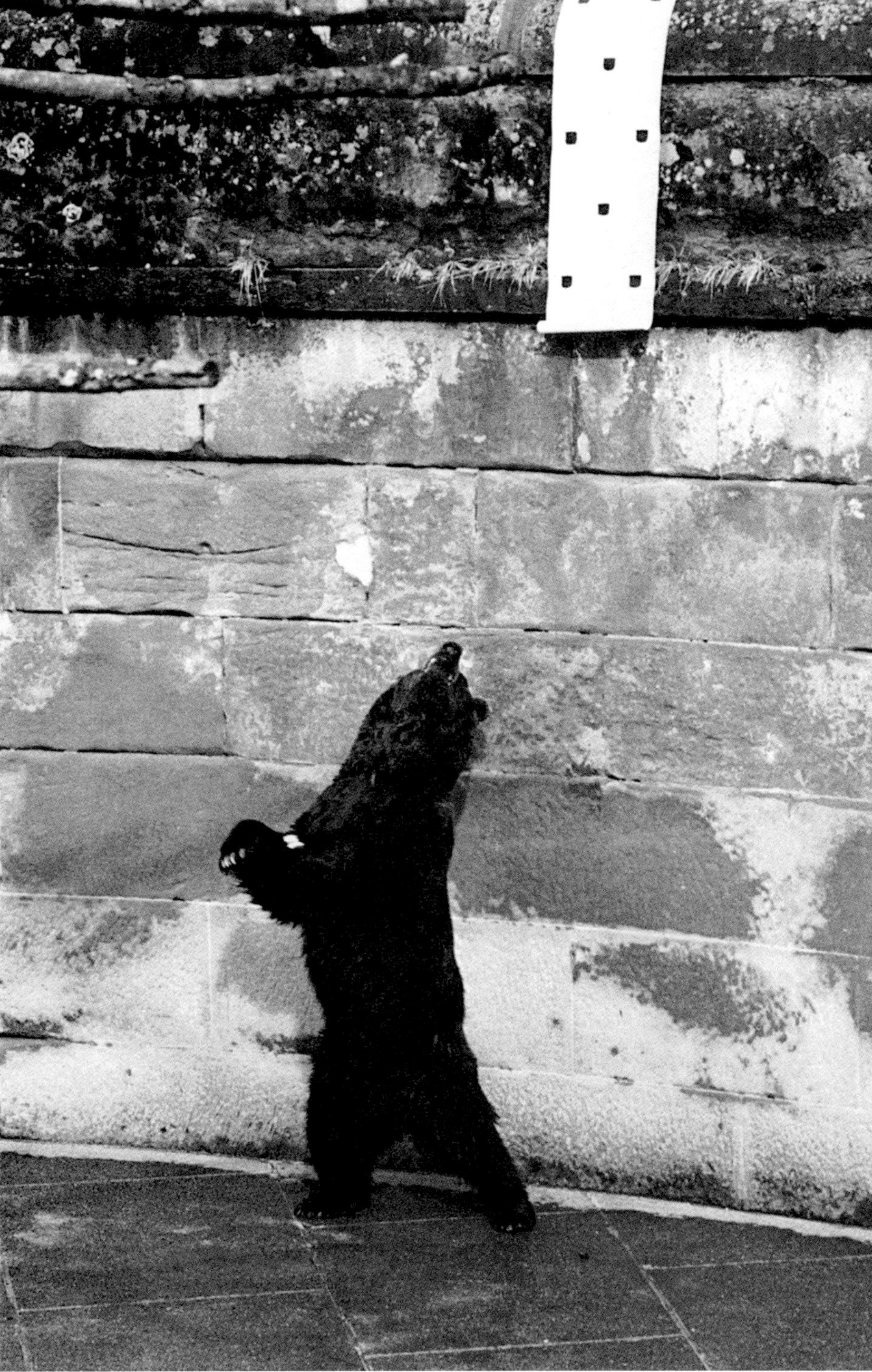

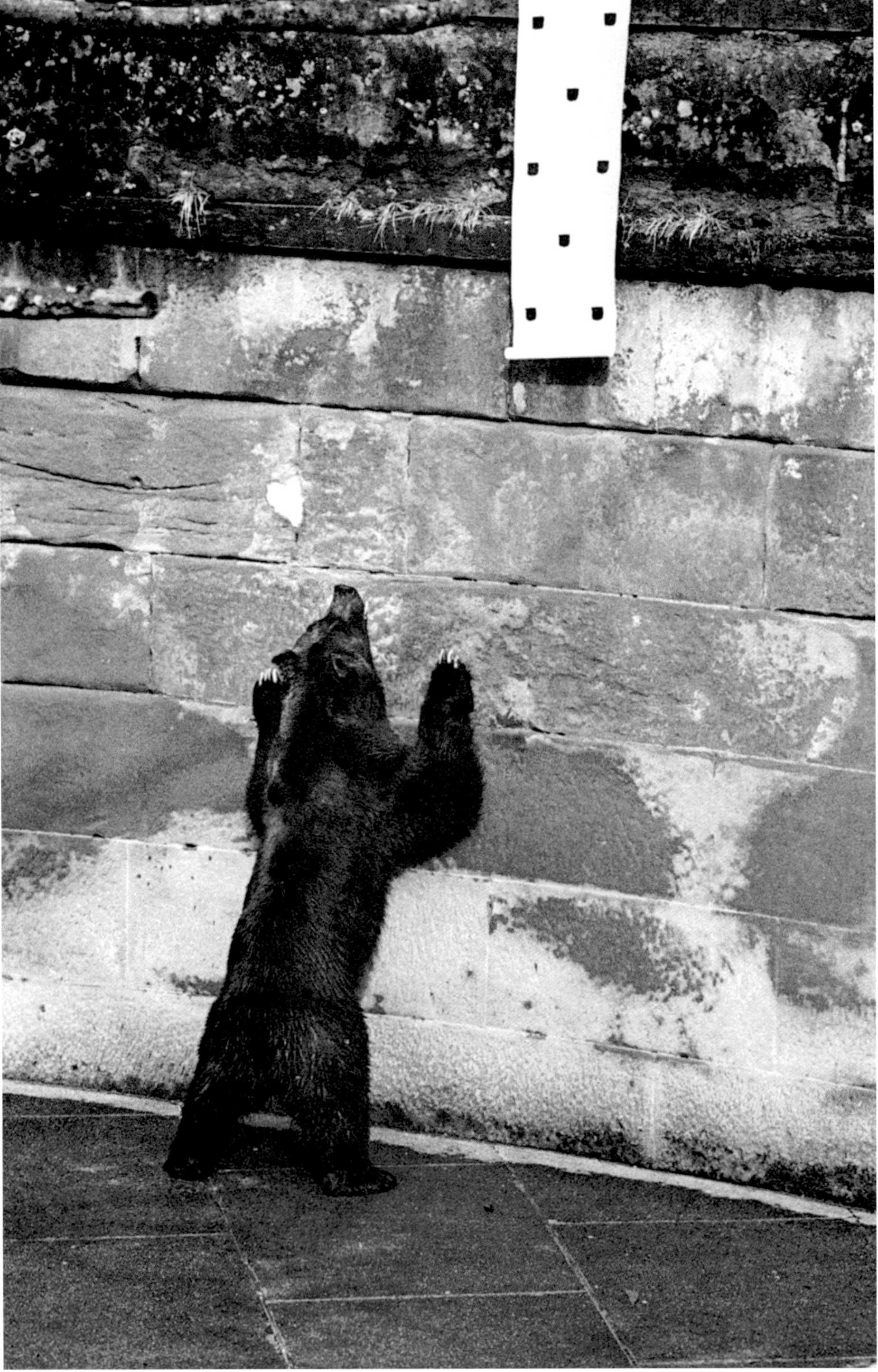

5 5

5

5 5

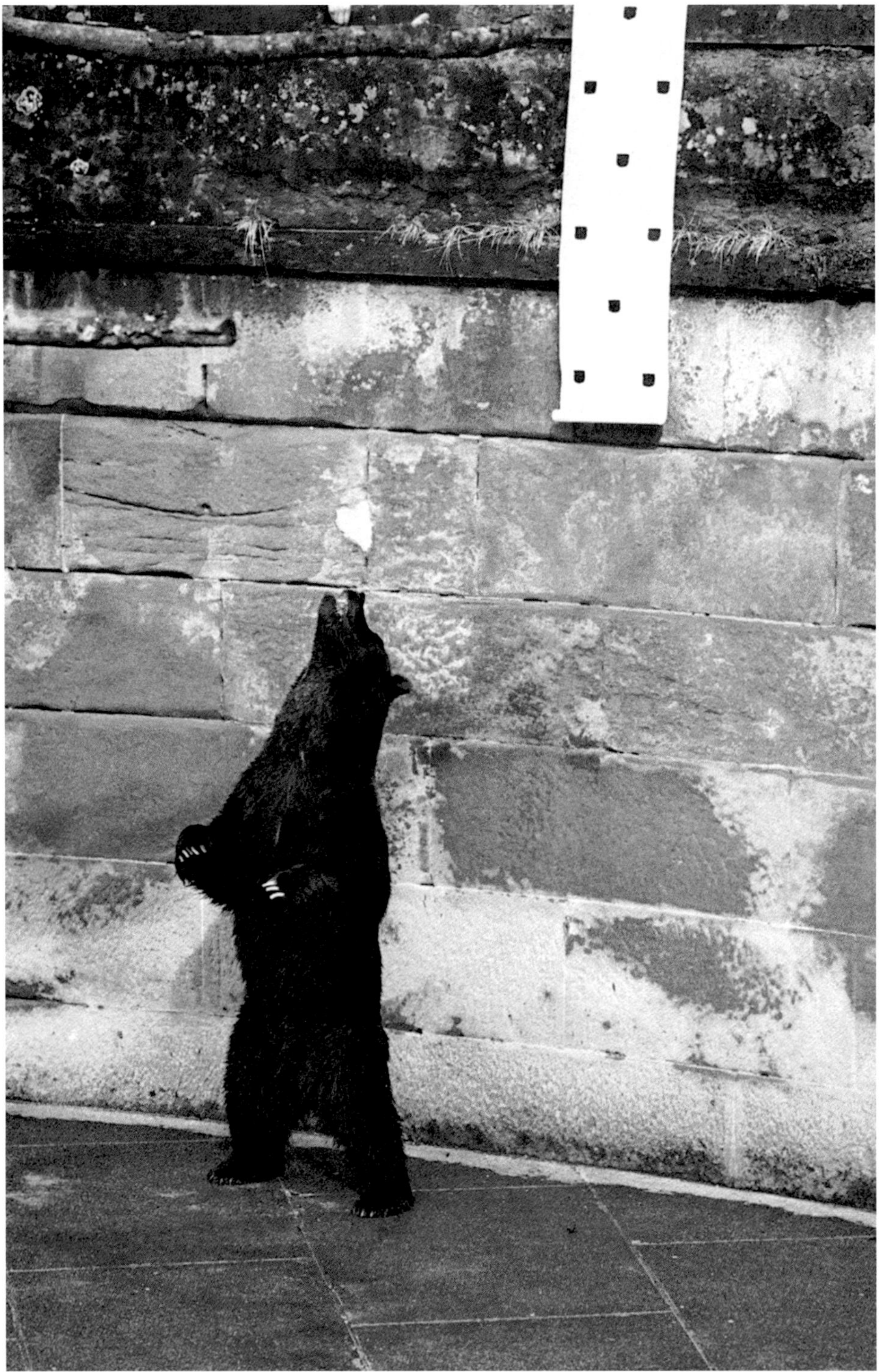

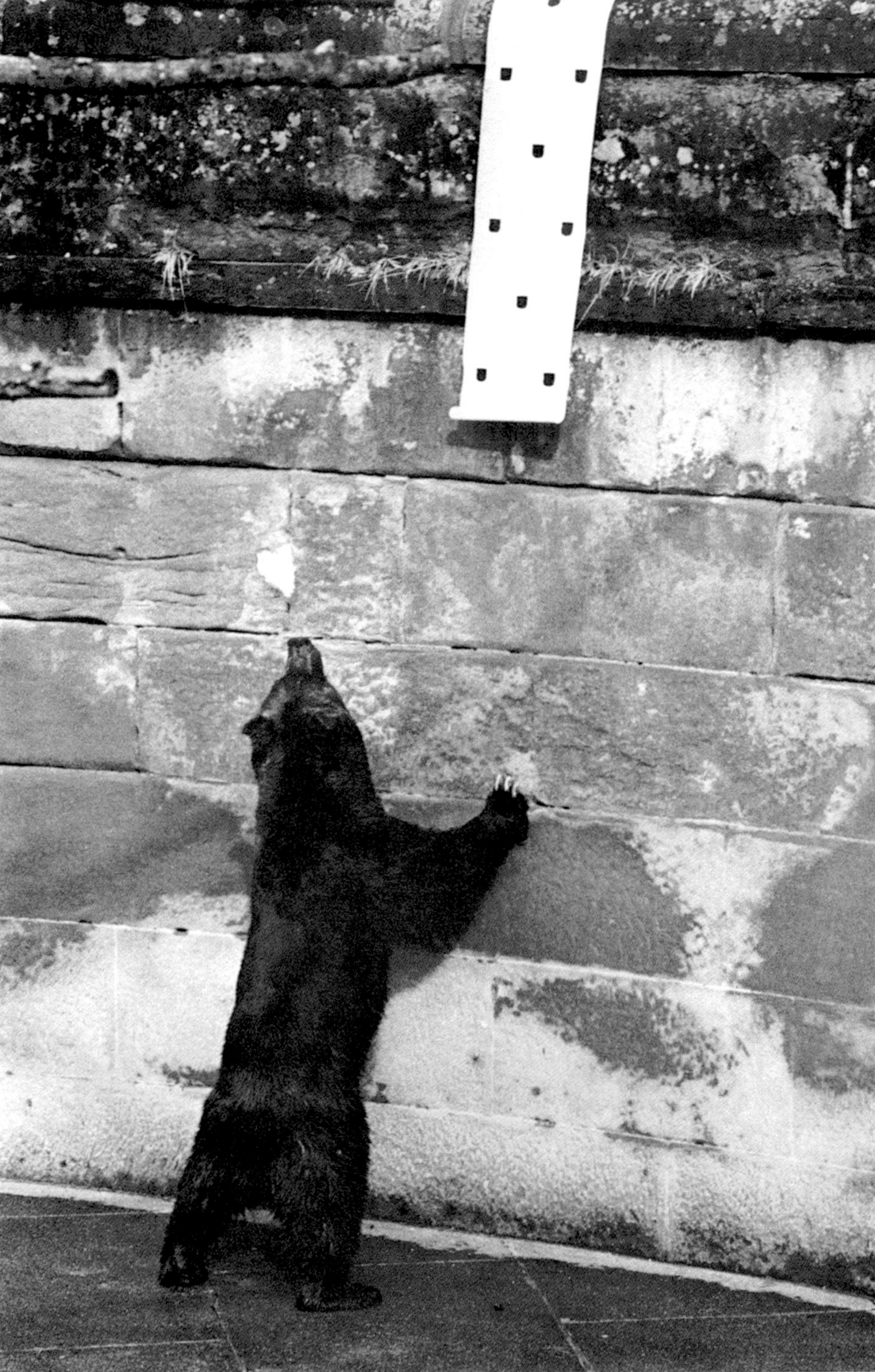

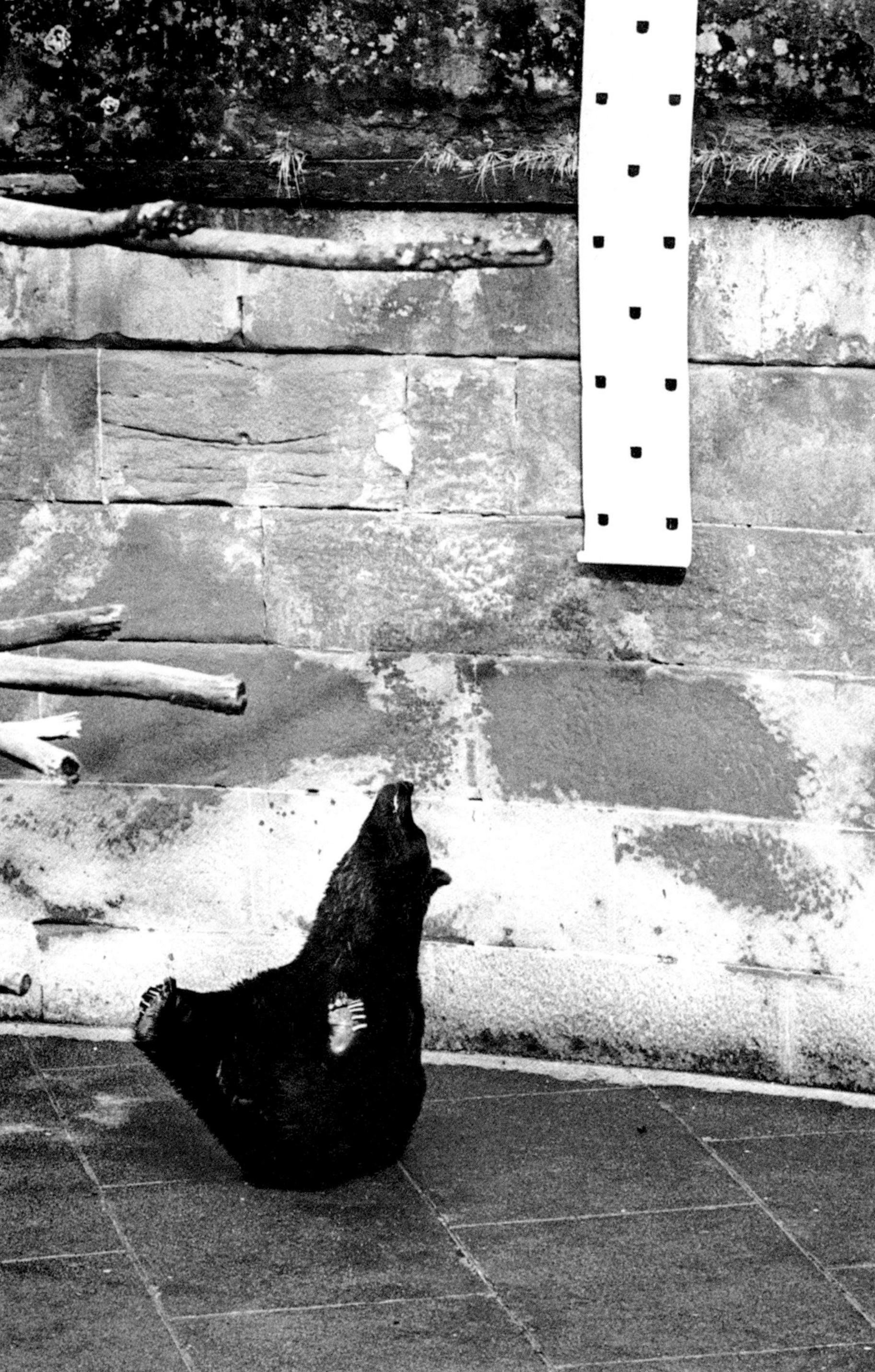

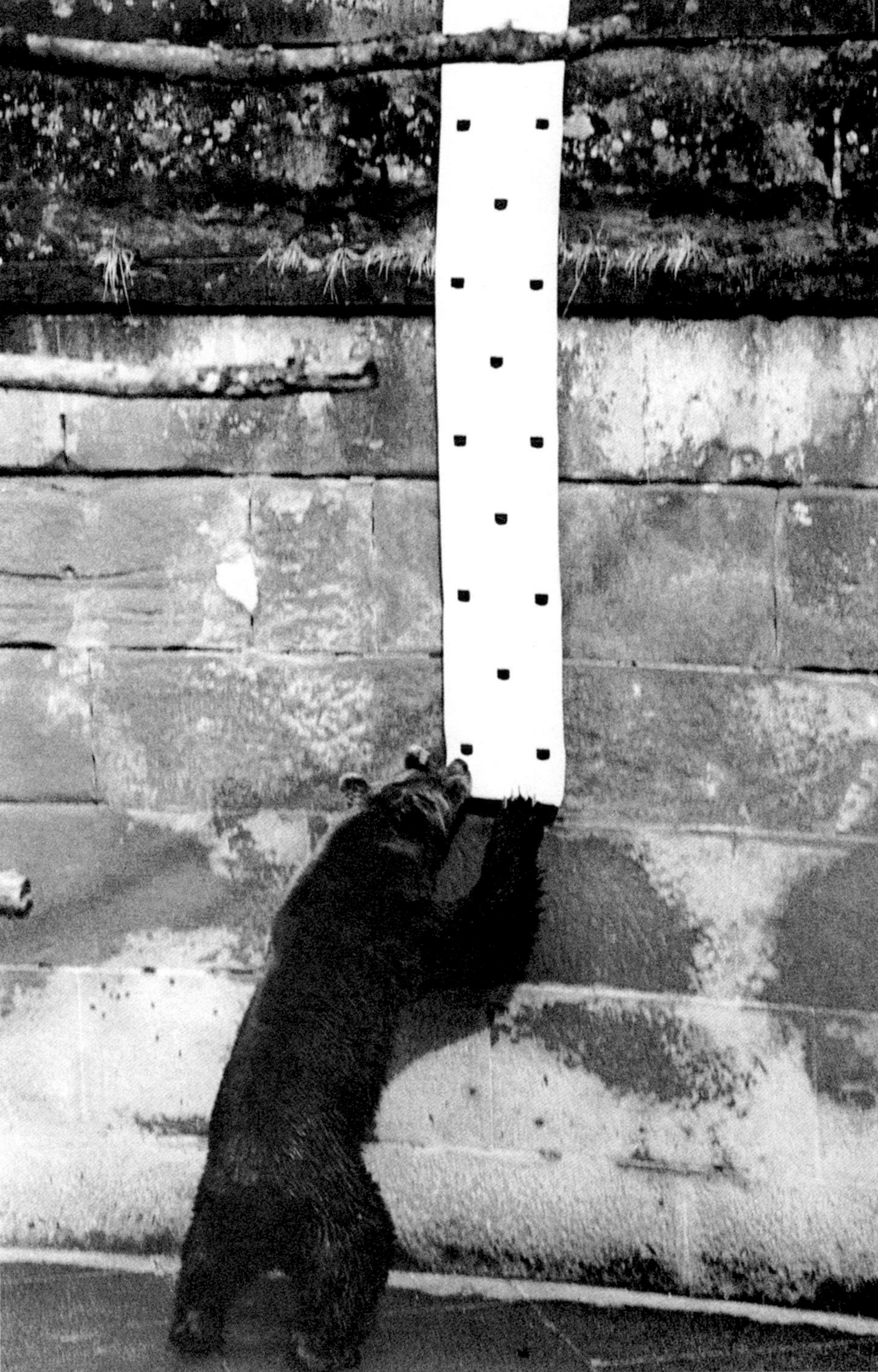

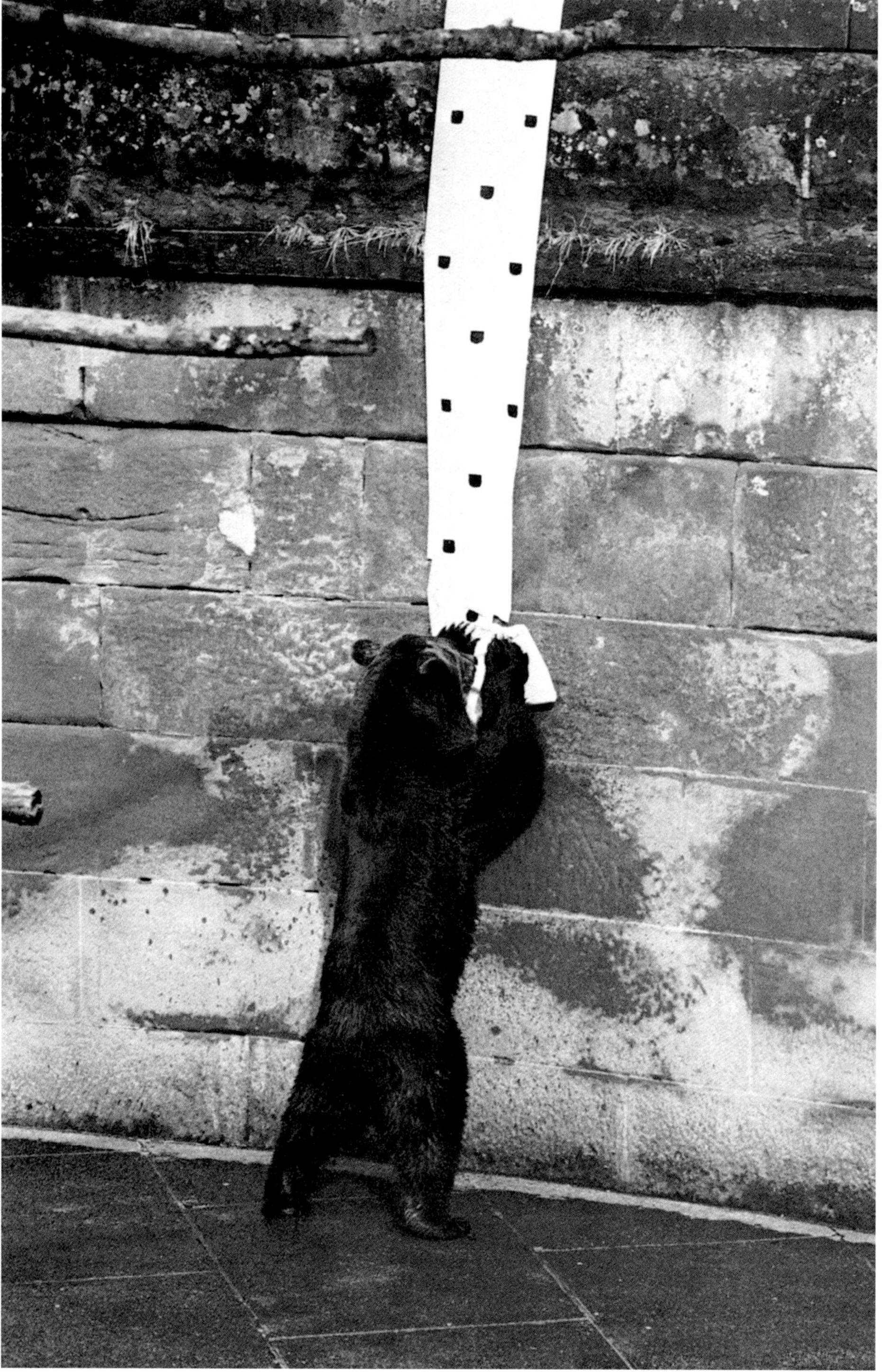

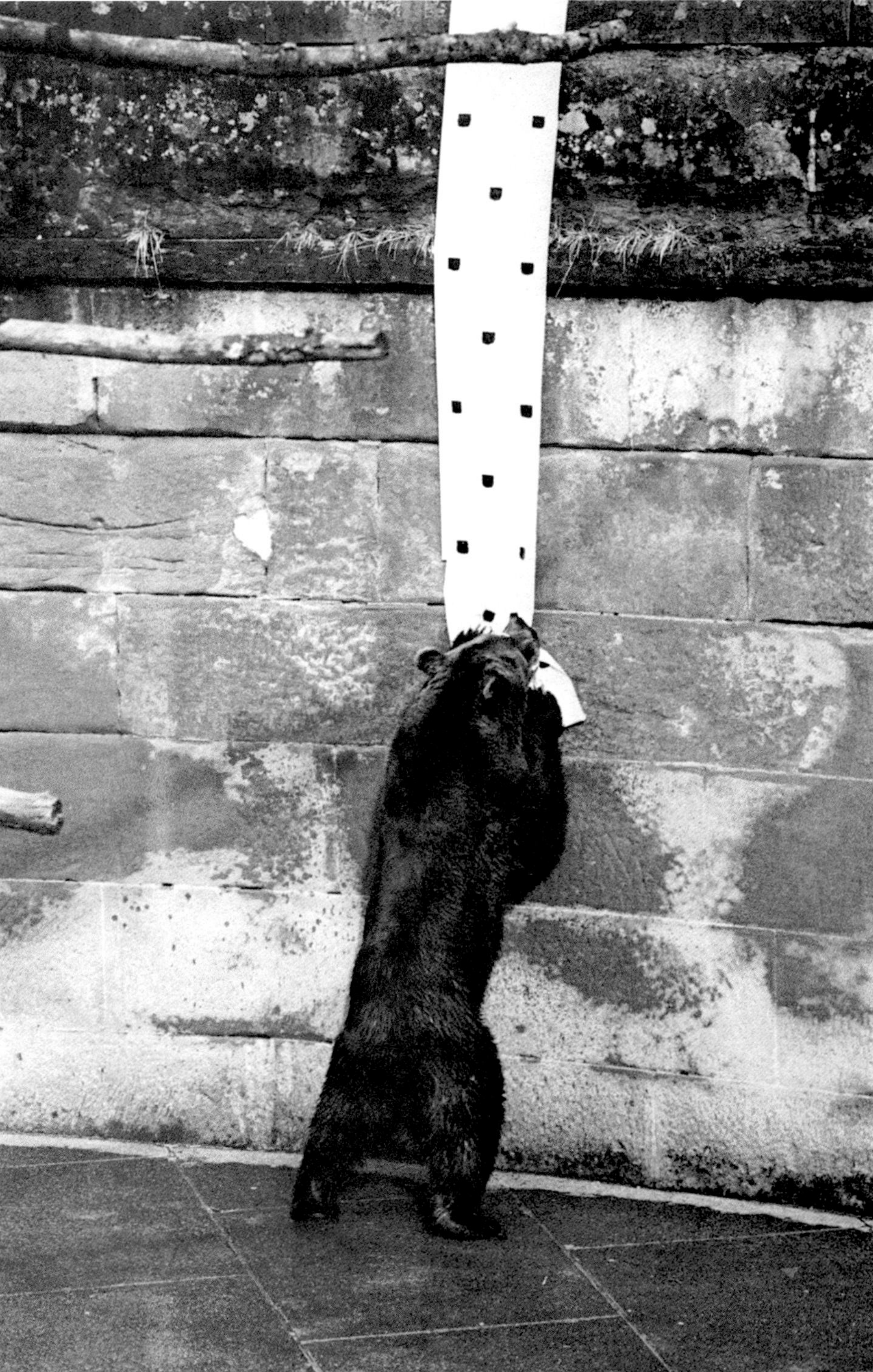

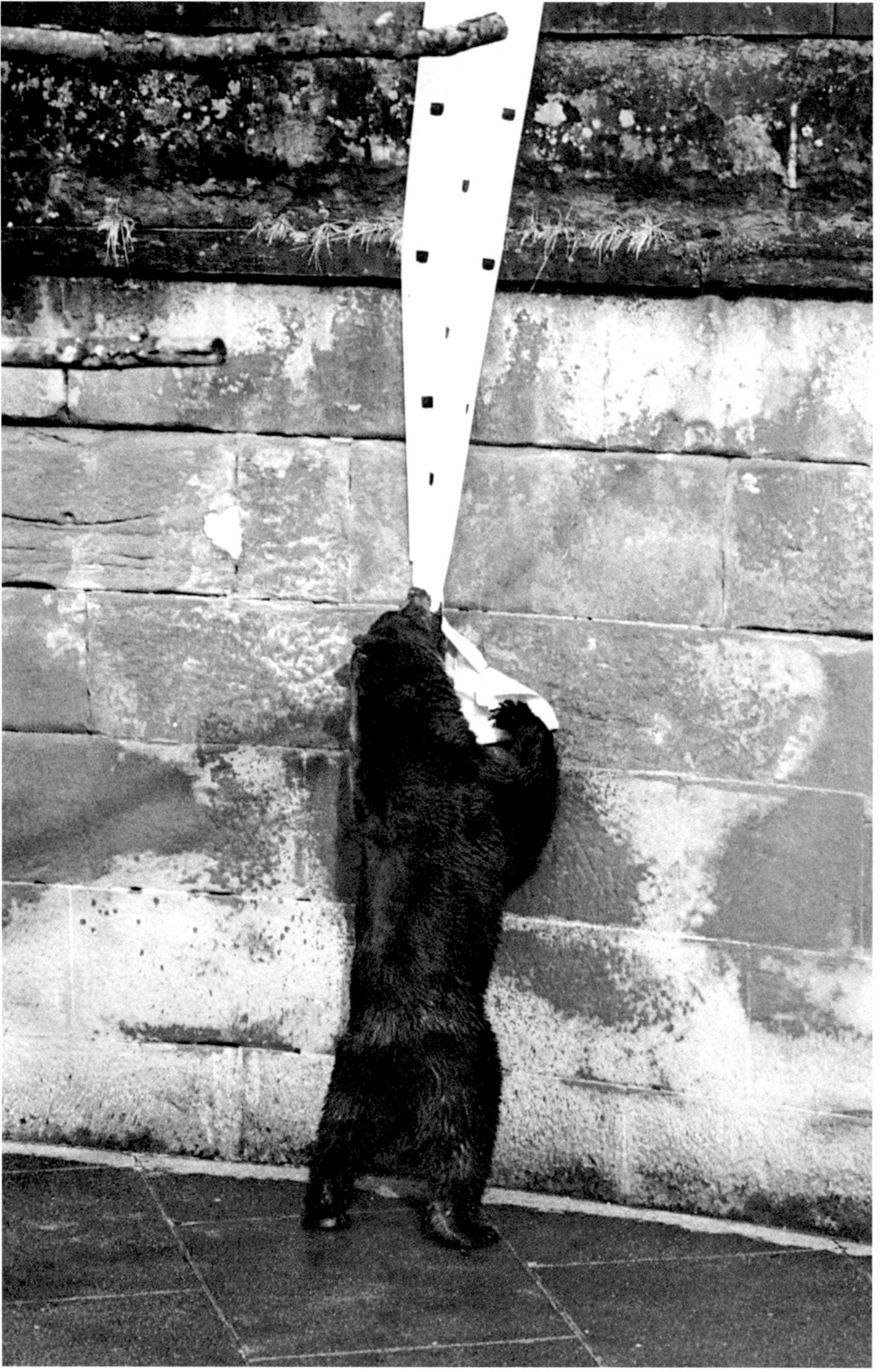

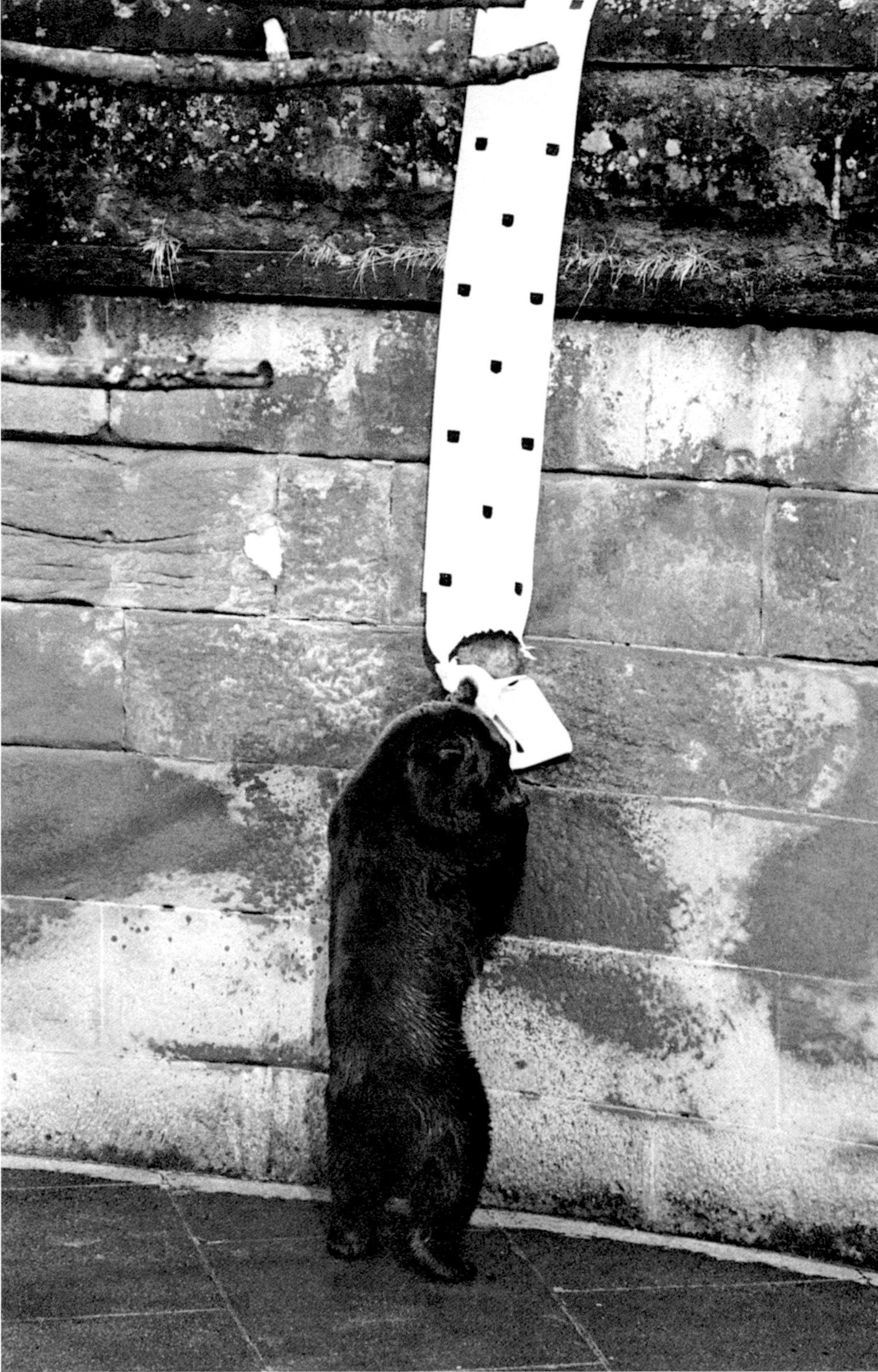

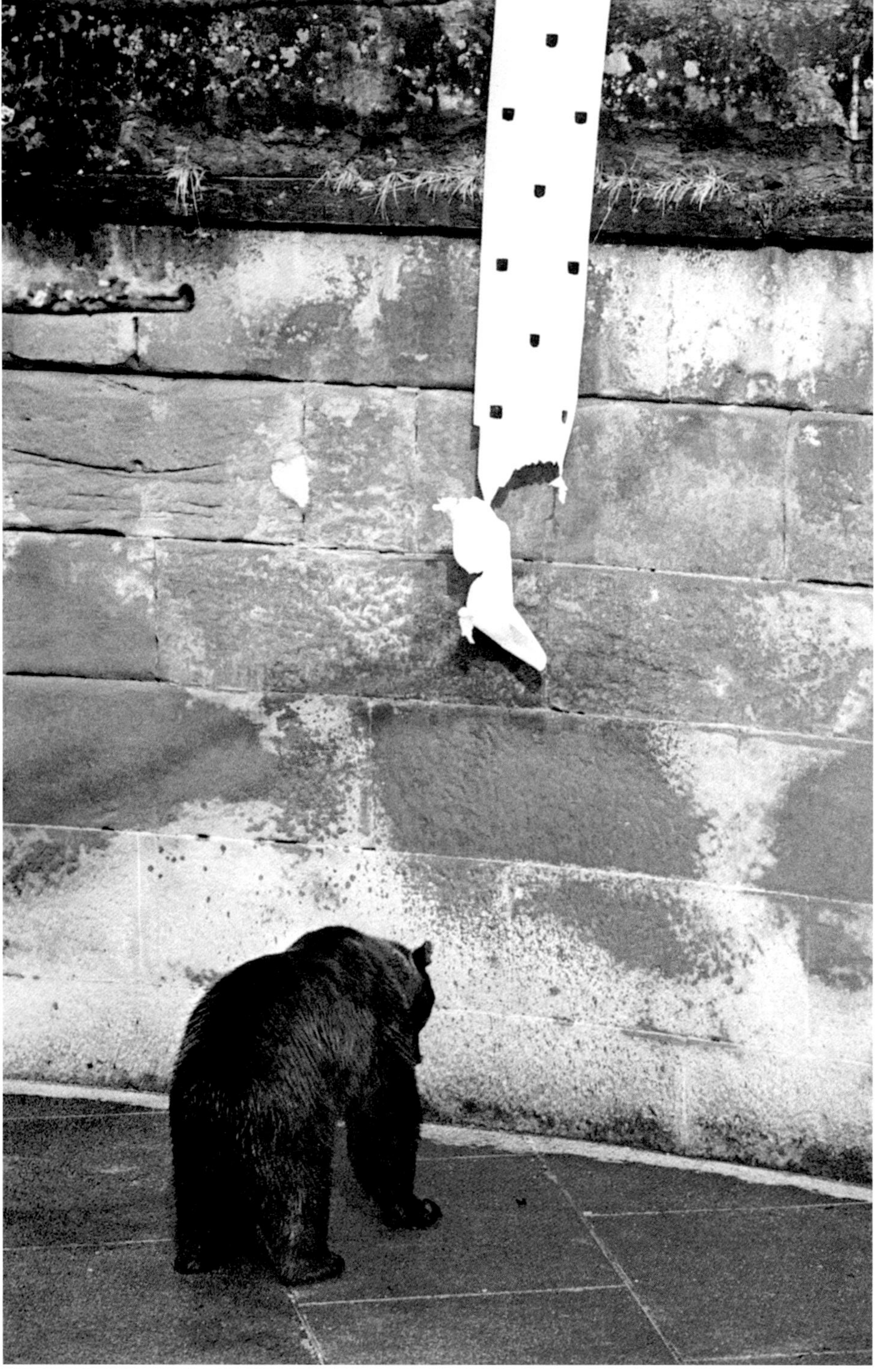

15 15

15

15 15

pp. 3-4, 6-14: Niele Toroni, *Dans la fosse aux ours*, Bern, 1978

Contents

Introduction

"There is the whole of the work, of which one only sees parts, cuts," Niele Toroni said in a 1988 interview.[1] His central role within contemporary art has prompted many occasions to see "parts and cuts," but very few to consider "the whole of the work." Over the last half century, Toroni has been the subject of numerous publications in French, German, Italian, and Japanese, and the artist himself has cleverly examined details of his own work through the making of artist's books. Yet, remarkably, there has never been a publication in English that provides an artistic and critical understanding of his work. Seeking to correct this omission, this book is the first English-language publication on the artist and the most comprehensive in print, and includes historical as well as newly commissioned essays connecting several schools of painting and thought. To further deepen an appreciation of this influential artist, this book also incorporates Toroni's handwritten letters, and a selection of writings from 1962 to 1994, which the artist himself chose, revealing a sharp clarity of vision tempered by accumulated knowledge.

This book is structured around four sections of chronological images that document Toroni's exhibitions from 1967 to 2002, along with a fifth section of his most recent exhibition in New York at Swiss Institute, which together provide crucial insight into both the developments and constants that have persisted in the artist's practice. These sections are interspersed with essays. In the first, "Fini Non Fini Infini Fin," art historians Joachim Pissarro and Annie Wischmeyer trace the lineage of Toroni's artistic practice back to postimpressionist painting and the 1927 installation of Monet's *Nymphéas* suite at the Musée de l'Orangerie—an especially fitting reference since, on the occasion of his Swiss Institute exhibition, Toroni mused that the main gallery invoked his own Orangerie. The second essay, written by renowned curator Harald Szeemann in 1991 on the occasion of Toroni's exhibition at the Museo Comunale d'Arte Moderna Ascona, elucidates the clarity and depth of Toroni's work: "Anyone who knows Niele Toroni," Szeemann writes, "knows another quality of methodological economy: it gives and creates time to live, to think, time for the oral tradition, and thus time to get rid of any overburdenedness."[2] In the book's final essay, Alex Bacon compares Toroni to his conceptualist peers, discussing his interpretation of the brushstroke and site specificity. Bacon concludes by relating Toroni's practice to that of a younger generation of artists working today as a testament to the lasting influence of his practice.

Contacting Niele Toroni requires a certain degree of intentionality. He has neither an e-mail address nor a cellphone; communication is only possible in the form of a precisely timed phone call or handwritten letter. So it is apt that we close this publication with letters and writings sent by the artist to Swiss Institute over a wintry three months at the beginning of 2016, in which Toroni discusses some of his favorite writings on his work, from authors such as René Denizot and Bernard Marcadé, and provides a rare look into how he perceives his own practice.

This correspondence also marked the beginning of a fruitful collaboration, leading to several artistic interventions by Toroni that are included in this very publication, blurring the distinction between monograph and artist's book. He is particularly drawn to the number five, which he always chooses when betting on unfamiliar horses and often plays when at the roulette table. To interrupt the flow of the book, Toroni decided that every time a page number included a five, that page would be covered with a repetition of the page number in the pattern of an X. The endpapers are covered with the same pattern, but instead of fives, the artist decided to use Swiss Institute's logo. He also chose to insert blank pages printed in the vibrant orange of the mineral minium. This particular hue is of yesteryear's antirust paint, which Toroni says is much more joyous than the black or white usually painted over it. For him, it is a simple, vernacular color that lies hidden beneath the surface. As mentioned in Pissarro and Wischmeyer's essay, orange was also significant for the exhibition at Swiss Institute, where the artist used this color for many of his imprints.

The Swiss Institute exhibition marked Toroni's first institutional exhibition in the United States in over twenty-five years, and was his very first institutional solo show in New York City. Like a retrospective in miniature, the exhibition spanned over five decades of his career, represented by four existing works and three "interventions," a term used by the artist to describe site-specific applications of imprints in different geometric configurations. The main gallery was devoted to a monumental scroll from 1968, a series of twenty-five square canvases from 1987, and seven single imprints from 2014, each one on a piece of computer paper attached to a thin strip of plywood. To accommodate the scroll, the stairs had to be removed from the platform that divided the main gallery, rendering the platform an expansive pedestal that connected each work exhibited in that space.

With the exception of a series of imprints made on pieces of scrap paper, the lobby gallery was devoted to a crucial series of new, site-specific interventions. On a panel of the building's glass garage door, Toroni impressed three white markings that heralded the exhibition. Positioned over the passage between the lobby gallery and the main gallery was a collection of twenty-eight black imprints arranged in the form of a triangle. And, tucked away just beside the entrance, Toroni painted two chevrons on the door of the gallery's electrical panel in the same cerulean hue as the DGA logo that brands the control panel of the security system. Collectively, these interventions exact a close observation of the architecture and infrastructure in which they exist on both macro and micro scales. The tension between playful nuance, seen in the works on the garage door and the security panel, and grand gesture, manifested in the large triangle formation, typify Toroni's imaginative observations of the spaces we inhabit, which often remain unnoticed.

It is a privilege to grant English speakers new awareness of Toroni's complex universe, and to offer a sense of chronological scale to a practice that has discreetly unraveled over five decades. It is with vast creativity that Toroni has devoted himself to the simple gesture of applying a paint-dipped brush to a surface, but it is with precisely this mark that the artist has created multitudes of inflections and permutations, a brush with the infinite.

Simon Castets
Director, Swiss Institute

Notes

1. Niele Toroni, interview by Catherine Lawless, "Entretien avec Niele Toroni: à propos de 'Empreintes De Pinceau No50 Répétées à Intervalles Réguliers De 30 Cm.' 1967," *Les Cahiers du Musée National d'Art Moderne*, no. 25 (Autumn 1988): 107-114, translator unknown.
2. From Harald Szeemann's untitled essay on pp. 113-114, 116.

Exhibitions: 1967–1977

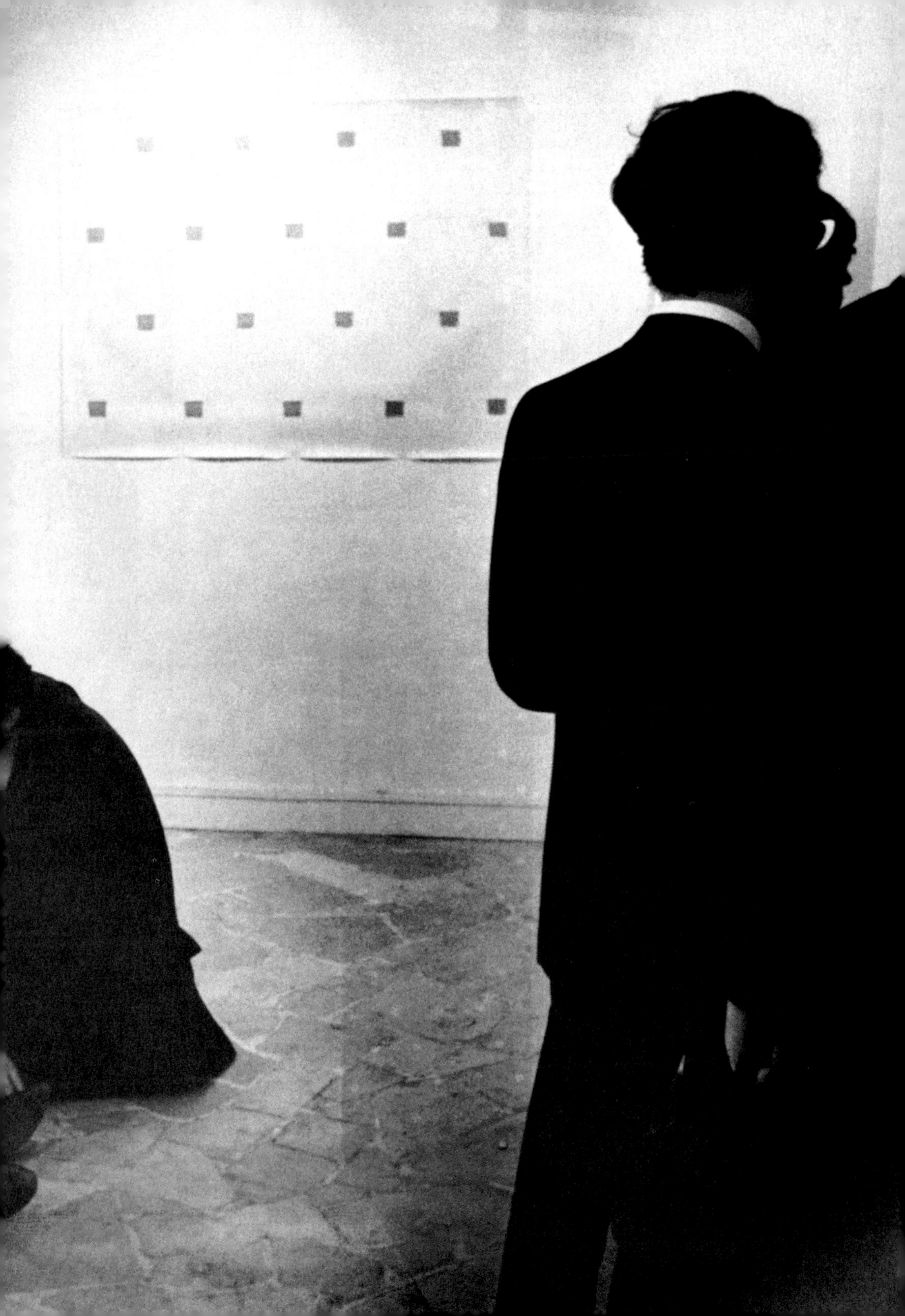

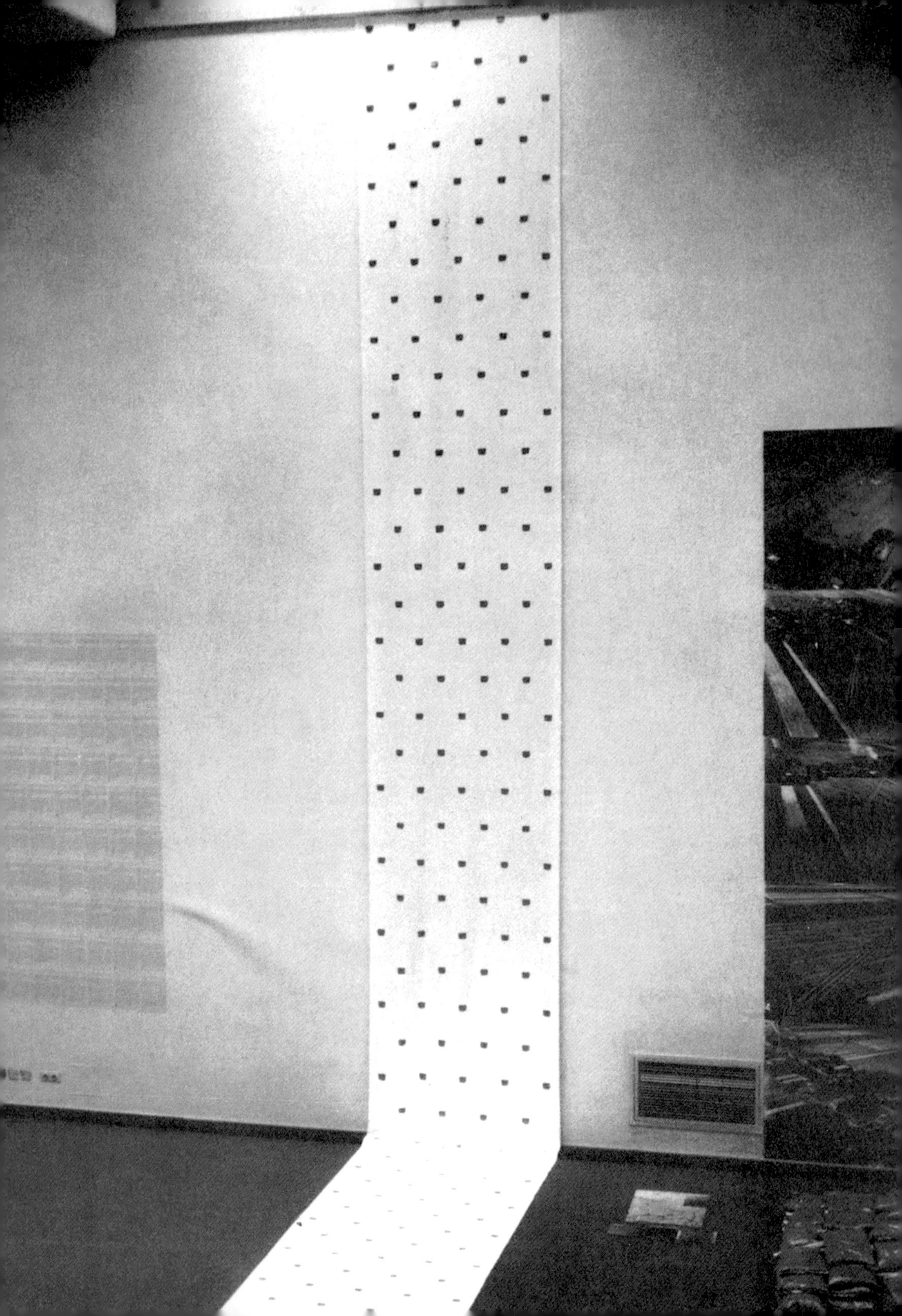

25 25

25

25 25

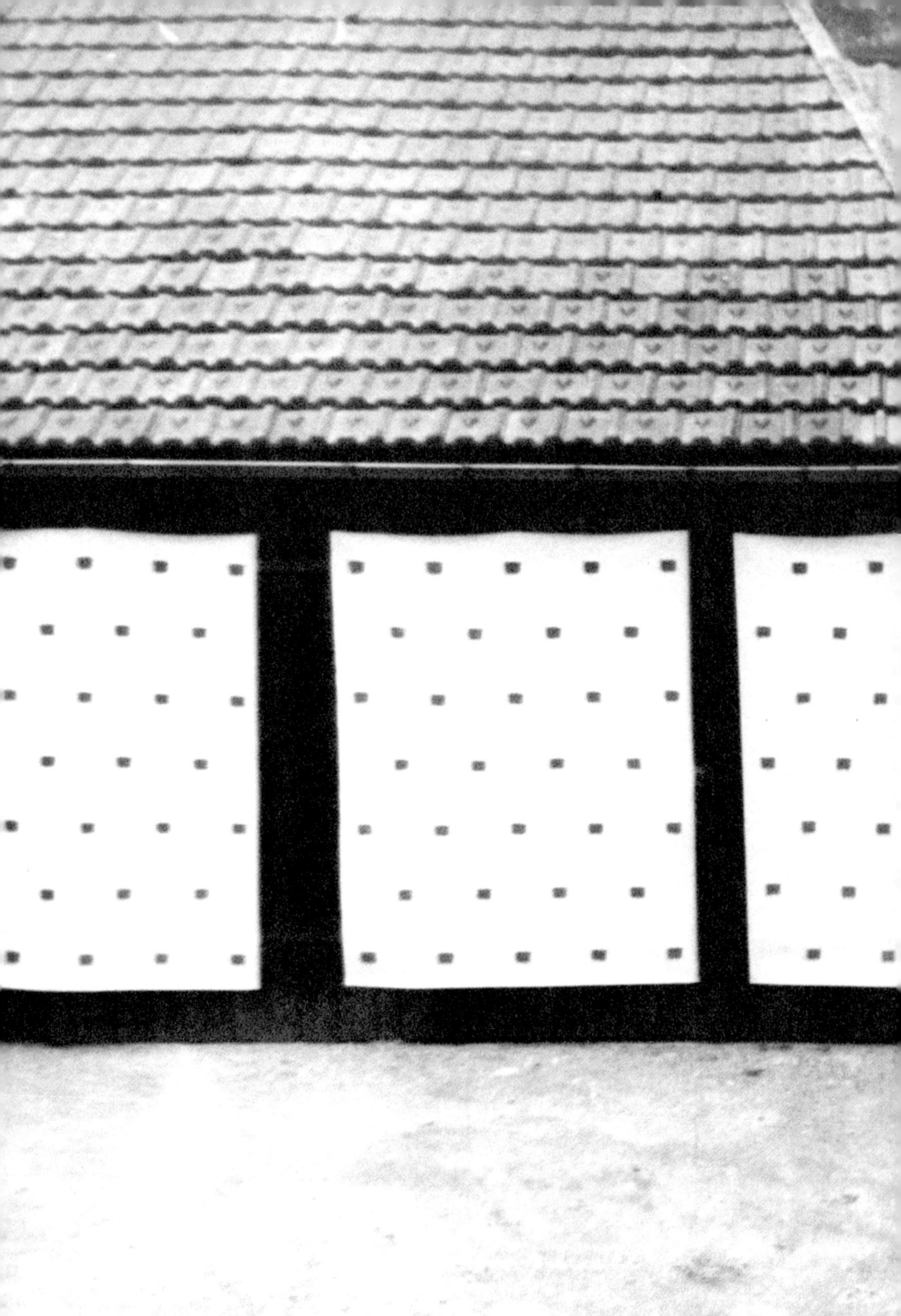

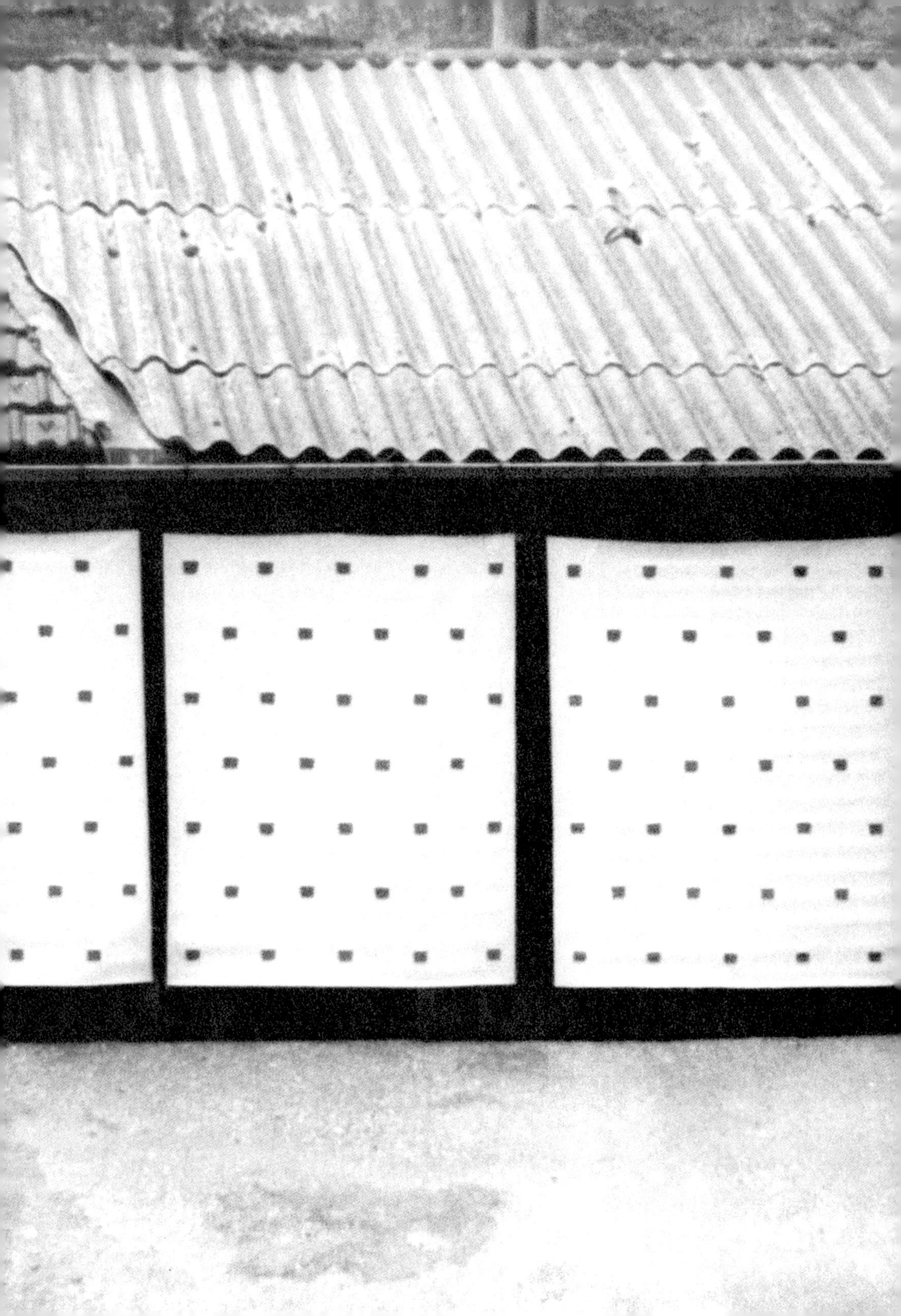

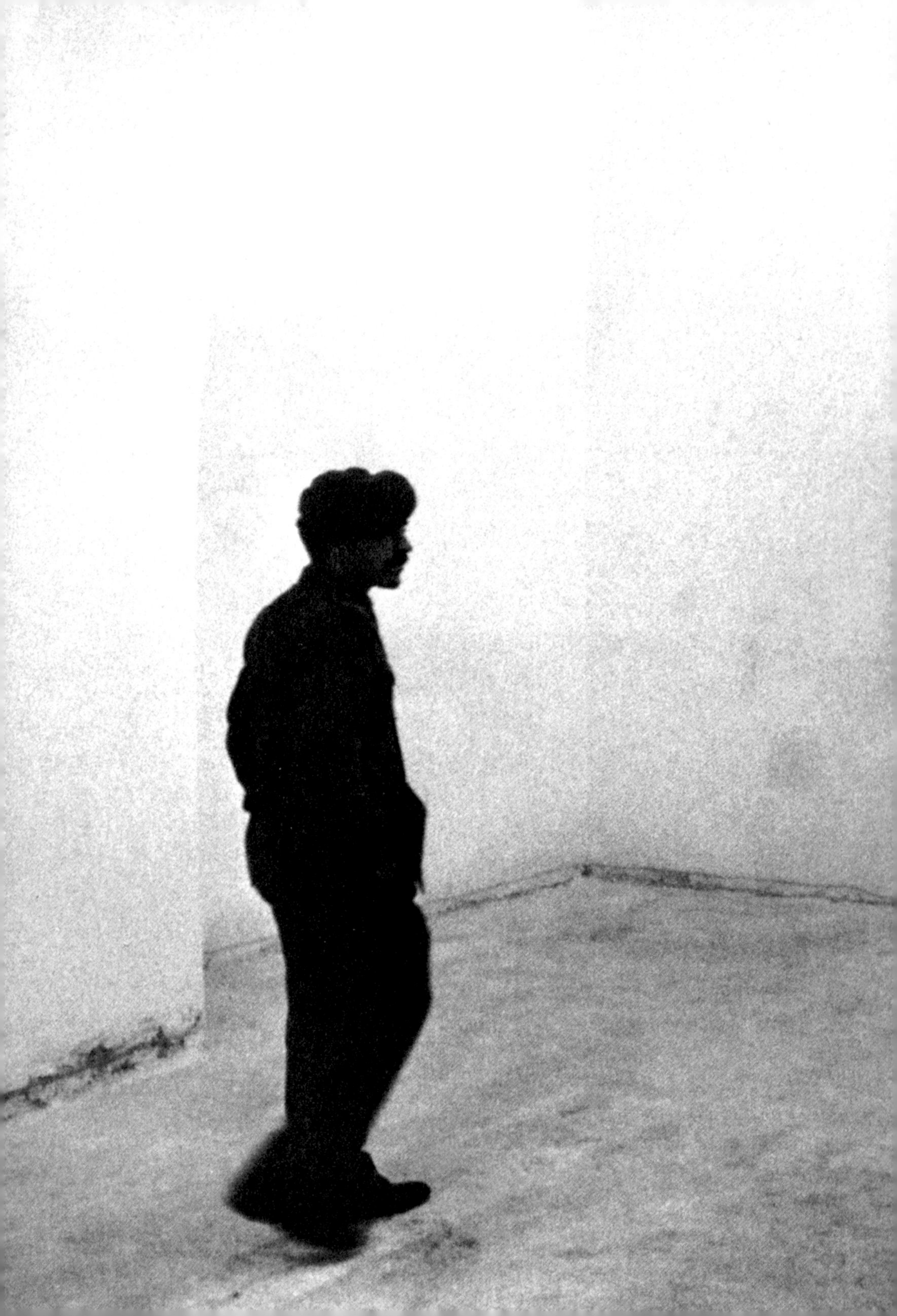

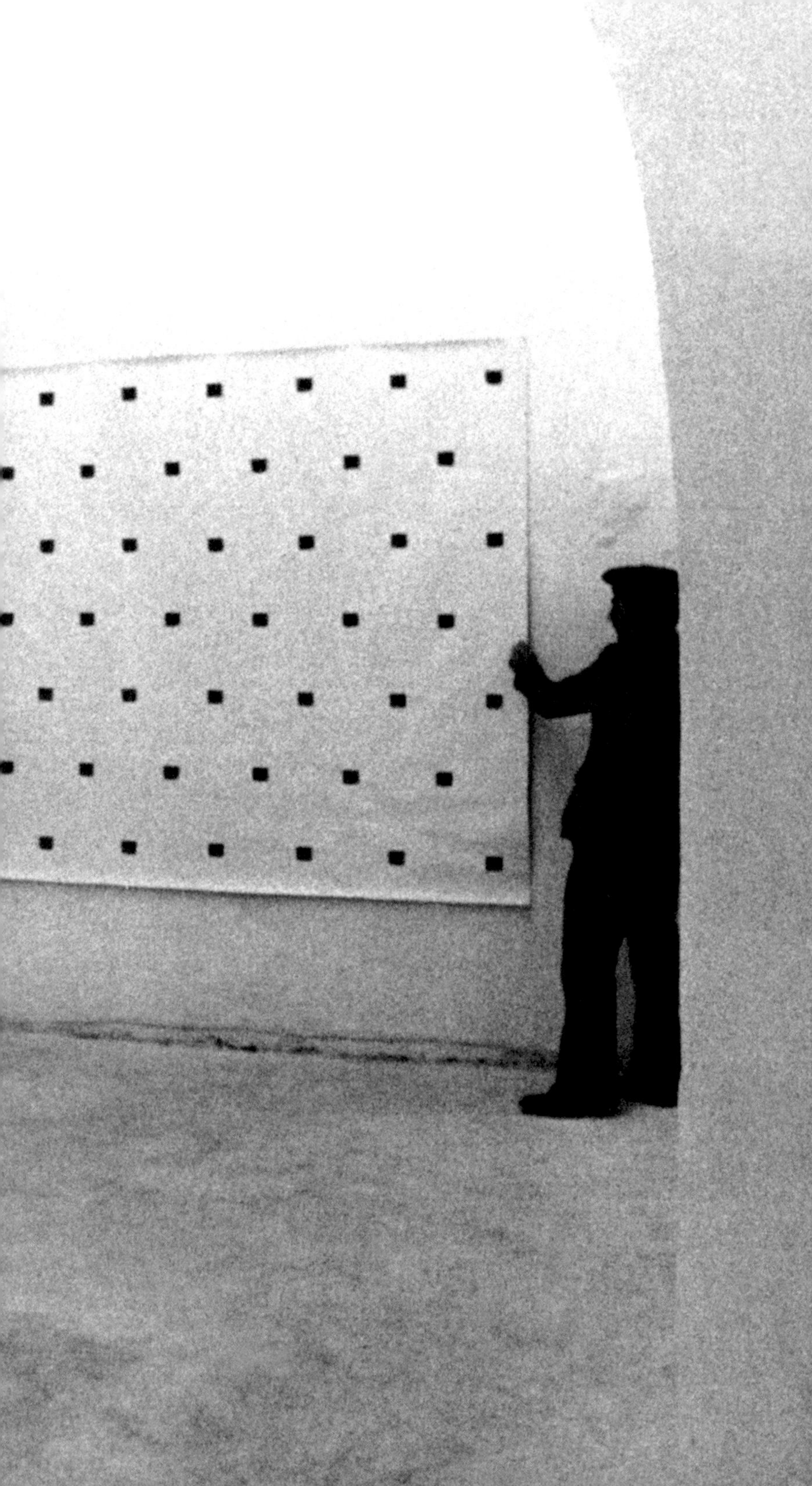

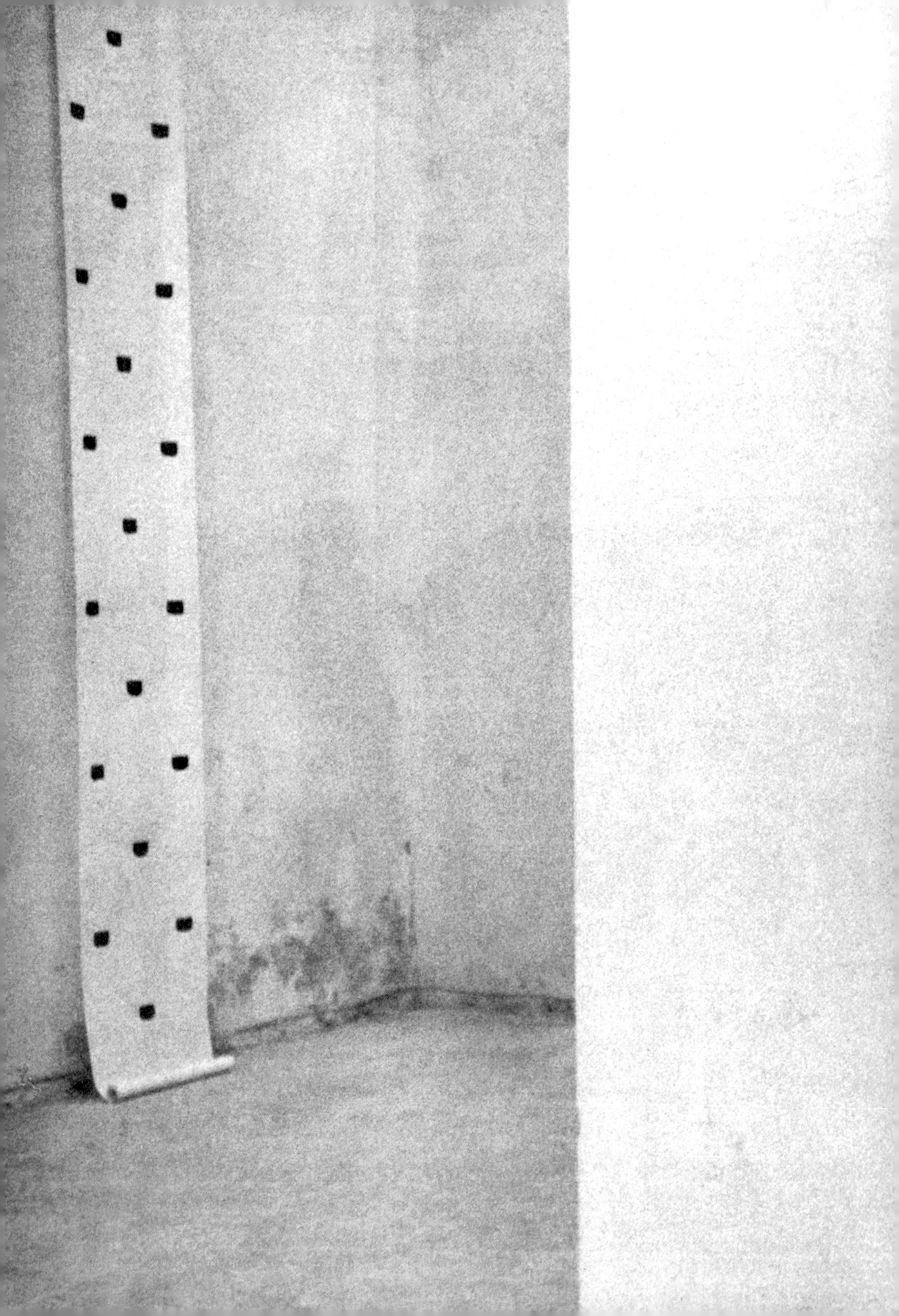

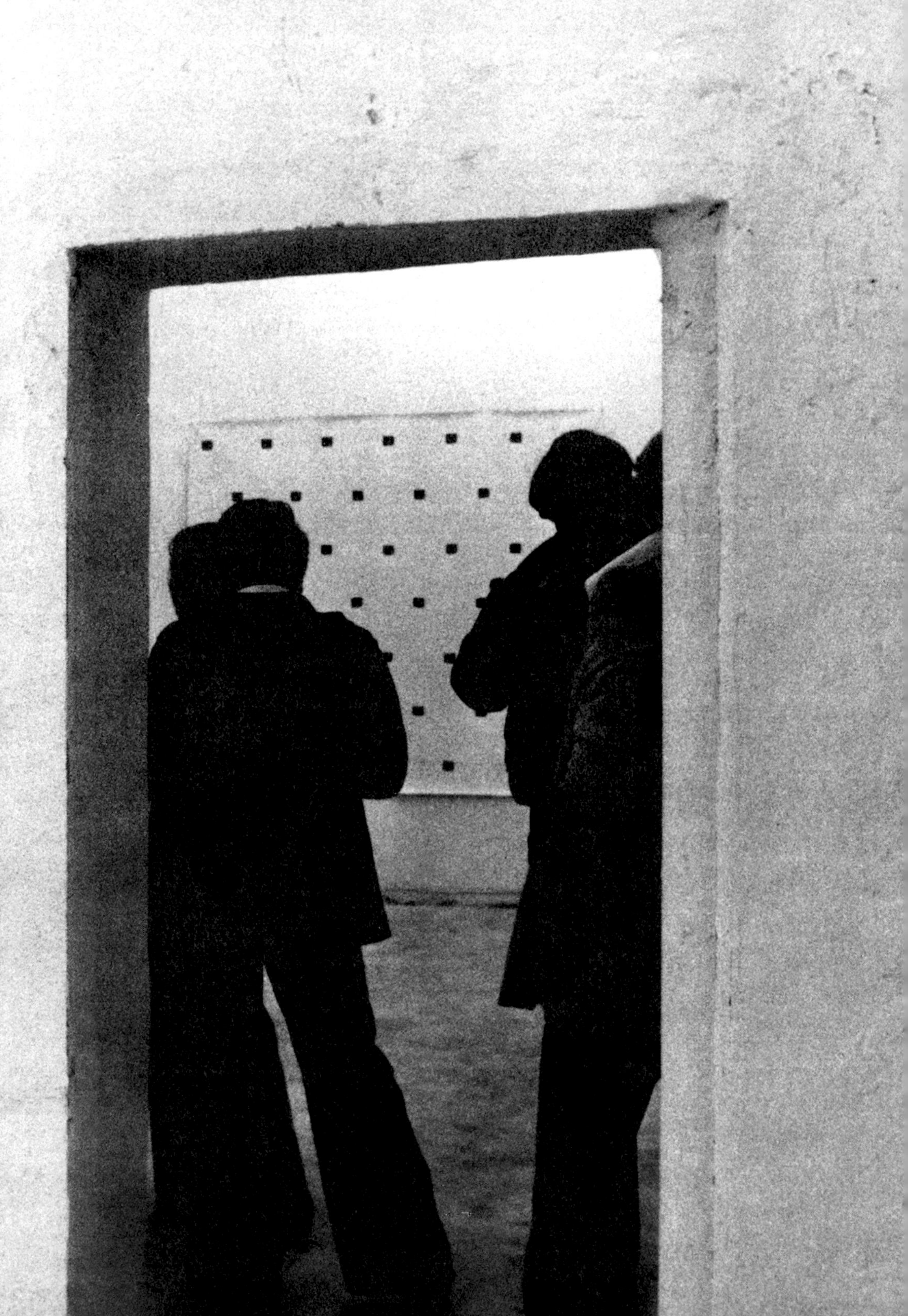

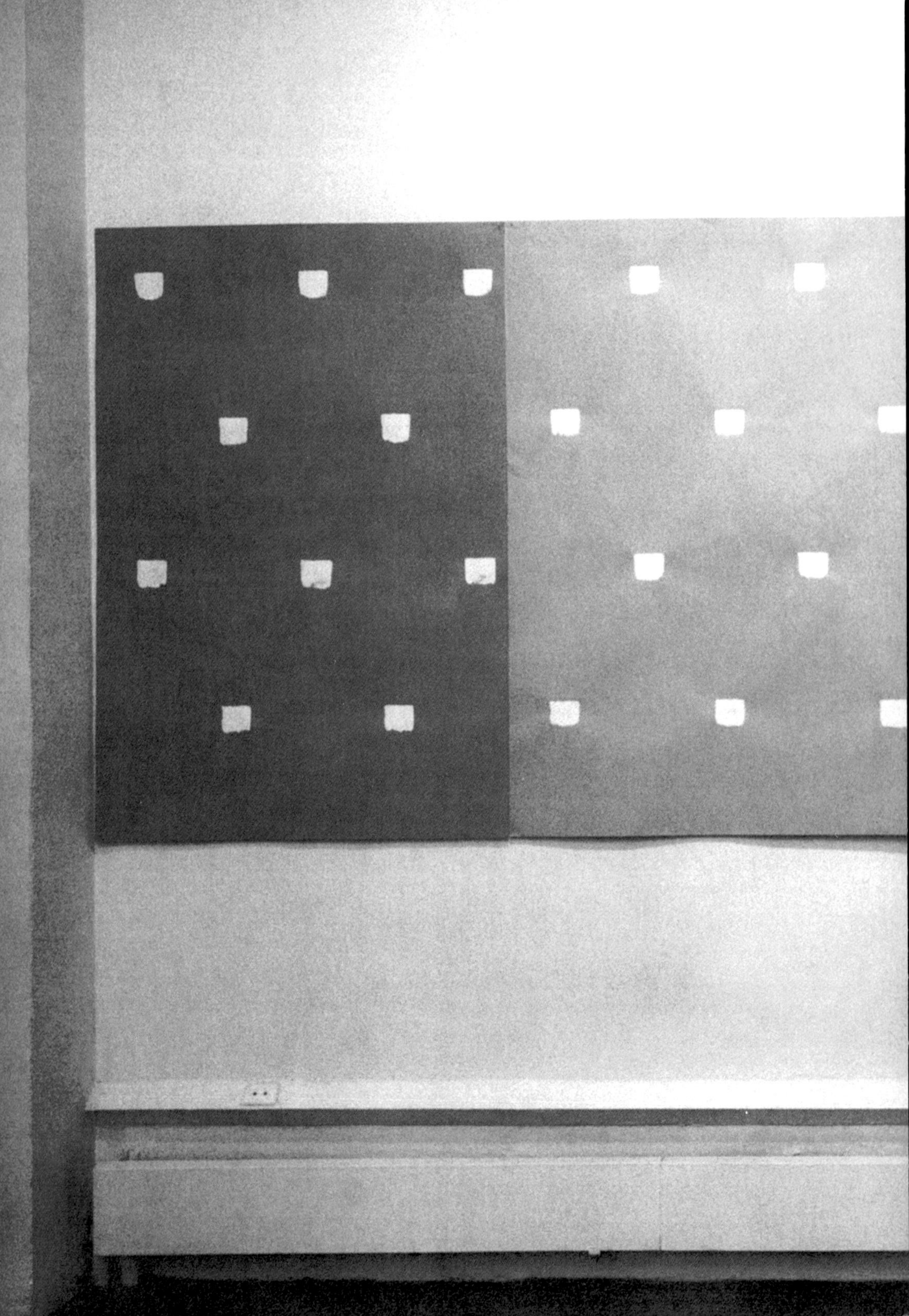

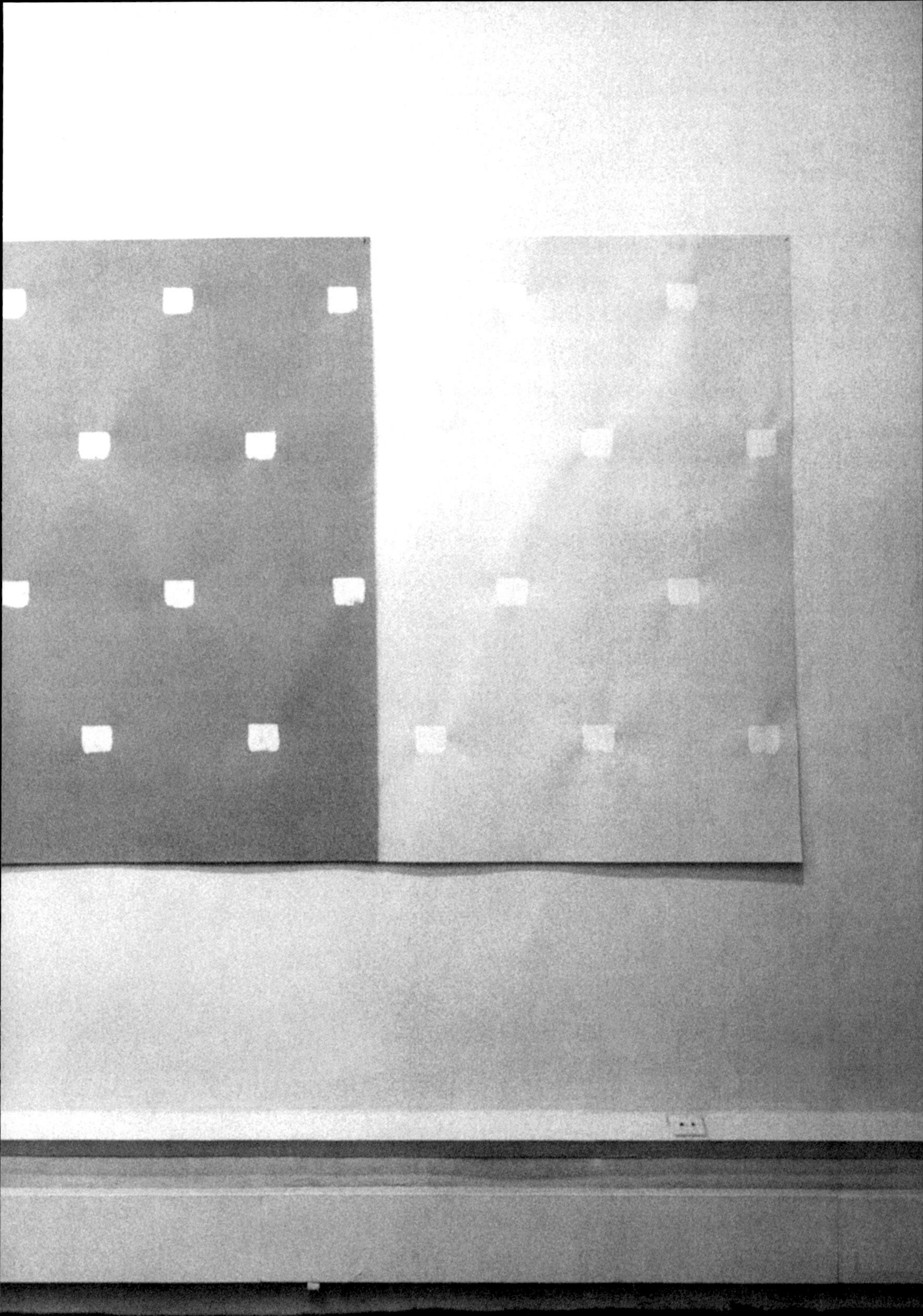

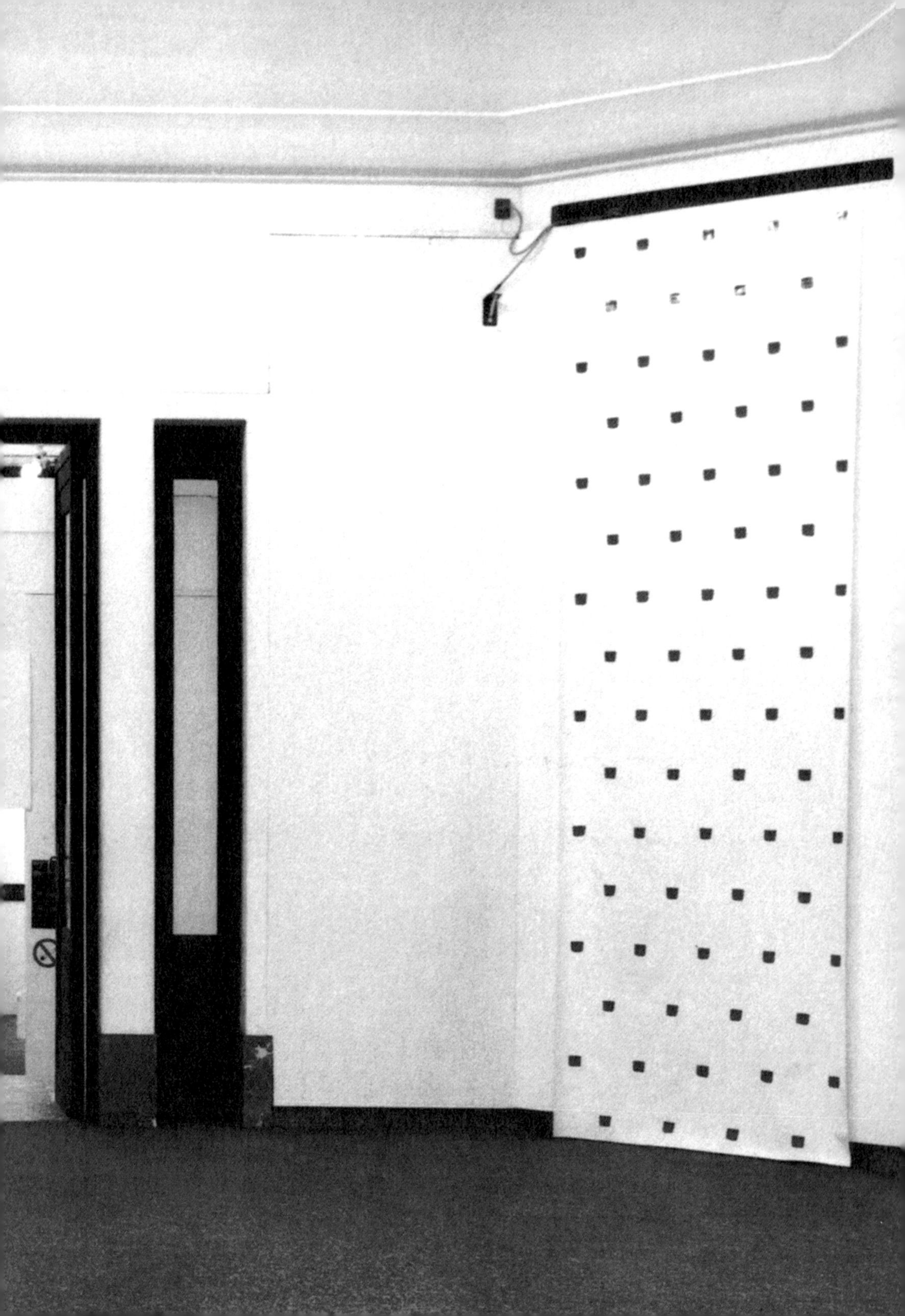

35

35

35

35

35

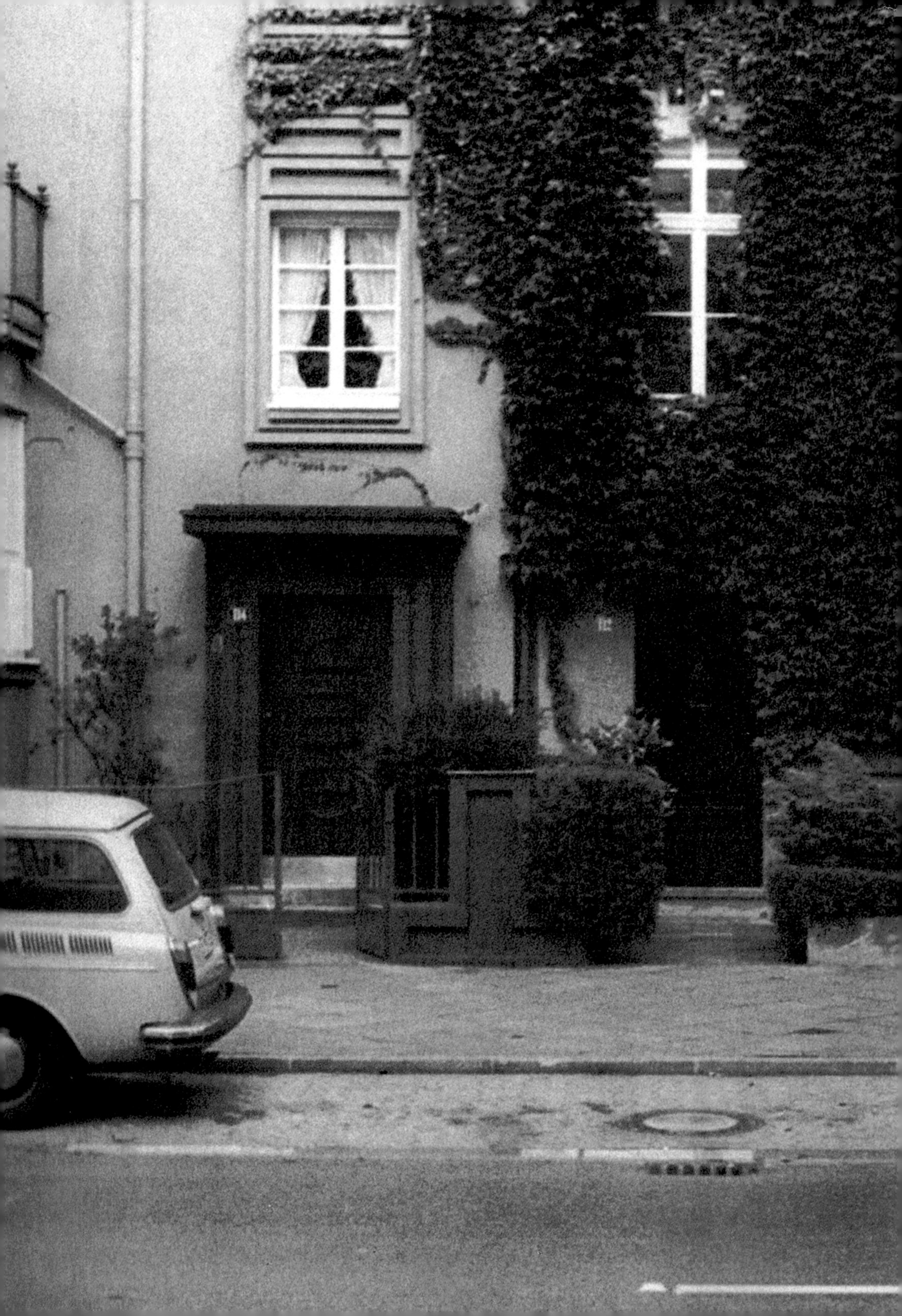

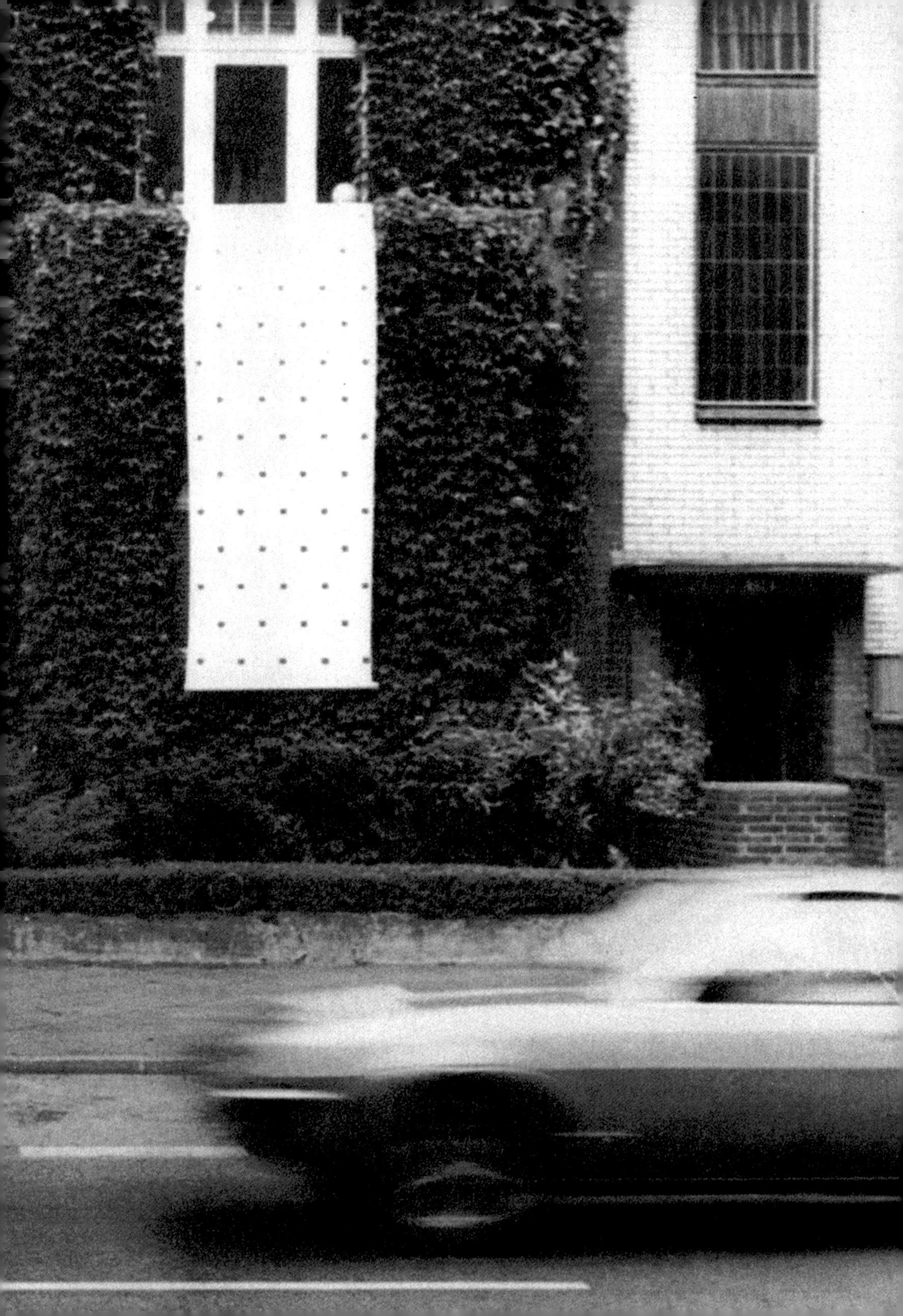

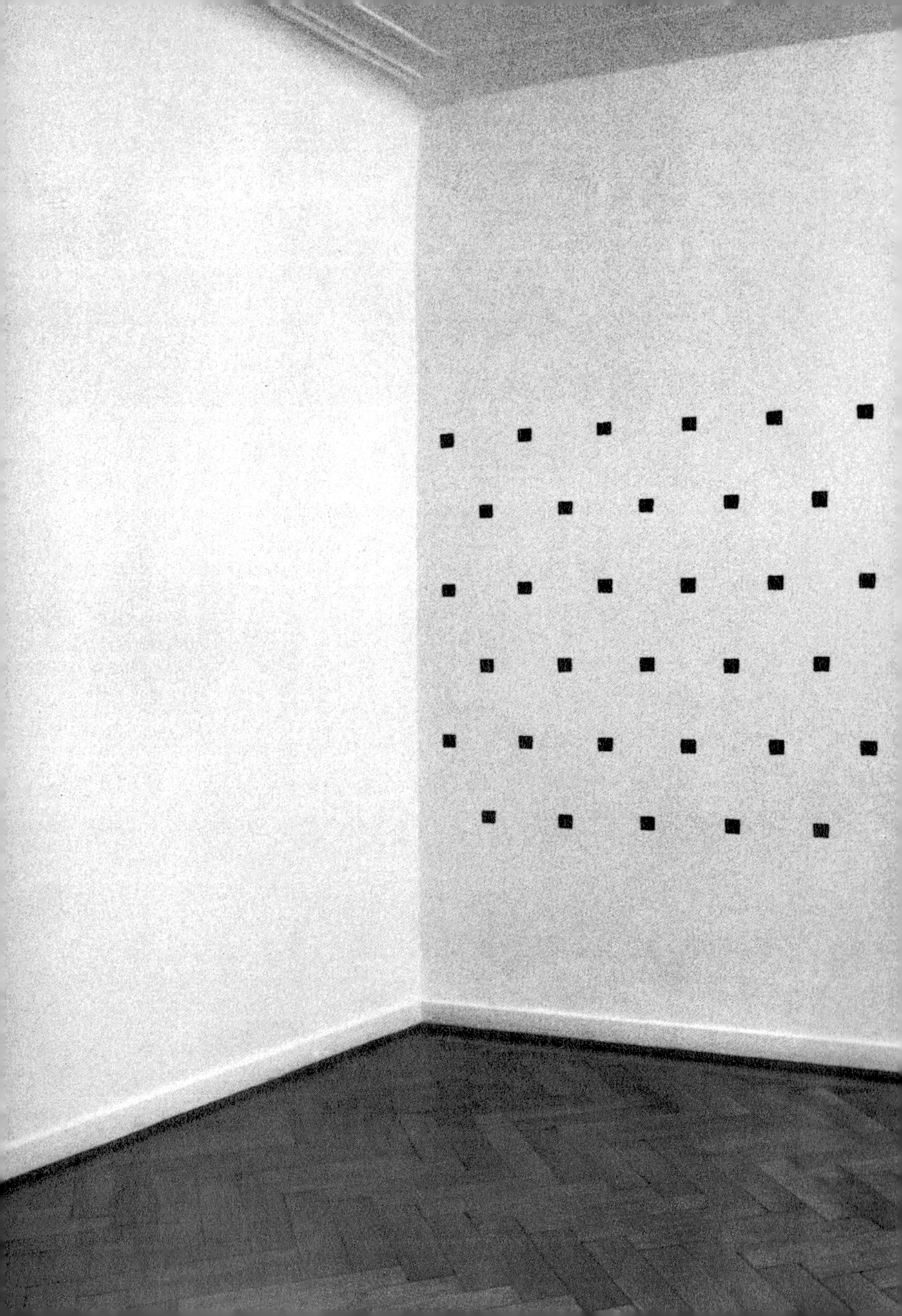

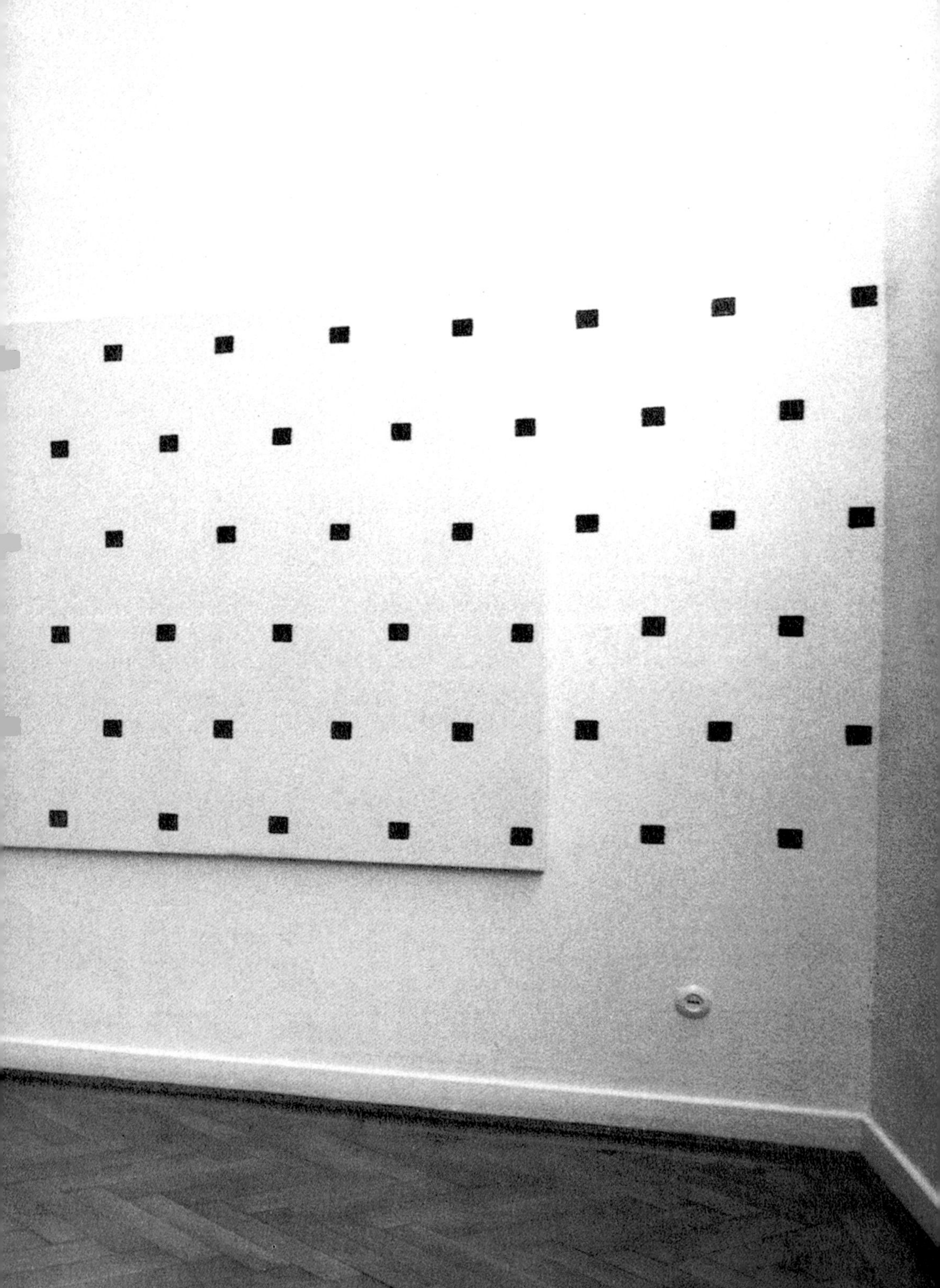

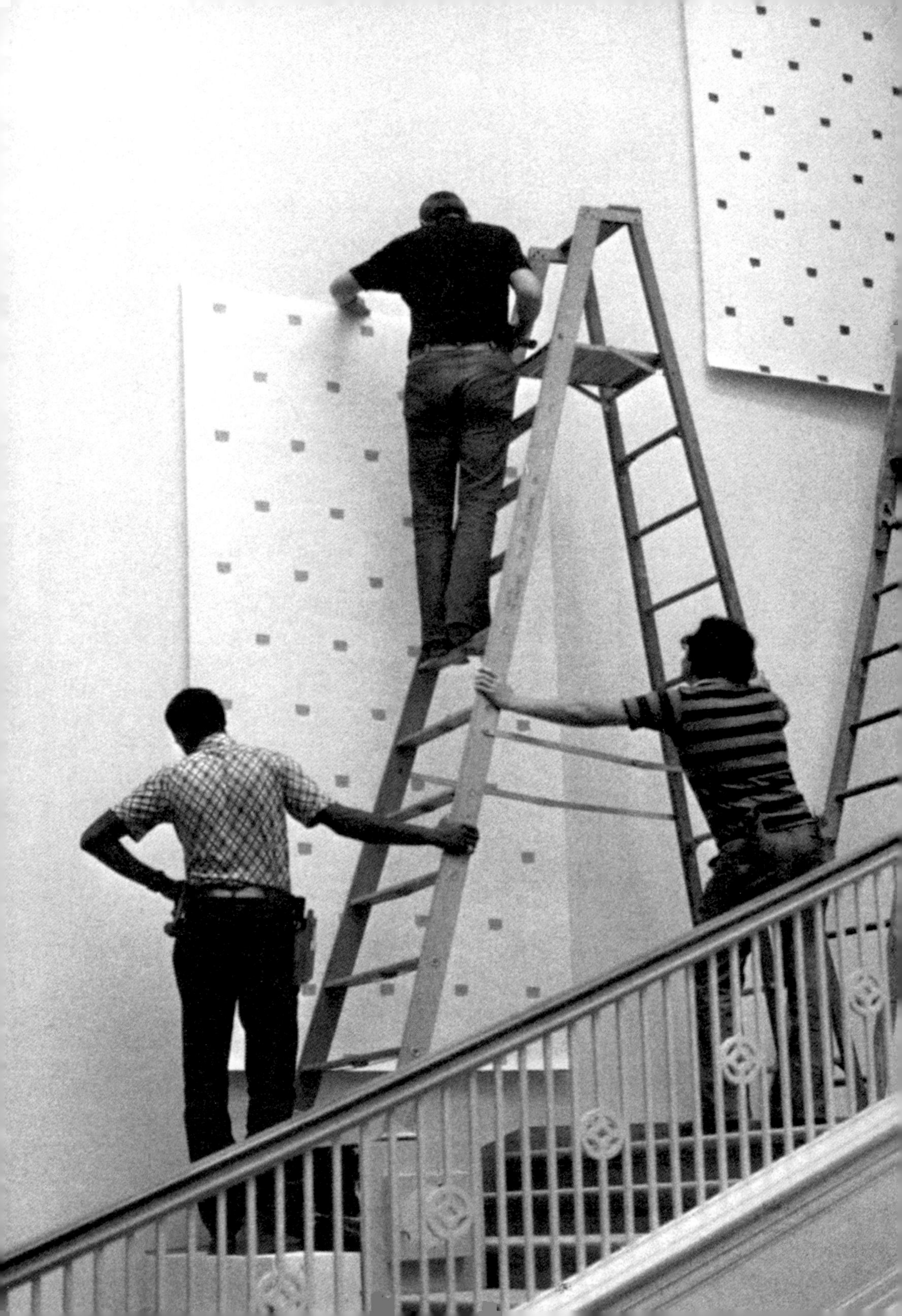

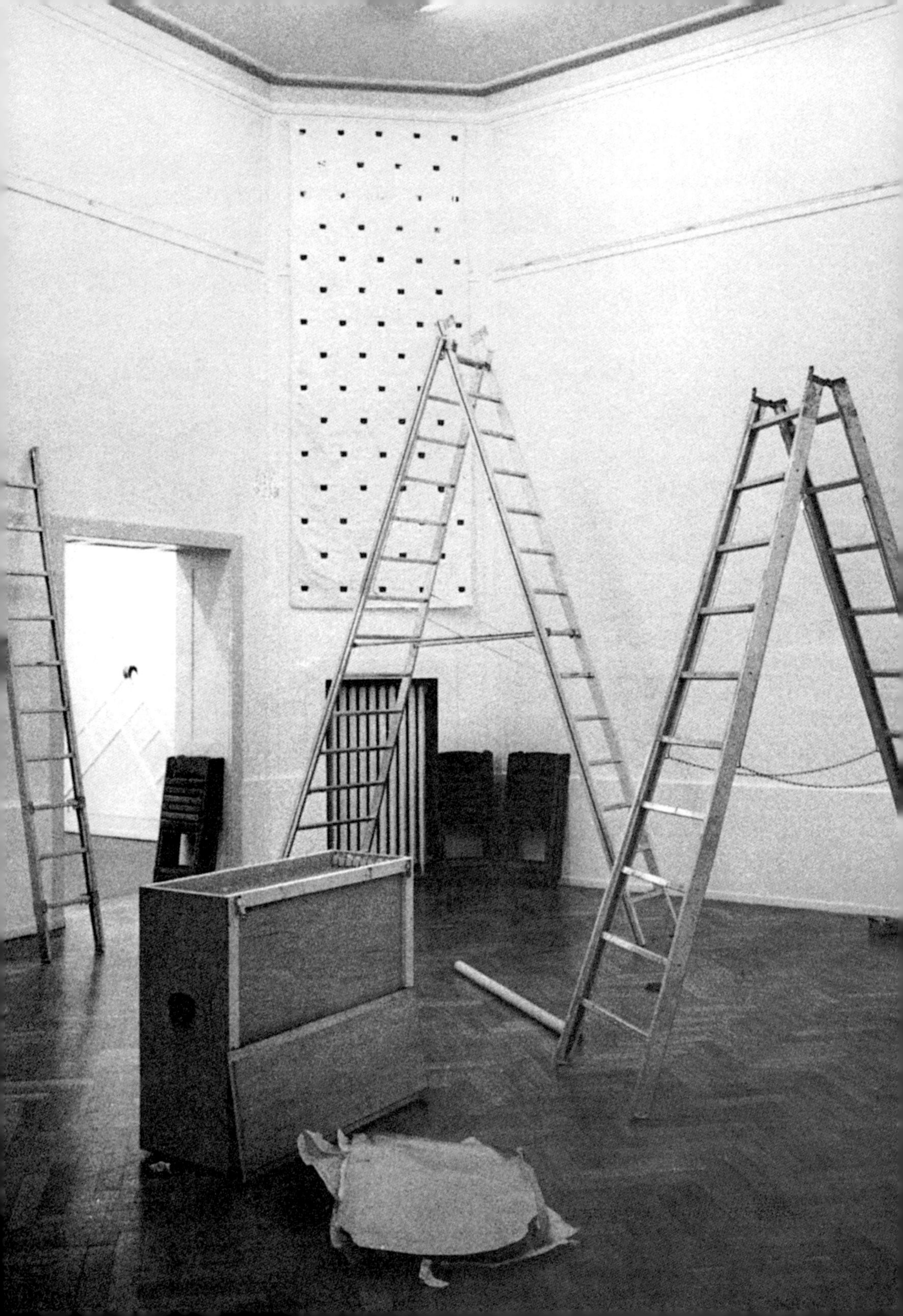

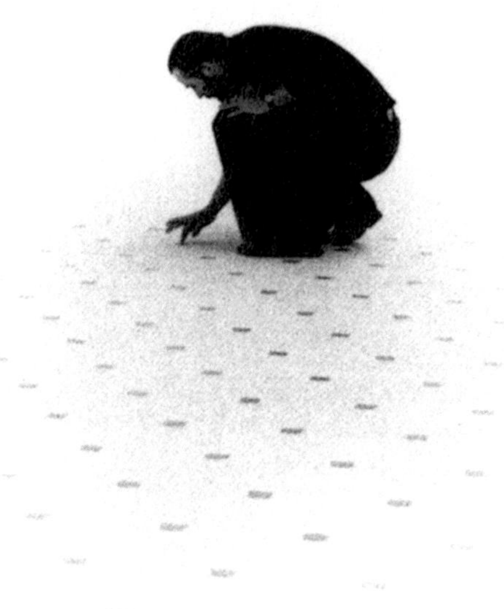

45

45

45

45

45

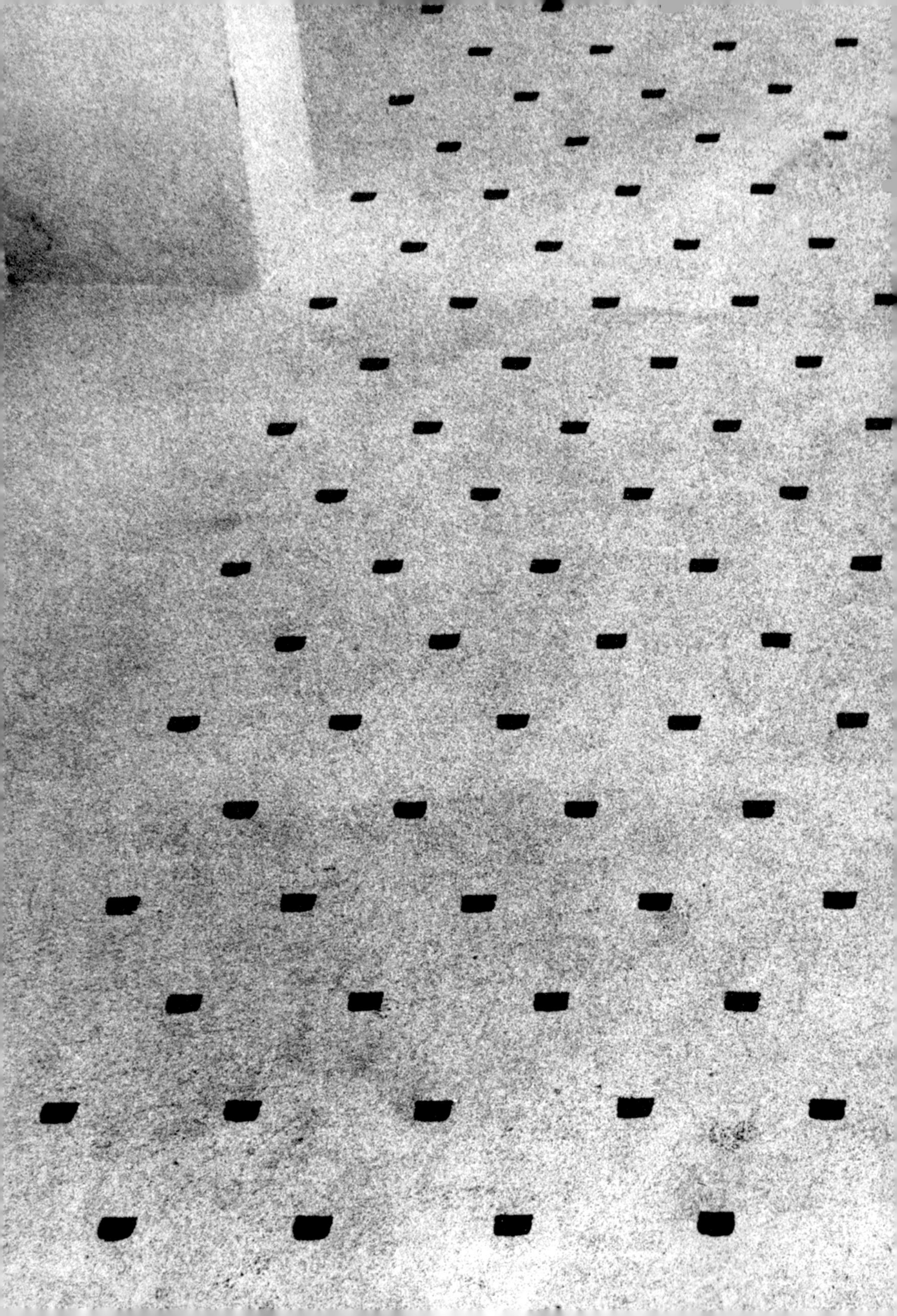

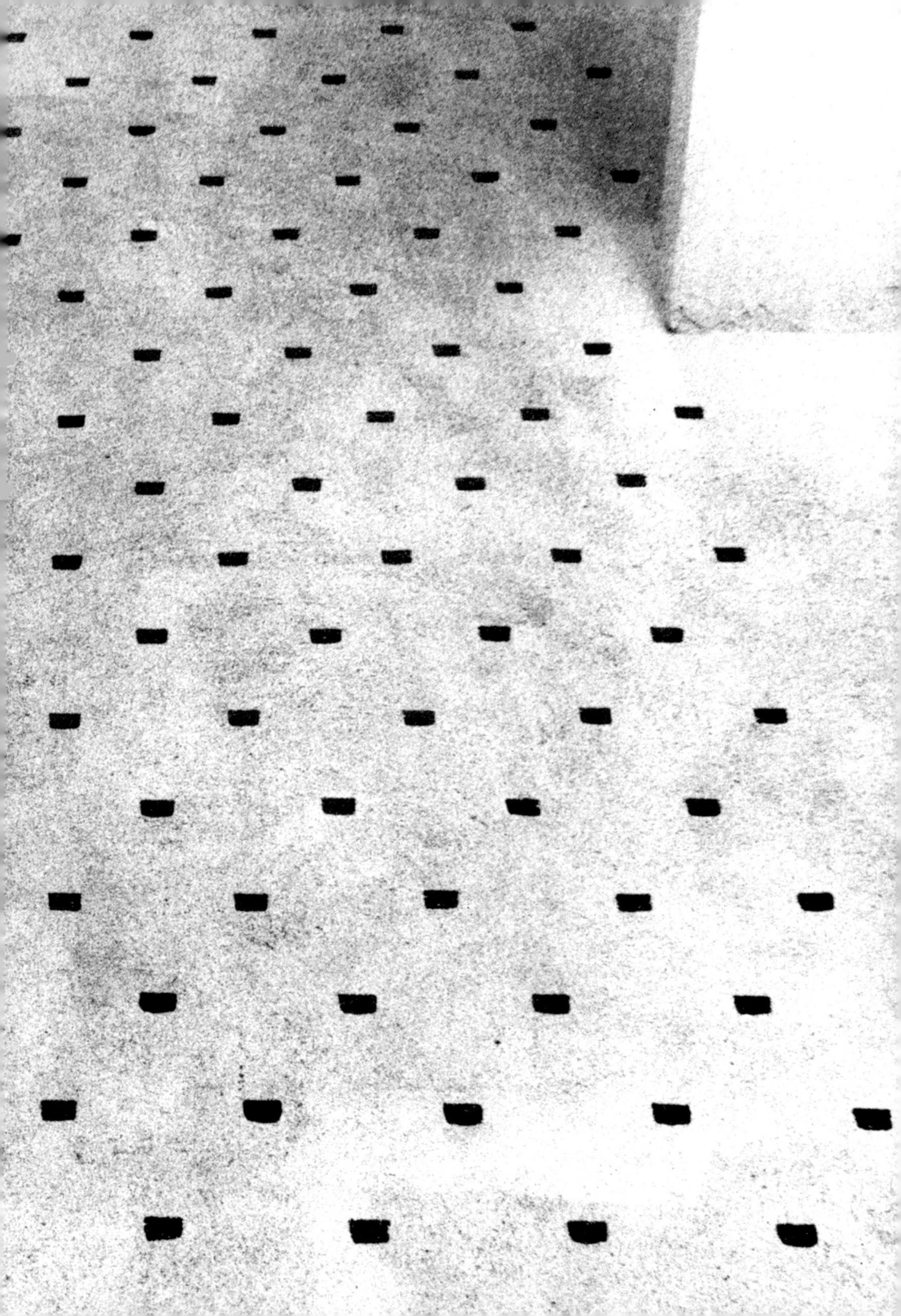

p. 23: Musée d'Art Moderne de la Ville de Paris, Paris, 1967

p. 24: Prospect 69 (Städtische Kunsthalle), Düsseldorf, 1969

pp. 26-27: 16 Rue Castagnary, Paris, 1969

pp. 28-31: Collection D'Alessandro, Rome, 1974

pp. 32-33: Galerie Yvon Lambert, Paris, 1975

p. 34: Palais des Beaux-Arts, Brussels, 1975

pp. 36-37: Galerie Kiki Maier-Hahn, Düsseldorf, 1976

pp. 38-39: Galerie Paul Maenz, Cologne, 1976

p. 41: Art Institute of Chicago, Chicago, 1977

p. 43: Kunsthalle Bern, Bern, 1977

pp. 44, 46-47: Galleria D'Alessandro-Ferranti, Rome, 1977

50

50

50

50

50

51

51

51

51

51

52

52

52

52

52

53

53

53

53

53

54

54

54

54

54

55 55

55

55 55

56

56

56

56

56

57 57

57

57 57

58 58

58

58 58

59 59

59

59 59

Fini Non Fini Infini Fin
Joachim Pissarro and Annie Wischmeyer

LE FINI

Since 1967, Niele Toroni has been making the same mark. "What I see in my work is, first of all, imprints [*empreintes*] of a no. 50 brush repeated at regular intervals of 30 centimeters. I think that what people see when they look at my work is first of all this evidence . . . What I mean is that through the imprint I try to show painting."[1] Referring to this body of work as *travail/peinture*, or "work/painting," Toroni has sought to lay bare the mechanisms of painting and the physical act of creation. "It is not out of 'workerism' that I bracket the two terms together, but to bring home the fact that my painting does not exist without the work involved in making it."[2] His adherence to the fundamental nature of the medium takes on a quality of defiance through his stubborn, repetitive assertion.

The *empreinte* is not an impressionist *tache* or expressionist gesture, but in the same way that those methods were the marks of their times, so is Toroni's refusal of their conceptual and formal implications. Unburdening the imprint of its subordinate role in image making, he makes the subject of the work the evidence of its own process of becoming. Short of the blank canvas, the solitary mark is the radical limit of the pictorial, the zero degree, the proverbial end of painting, the *fin*.

Taking the liberation of the imprint a step further, Toroni often abandons the traditional canvas substrate altogether, instead painting on the wall, intervening directly with the architecture. Responding to the particularities of specific spaces, and often made in unconventional places (a high corner of a room, perhaps), the imprints work in concert with the architecture rather than imposing on it. Demurring in both form and ego, the humble process of applying paint to surface takes precedence.

This concern with architecture is manifested in Toroni's installation at Swiss Institute. At the opening of this exhibition, Toroni quipped, in passing, "C'est mon homage à l'Orangerie" (It is my homage to the Orangerie), referring to the installation of Monet's *Nymphéas* (Water Lilies) suite at the museum in Paris of that name. This offhand remark, however, offers an unexpected lens through which to examine and understand his work. The main exhibition space at Swiss Institute, ringed in a continuum of orange-imprinted canvases, indeed bore an implied reference to this icon of impressionist painting and the museum it occupies. This visual and verbal pun betrayed an affinity and perhaps affection for a group of artists who championed subjectivity and sensorial indeterminacy. At first glance, the dreamlike paintings of the impressionist masters seem to be an antithetical, anomalous reference for Toroni, a man who has devoted the past fifty years to the same rigid, dogmatic concept. However, going beyond the superficial dissonance, one finds rhymes and sympathies in both method and thought.

LE NON FINI

In 1874, Monet first exhibited *Impression, soleil levant* (Impression, Sunrise) at the inaugural exhibition of independent artists in Paris. Borrowing from the painting's title, critic Louis Leroy pejoratively referred to the exhibiting group of artists as "impressionists," bemoaning the unfinished quality of the works. Beginning as an experiment as to how best to capture the effect of light reflecting off water while painting en plein air, the method of rapid brushwork in pure hues was quickly translated into other subject matter, becoming what we now recognize as the impressionist style. The effect was one of perceptual immediacy, rather than academic accuracy. "They are impressionists in the sense that they render not the landscape, but the sensation produced by the landscape," wrote Jules-Antoine Castagnary, a critical champion of the movement at the time.[3] Ignoring traditional laws governing the formal structure of a composition, the impressionists instead focused on color and the individual brushstroke, resulting in canvases that lacked conventional perspectival space and hierarchies of forms. Thus, the completed works had a tenuous quality, with surfaces that threatened to disintegrate, both physically and conceptually, into a chaos of discrete marks. The dislodging of the unitary mark from the synthesis of the whole, disregarding the concern for traditional cohesion, signaled a turn toward an almost Byzantine material realism in its emphasis on the physicality of the medium.

The term *non fini* is best translated as the *un*finish, rather than the unfinish*ed*, signifying it as a deliberate incompleteness, an intentional conceptual gesture, and not merely an incomplete work. Traditionally, in the history of Western art, a piece was considered complete only when the artist achieved a certain level of finish to the surface—erasing brushwork or polishing away rough chisel marks, essentially obscuring the process through which the final product was created. Of course, the impressionists were not the first to employ the *non fini*. A number of works from the Renaissance have survived to the present day in various states of unfinish. Giorgio Vasari expressed a certain interest, even admiration, for the boldness and vitality found in underpaintings and incomplete sculpture, a quality lost in the refinement of the completed work. His appreciation of the immediacy of the brushwork or roughly modeled marble feels modern, and reminiscent of more contemporary assessments of the impressionists.[4] Édouard Manet's uncouth outlines and J. M. W. Turner's sublime storms also bear witness to this history; however, it was the impressionists that took the *non fini*, as a stylistic trope, to the verge of mannerism.

Although Toroni directly referenced the particular installation by Monet at the Orangerie, his work in terms of concept, execution, and temperament bears a closer relationship to the postimpressionist painter Paul Cézanne. While maintaining a similar formal quality of unfinish, postimpressionism rejected the impressionists' concern for capturing the perceptual effects of light and color, moving instead toward abstraction, formal order, and symbolic content. For Cézanne, this meant canvases constructed of deliberate and methodical brushstrokes, resulting in works with an architectural sensibility. The rhythmic surfaces of these later works address technical aspects of the medium, and concern themselves not with the translation of perception, but with the formal structure of the painting as a whole. Cézanne's use of paint becomes nearly objectlike, giving the works the effect of having been designed and assembled. This can be clearly seen in his paintings of Mont Sainte-Victoire (a favorite and repeated subject of his) from the early 1900s. Lacking atmospheric perspective, the image clings to the surface of the painting, behaving more like a wall than a window. Contributing to the disruption of the illusion of space in these later works, Cézanne often left moments of bare canvas in the finished paintings, allowing the visible substrate to reinforce the process of making.

In a letter to his wife in 1907, the German poet Rainer Maria Rilke described attending the Salon d'Automne with the artist Mathilde Vollmoeller-Purrmann. Encountering Cézanne's *Still Life with Apples*, she proffered an explanation for the unusual passages of blank canvas in the painting: "Here, this is something he knew, and now he's saying it (a part of an apple); right next to it there's an empty space, because that was something he didn't know yet. He only made what he knew and nothing else."[5] These lacunae in the surface of the painting are indicative of Cézanne's process and the deliberateness with which he worked. In an oft-quoted interview in *ArtNews* in 1959, the enigmatic Russian expatriate artist known only as Woks said,

"I believe that we are living a critical moment in the history of painting. Since Cézanne, it has become evident that, for the painter, what counts is no longer the painting but the process of creation . . . Henceforth, the essential aim of painting must be the process of creation; the viewer must no longer be made to look at the painting alone, but the very process of making it."[6]

For Toroni, the process of making is made visible by the *non fini*. "The space between imprints, the 30 centimeters, is what makes the imprints appear, and it is not painted," he says, and continues: "So, this is in relation to the role of space, the architecture of the room, which makes the painting appear. This I never painted so I don't create it, I don't invent anything."[7] The withholding of paint from the canvas becomes an act of generosity, allowing physical and conceptual space for a purposeful mark to be made. Toroni posits, "It's the relationship between the painted and the non-painted: each reflects the other."[8] Going beyond the simple formalism of the figure-ground relationship, the mutual dependency of the imprint and the bare surface operates as an iterative mechanism by which the subject—the *work* of the painting—is made apparent in an endless loop of the *fini* and the *non fini.*

L'INFINI

In 1922, working alongside the architect Camille Lefèvre, Monet orchestrated the architectural designs for the display of his *Nymphéas* suite at the Musée de l'Orangerie in Paris. At the heart of the final design are two ovoid rooms, deliberately evoking the mathematical symbol of infinity. Carefully planning the scale, rhythm, and spacing of the canvases, Monet intended that the works themselves would echo the architecture, giving the "illusion of an endless whole, of a wave with no horizon and no shore."[9]

Circling back to Toroni's reference to Monet's Orangerie, the concept of the *non fini* can also be considered in terms of temporality, or *infini*: the sustained, ongoing, incomplete project. The repetition of the specific gesture unburdens it of expressive meaning, returning it through banality to a conversation of labor and process. Beyond the instance of the brushstroke, it is the accumulation of works, of imprints, stretched out over decades, that is the ultimate import of Toroni's oeuvre. To this end, Toroni's work can be seen as both the final mark, or as a radical proposition in a perpetual state of beginning.[10]

FIN

65

65

65

65

65

Notes

1. Interview with the artist by Jean Siegel, *Arts* Magazine (October 1989): 47.
2. Bernard Marcadé, interview with the artist, *Niele Toroni* (Bordeaux: CAPC Musée d'Art Contemporain de Bordeaux, 1997), 145.
3. Jules-Antoine Castagnary, "L'Exposition du boulevard des Capucines: Les Impressionistes," *Le Siècle*, April 29, 1874, reprinted in Hélène Adhémar, "L'Exposition de 1874 chez Nadar (rétrospective documentaire)," *Centenaire de l'impressionnisme* (Paris: Secrétariat d'État à la culture and Éditions des Musées nationaux, 1974), 265.
4. Creighton E. Gilbert, "What Is Expressed in Michelangelo's 'Non-Finito,'" *Artibus et Historiae* 24, no. 48 (2003): 57-64. See also Paola Barocchi's notes to her edition of Giorgio Vasari, *La Vita di Michelangelo nelle redazioni del 1550 e del 1568*, vol. 4 (Milan: R. Ricciardi, 1962), 1,645-1,670.
5. See Rainer Maria Rilke, *Letters on Cézanne*, ed. Clara Rilke, trans. Joel Agee (New York: Fromm, 1985), 46.
6. Excerpt from an interview with Woks, *ArtNews* (March 1959): 62.
7. Siegel, 50.
8. Marcadé, 148.
9. Claude Monet, quoted in Robert Gordon and Andrew Forge, *Monet* (New York: Abrams, 1983), 224.
10. See also Marcadé, 146, and René Denizot, "An Imprint Is Never Alone," *Artforum* 19, no. 4 (December 1980): n.p.

Exhibitions: 1978–1983

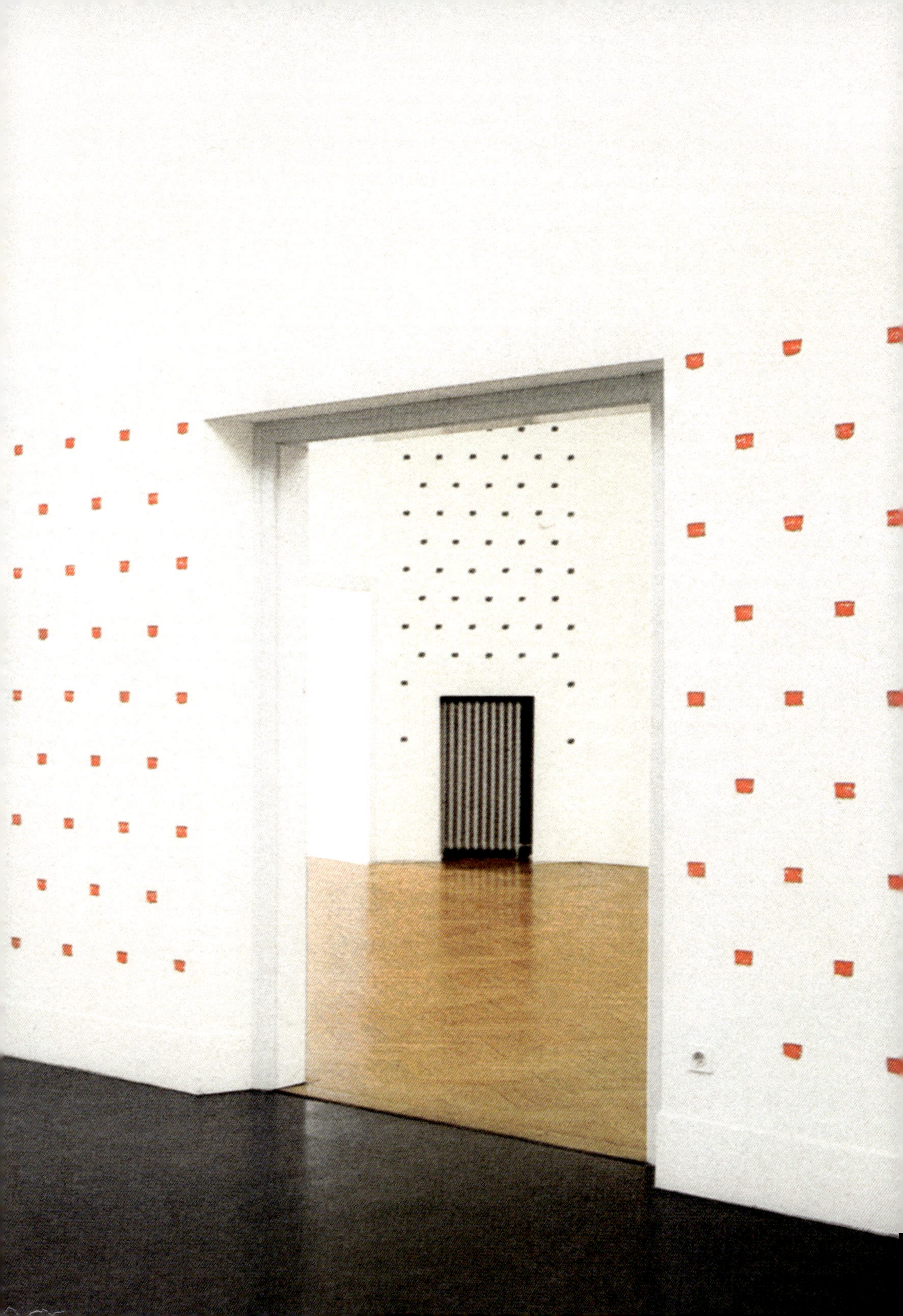

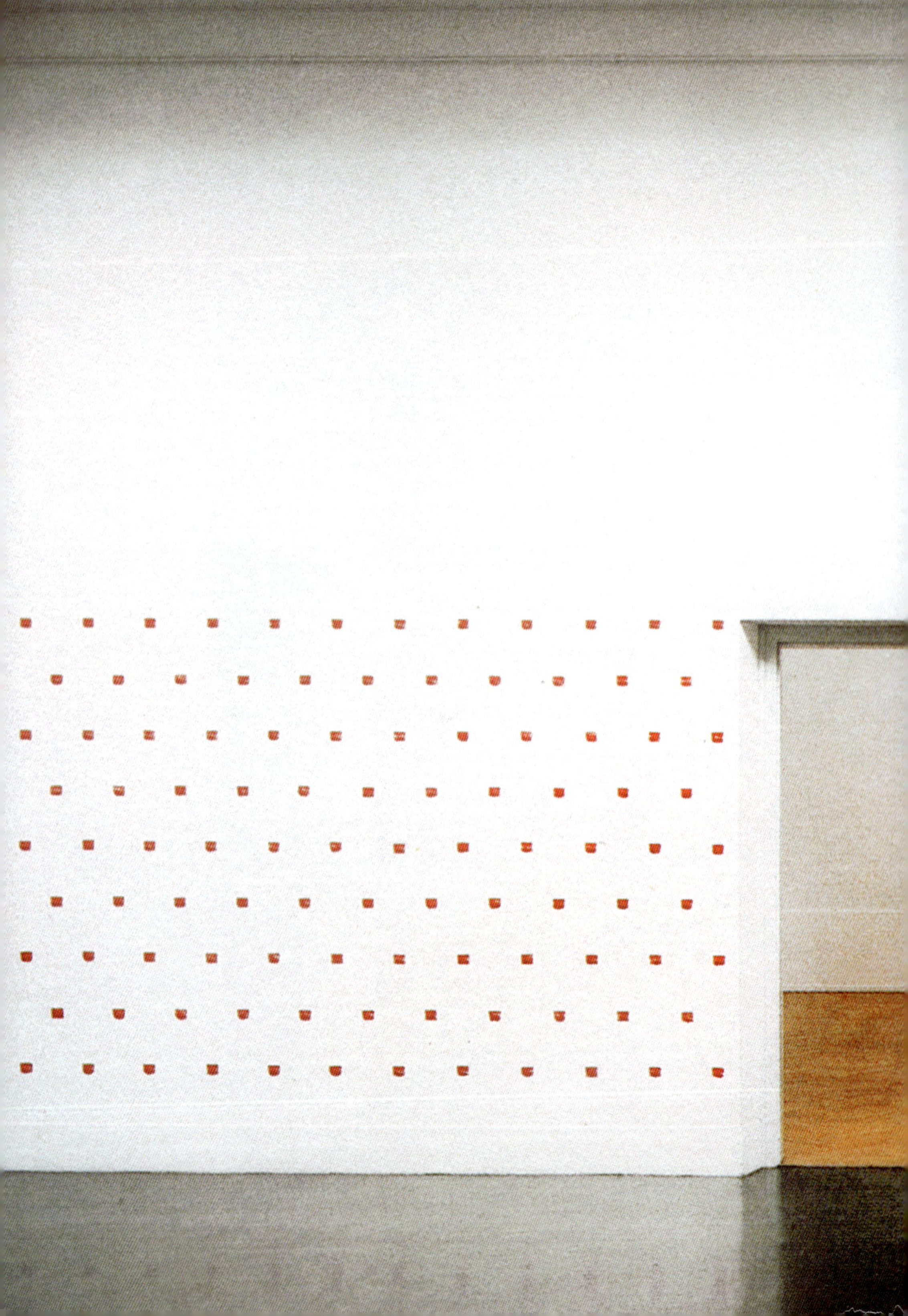

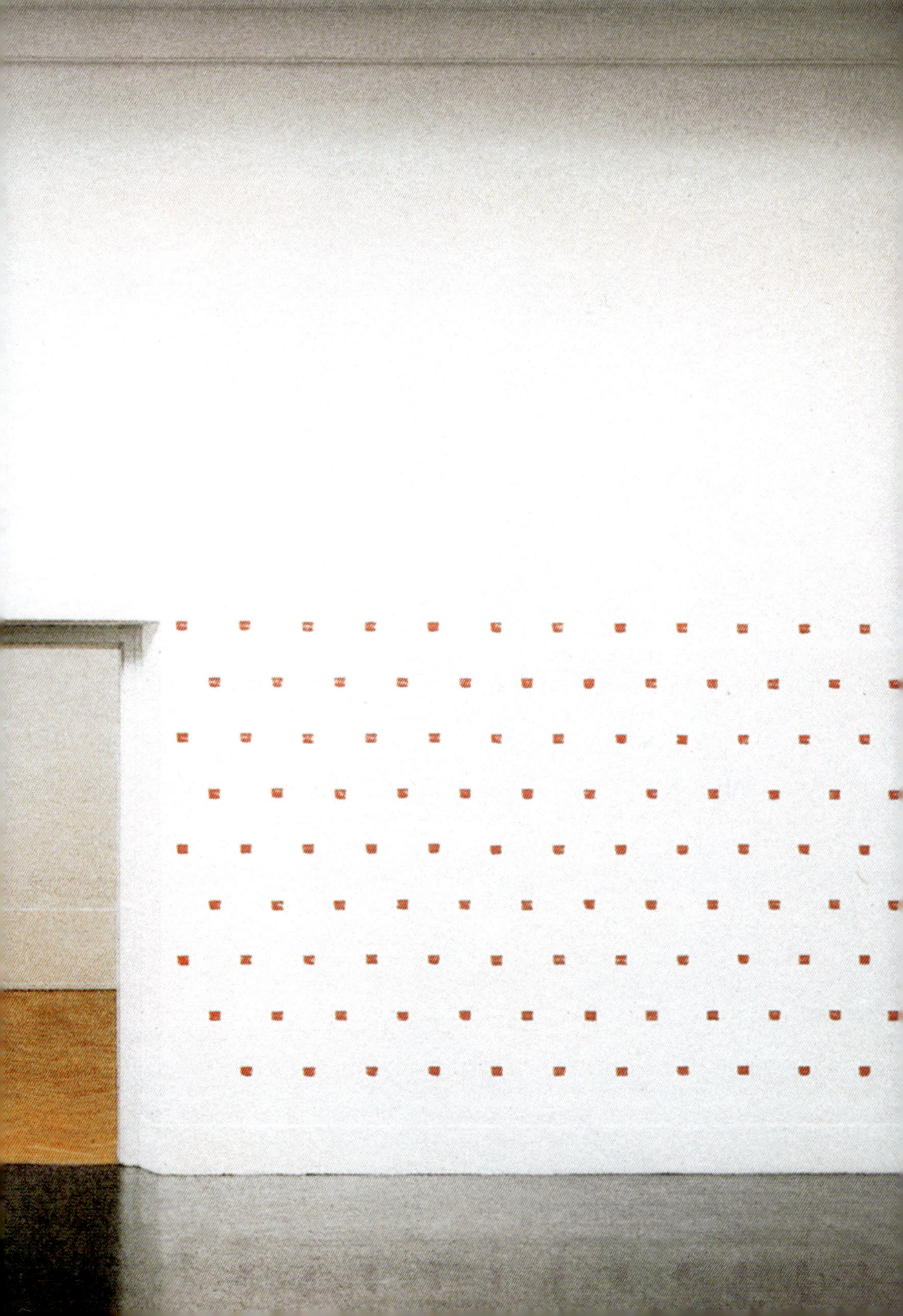

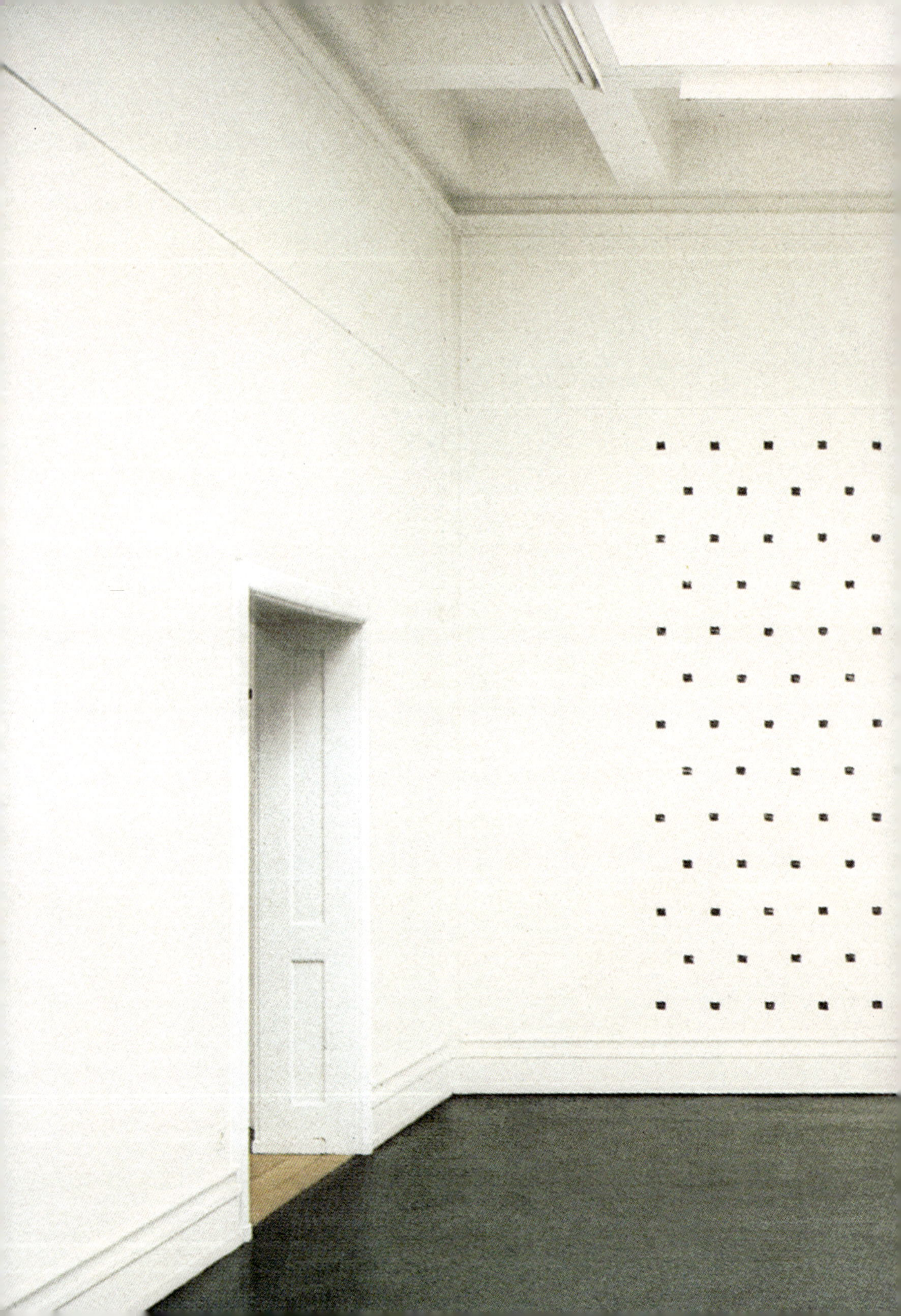

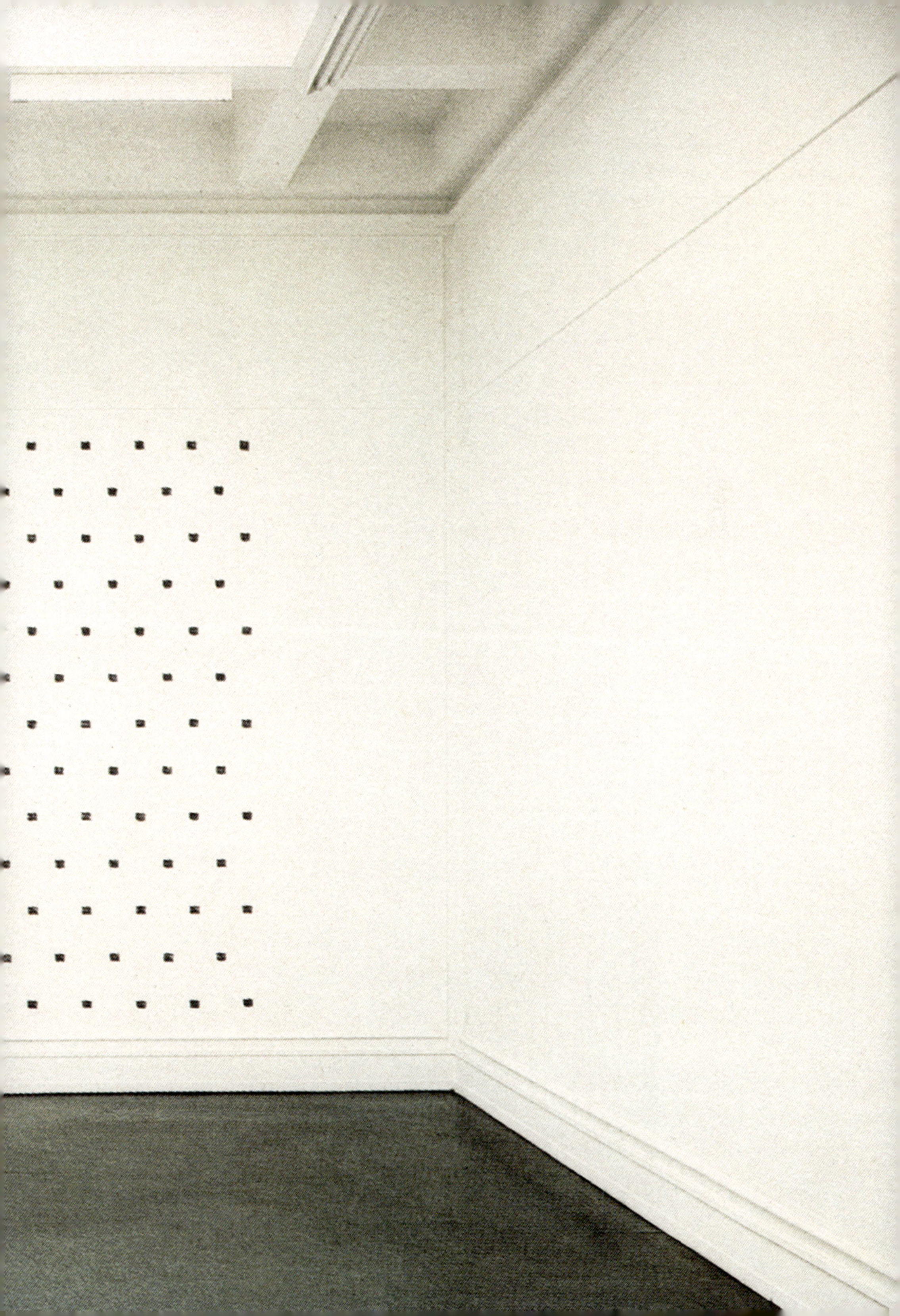

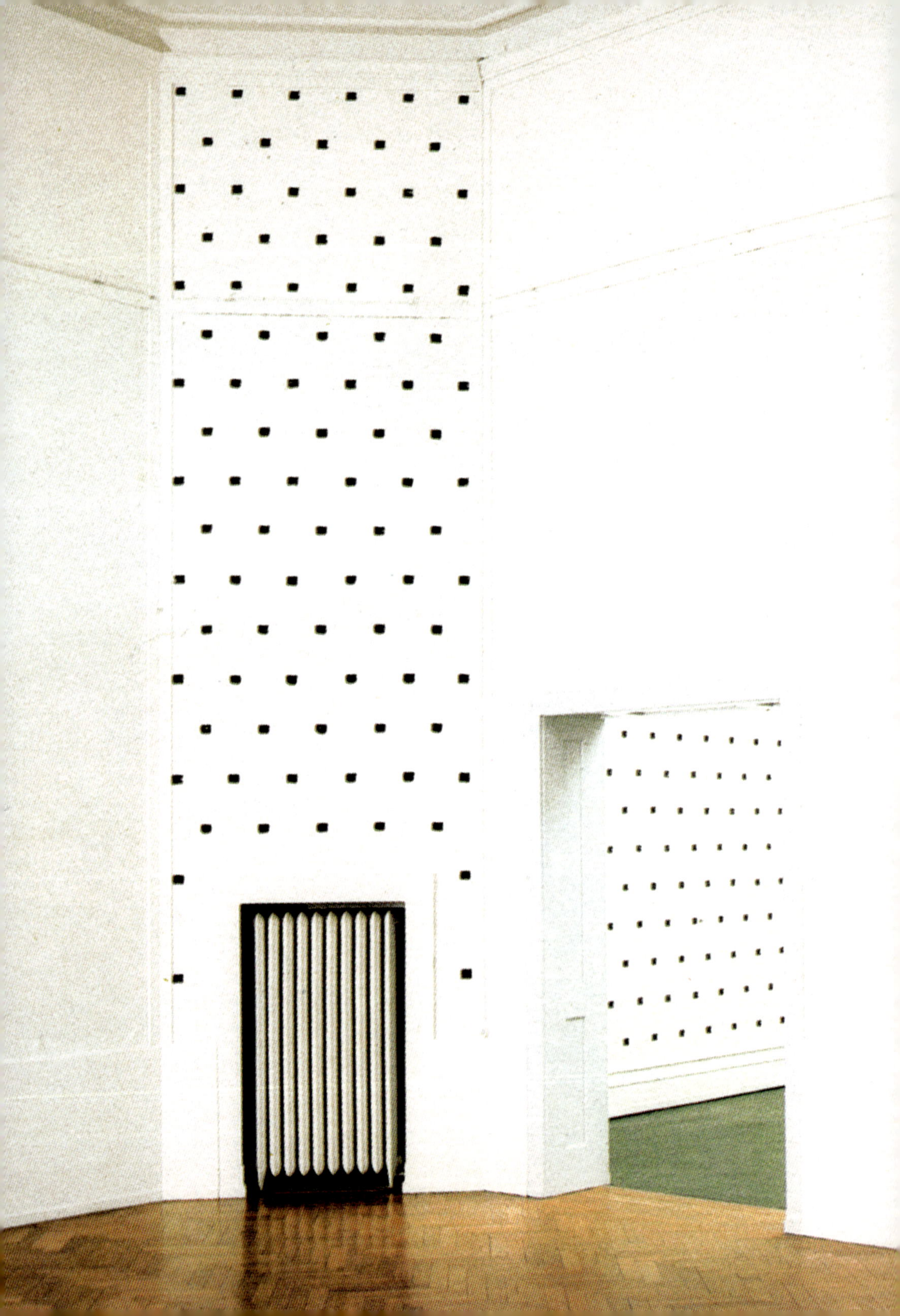

75 75

75

75 75

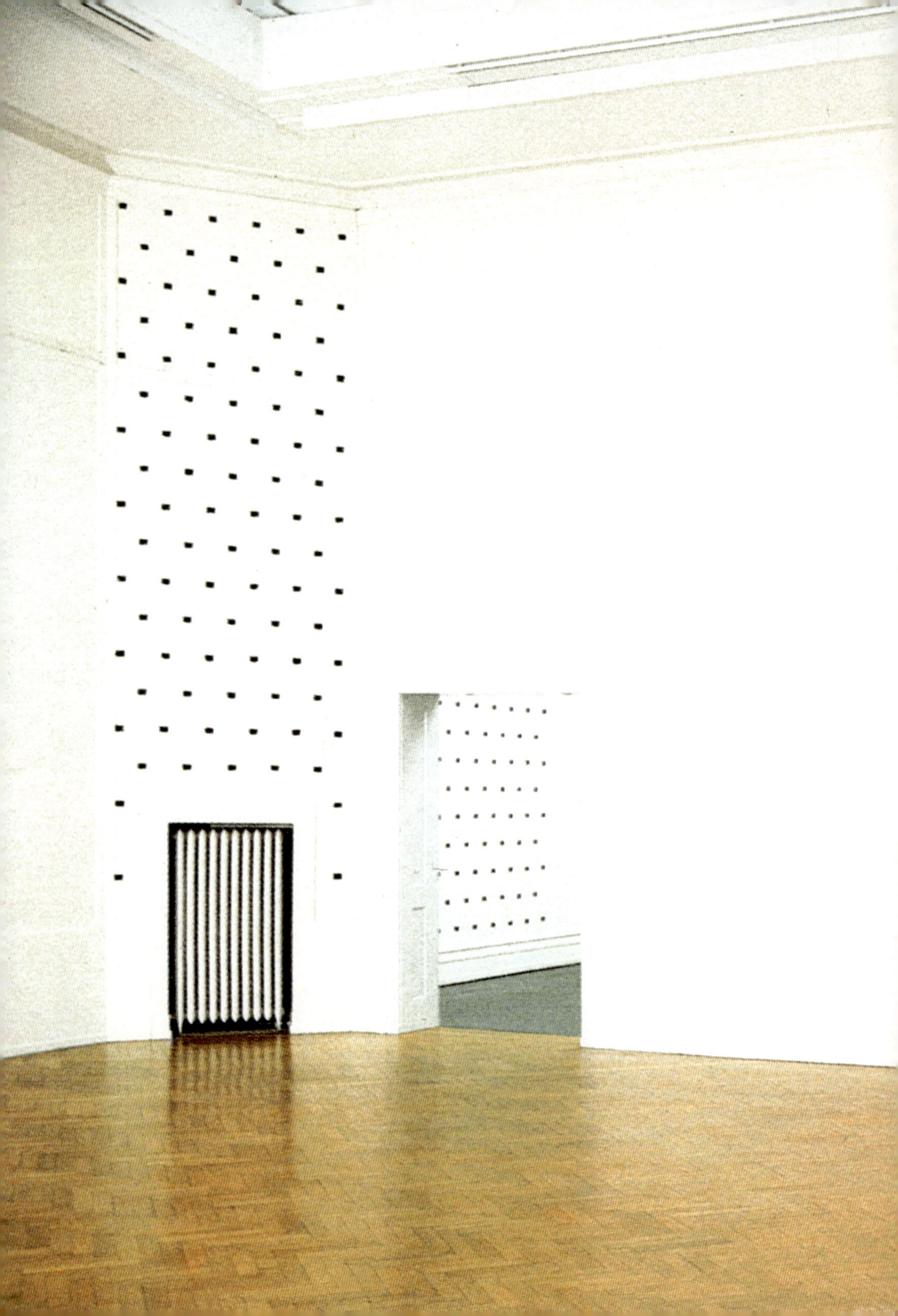

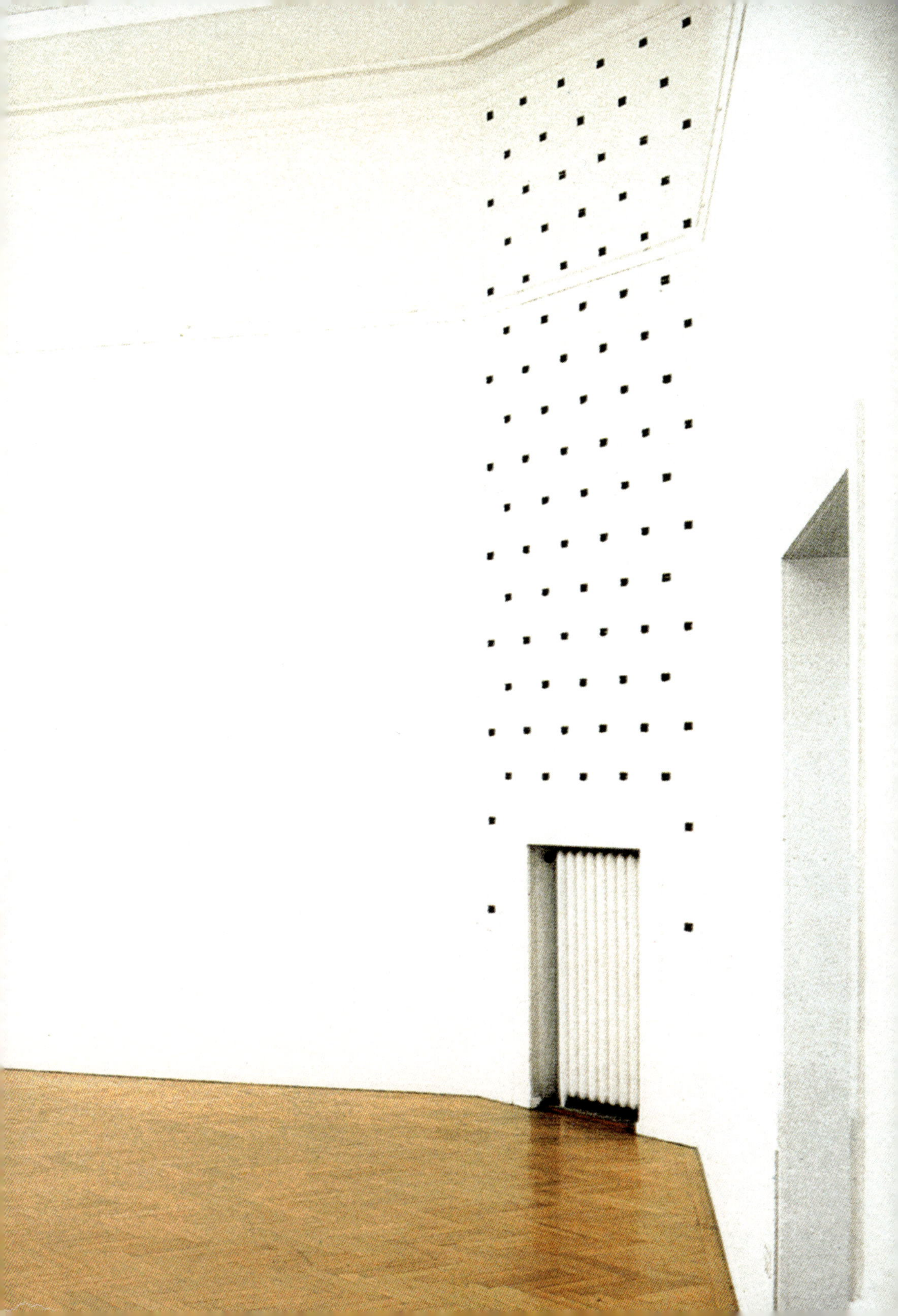

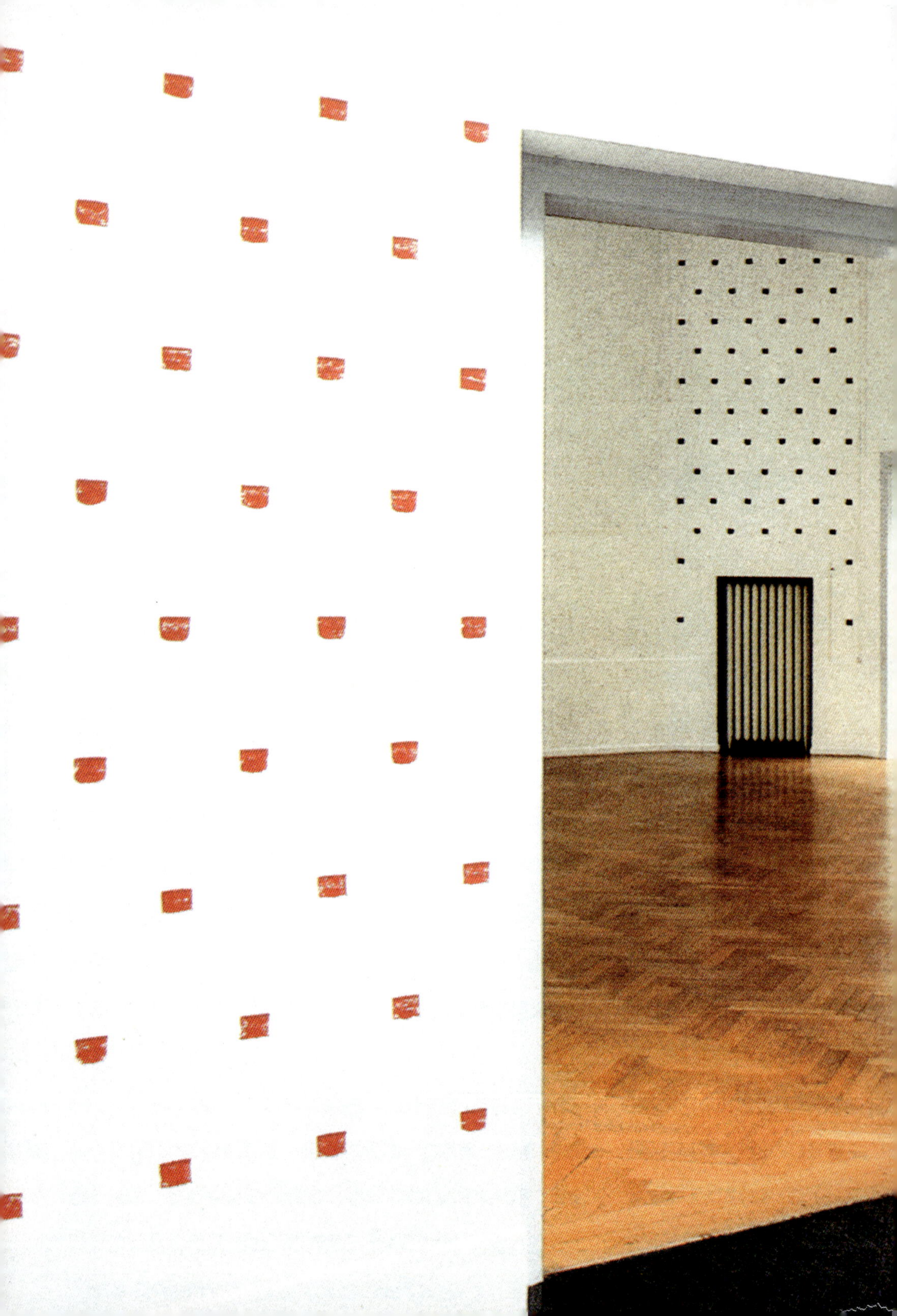

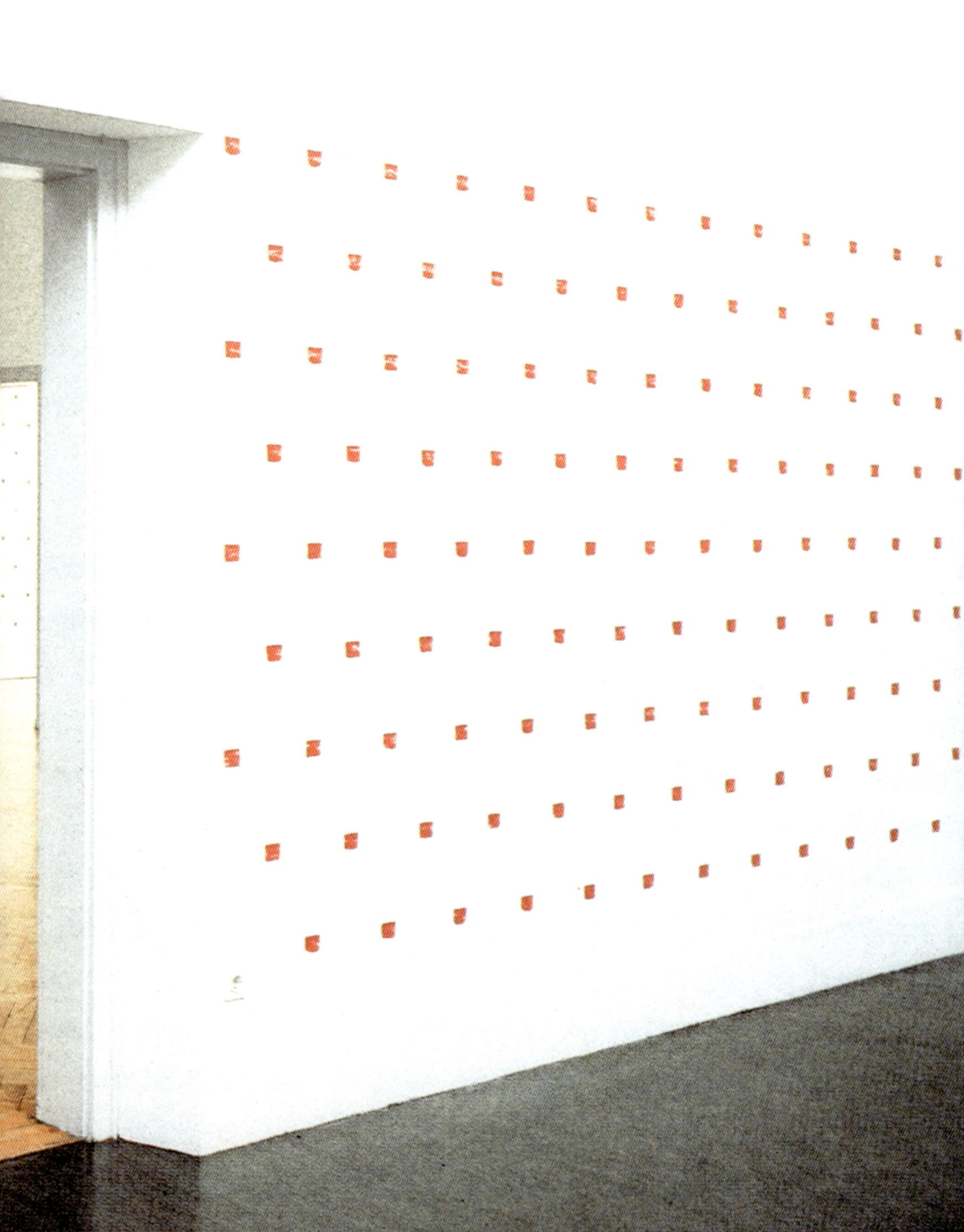

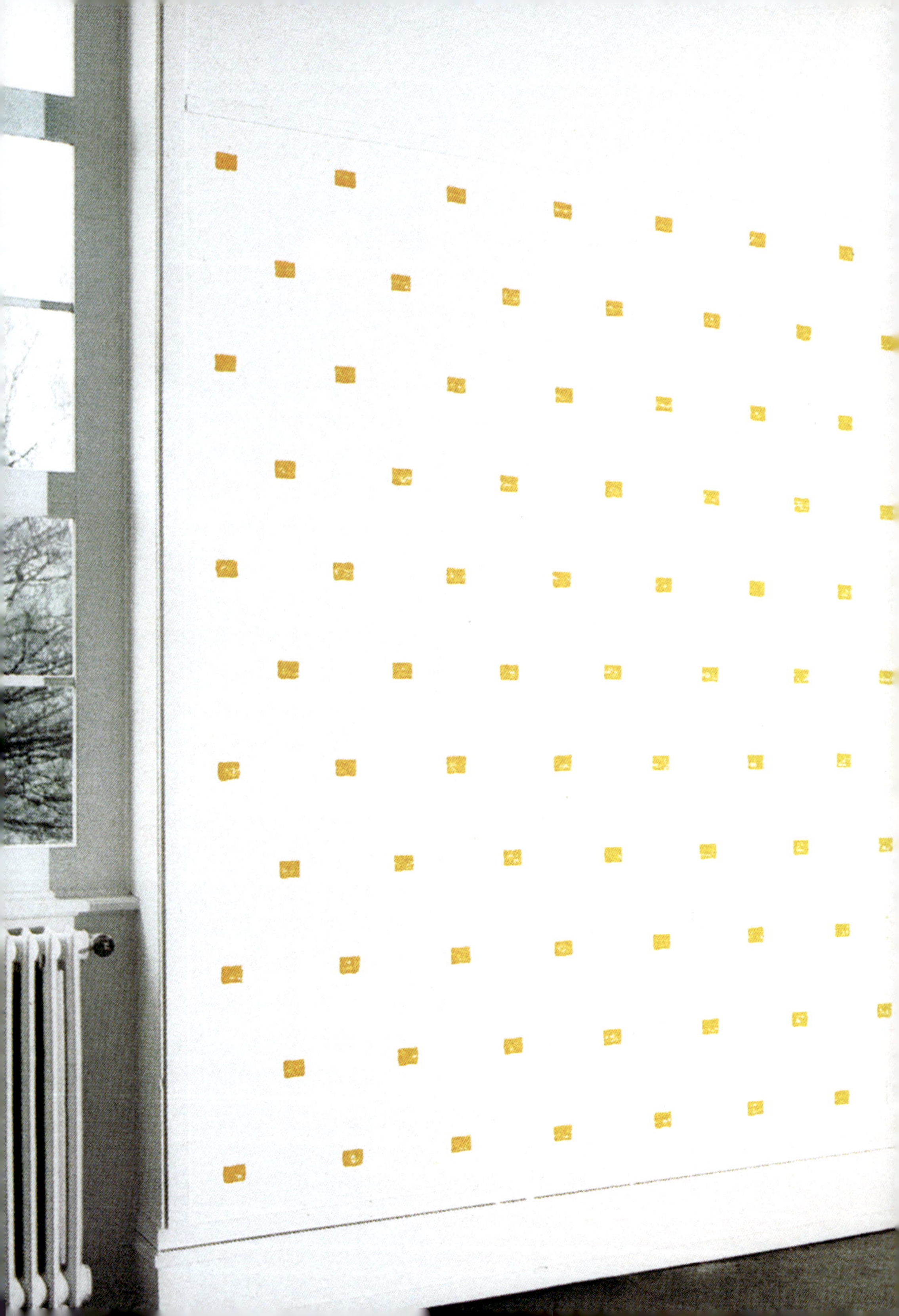

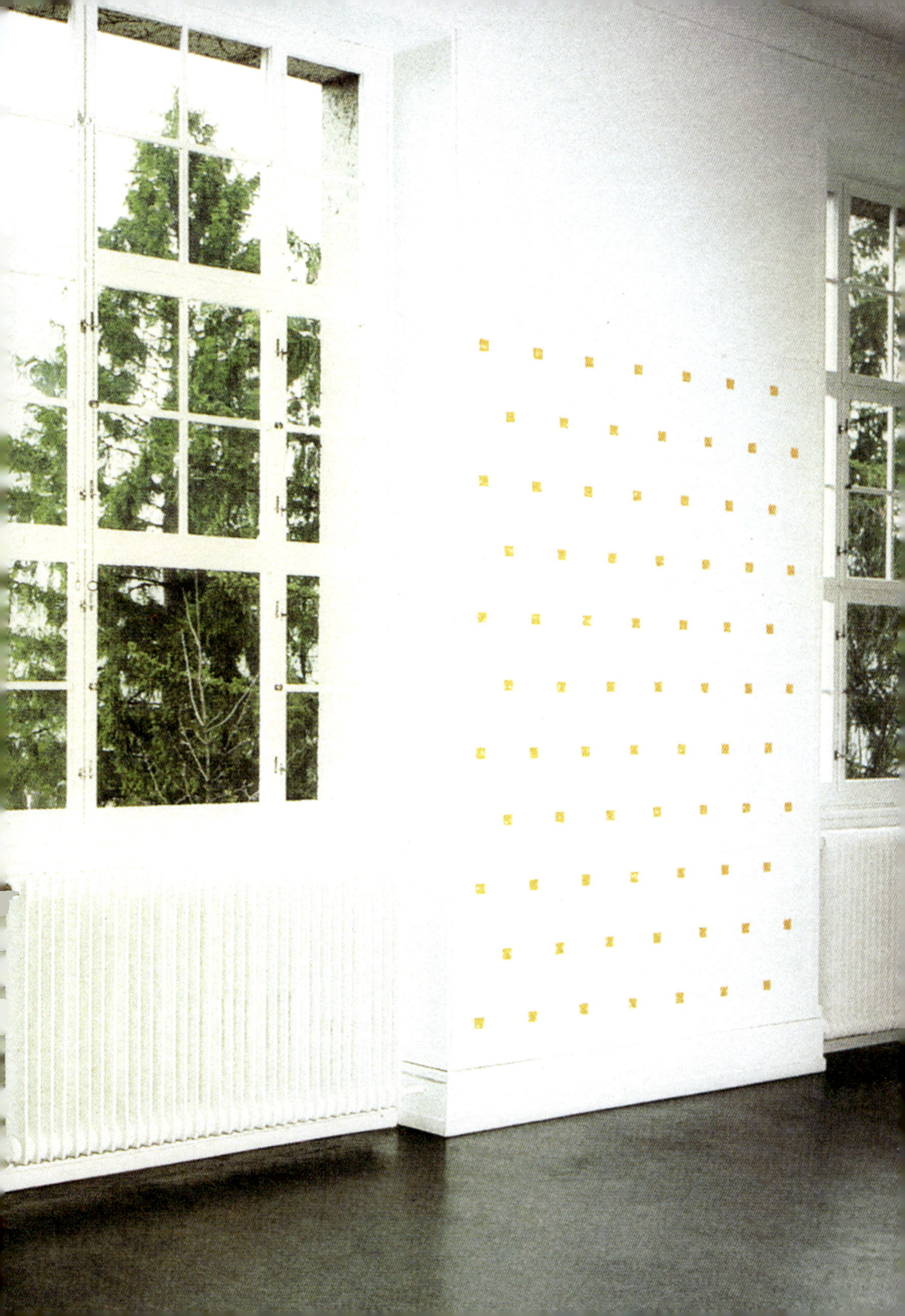

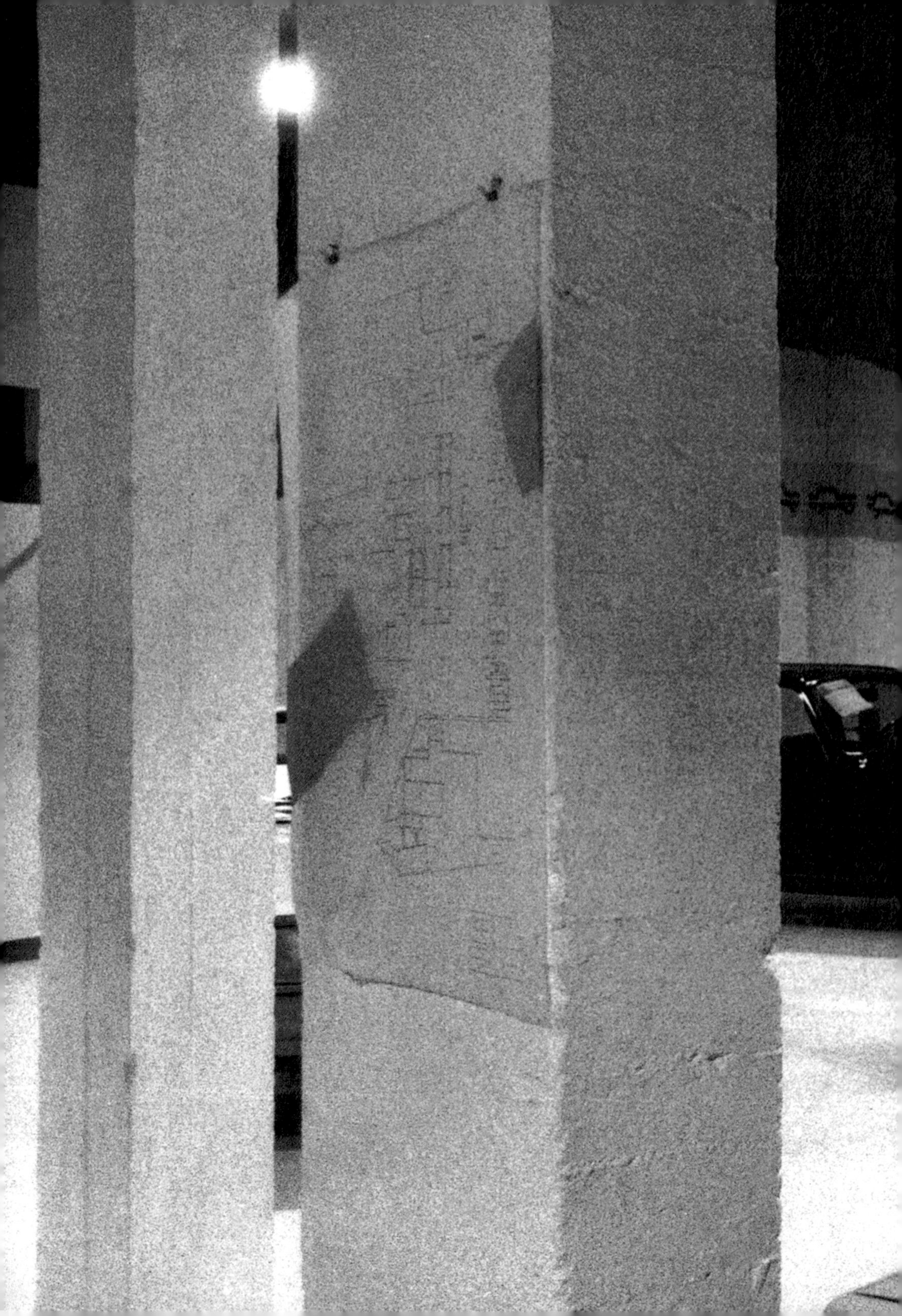

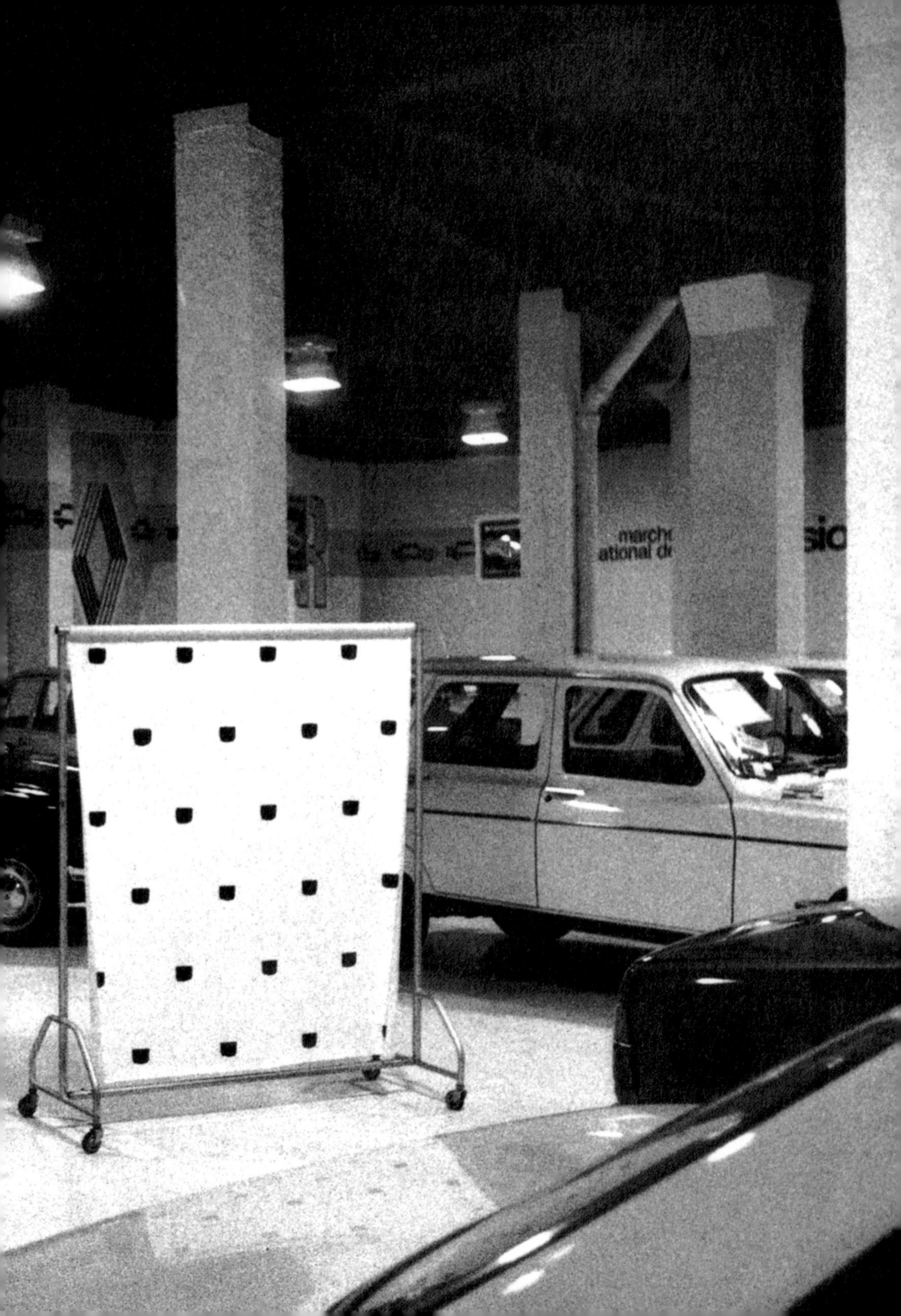

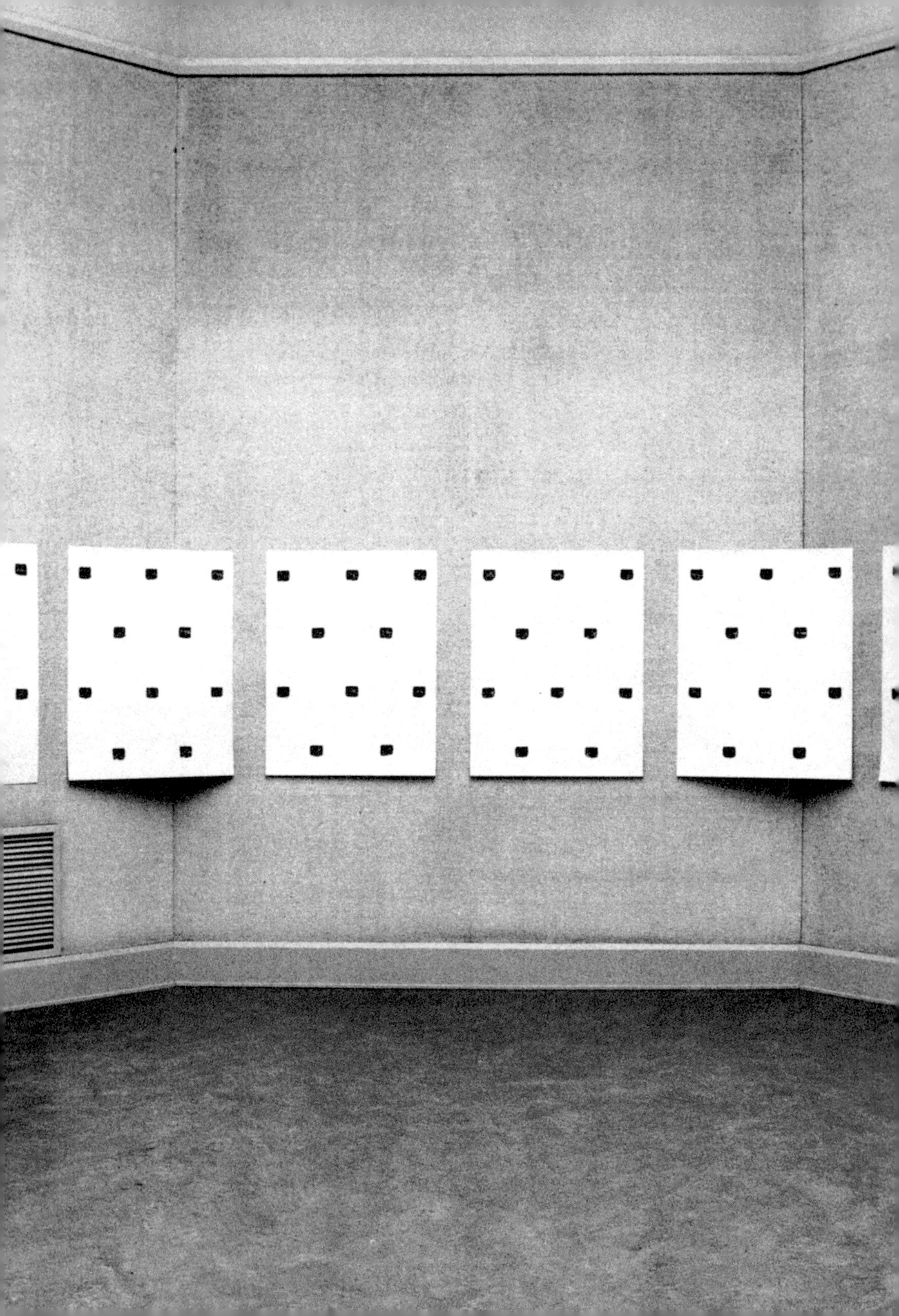

85

85

85

85

85

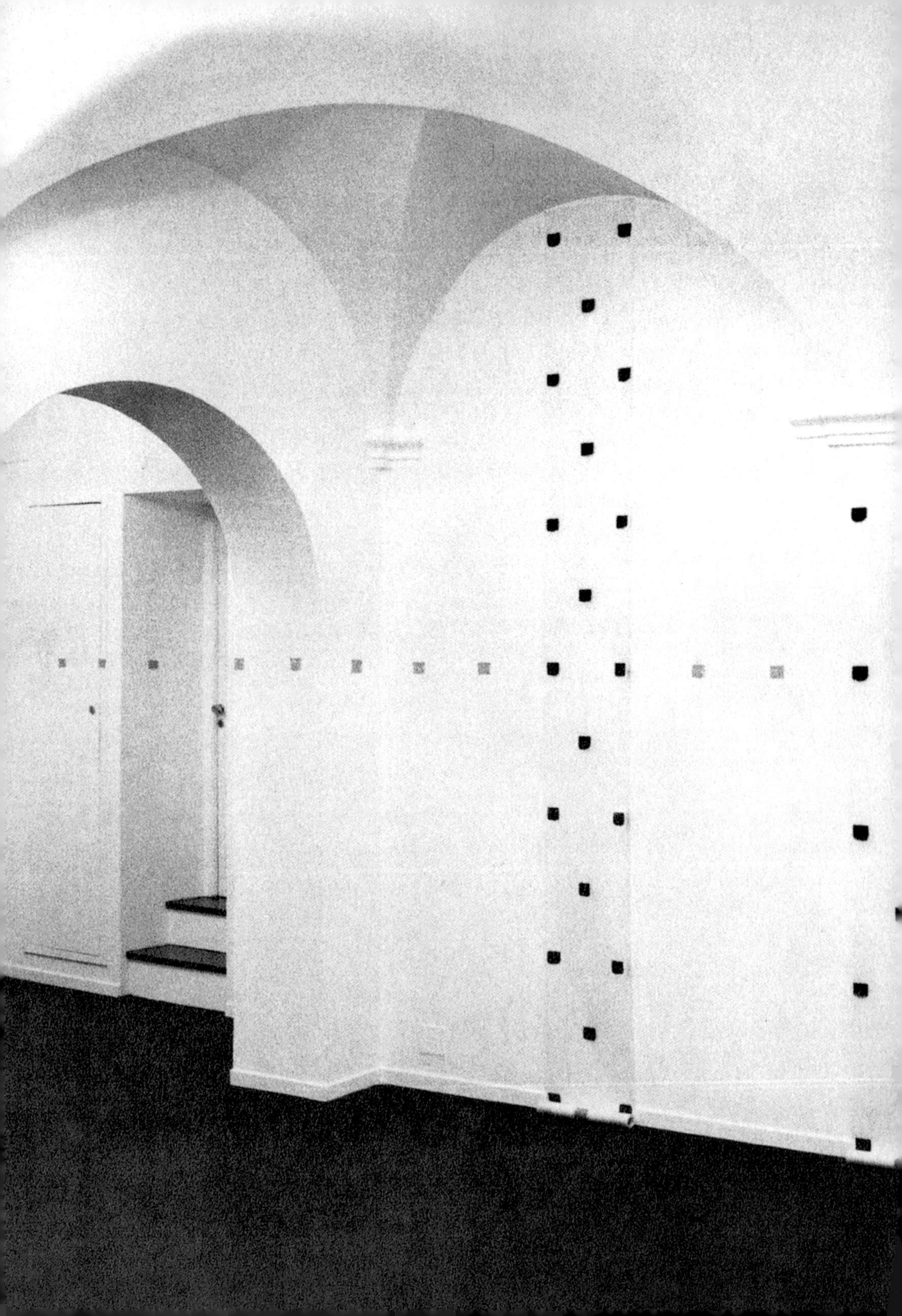

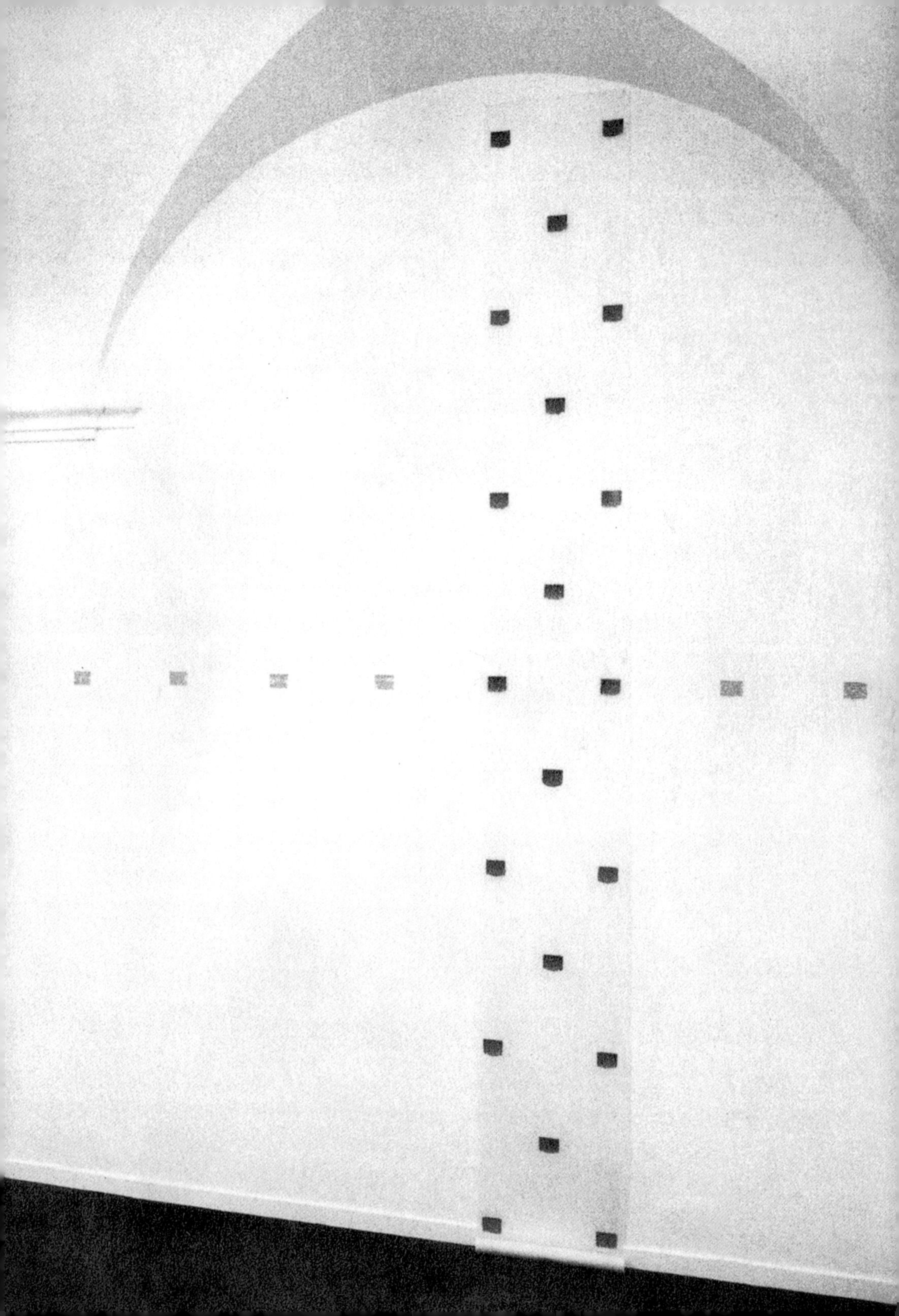

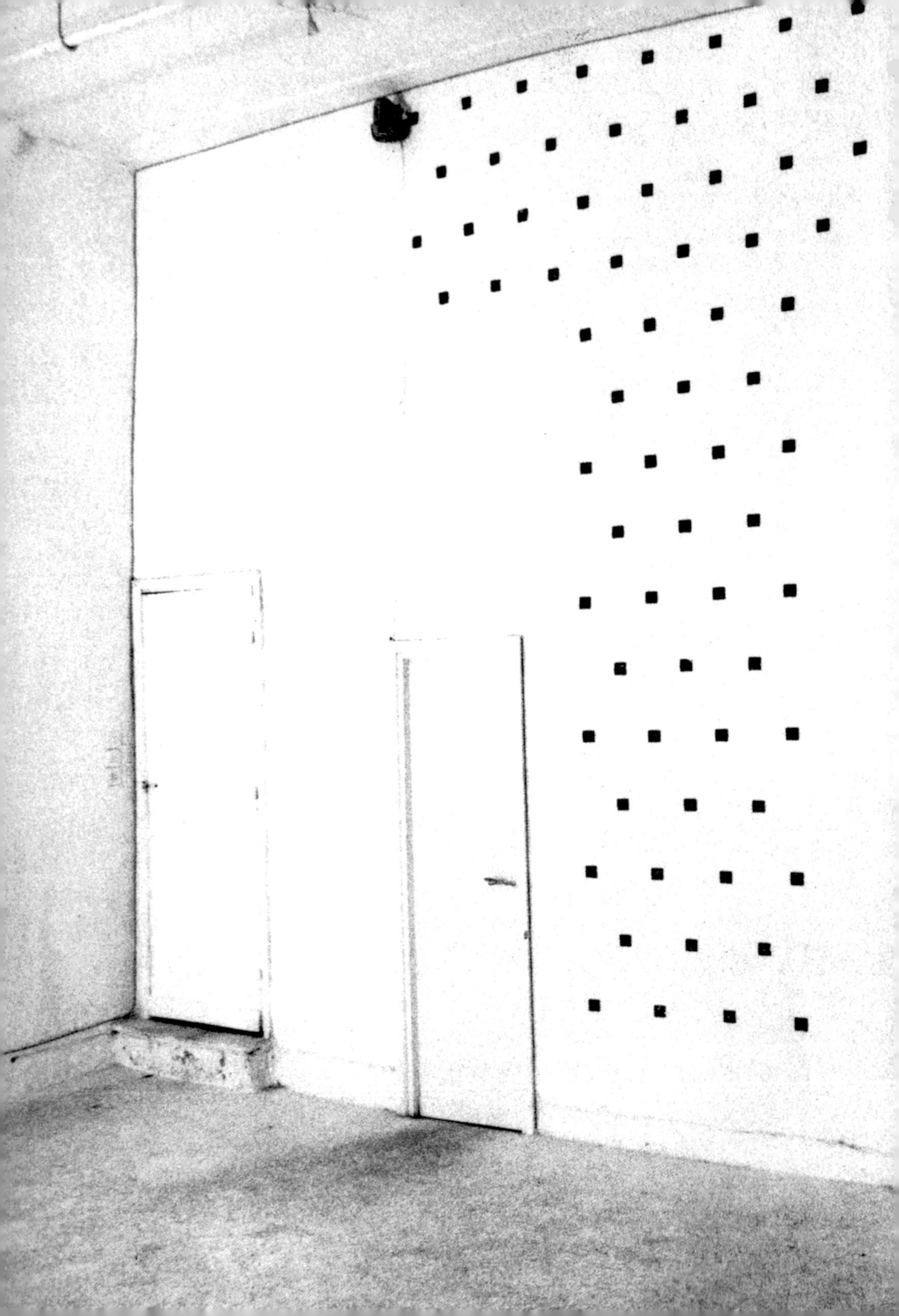

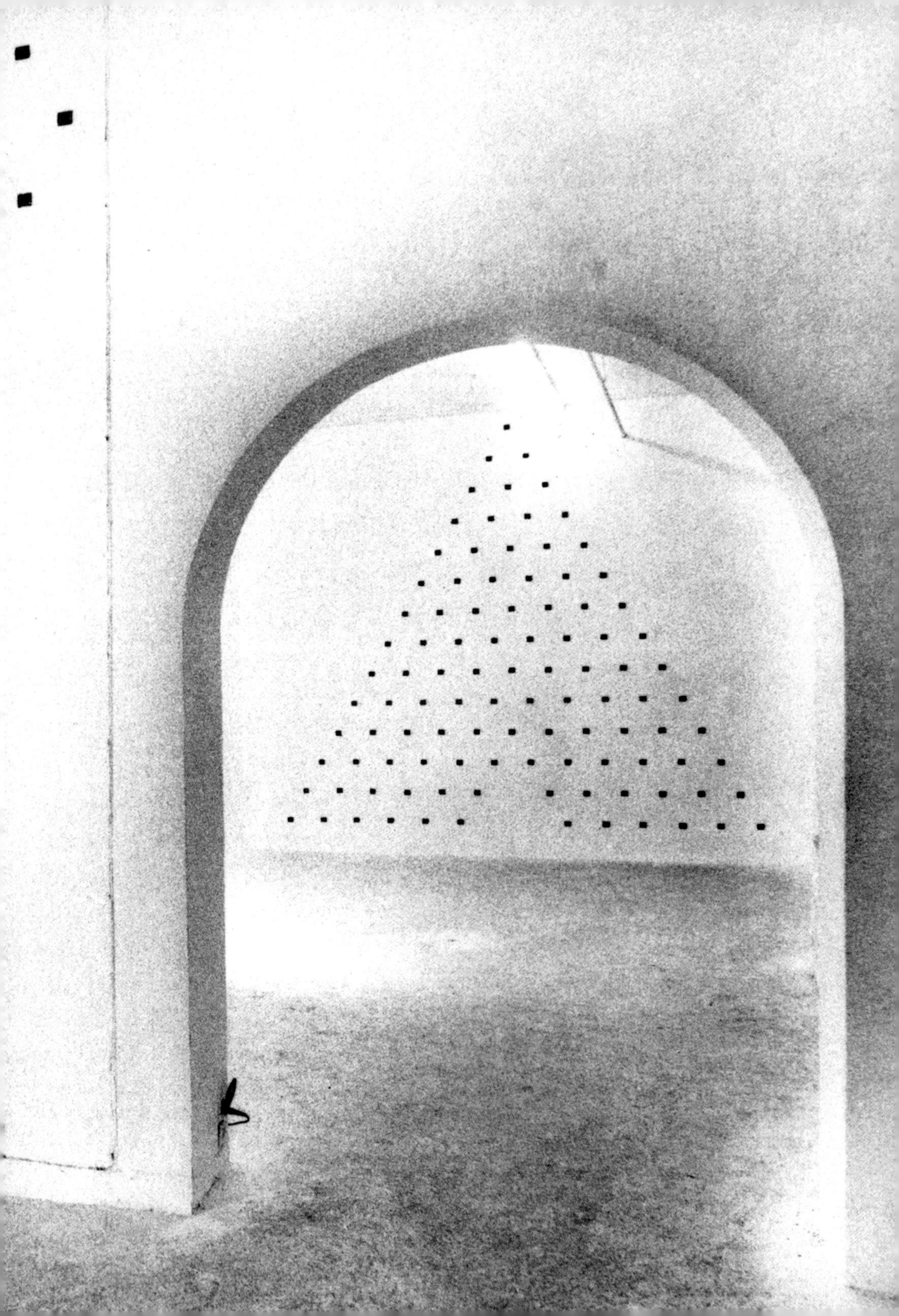

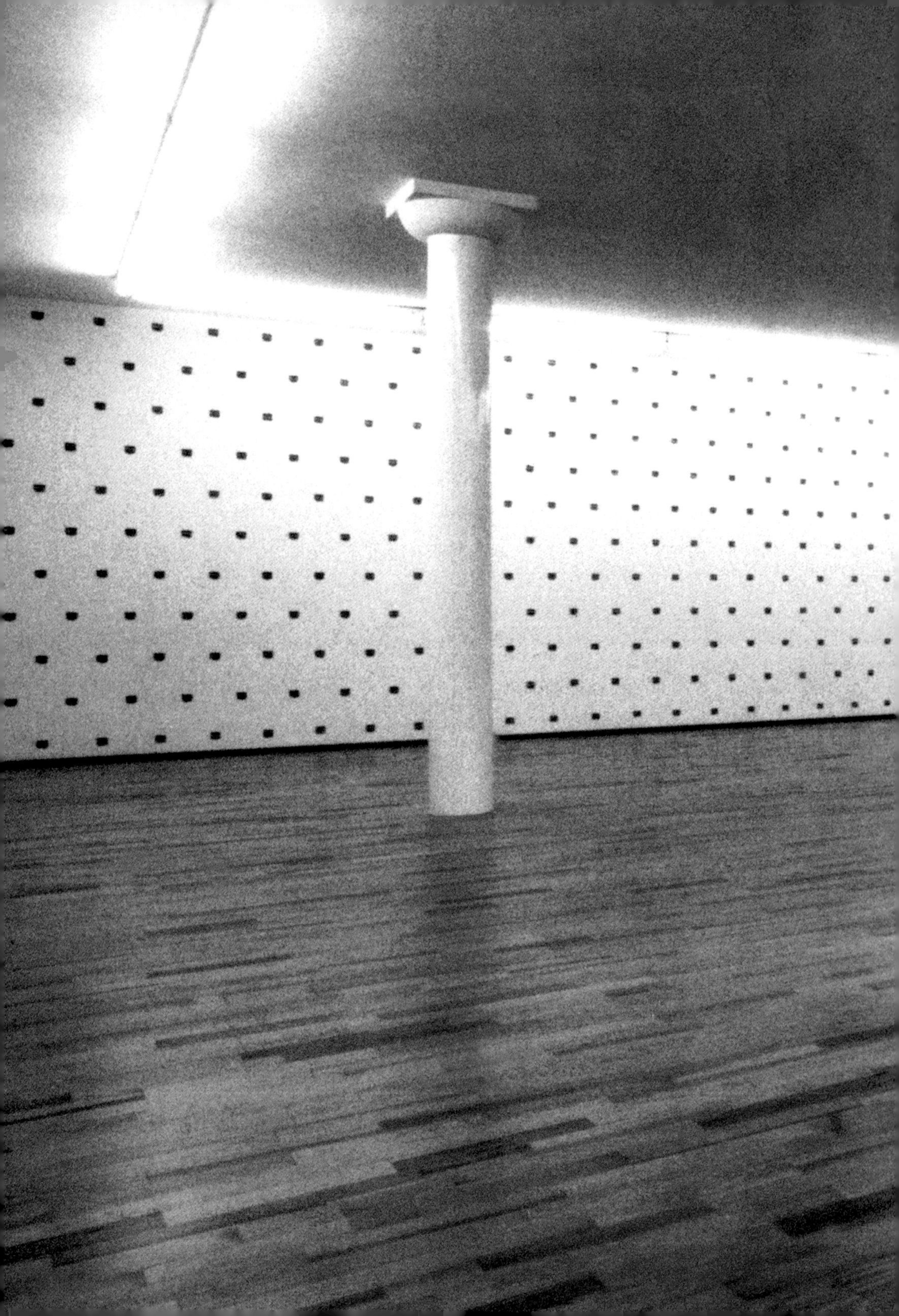

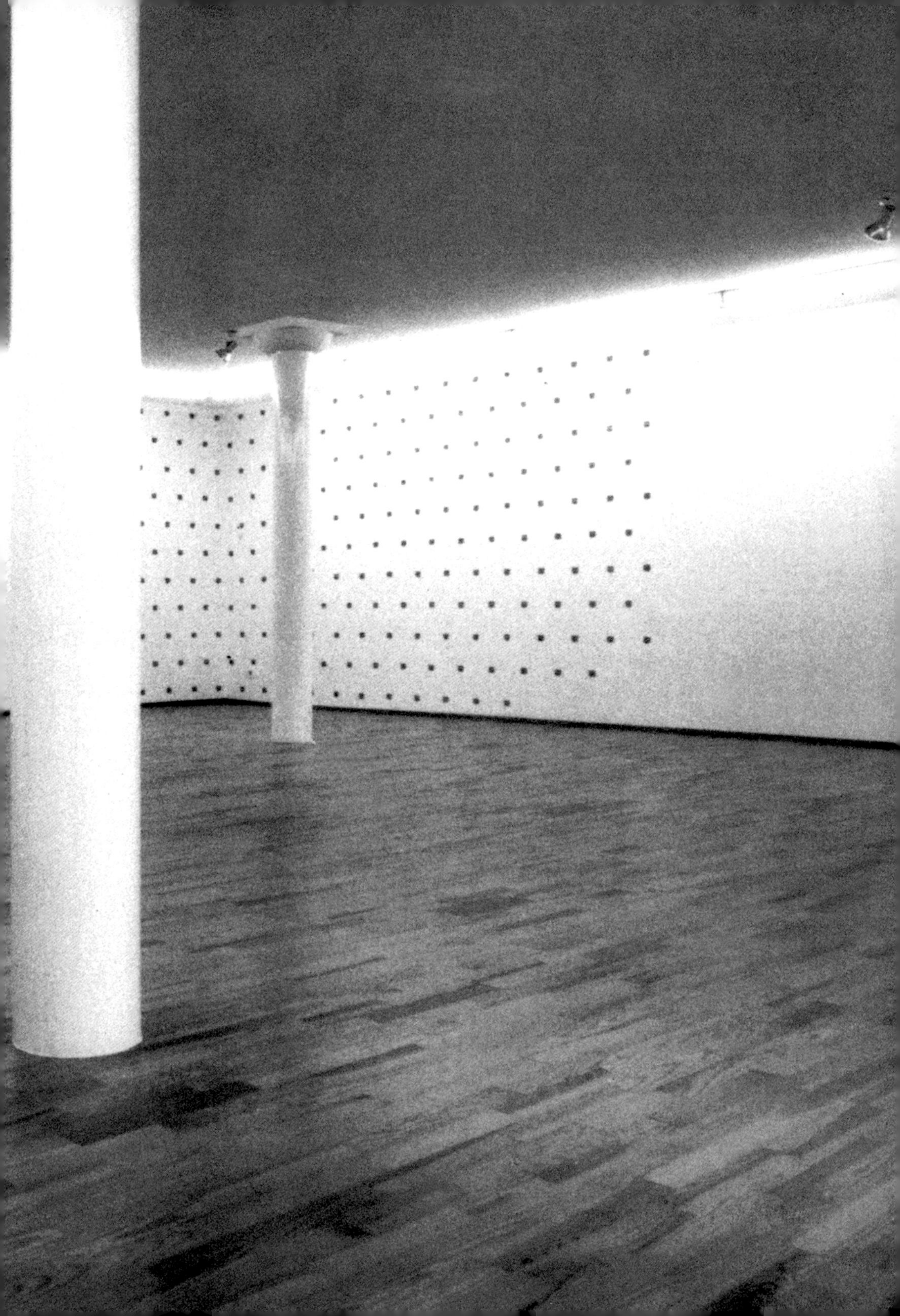

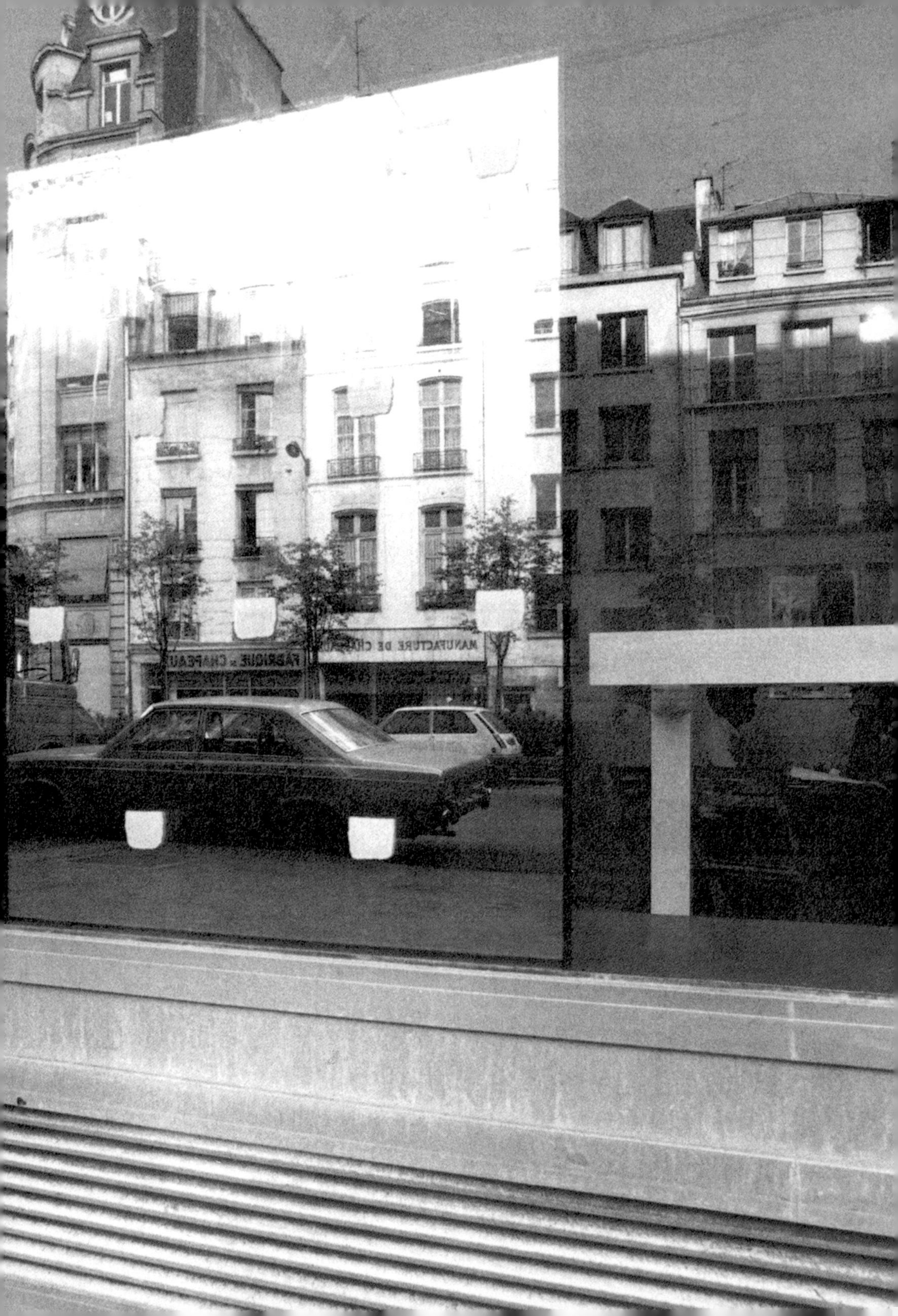
MANUFACTURE DE
FABRIQUE

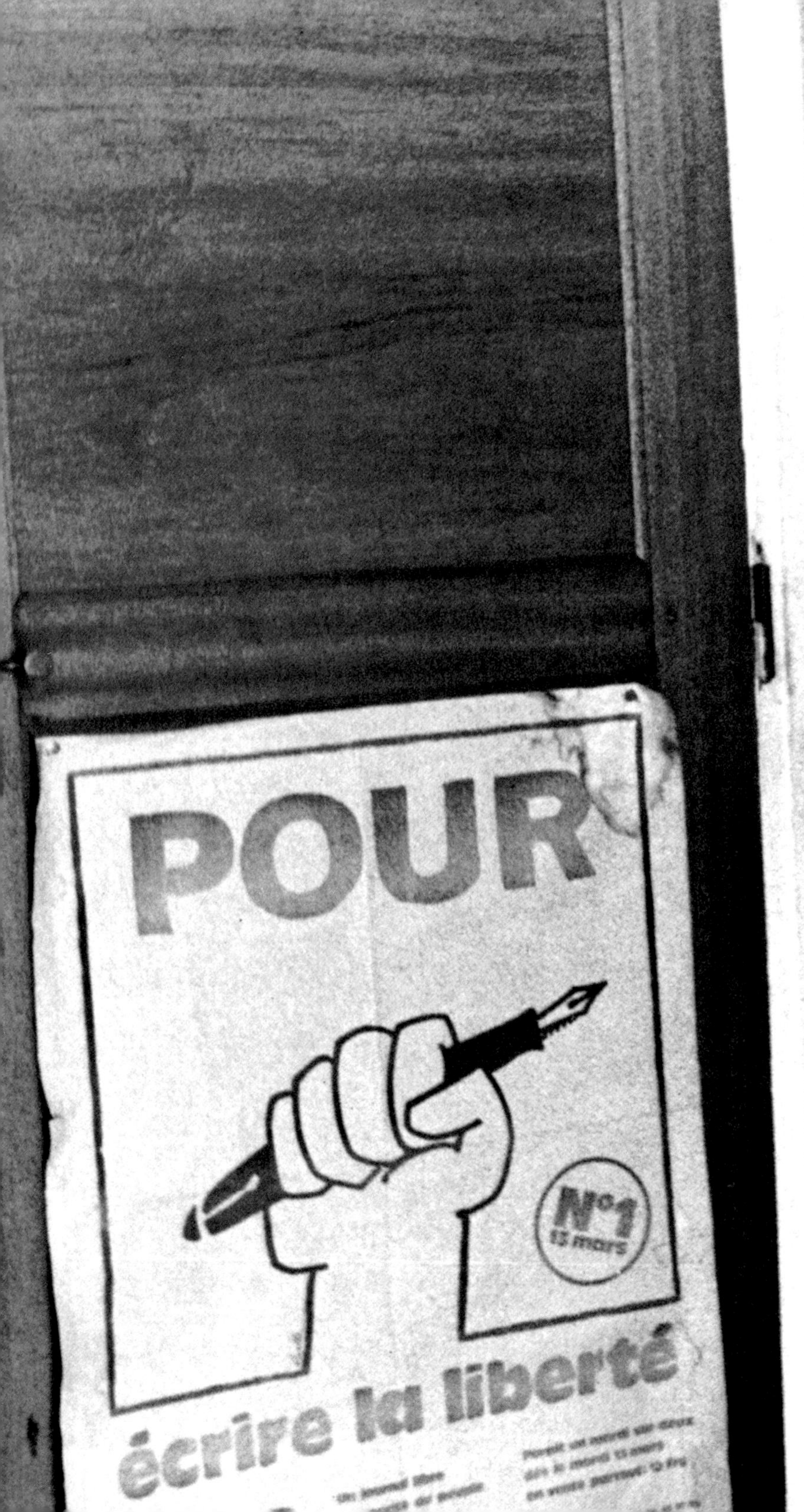
POUR
N°1
13 mars
écrire la liberté

95

95

95

95

95

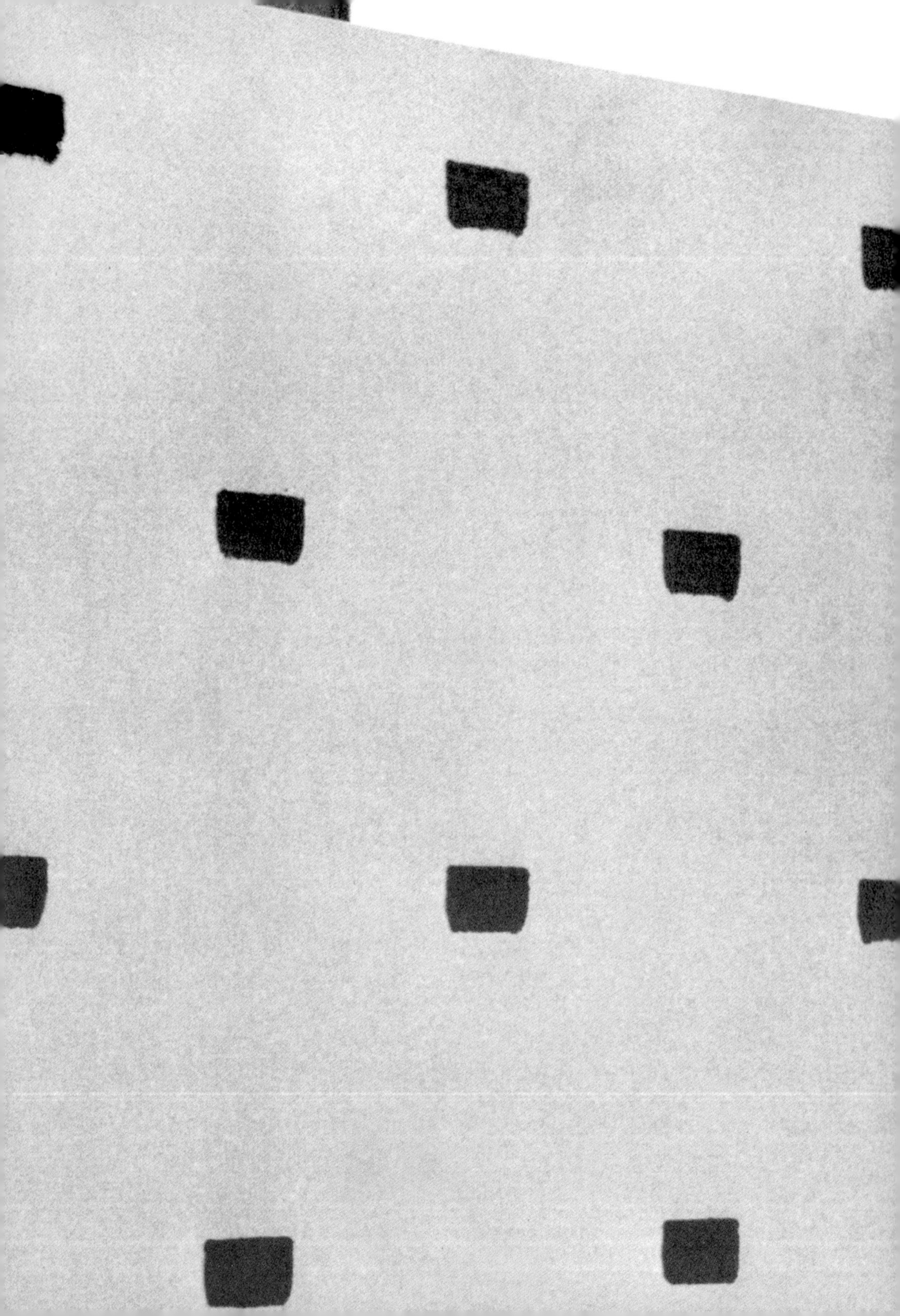

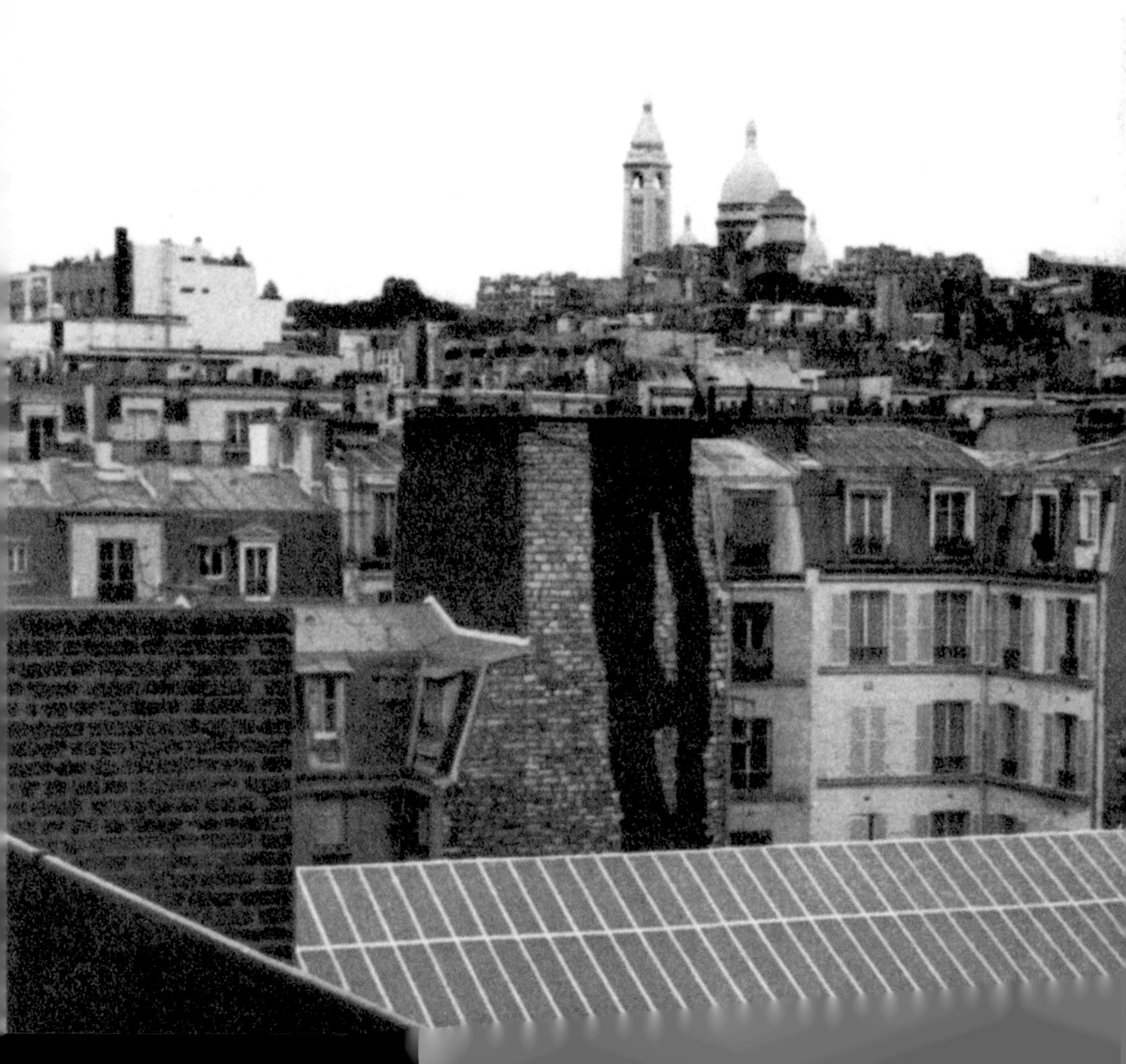

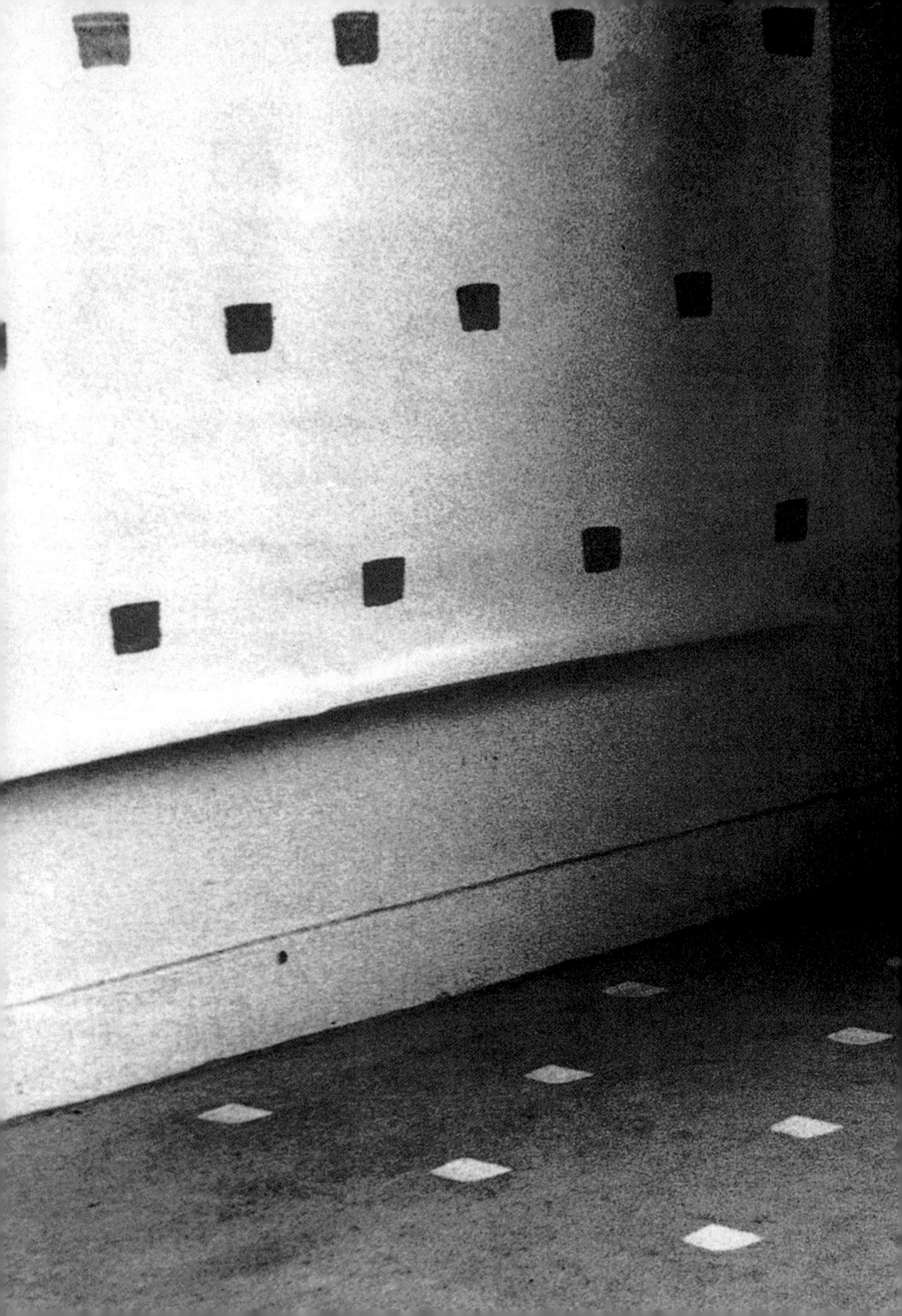

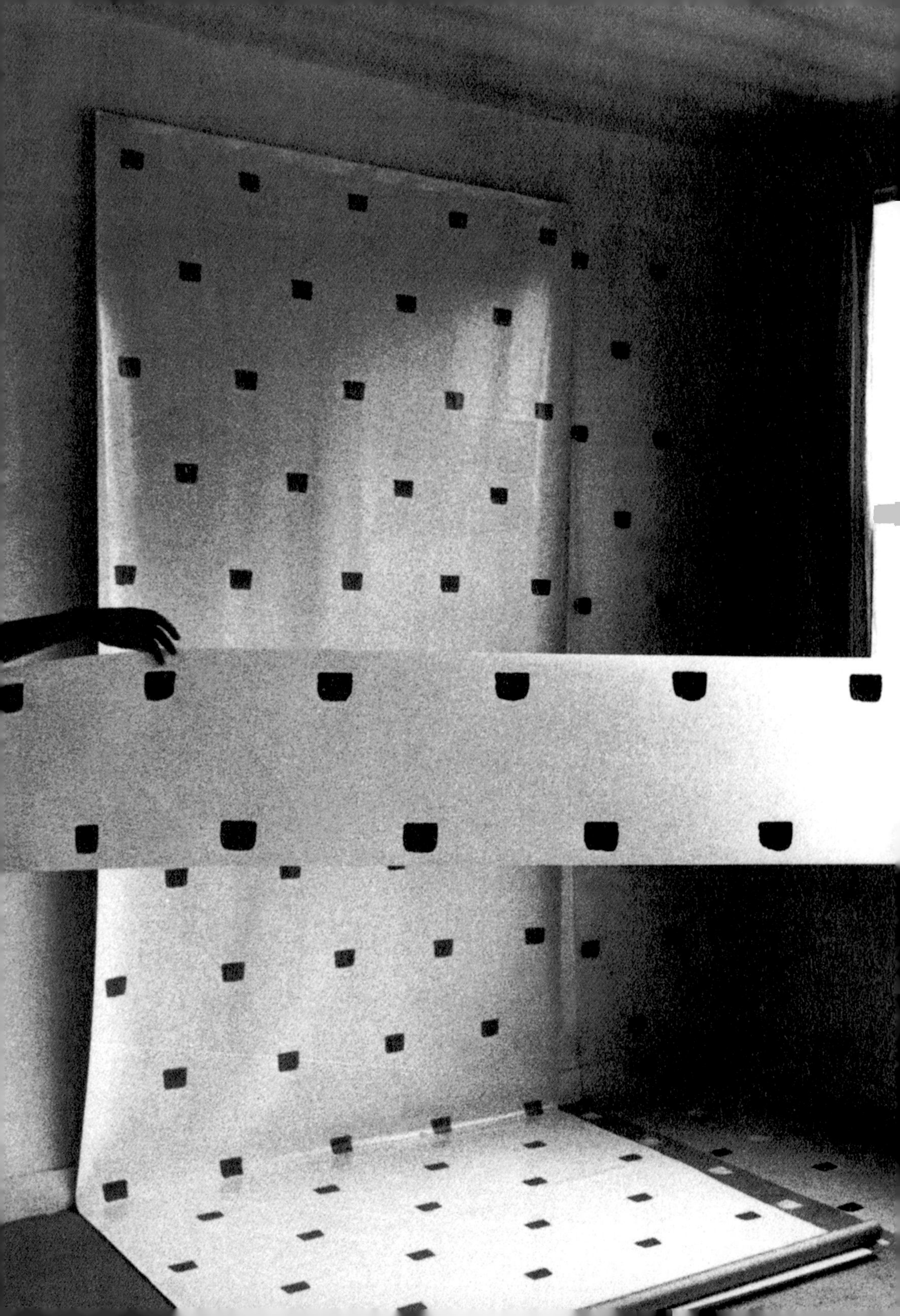

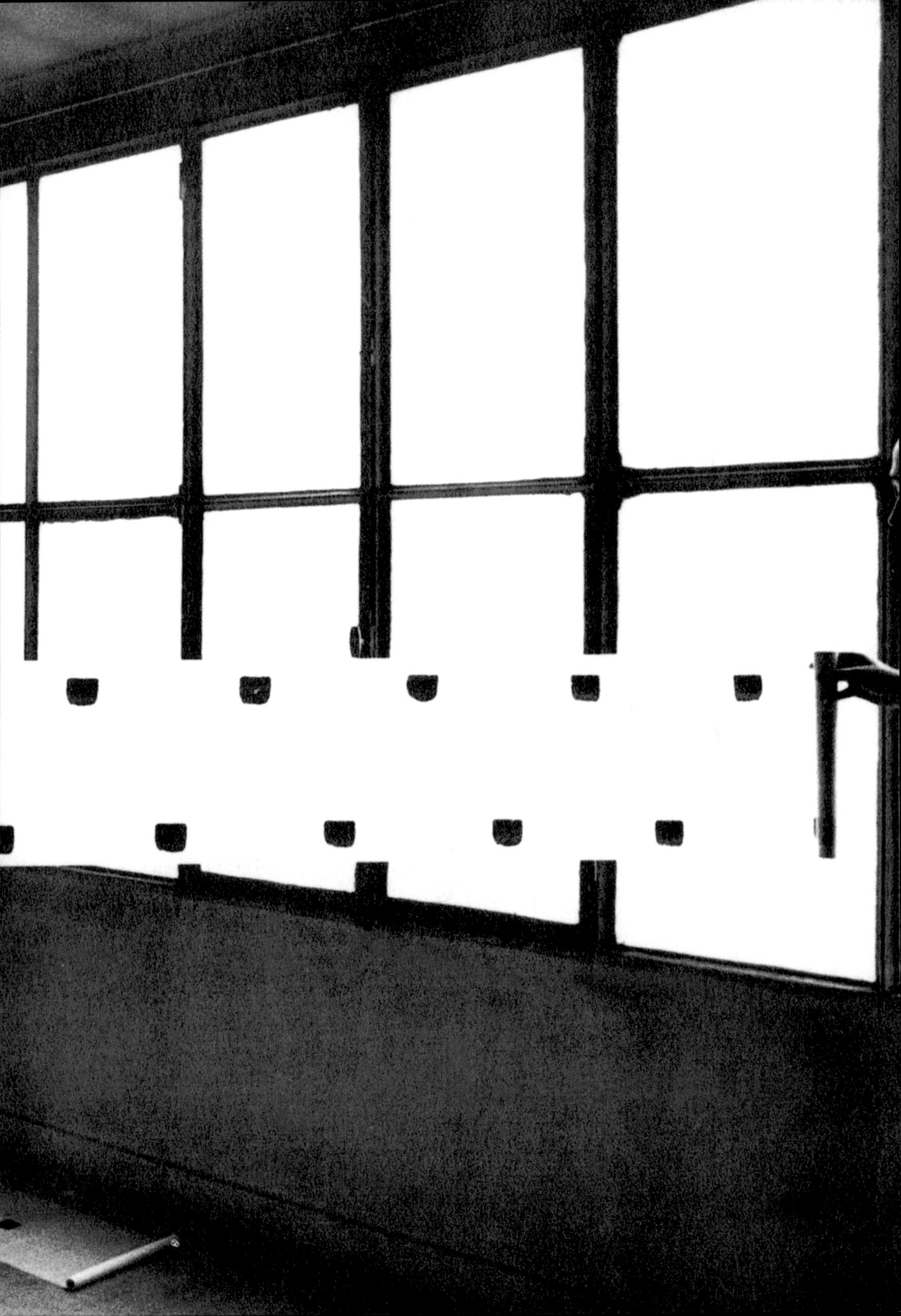

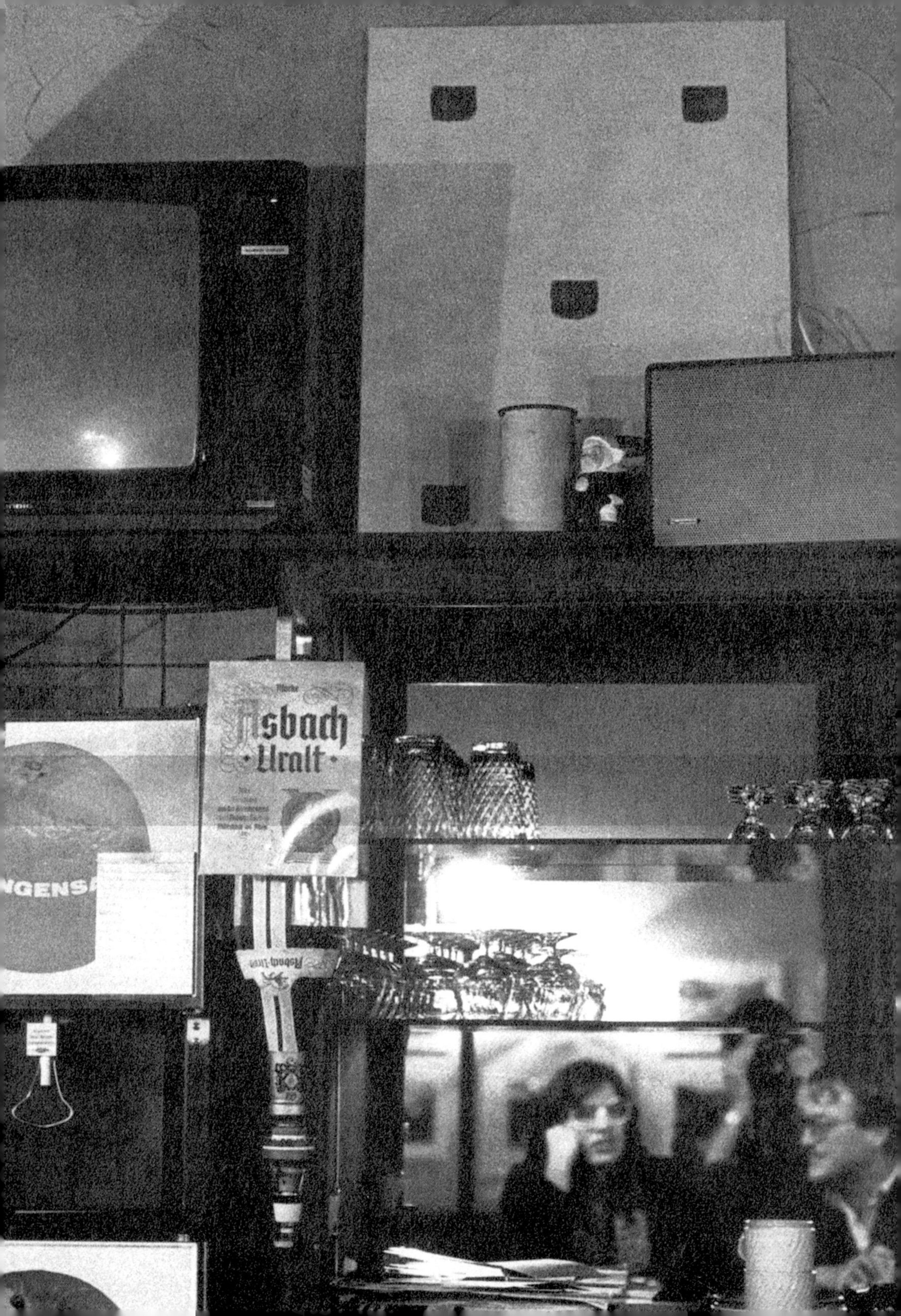
Asbach
Uralt

105

105

105

105

105

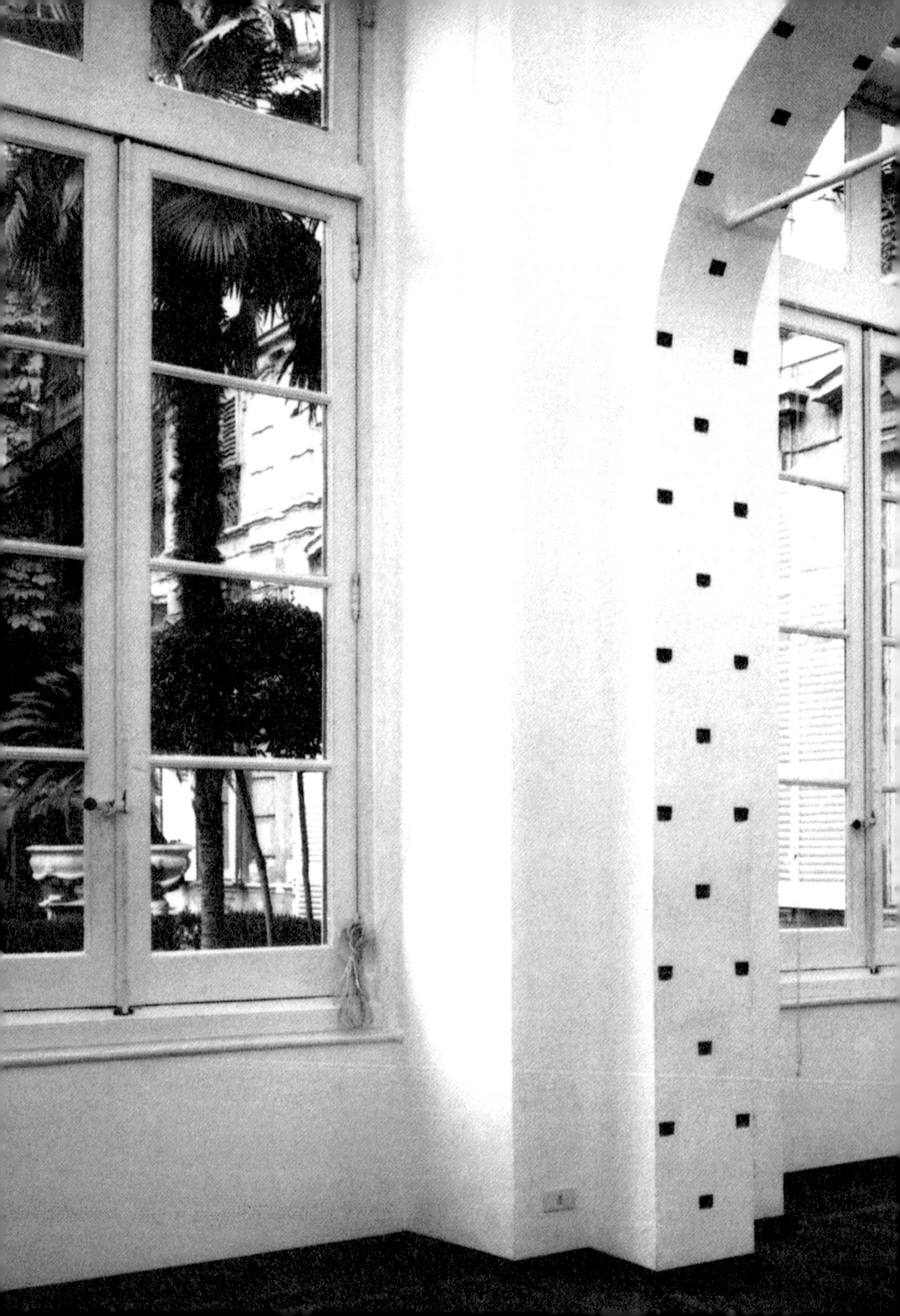

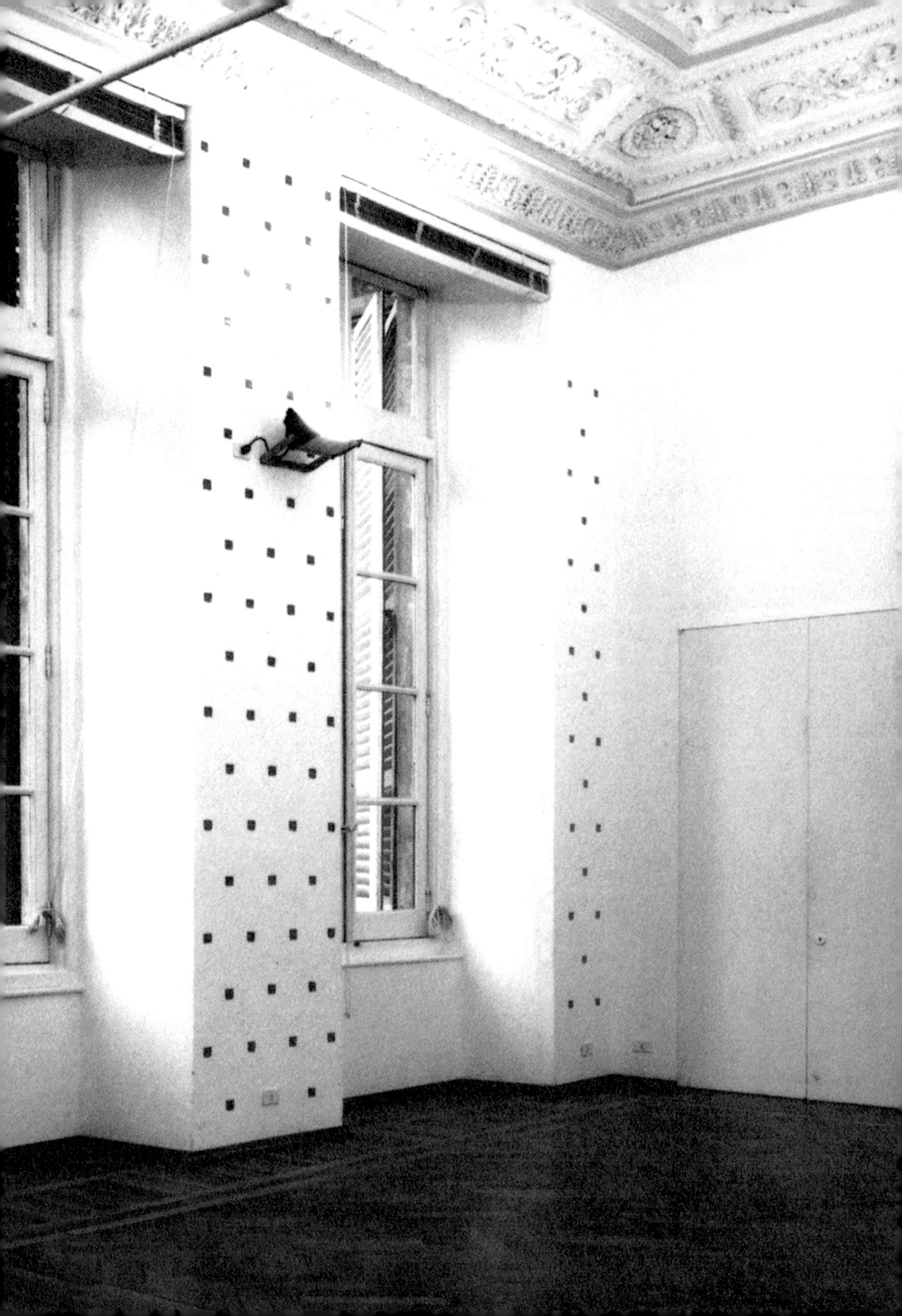

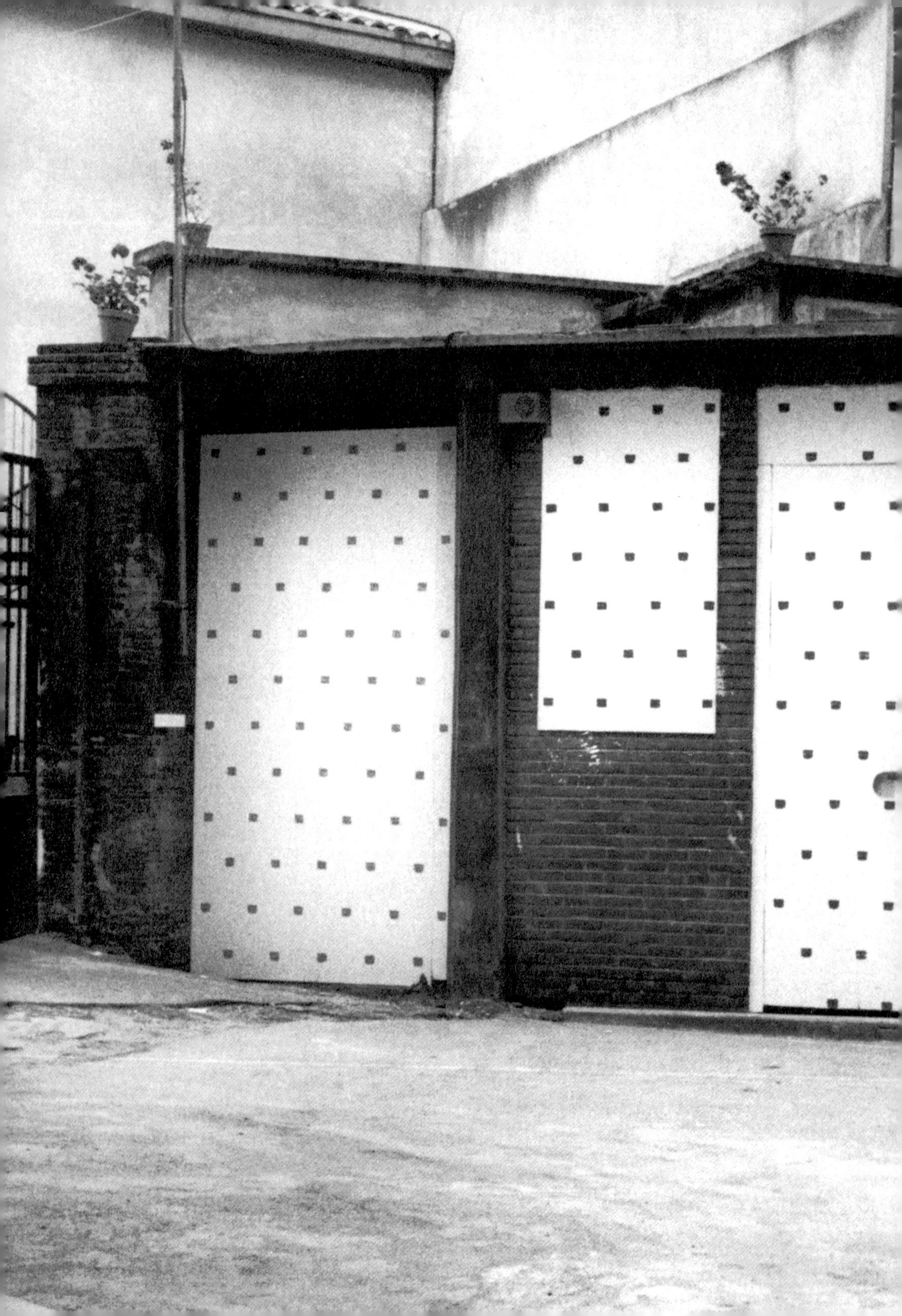

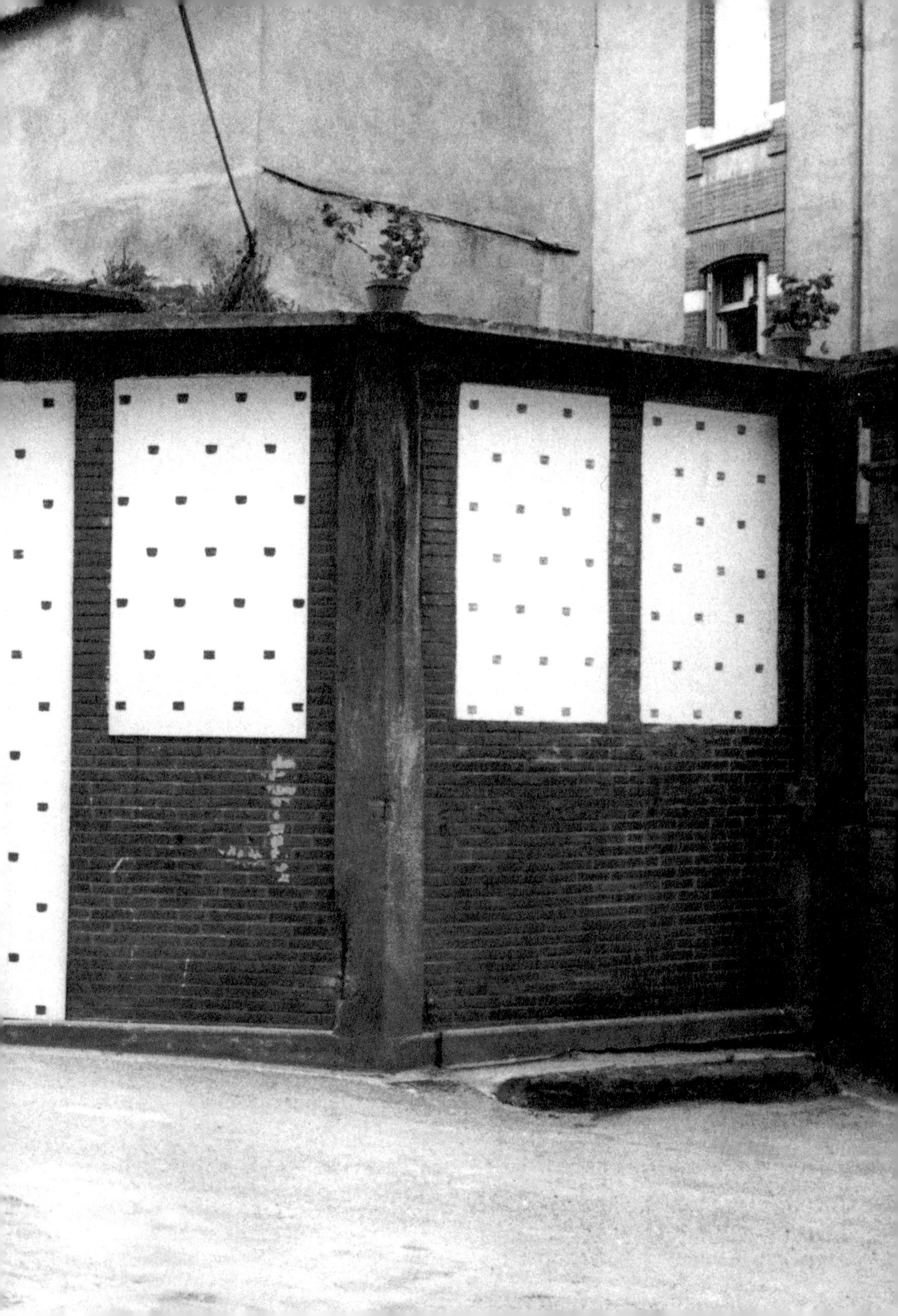

pp. 69-74, 76-81: Kunsthalle Bern, Bern, 1978
pp. 82-83: Garage Escoffier, Paris, 1978
p. 84: Van Abbemuseum, Eindhoven, 1978
pp. 86-87: Samangallery, Genoa, 1978
pp. 88-89: Galleria Ugo Ferranti, Rome, 1979
pp. 90-91: Galerie Paul Maenz, Cologne, 1979
p. 93: Galerie Yvon Lambert, Paris, 1979
pp. 94, 96-101: Artist's studio, Paris, 1980
pp. 102-103: Bundesplatz 4, Bern, 1981
p. 104: documenta 7 (Orangerie), Kassel, 1982
pp. 106-107: Palazzo Bianco, Genoa, 1982
pp. 108-109: Location unknown, Toulouse, 1983

Untitled
Harald Szeemann

I. A ROSE IS A ROSE IS A ROSE . . .

Who doesn't know Gertrude Stein's poem, in which, through repetition, the image of the rose is first evoked by the word, before being transposed into a purely verbal image and becoming fragrant poetry?

Niele Toroni has been repeating his paintbrush imprint in time and space since 1967. And it's never the same twice, because the same is the same is the same is irreducibly dissociated from identicality. The pleonasm becomes a battery; the energy of the iteration becomes an open structure. It is not the highs and lows of the artist's soul that are the inhibitors of identity, but the sites of explicitation of the method. The performance of true painting, rid of the junk of all the value judgments and all the old winks and nudges, is the constant: it finds its essence in each artwork by returning back to that essence. The world is not reduced to two dimensions the way it otherwise is in a picture, but painting is a fixed situation, and it thus becomes an open structure that can be freely reimagined in every aspect.

The wall is the "picture" and the picture is the life of the wall; the individual imprint becomes an alliance. The radical retracing of a practice to the visualization of a method spills into the essentials and "painting" comes into existence: it is different and varied like the abundance of the apparitions created by a given limitation, which is nonetheless inwardly open in all directions. Modesty and wild claims, imagination and order, reflection, visionariness and inertia—everything finds a place in the method as soon as it is revealed. Having been launched first as a concept in a direct clash with the art world, the method becomes a vital topos. Tribes of imprints of a no. 50 paintbrush, replaced at intervals of 30 centimeters, survive in spite of their ephemeral fate. The walls preserve the memory of their presence (identification and superimposition) and their value as indicators of open structures. They are walls that paradigmatically show the way, born of the inclination to anonymity that is implicit in the concept, in a time of unrestrained affirmation of the ego. The artist who covered them lives his method fully, in the time allotted to him. The reduction of art to a method becomes the seed of transaesthetics and atemporality; it takes its place in history only in a person who has seen/experienced the artworks. The monk-painter of Muralto makes this epiphany possible. Through him, the museum metamorphoses from a container of paintings into an artwork. The walls give thanks.

II. THE SENSUAL JOY OF THE MEDIUM GIVEN BY THE CONTACT AT REGULAR INTERVALS

He comes from the great tradition of wall builders (Borromini), and of artists who ennobled the walls with frescos or stucco (Serodine), from the crowd of purifiers of the walls (chimney sweeps and decorators), who, to date, alongside a myriad of architects, mark out the art of southern Switzerland. But in his case too, the Ticino region saw another of its great sons depart abroad, to Paris, in 1959. Like his predecessors, he keeps his love for the wall very much alive, making it a resonant painting medium. Nonetheless, he radically breaks with the representation of a given thing, apart from what there is to see as a result of his working method; he acts in tune with, and through the use of, what is available, that is to say preferably the walls of a neutral artistic context or of a piece of architecture that has grown over time, or even the floors, or more familiarly cloth, cotton, paper, oilcloth, or glass. The method that Niele Toroni applied for the first time in Paris in his thirties—in a joint exhibition with Daniel Buren, Olivier Mosset, and Michel Parmentier—is simple, readily imitable by others, but, like all simple things, highly complex, full of life, full of surprises, full of treachery, full of play. It is an action made visible, a work that can be as controlled as great freedom in painting; in the first instance, it can follow the format of cloth in a disciplined way, just as in other circumstances it easily covers large surfaces, alongside the differences between transparency and opacity. Faced with this method of "imprints with a no. 50 paintbrush repeated at regular intervals of 30 centimeters," all the criteria of art history becomes obsolete: the vibration of the artist's hand surely goes before anything else, as each brushstroke is different from the next, even if none of them stands out as the most expressive or the cleverest; the "modern" postulate of the opening-up of the painting space becomes superfluous before a method that can master any format, whose limits of application are suggested by the medium, and whose orchestration in space is defined by the artist in collaboration with that space. And then there is the composition: no problem here, it is part of the process of making the working method visible, and the same applies to the intensity of creativity, implicit in the method.

115

115

115

115

115

The creative act is incorporated into the equation of working time = painting time, the work ethic into what is visible, the torment of decision into the sensual joy of the medium and the great possibility amongst others; the celebration of the All finally ends in the ephemeral nature of the intervention-interaction in time; the artwork/painting is generally transitory, but even after being covered over, it remains unforgettable for anyone who saw it in that place, since now no ideology weighs down the dignity of the decoration. There is no respite: here it is perhaps not about the new, poetic, nomadic, and sedentary humanism that transports the radicality of the procedure to a new horizon and that leads, through "the eternal difference in the eternal same." And anyone who knows Niele Toroni knows another quality of methodological economy: it gives and creates time to live, to think, time for the oral tradition, and thus time to get rid of any overburdenedness; these are all qualities that shine, contained and proud, from the beloved medium, rigorously fertilized. The best iconology (neither God nor Marx nor Freud nor postmodernism) is its own iconography, regularly recurring in the repeated icon which, as an imprint, collectively resists any interpretation with ease. What remains is the reason for the location of the first and last imprint on the medium. This is the point. Understood? Where there is an imprint, there is generosity.

Exhibitions: 1984–1987

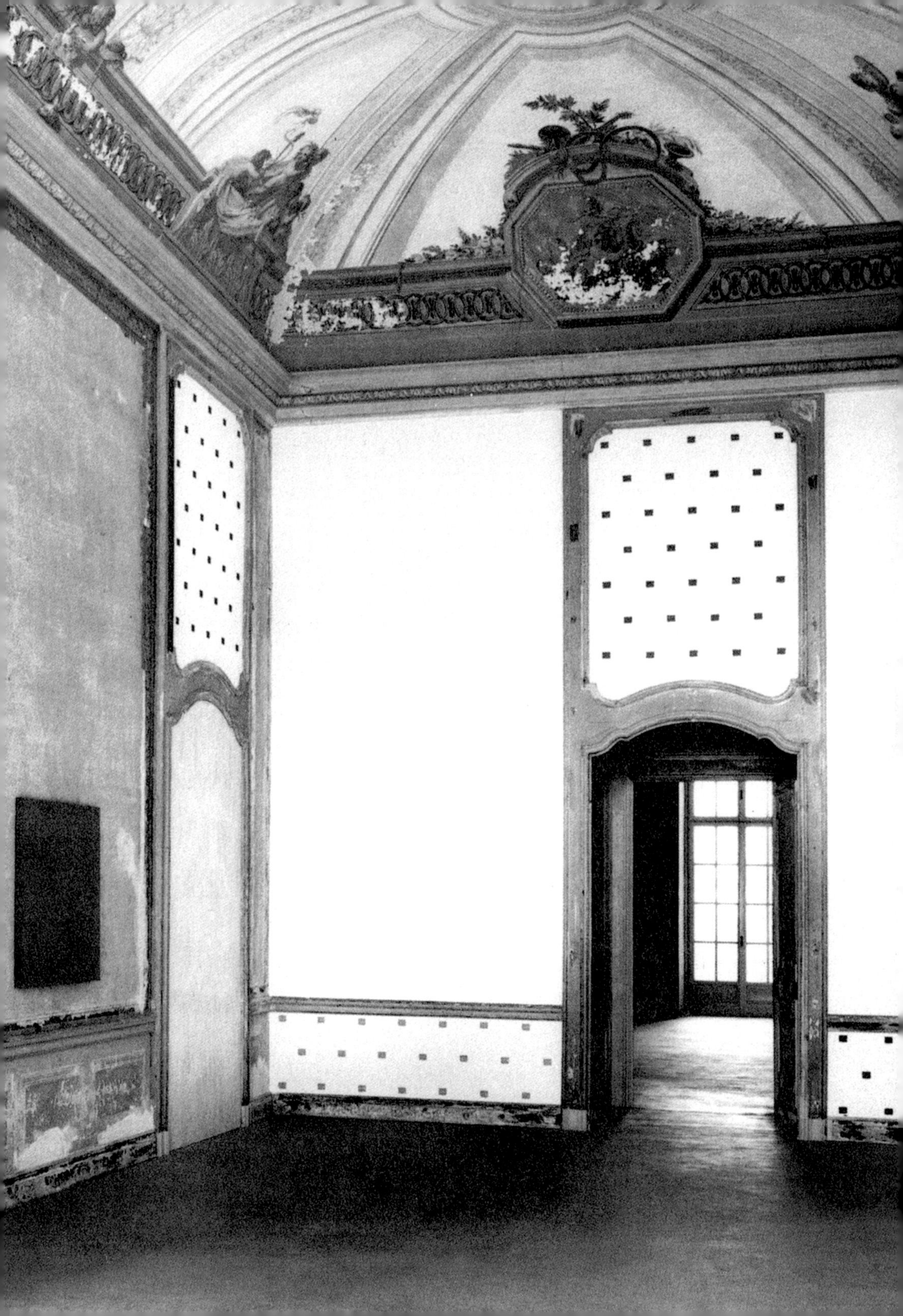

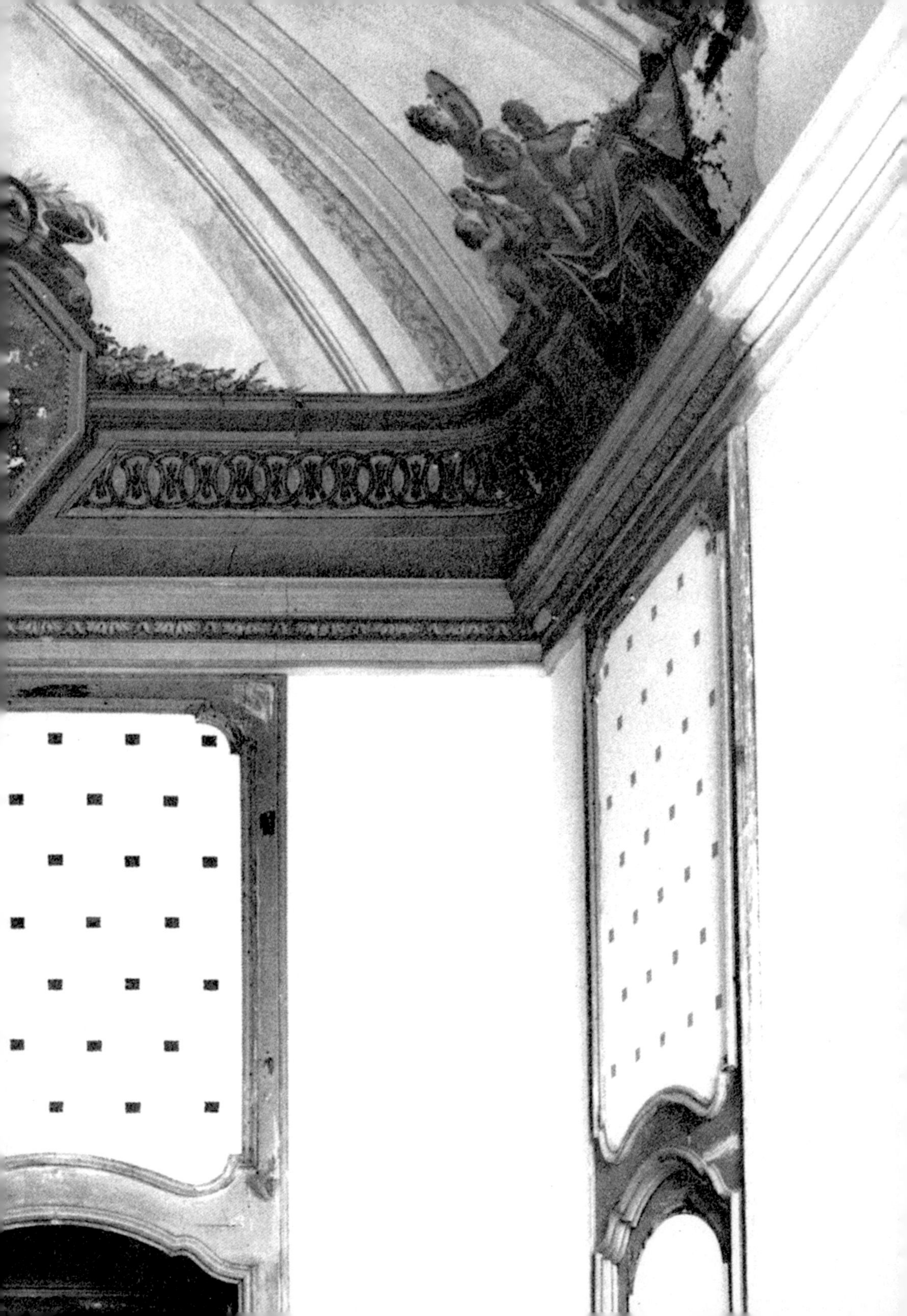

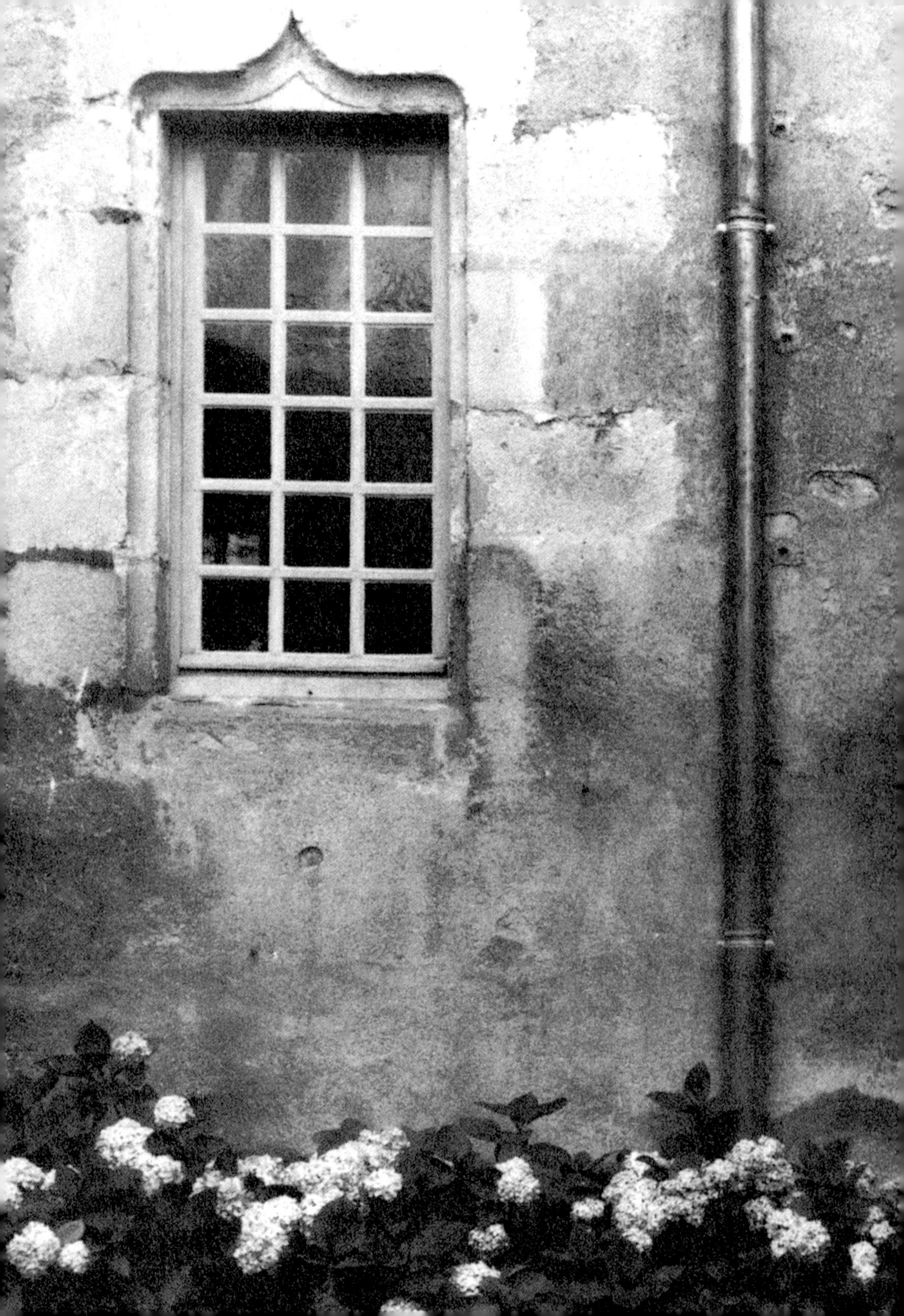

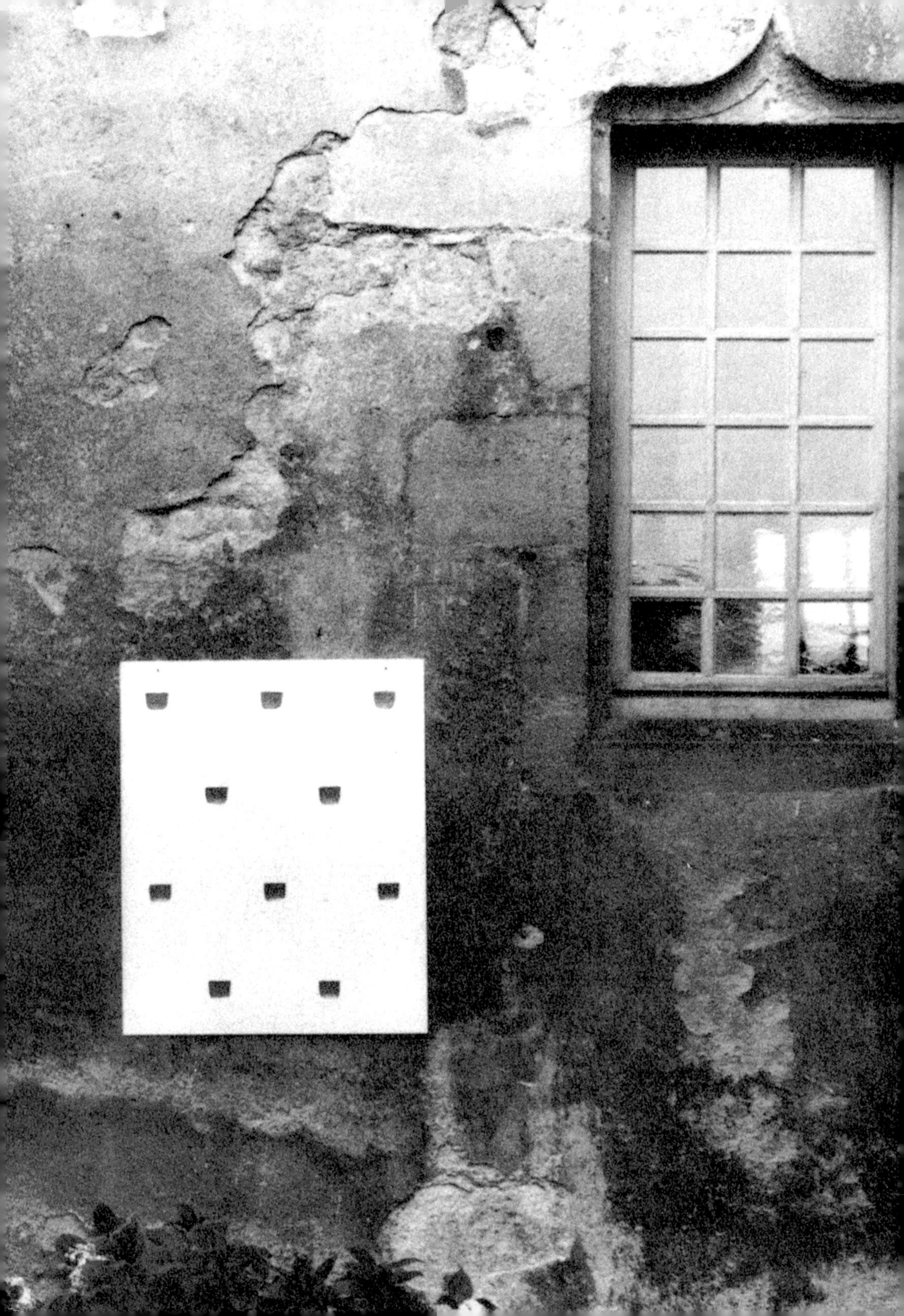

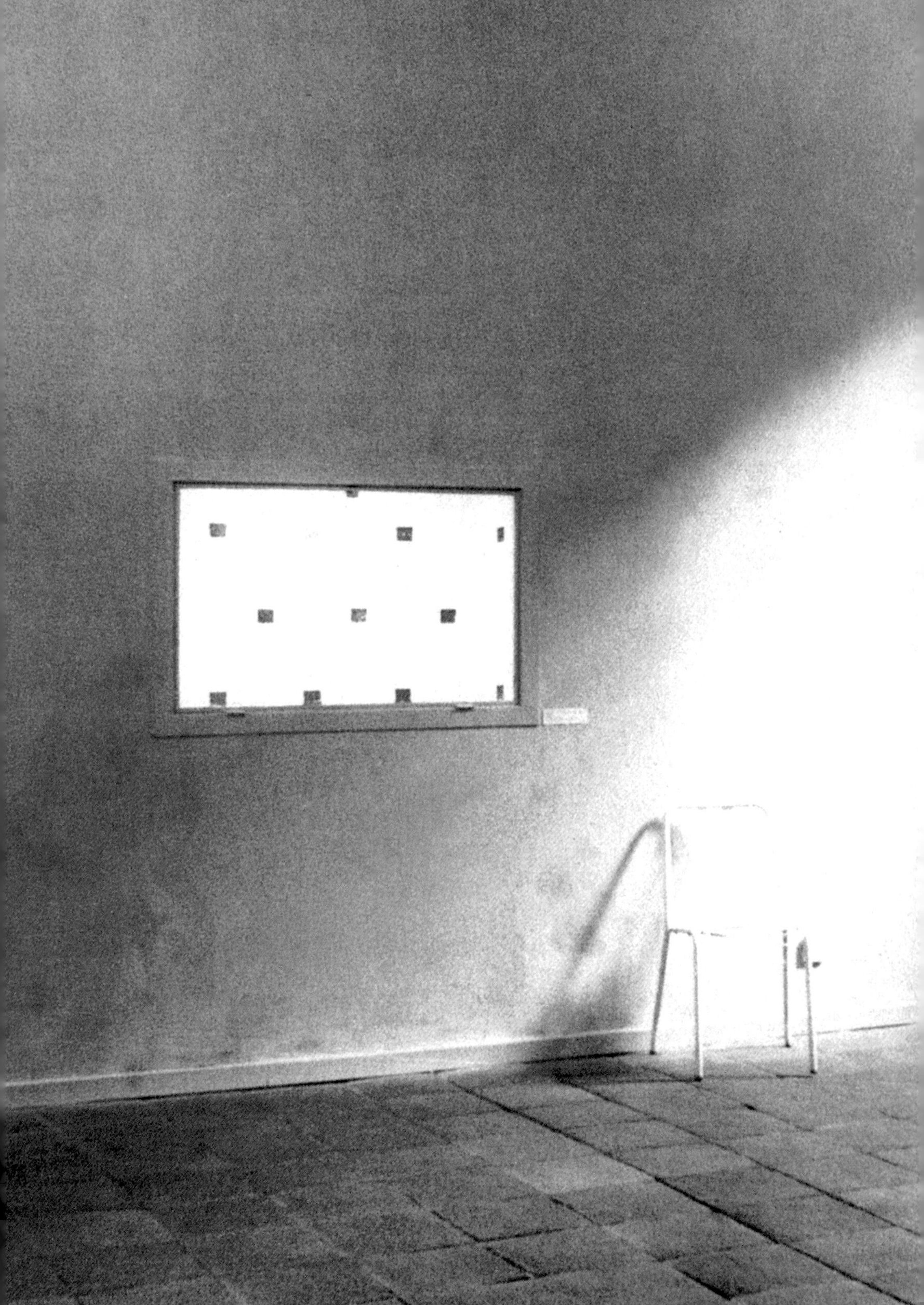

125 125

125

125 125

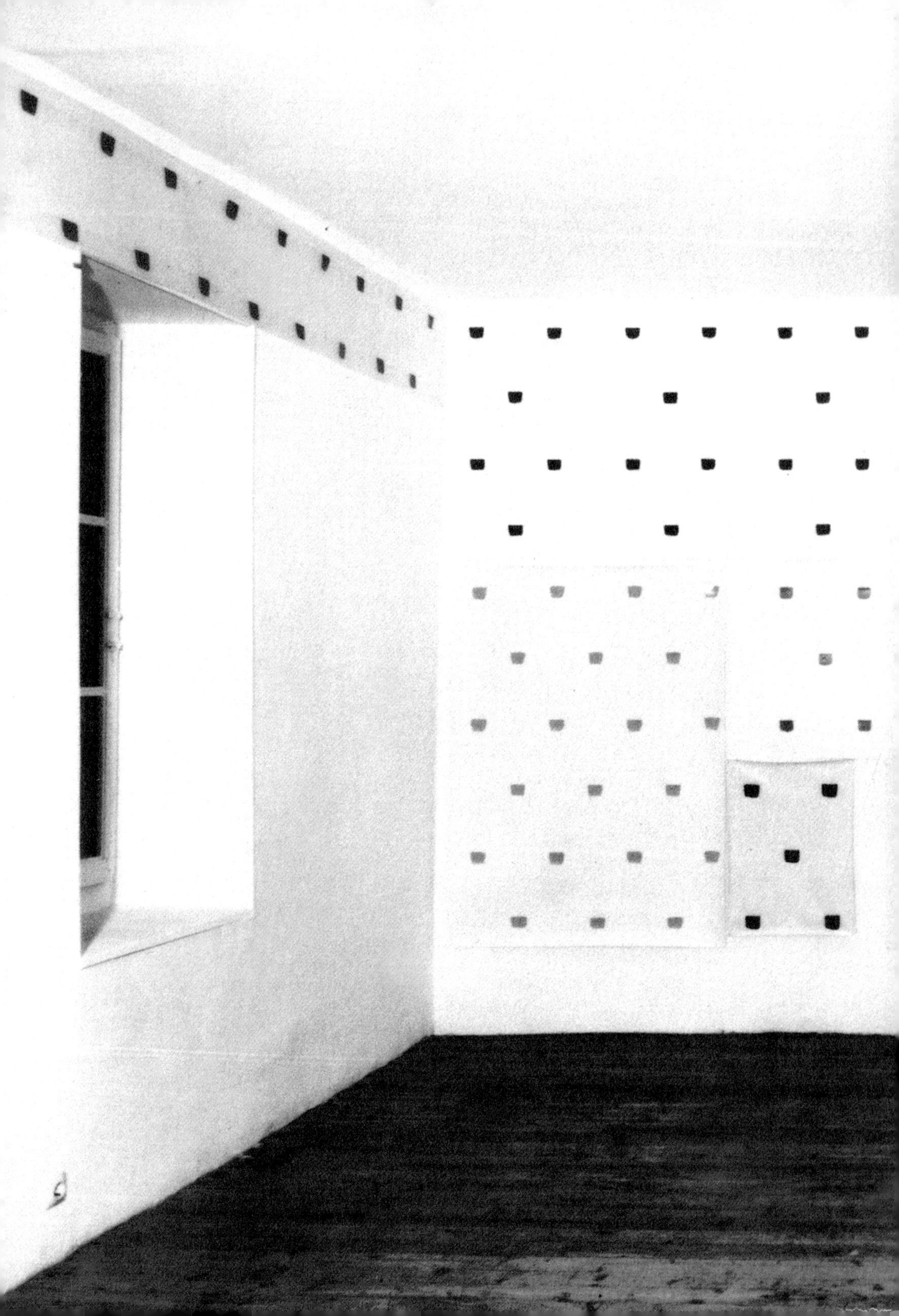

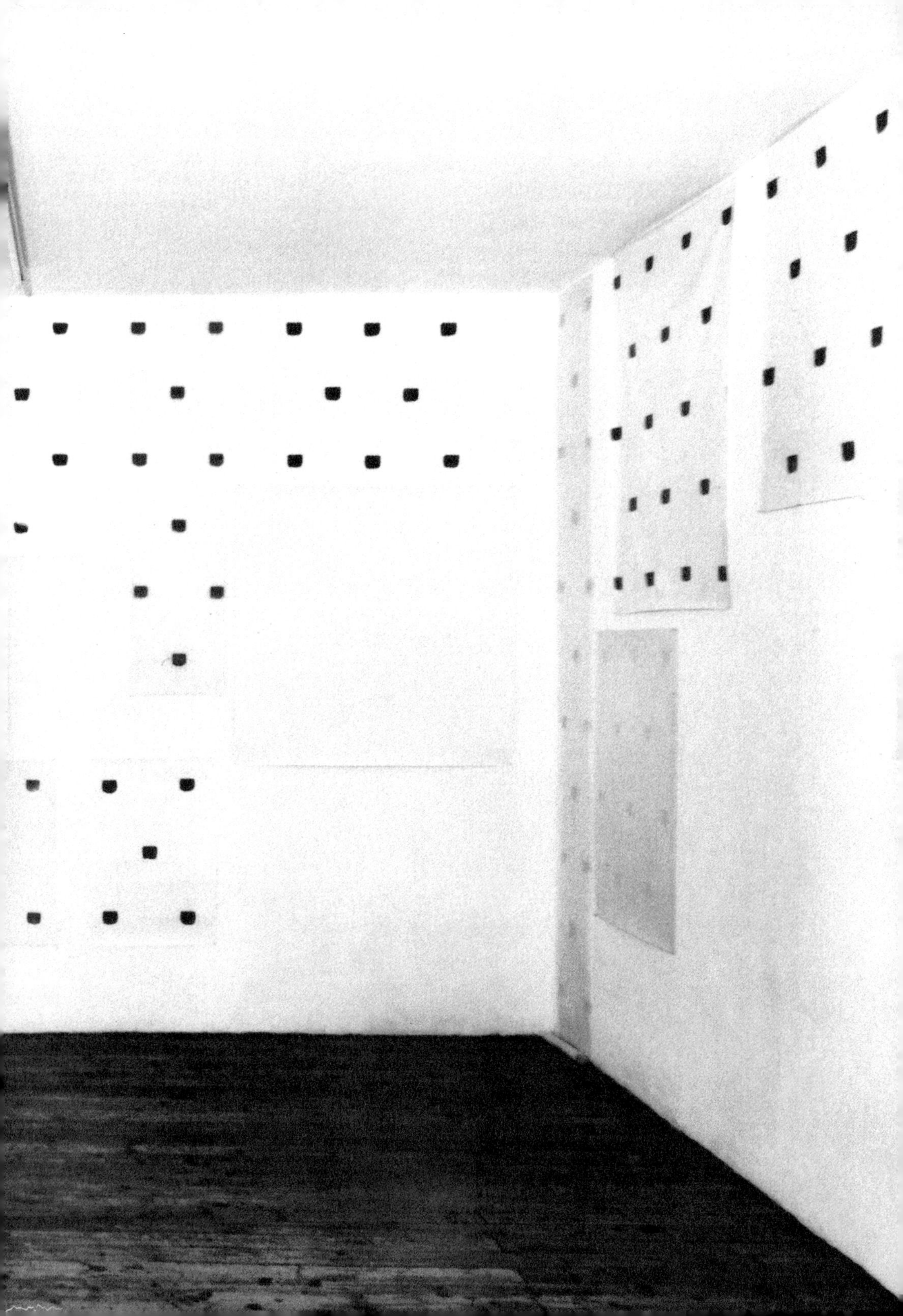

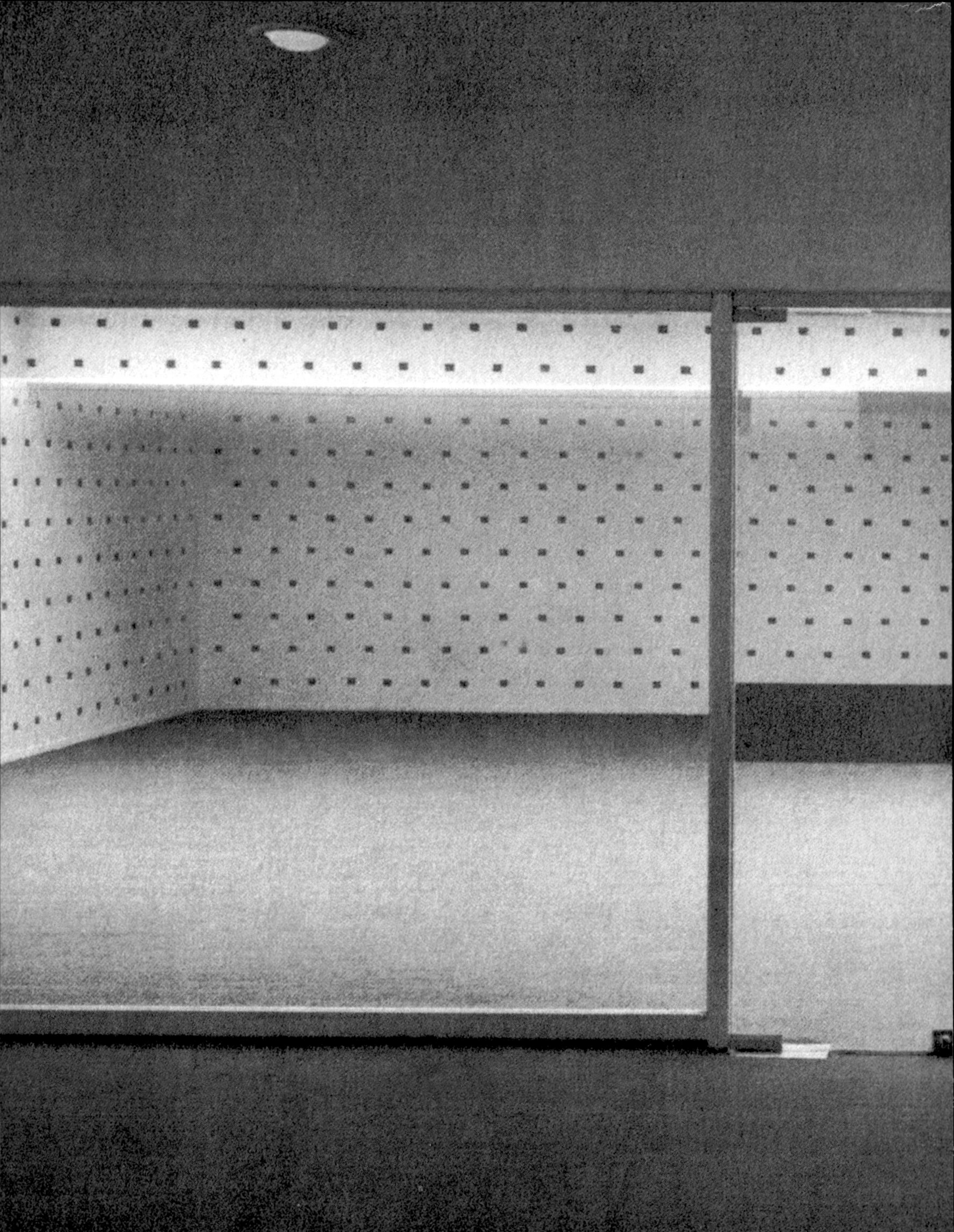

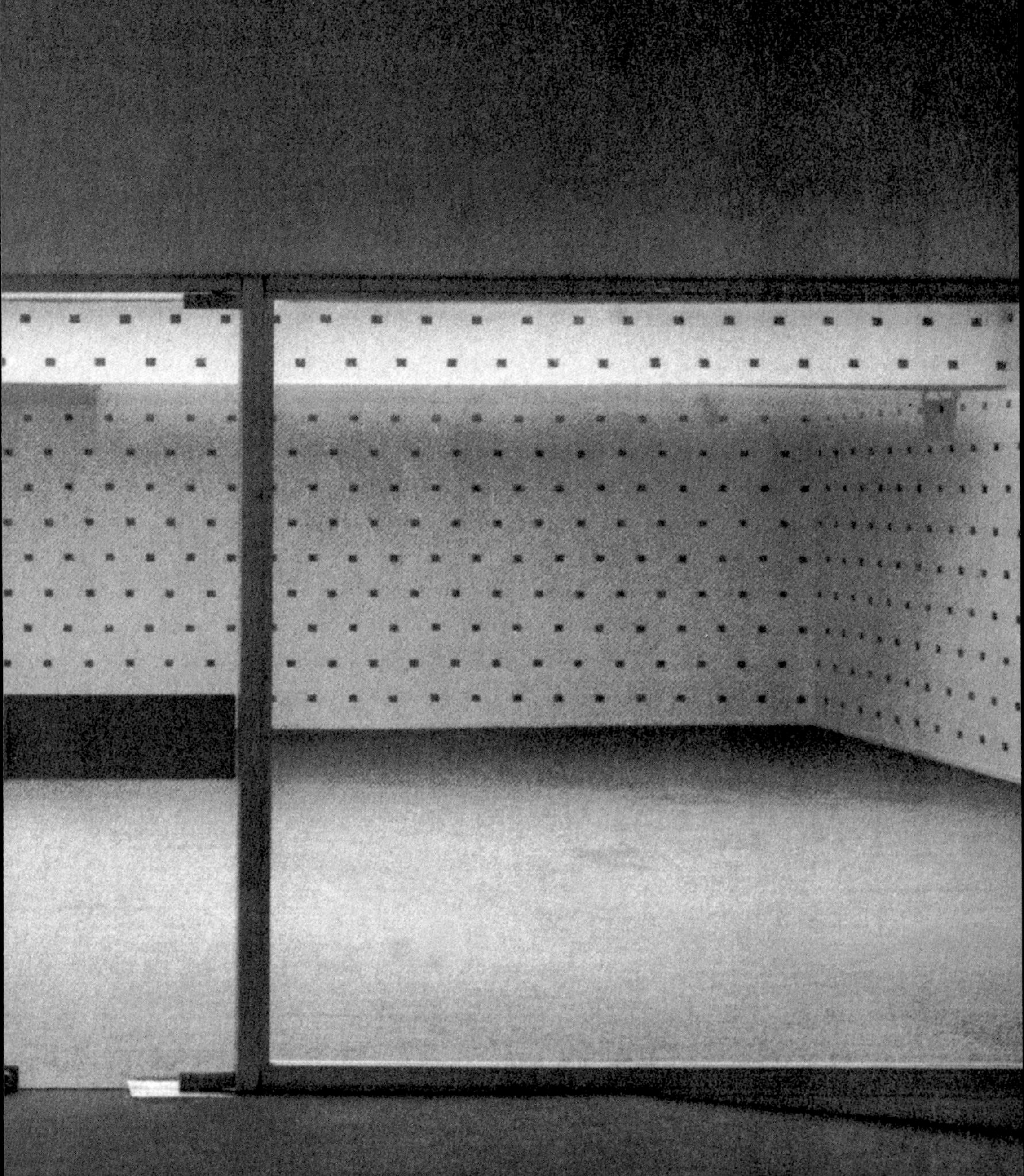

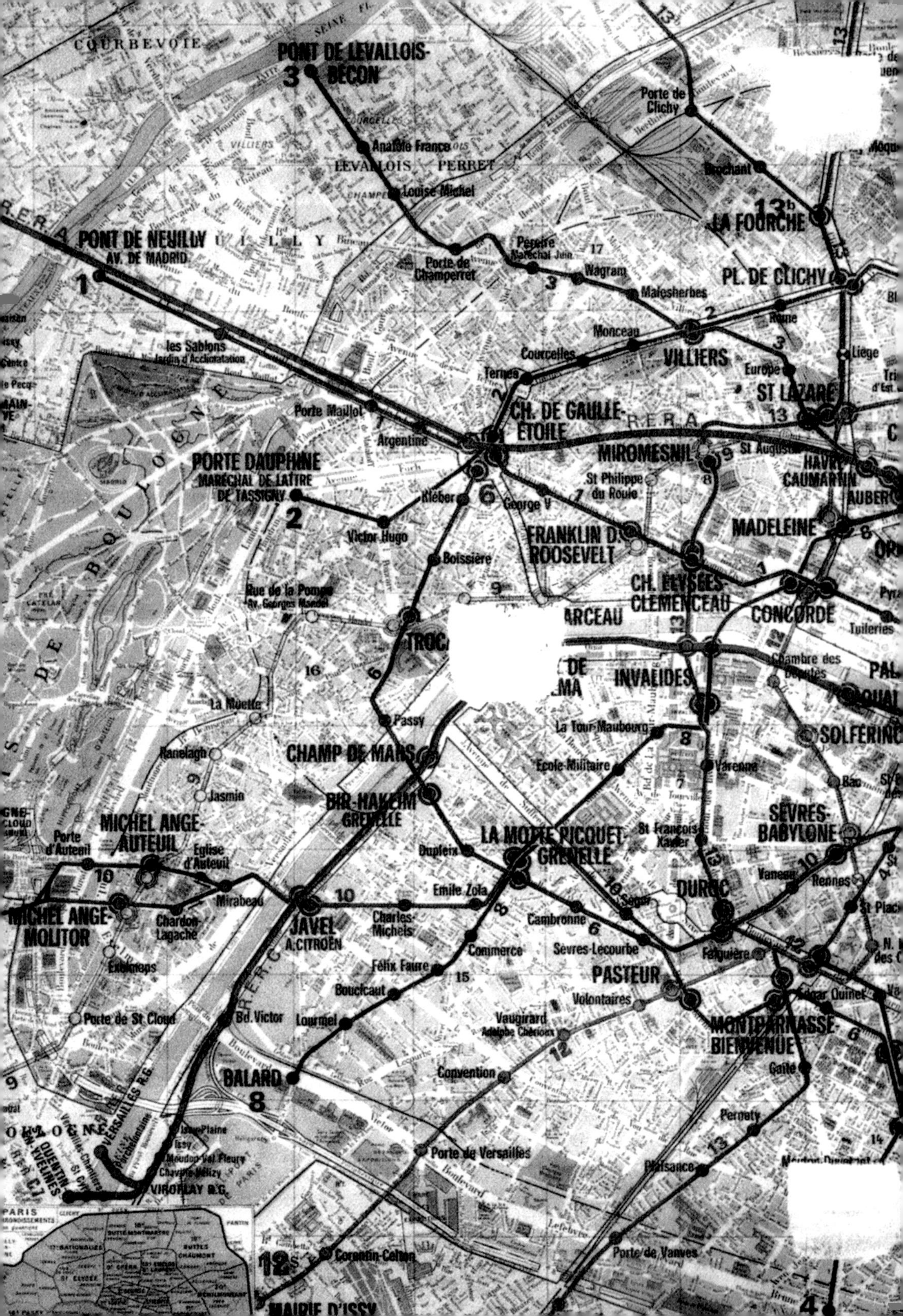

PONT DE LEVALLOIS-BECON
3
Anatole France
LEVALLOIS PERRET
Louise Michel
PONT DE NEUILLY
AV. DE MADRID
1
Porte de Champerret
Pereire
Wagram
Malesherbes
Monceau
VILLIERS
Courcelles
Ternes
Porte de Clichy
Brochant
LA FOURCHE
13b
PL. DE CLICHY
Rome
Liège
Europe
ST LAZARE
les Sablons
Porte Maillot
Argentine
CH. DE GAULLE-ETOILE
R.E.R. A
MIROMESNIL
St Augustin
HAVRE CAUMARTIN
AUBER
PORTE DAUPHINE
MARECHAL DE LATTRE DE TASSIGNY
2
Victor Hugo
Kléber
George V
St Philippe du Roule
FRANKLIN D. ROOSEVELT
MADELEINE
Boissière
CH. ELYSEES-CLEMENCEAU
CONCORDE
Tuileries
Rue de la Pompe
INVALIDES
Chambre des Députés
La Muette
Passy
Ranelagh
Jasmin
CHAMP DE MARS
BIR-HAKEIM GRENELLE
La Tour-Maubourg
Ecole Militaire
Varenne
SOLFERINO
Bac
SEVRES-BABYLONE
MICHEL ANGE-AUTEUIL
Porte d'Auteuil
Eglise d'Auteuil
Mirabeau
Chardon-Lagache
MICHEL ANGE-MOLITOR
Exelmans
Porte de St Cloud
LA MOTTE PICQUET-GRENELLE
Dupleix
St François Xavier
DUROC
Vaneau
Rennes
Emile Zola
JAVEL A.CITROEN
Charles-Michels
Commerce
Cambronne
Ségur
Sèvres-Lecourbe
Falguière
Félix Faure
Boucicaut
Lourmel
Bd.Victor
PASTEUR
Volontaires
Vaugirard
Edgar Quinet
MONTPARNASSE-BIENVENUE
Gaîté
BALARD
8
Convention
Pernety
Porte de Versailles
Plaisance
Viroflay R.G.
Porte de Vanves
Corentin-Celton
MAIRIE D'ISSY
12s
4

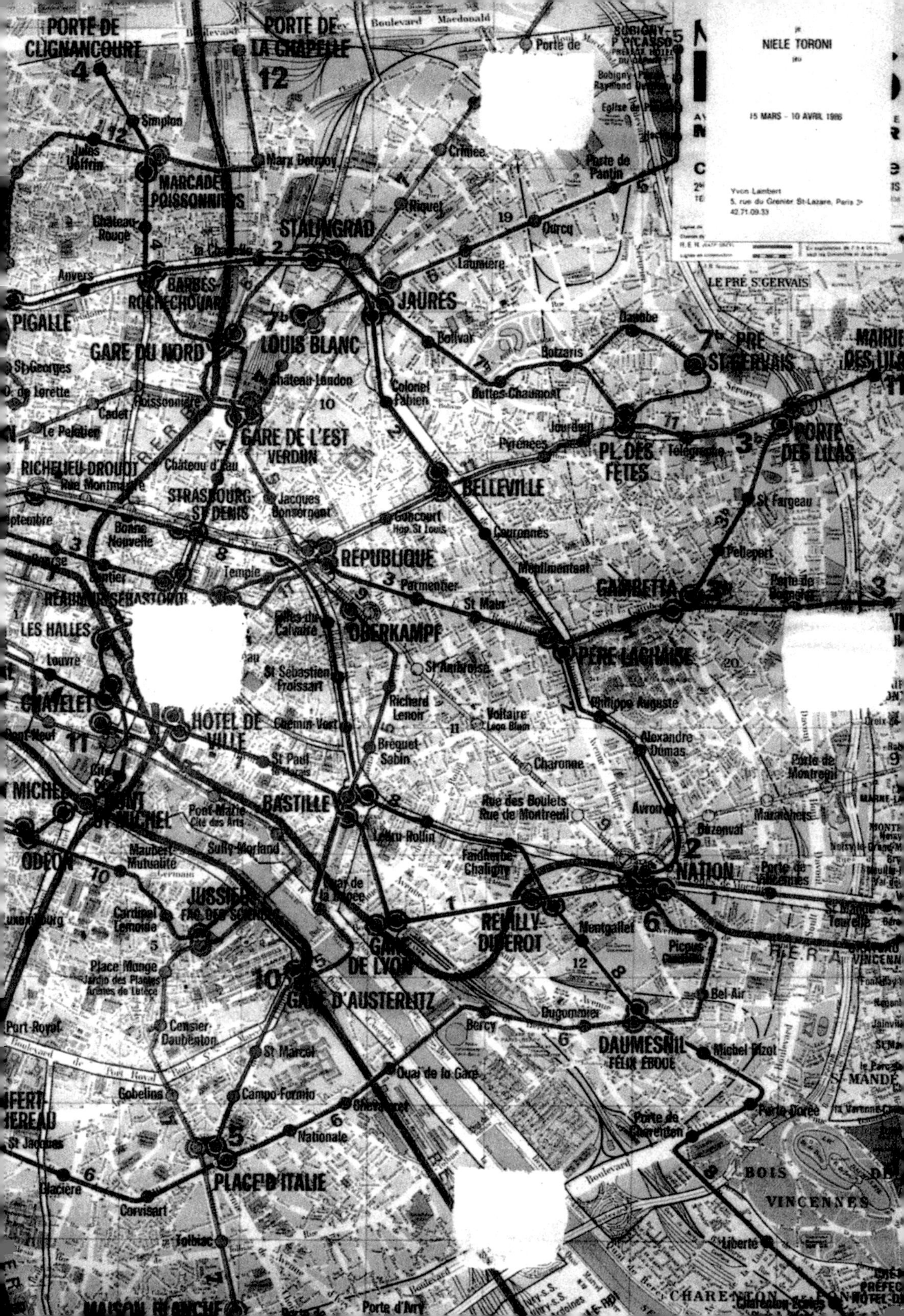
je
NIELE TORONI
jeu
15 MARS – 10 AVRIL 1986
Yvon Lambert
5, rue du Grenier St-Lazare, Paris 3e
42.71.09.33
PORTE DE CLIGNANCOURT
PORTE DE LA CHAPELLE
MARCADET POISSONNIERS
STALINGRAD
BARBÈS ROCHECHOUART
PIGALLE
JAURÈS
GARE DU NORD
LOUIS BLANC
LE PRÉ S.T GERVAIS
PRÉ S.T GERVAIS
GARE DE L'EST VERDUN
PL. DES FÊTES
PORTE DES LILAS
RICHELIEU-DROUOT
BELLEVILLE
STRASBOURG-S.T DENIS
RÉPUBLIQUE
GAMBETTA
LES HALLES
OBERKAMPF
PÈRE LACHAISE
CHÂTELET
HÔTEL DE VILLE
BASTILLE
NATION
ODÉON
REUILLY DIDEROT
GARE DE LYON
GARE D'AUSTERLITZ
DAUMESNIL FÉLIX ÉBOUÉ
PLACE D'ITALIE
BOIS VINCENNES
CHARENTON

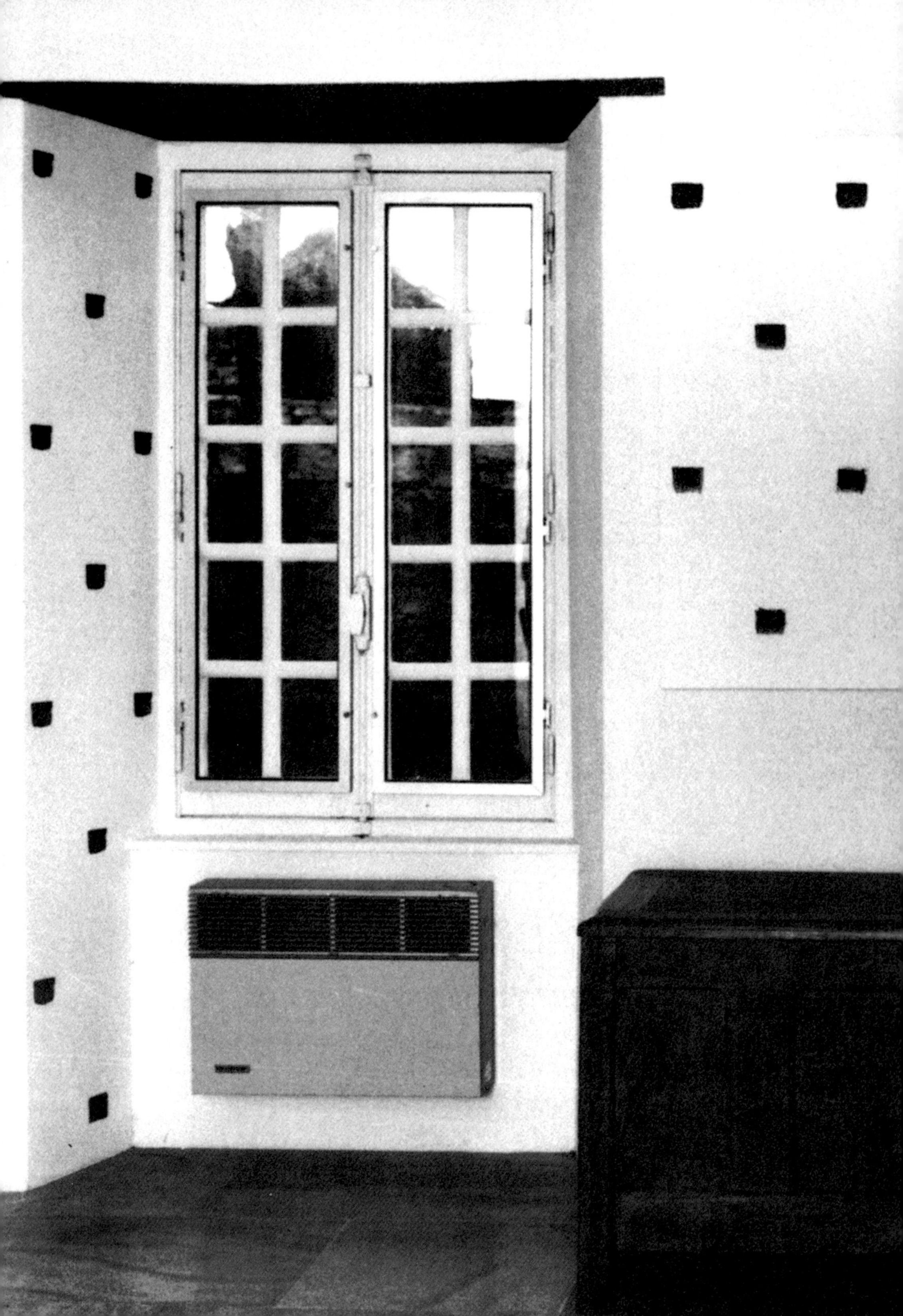

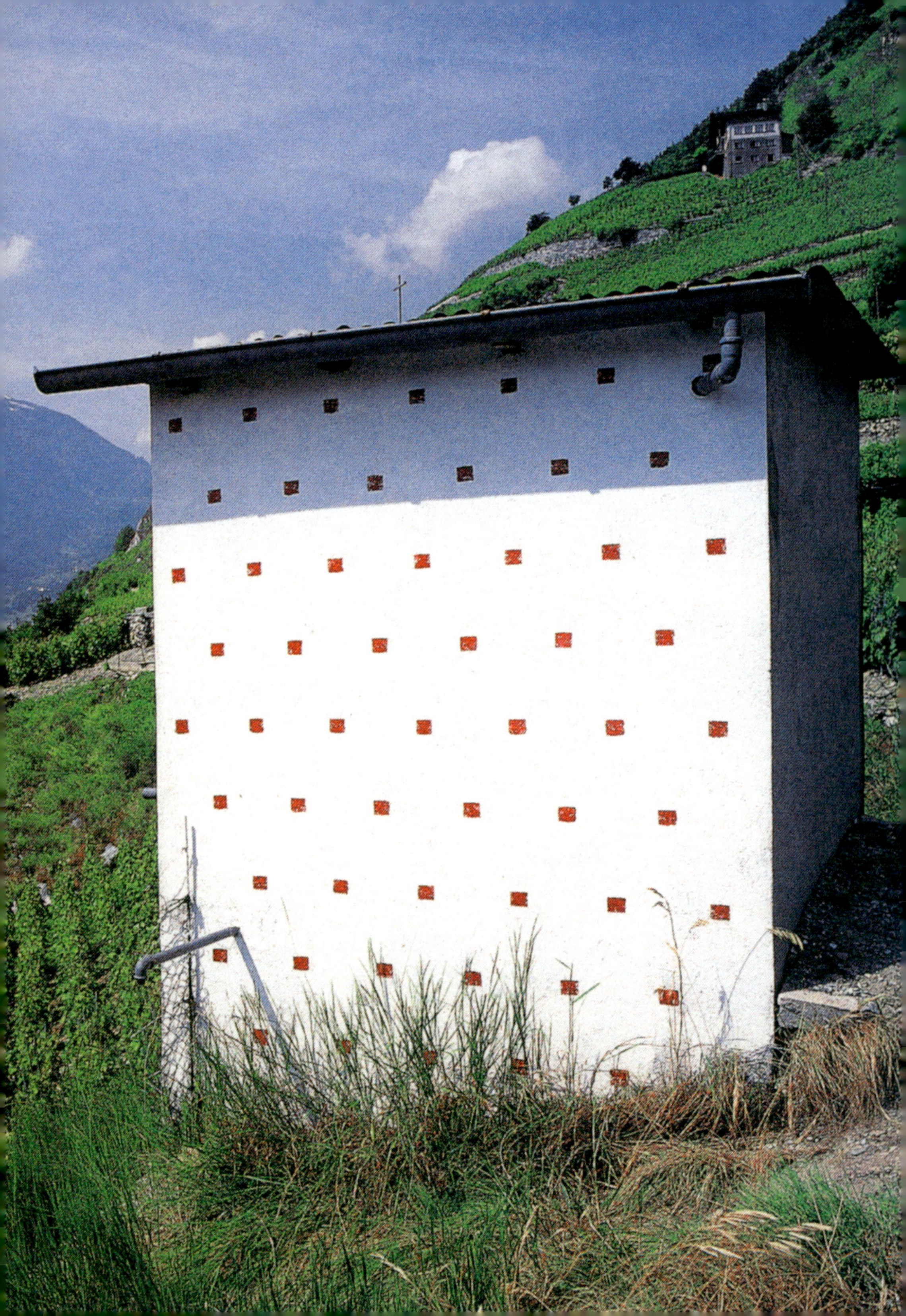

135 135

135

135 135

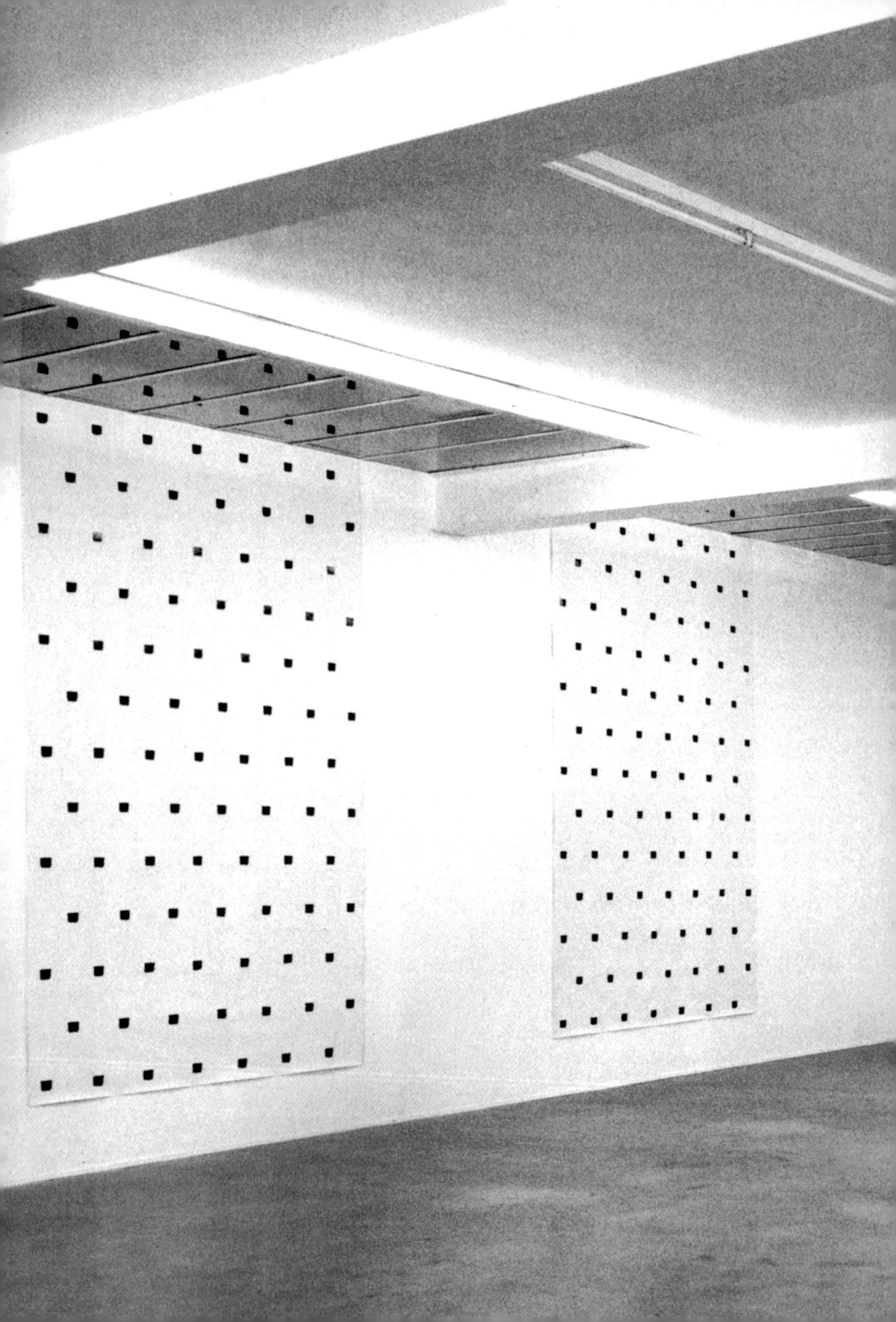

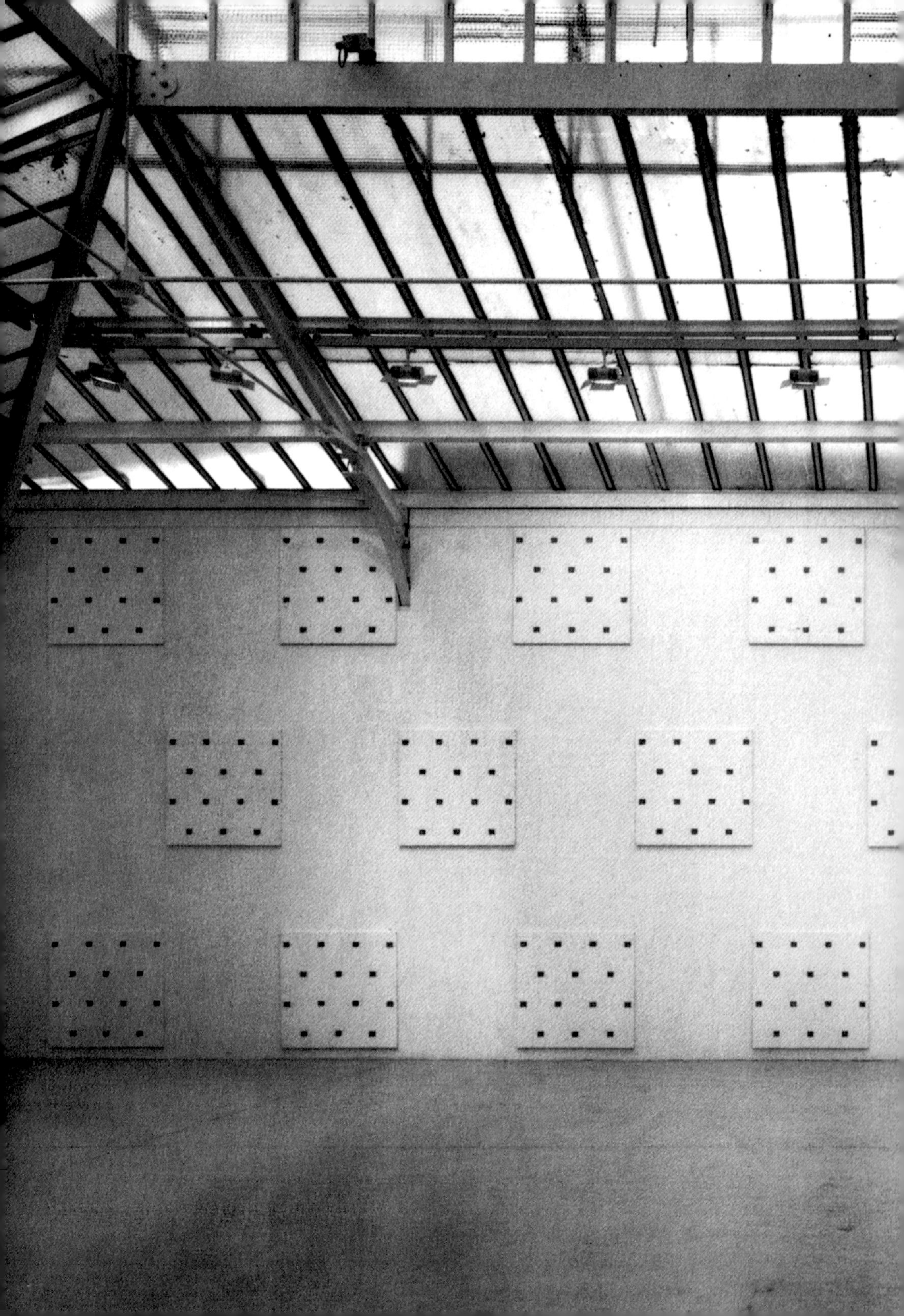

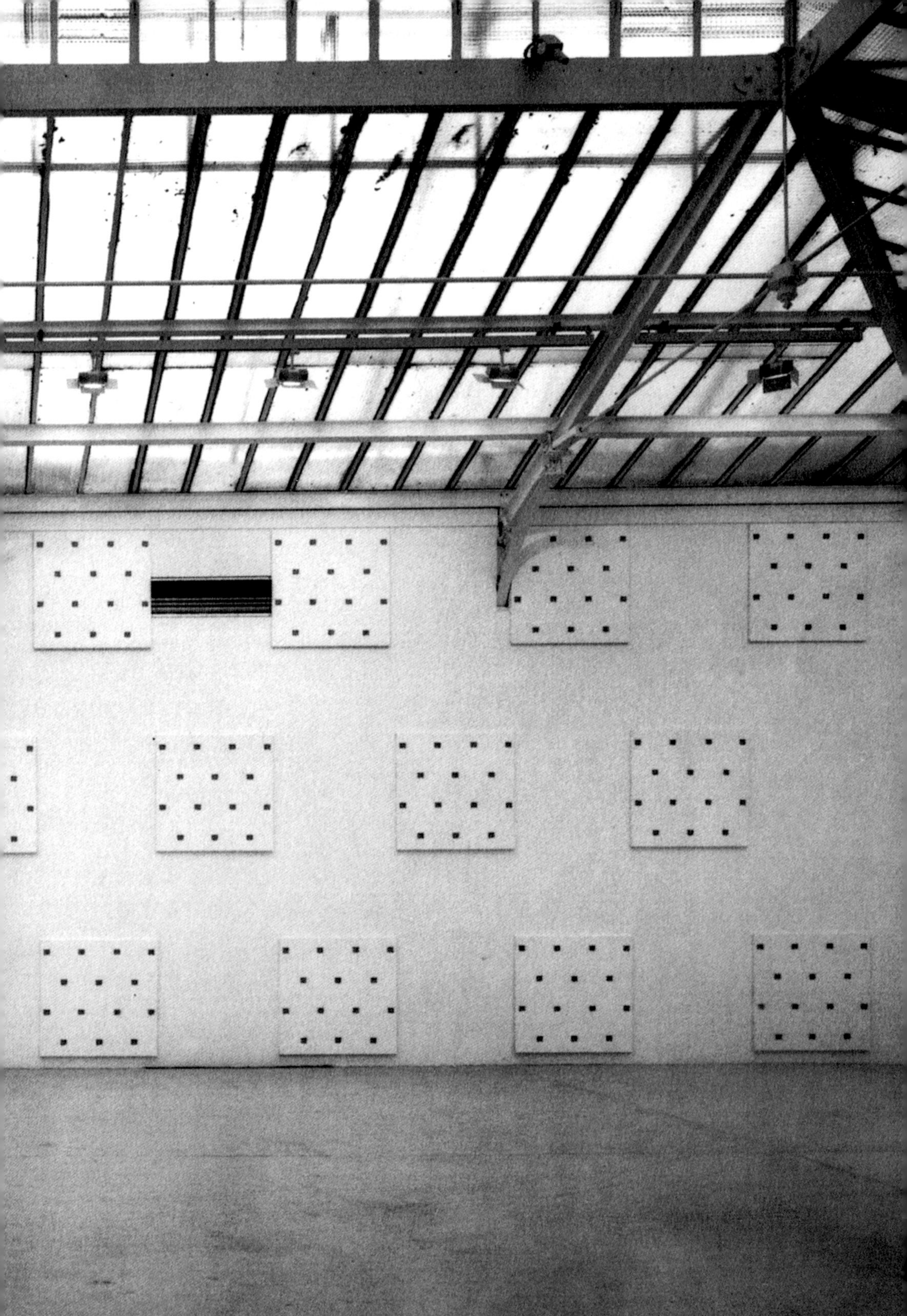

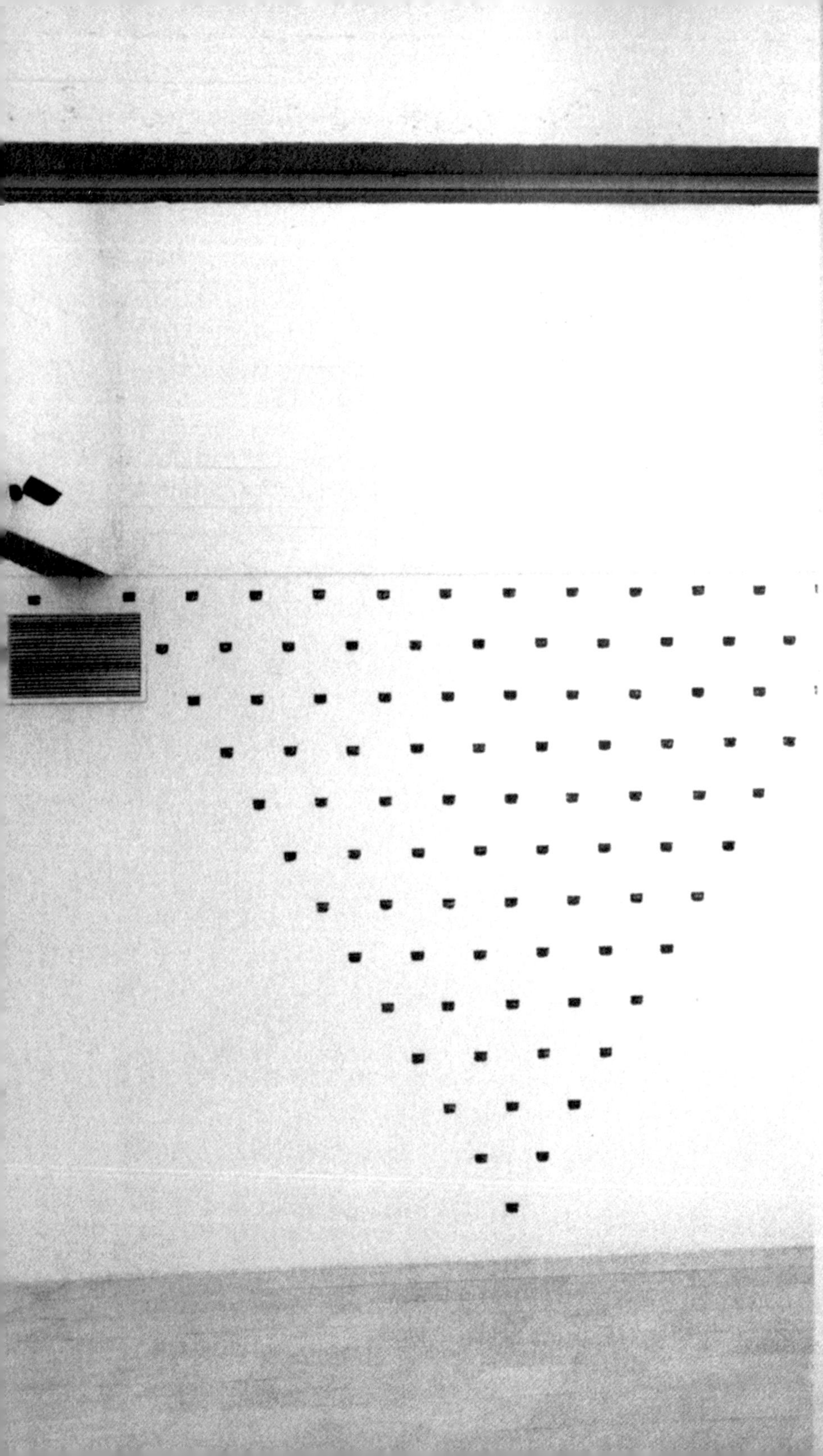

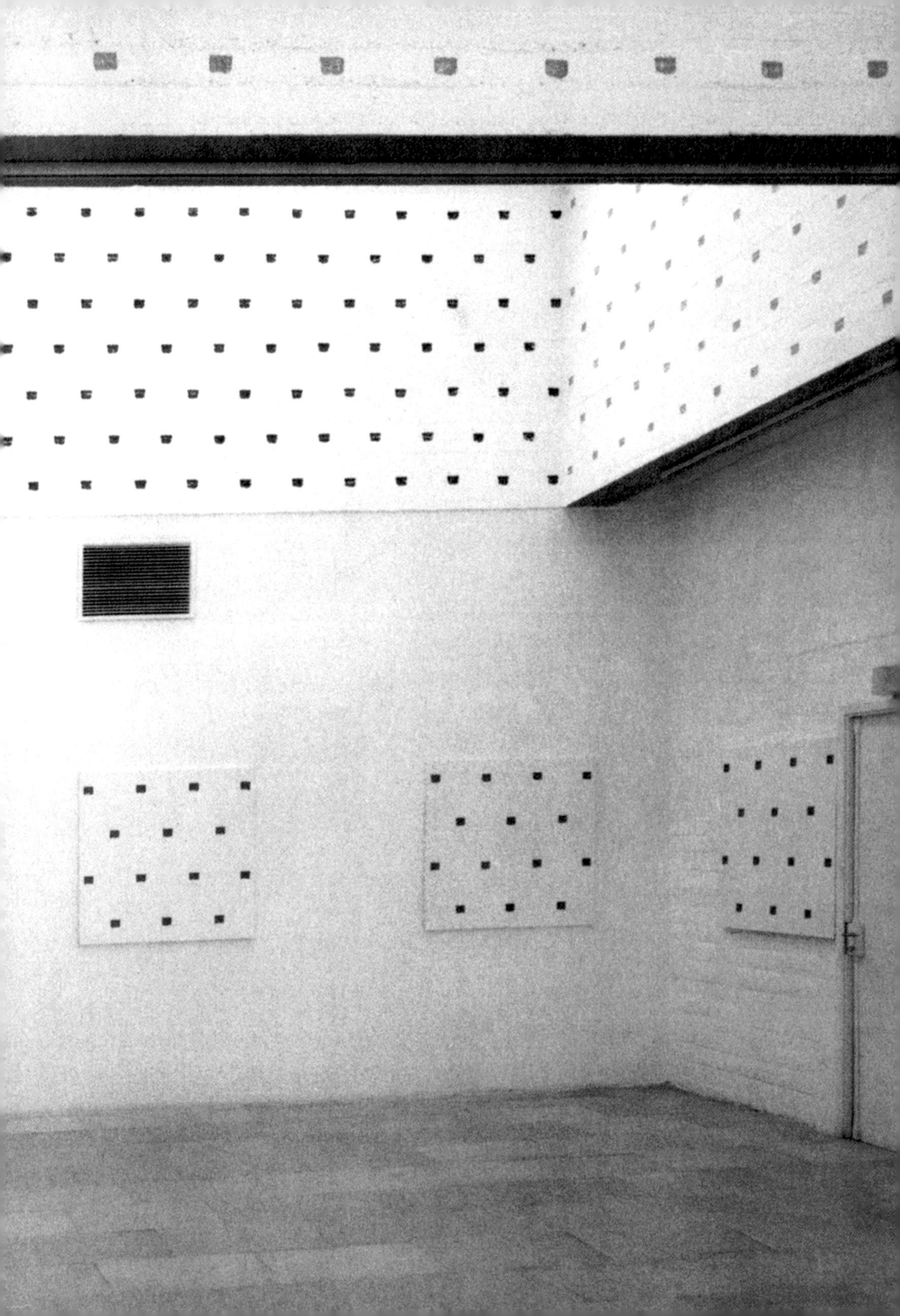

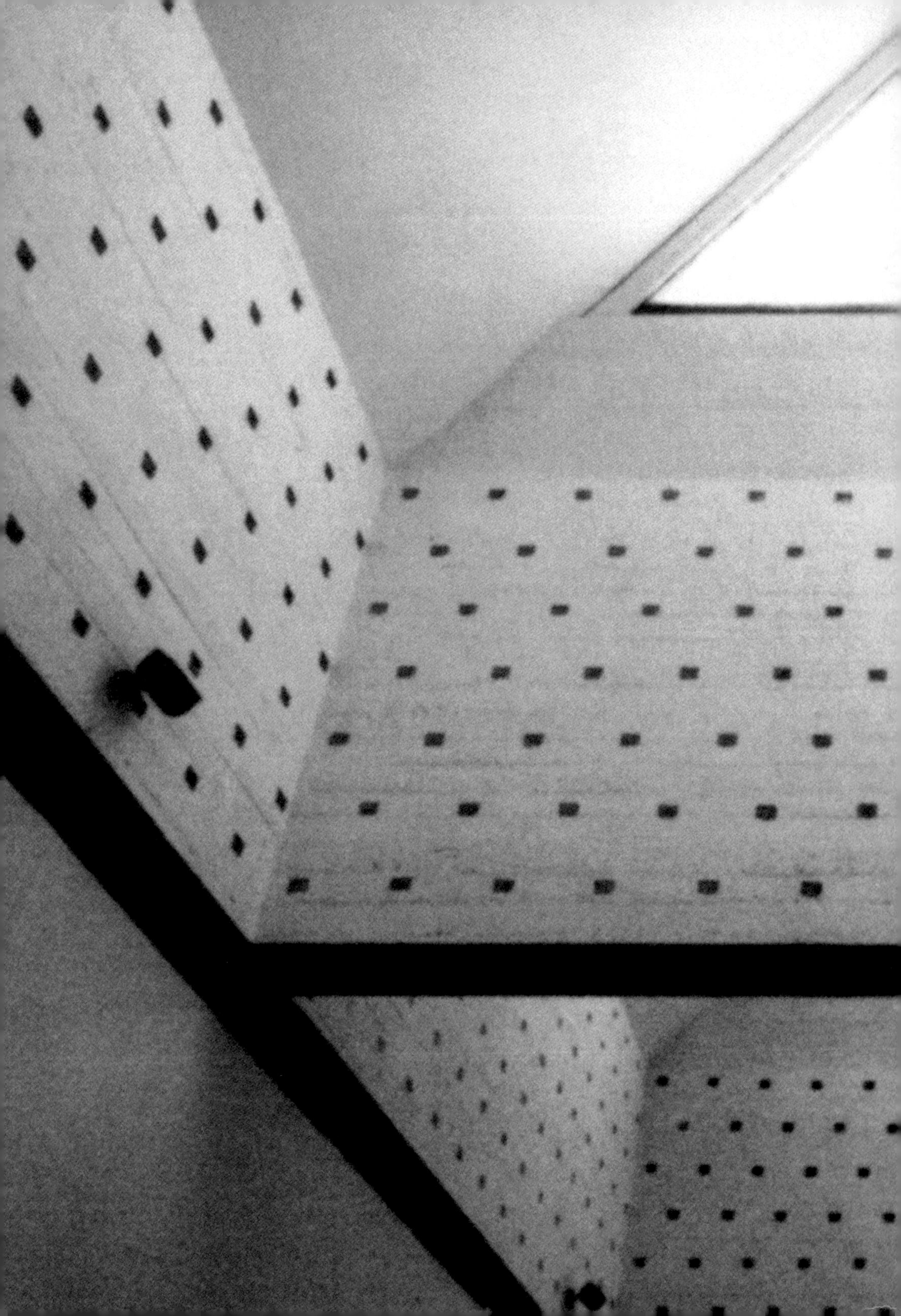

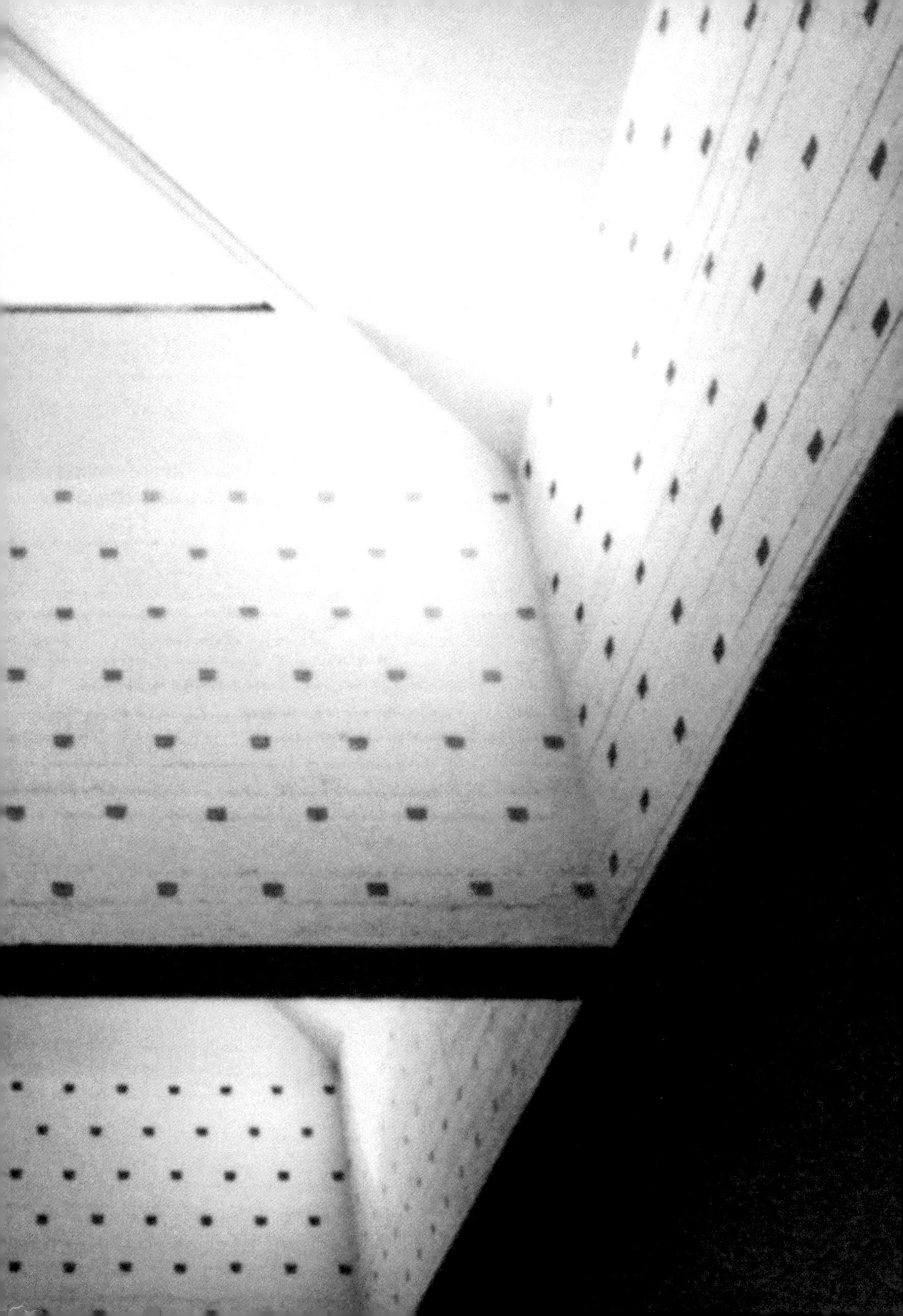

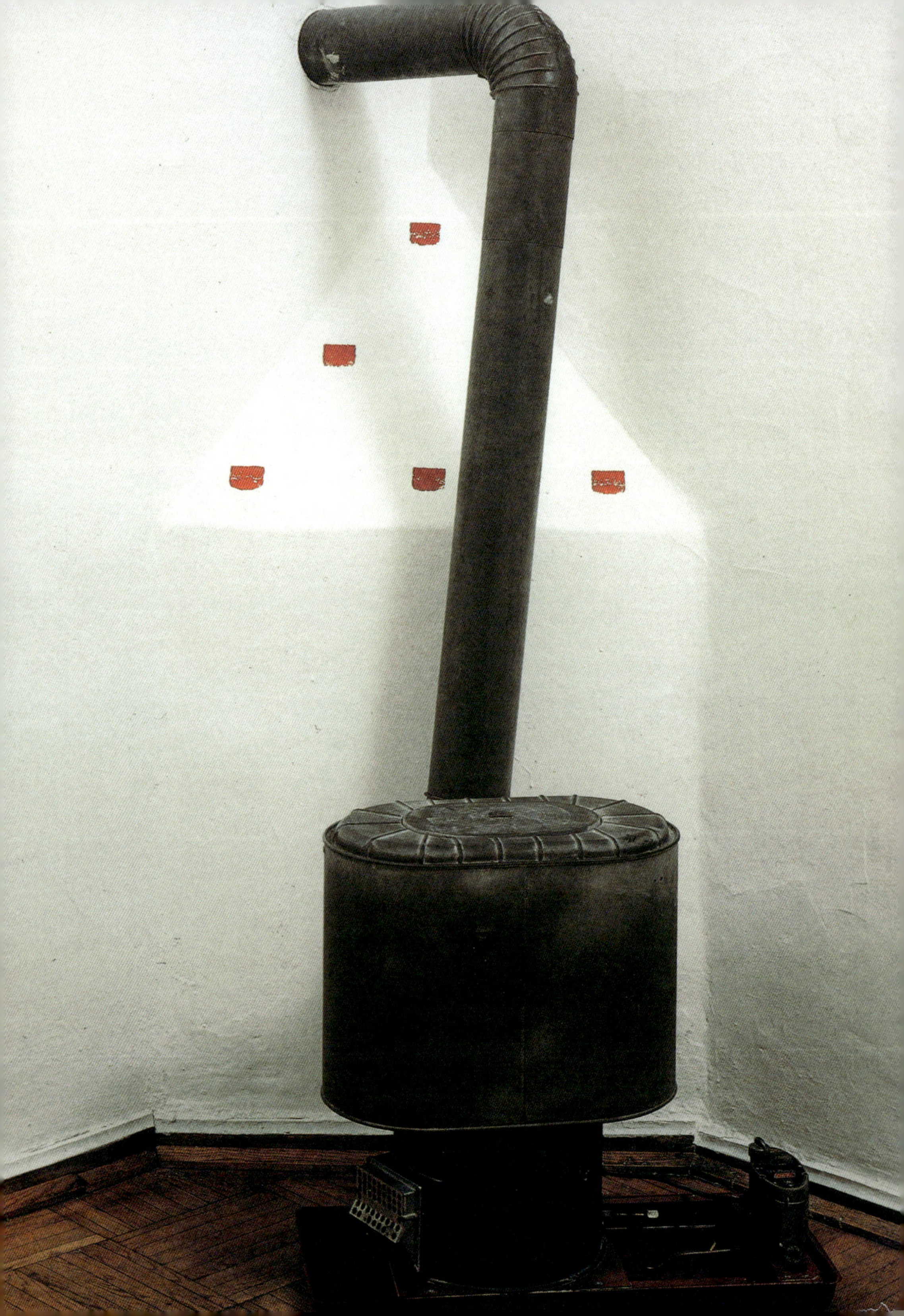

145

145

145

145

145

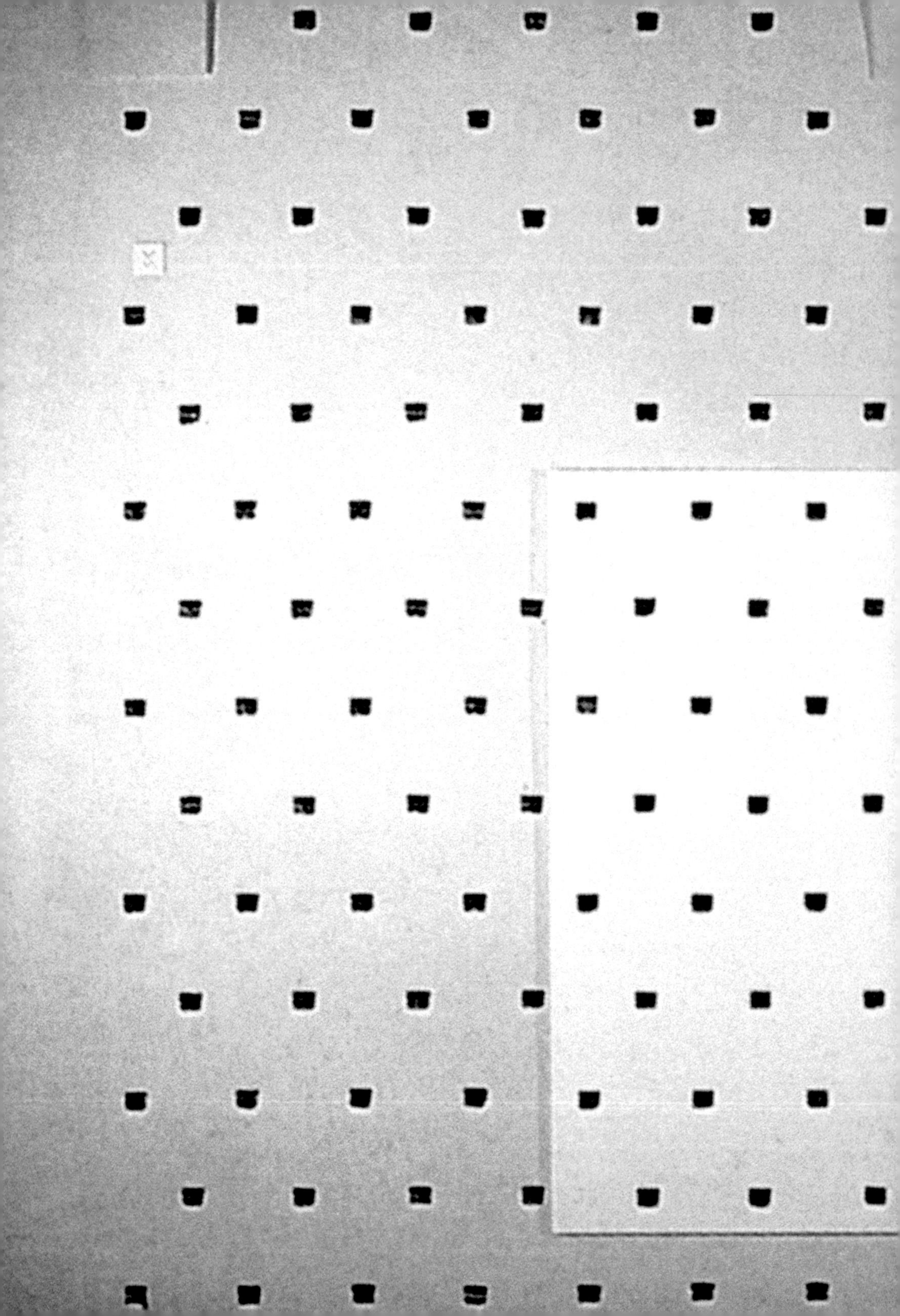

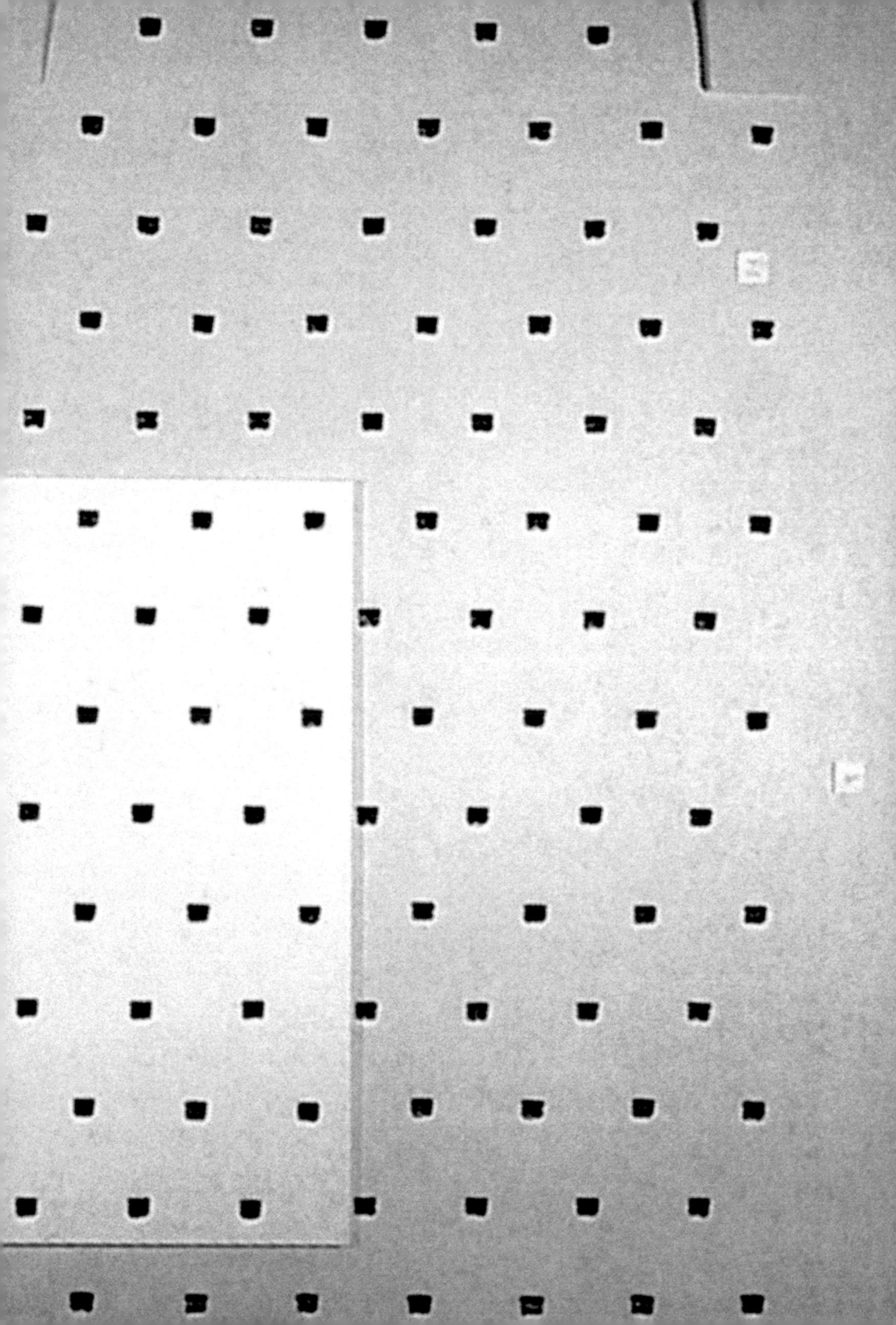

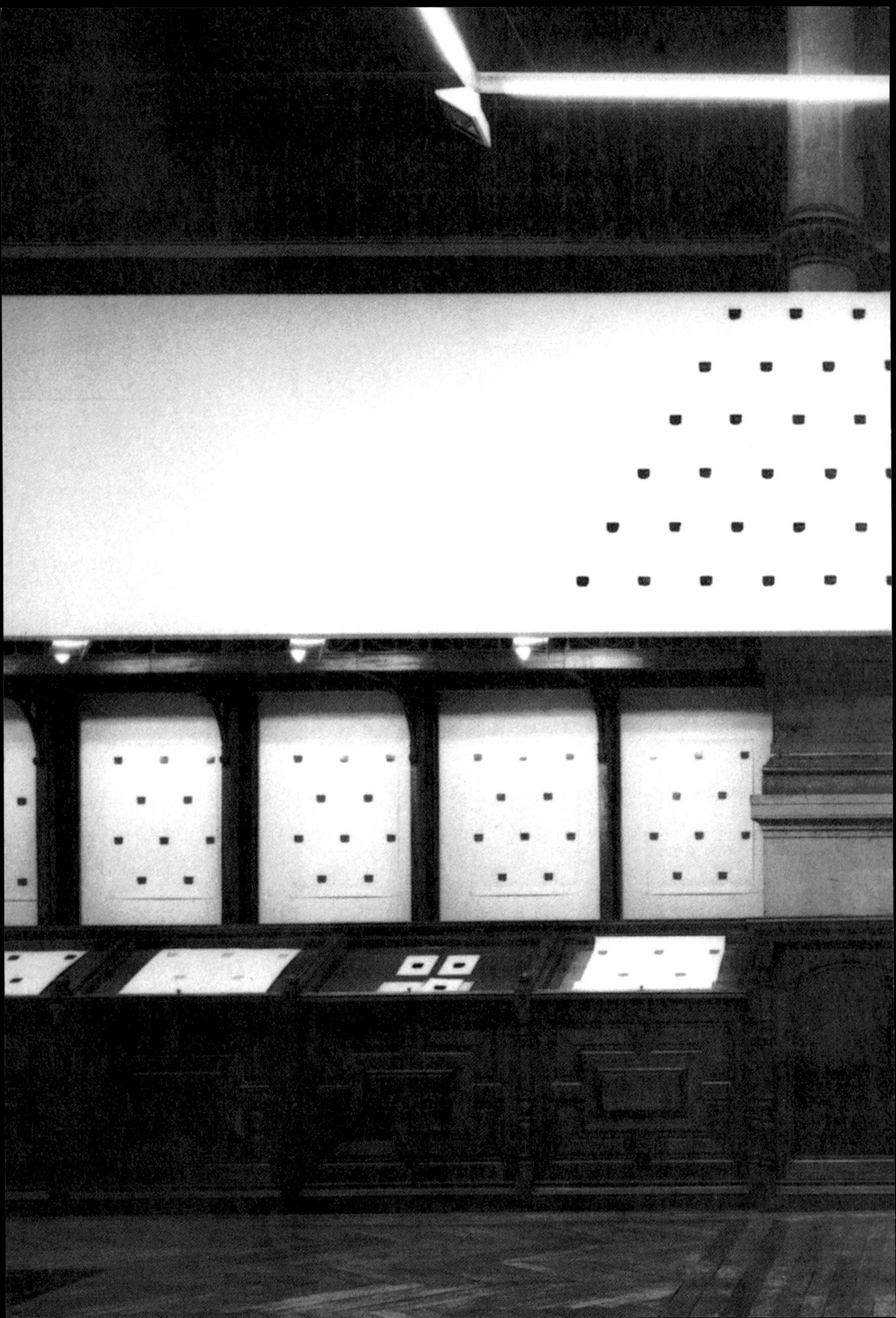

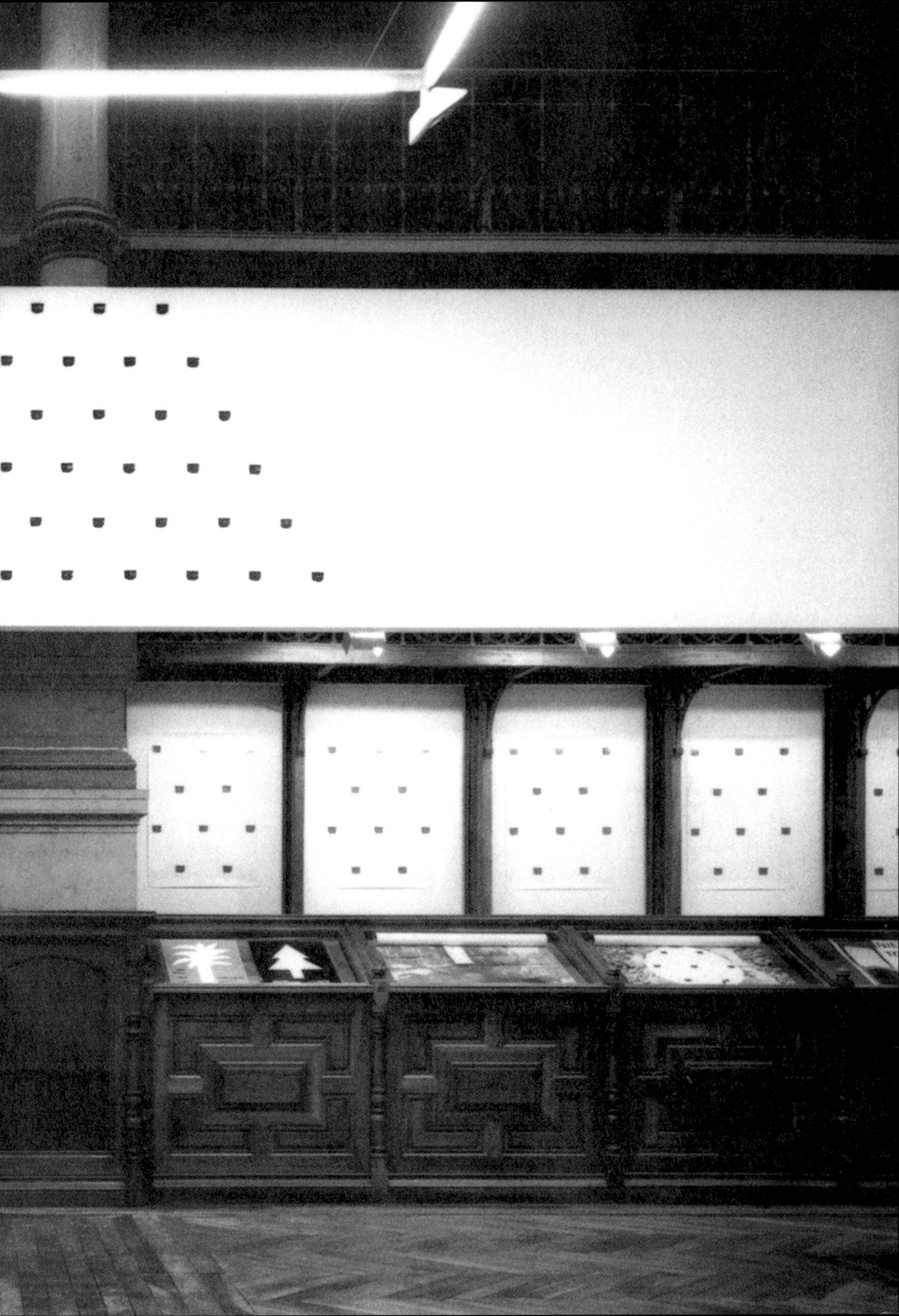

150

150

150

150

150

151

151

151

151

151

152

152

152

152

152

153 153

153

153 153

154

154

154

154

154

155 155

155

155 155

156

156

156

156

156

157

157

157

157

157

158

158

158

158

158

159 159

159

159 159

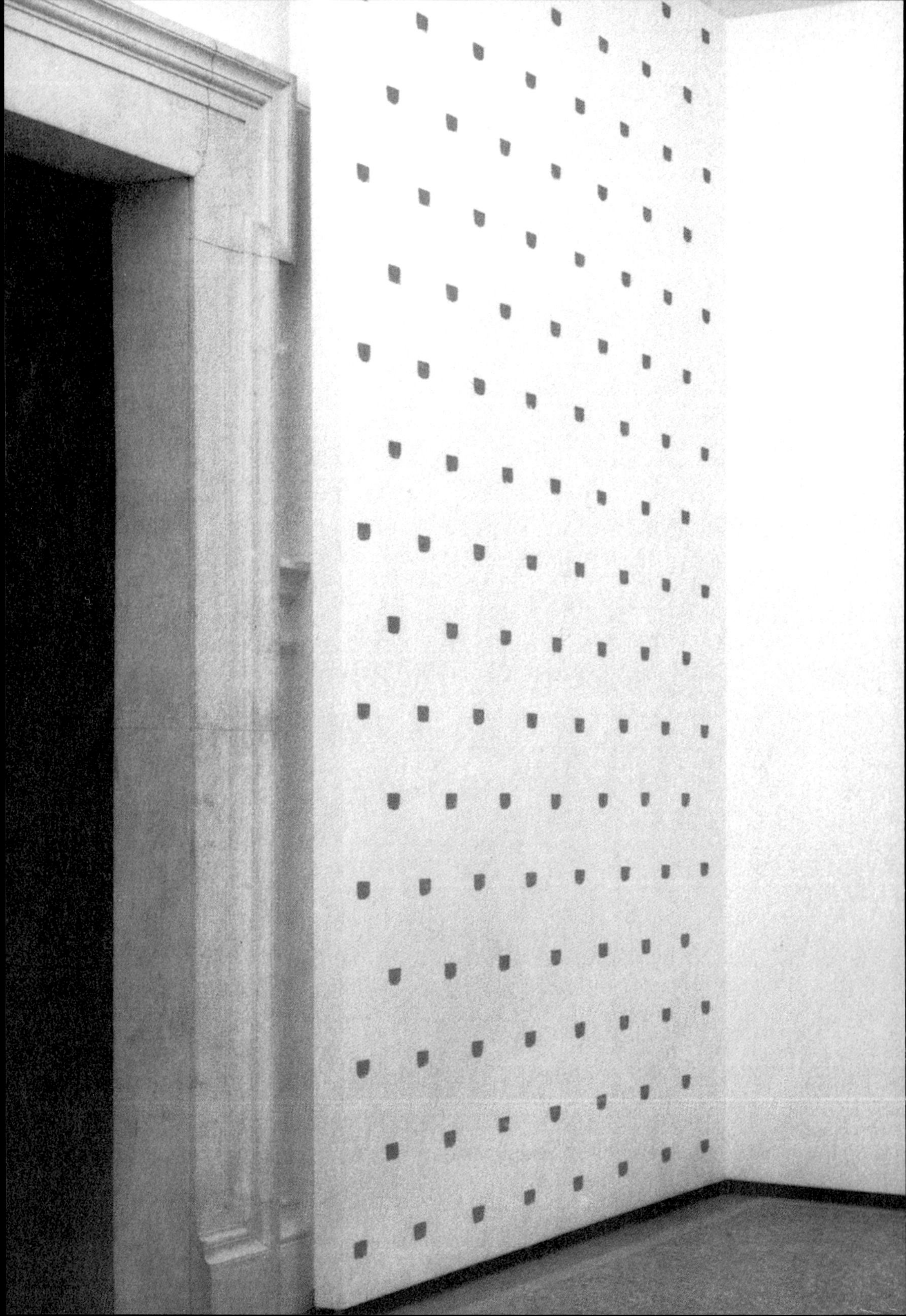

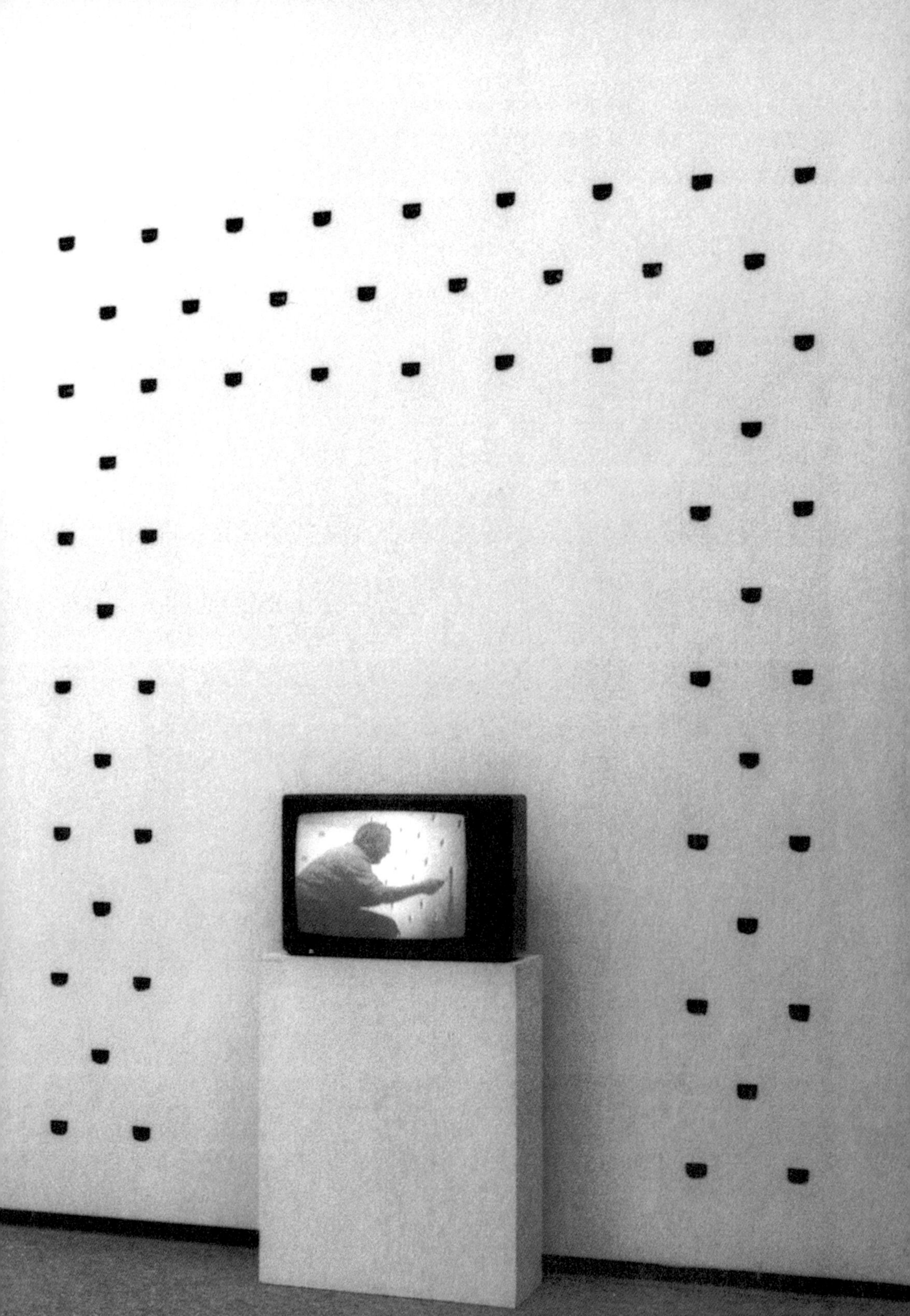

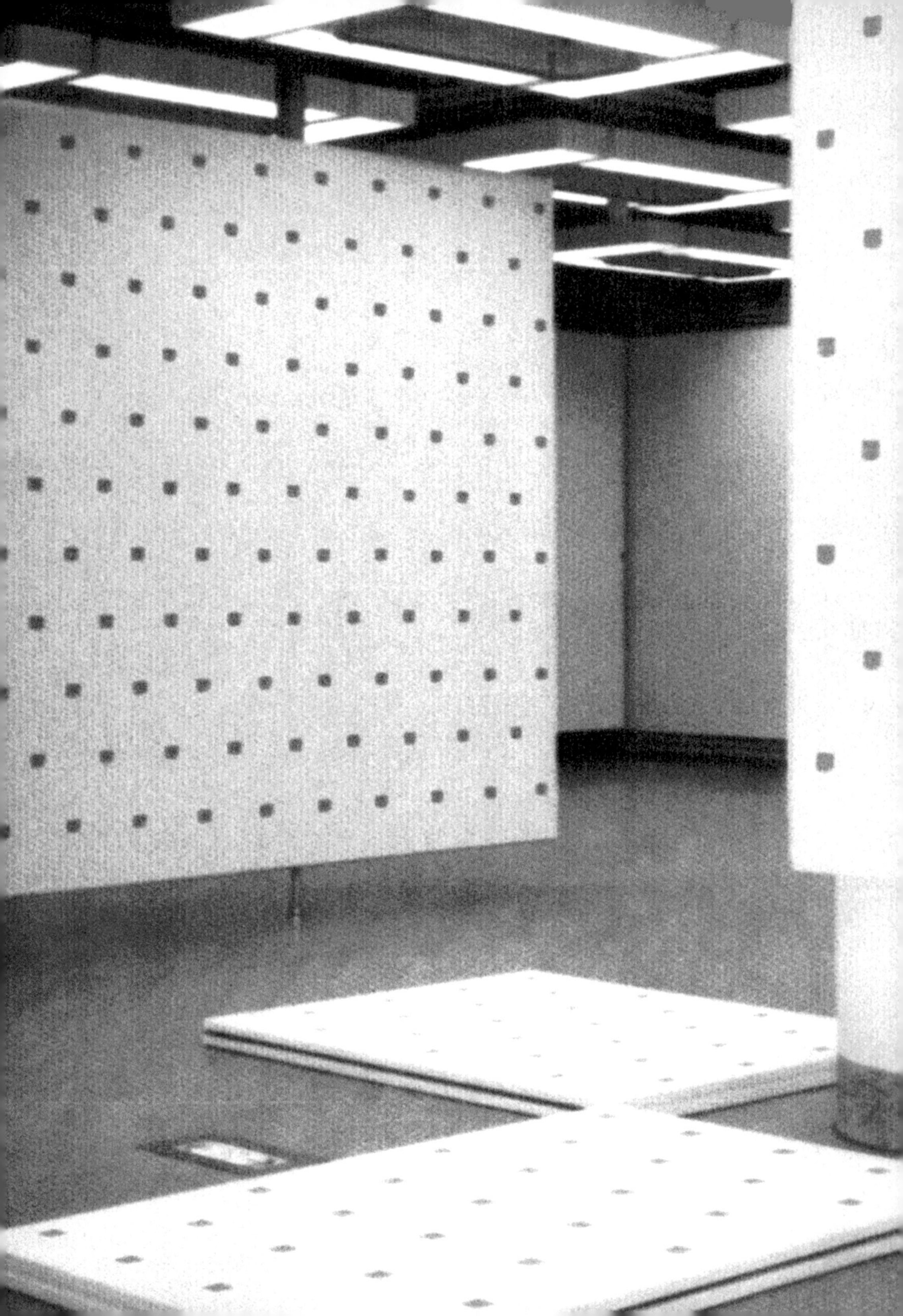

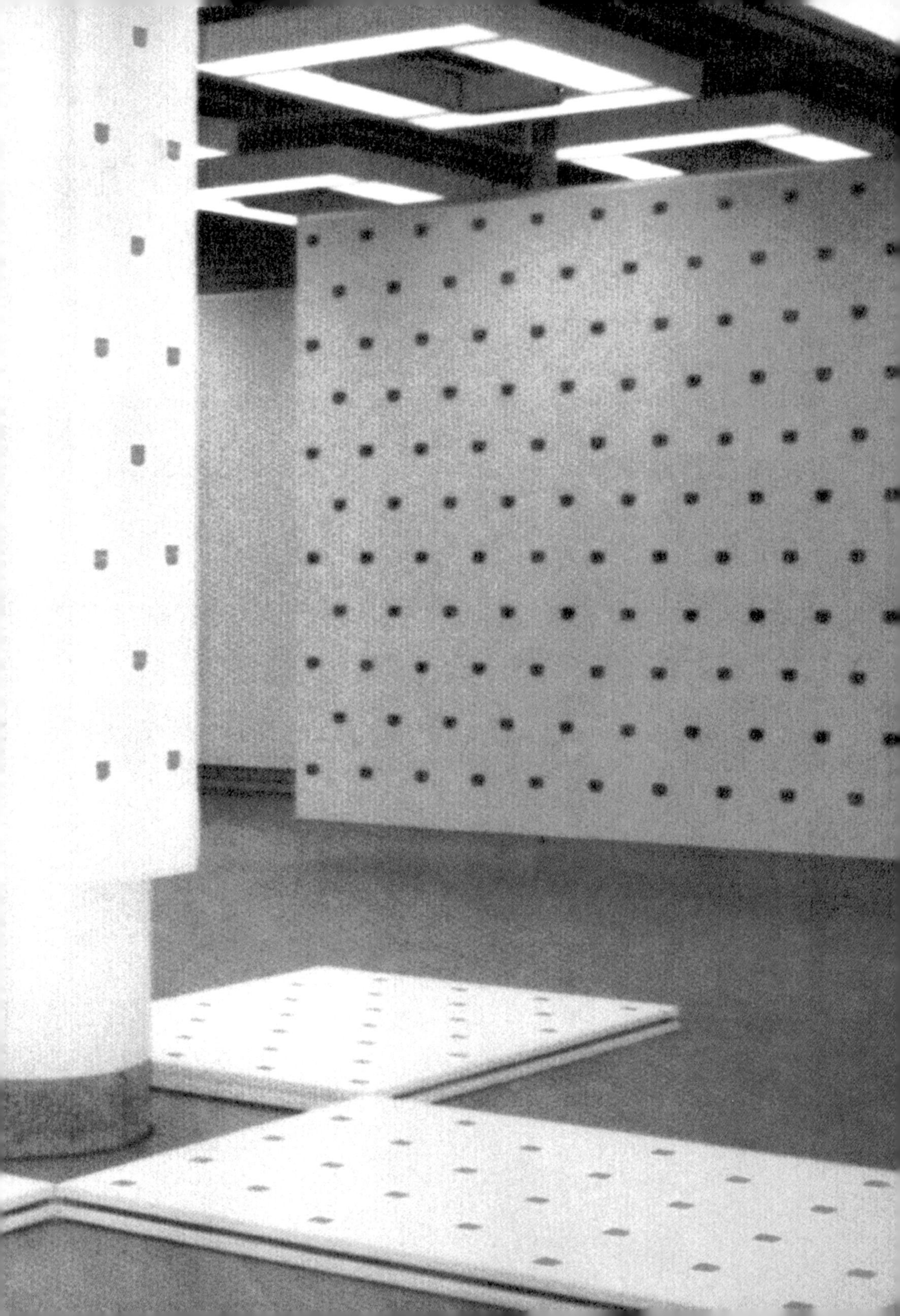

pp. 119-121: Castello di Rivoli Museo d'Arte Contemporanea, Turin, 1984

pp. 122-124: Musée Rolin, Autun, 1985

pp. 126-127: Galerie Pietro Spartà, Chagny, 1985

pp. 128-129: Musée d'Art Moderne de la Ville de Paris, Paris, 1985

pp. 130-131: Galerie Yvon Lambert, Paris, 1986

pp. 132-133: Collection B.L., Regnéville-sur-Mer, 1986

p. 134: Unknown vineyard, Martigny, 1986

pp. 136-137: Galerie Micheline Szwajcer, Antwerp, 1986

pp. 138-139: Galerie Yvon Lambert, Paris, 1987

pp. 140-143: Villa Arson, Nice, 1987

p. 144: Galerie nächst St. Stephan, Vienna, 1987

pp. 146-147: Museo Cantonale d'Arte, Lugano, 1987

pp. 148-149, 160-161: Museé de Peinture et de Sculpture, Grenoble, 1987

pp. 162-163: Meguro Museum of Art, Tokyo, 1987

165

165

165

165

165

Exhibitions: 1988–2002

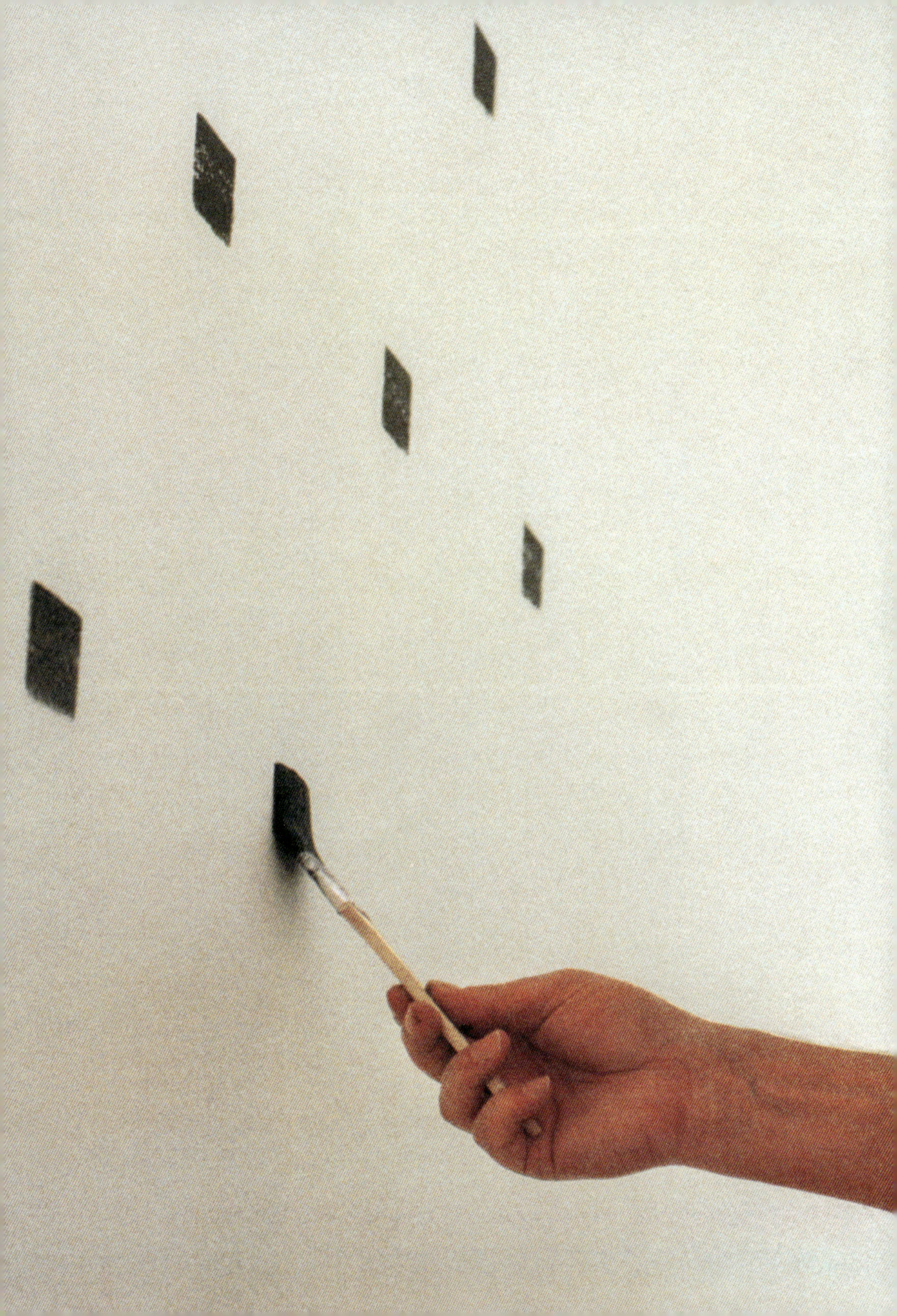

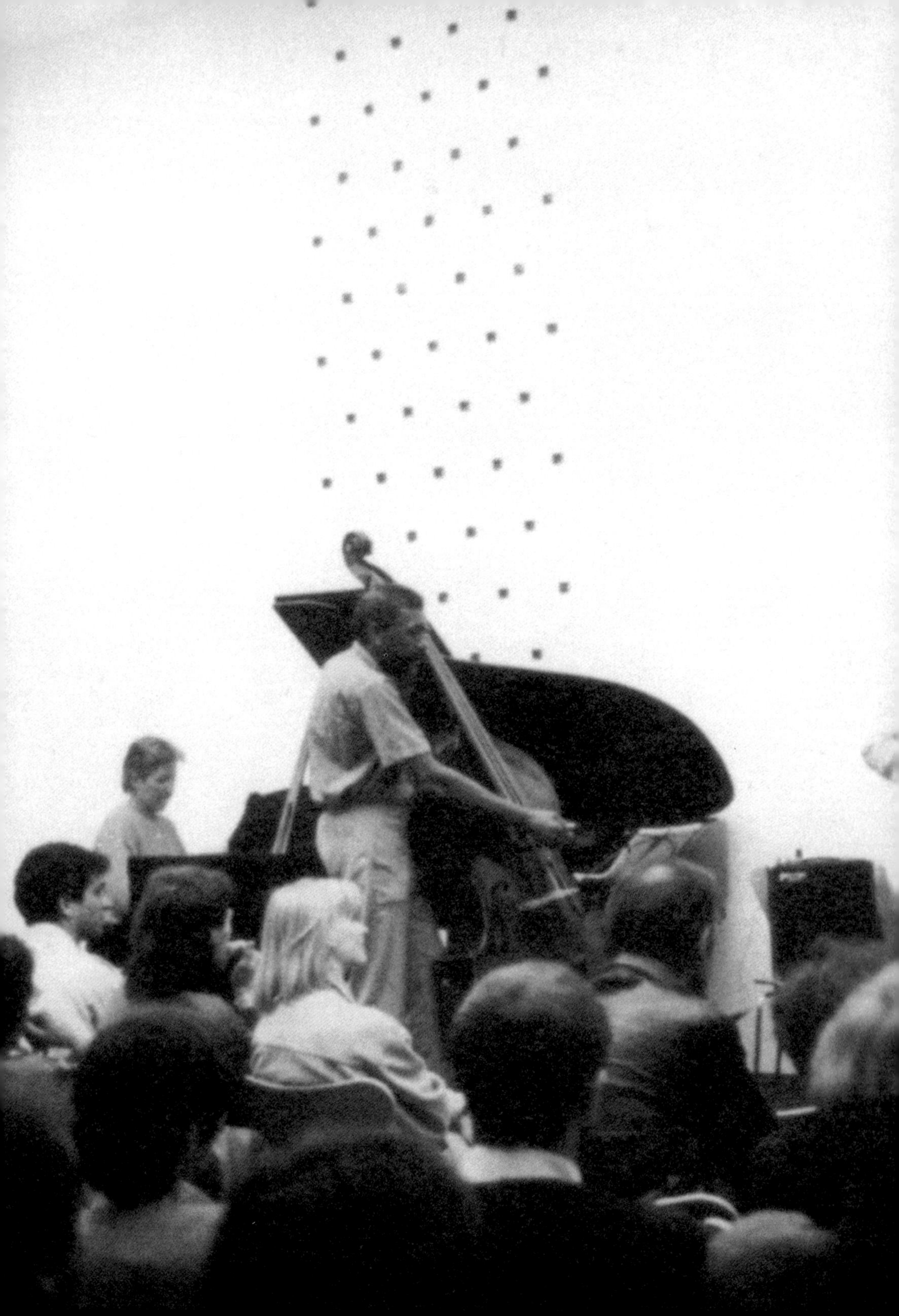

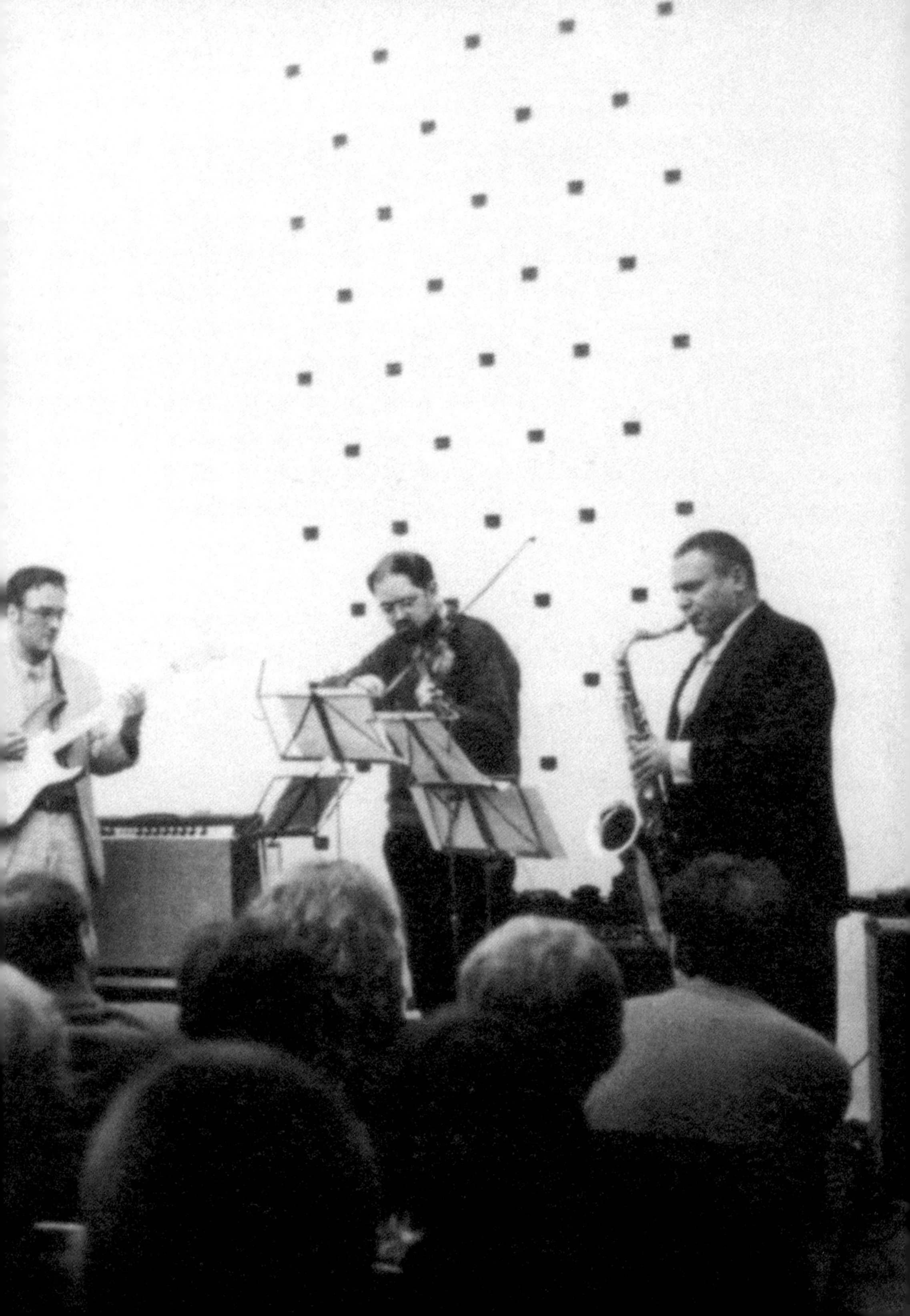

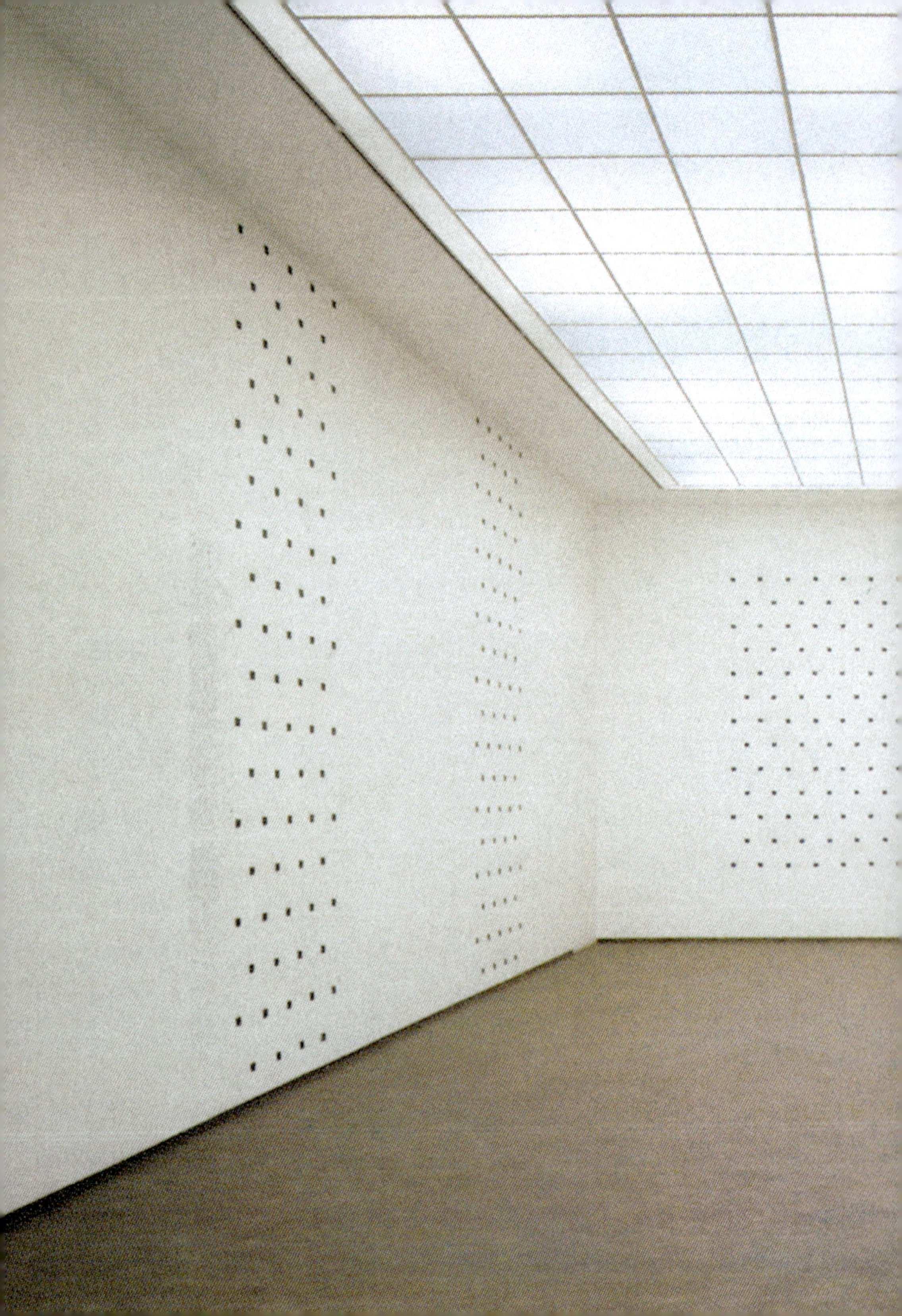

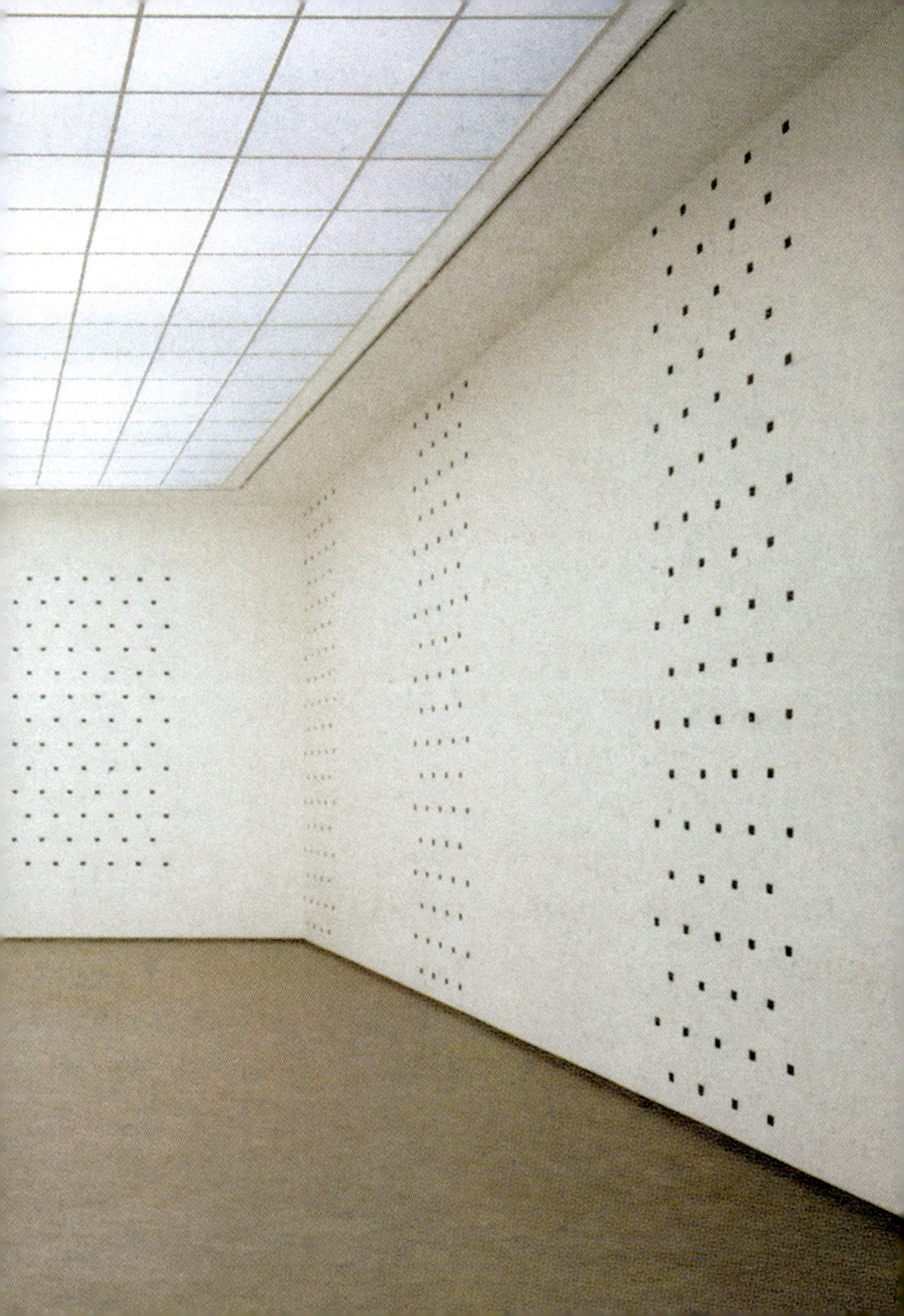

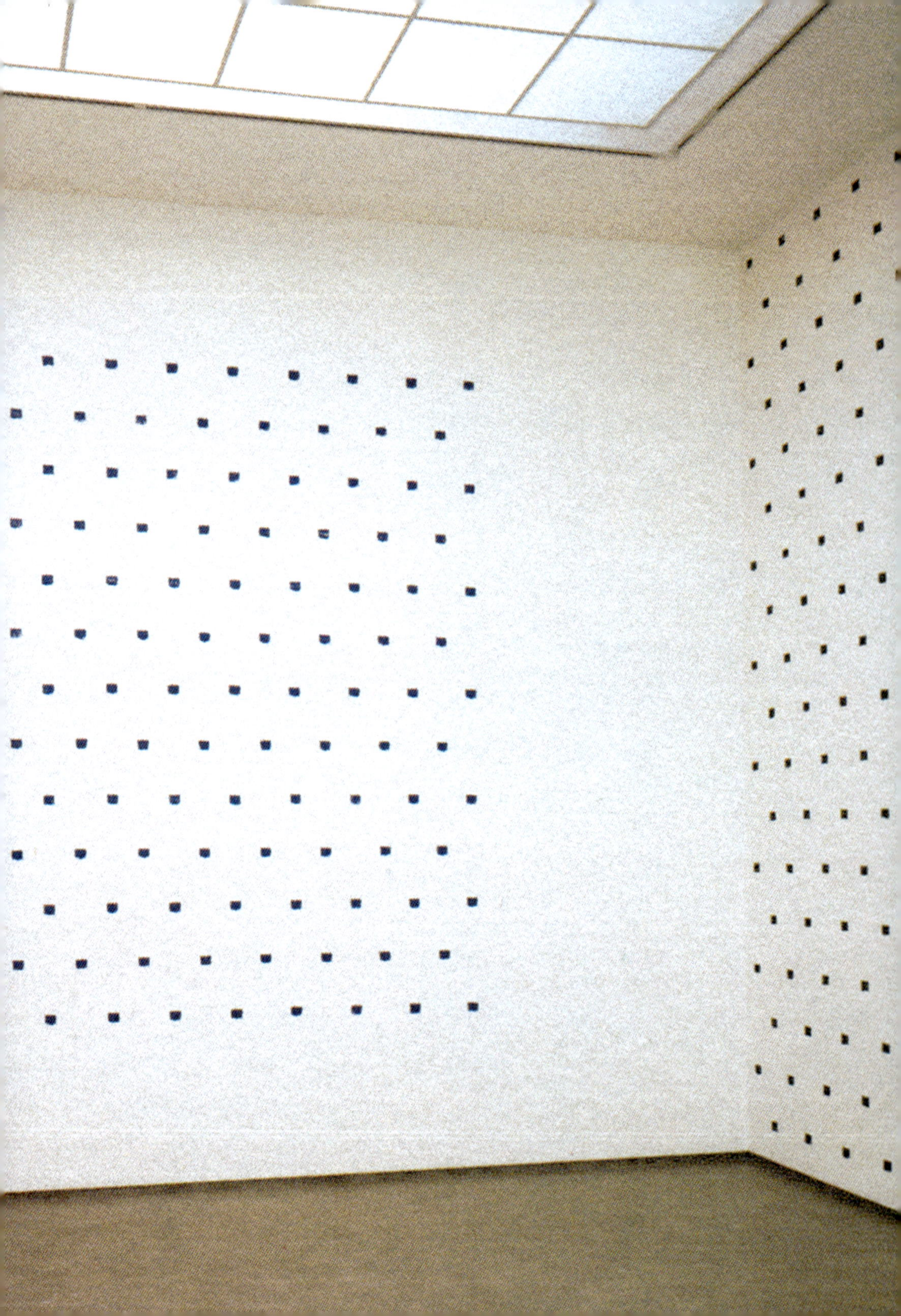

175

175

175

175

175

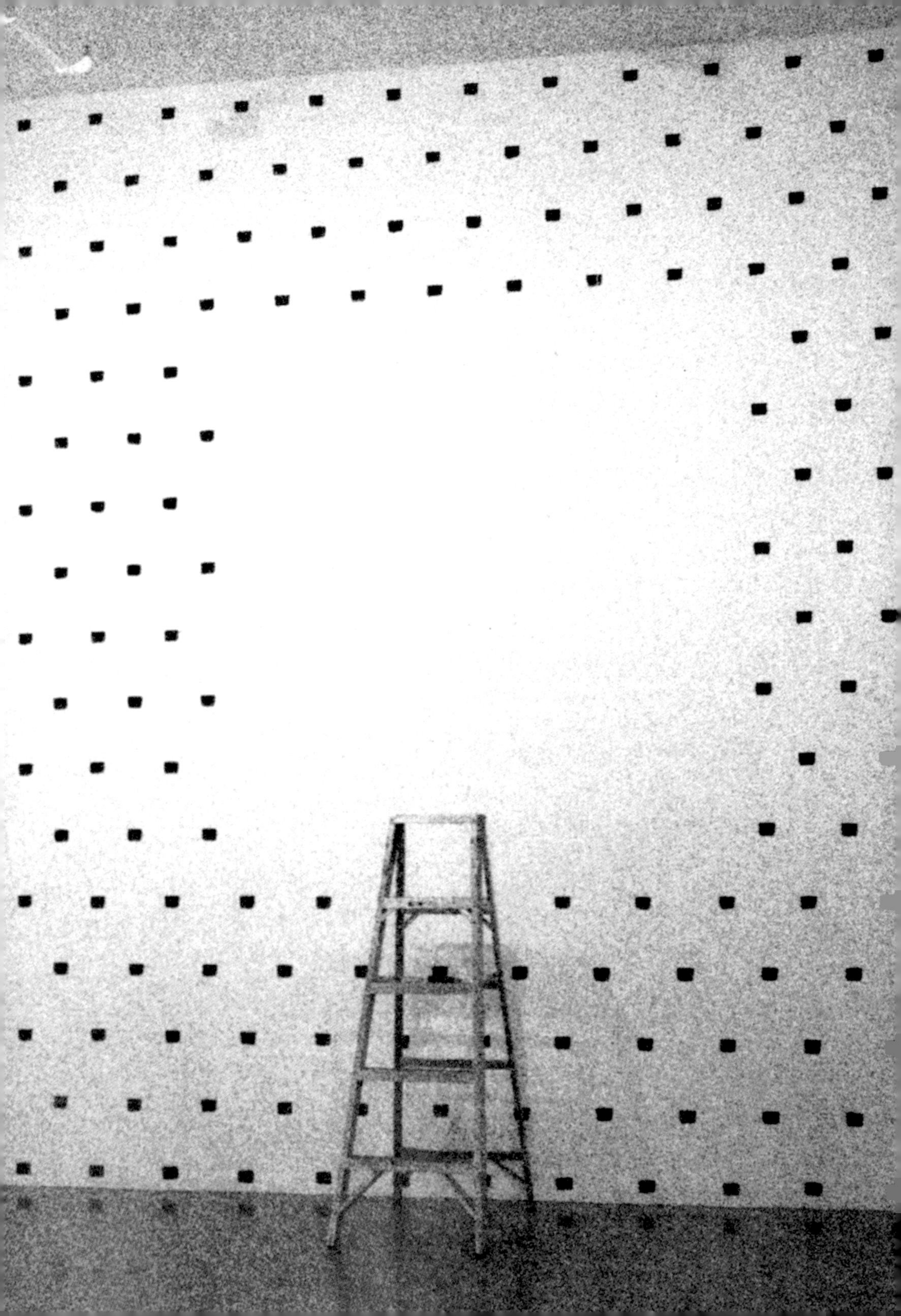

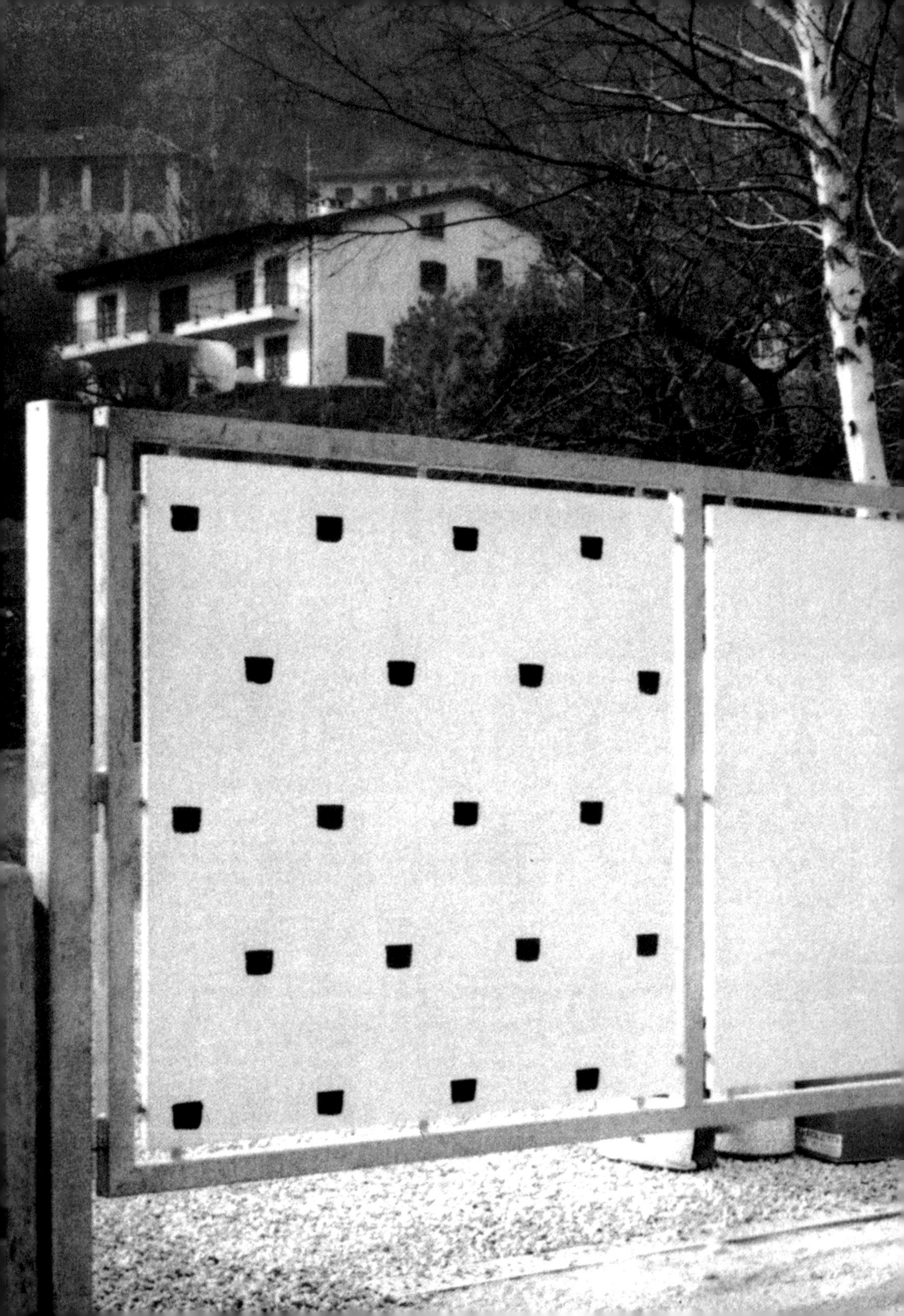

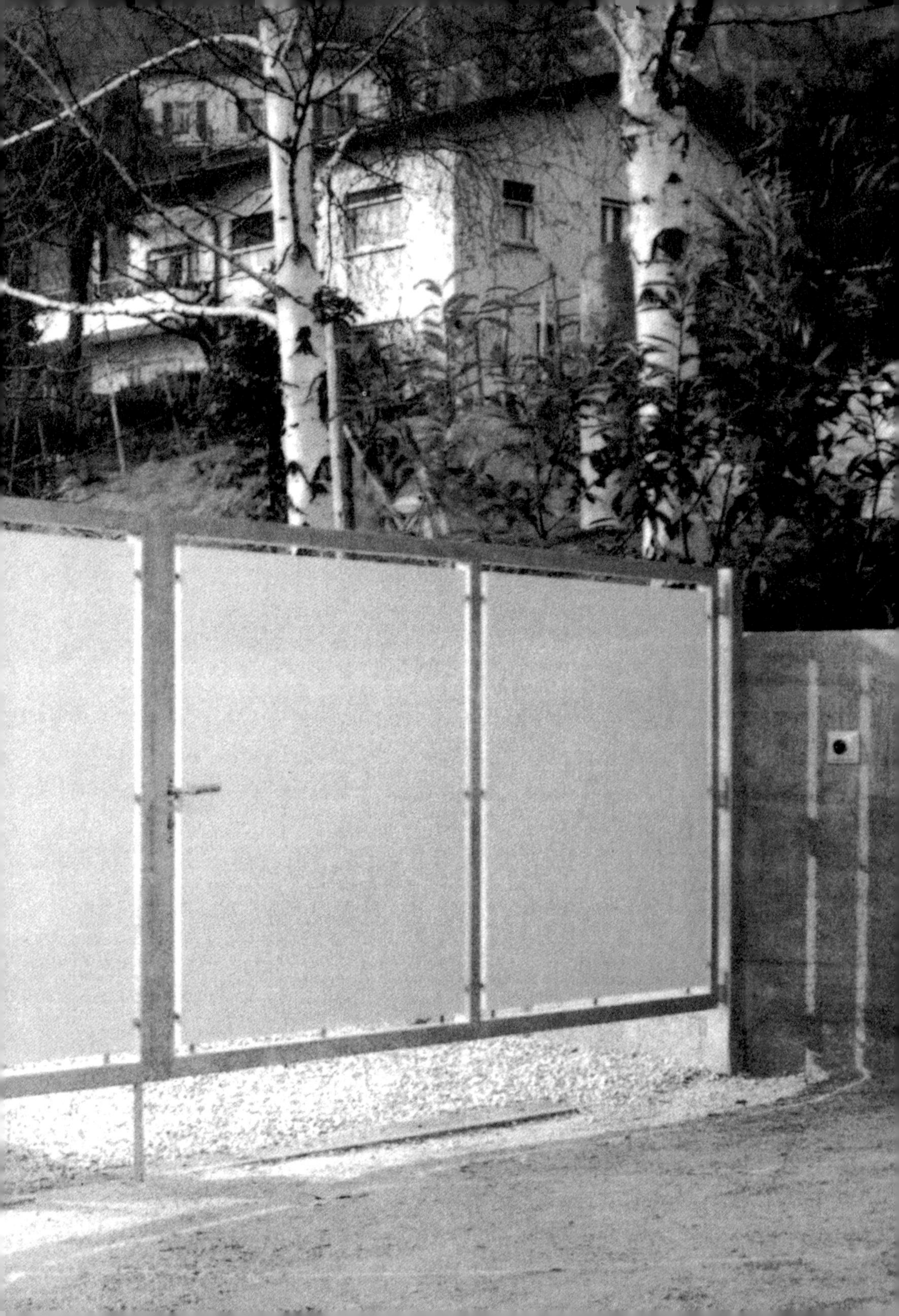

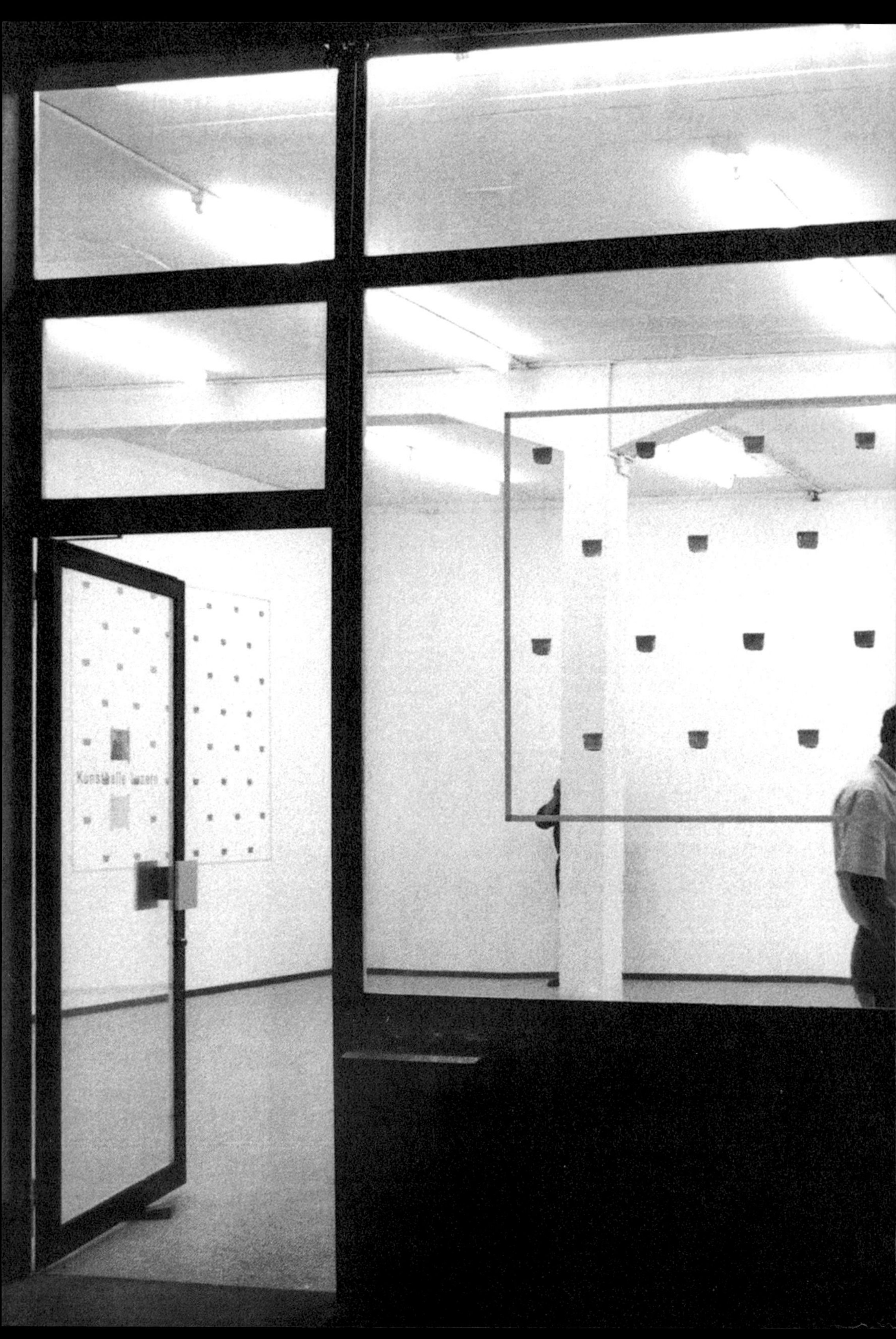

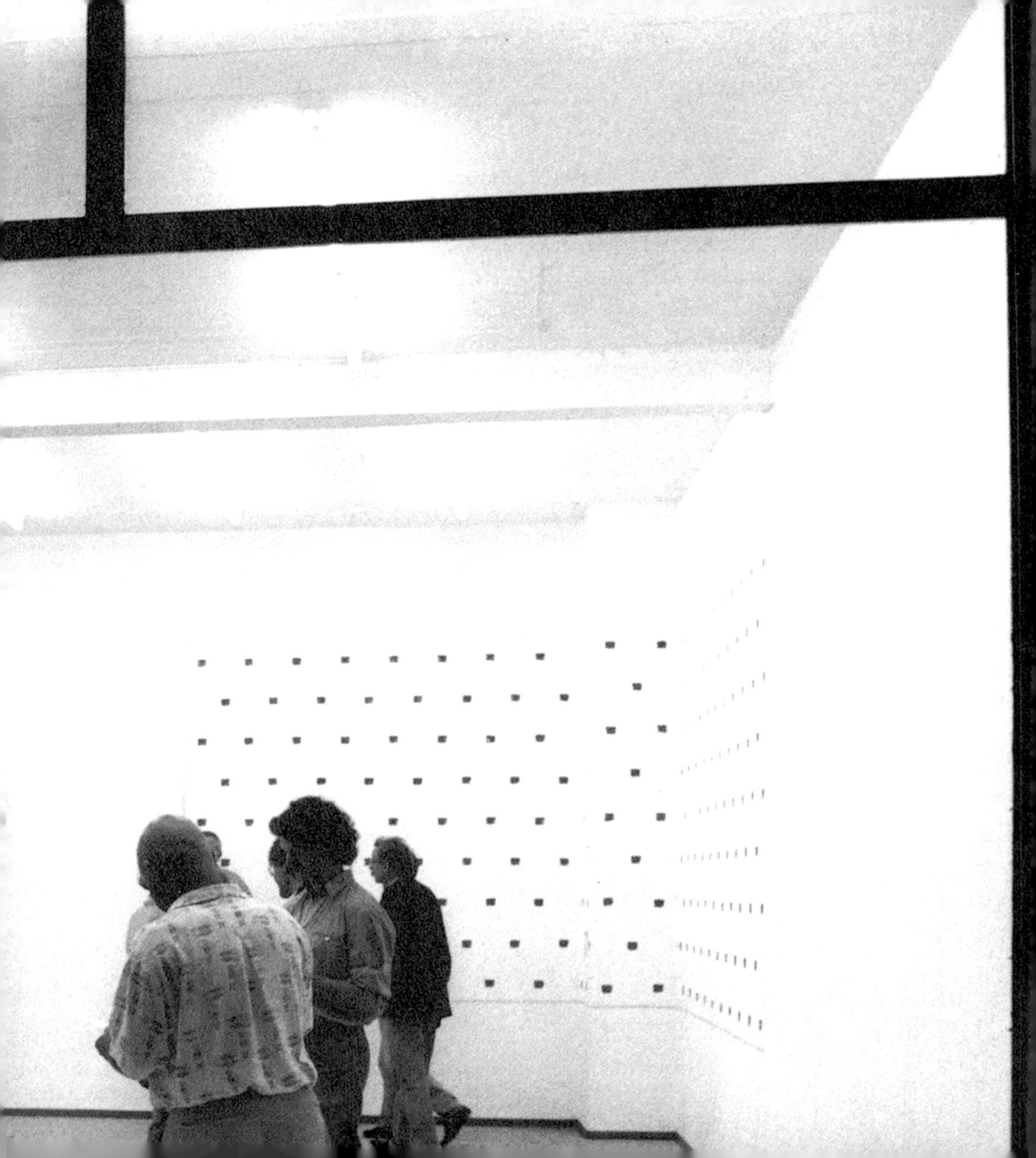

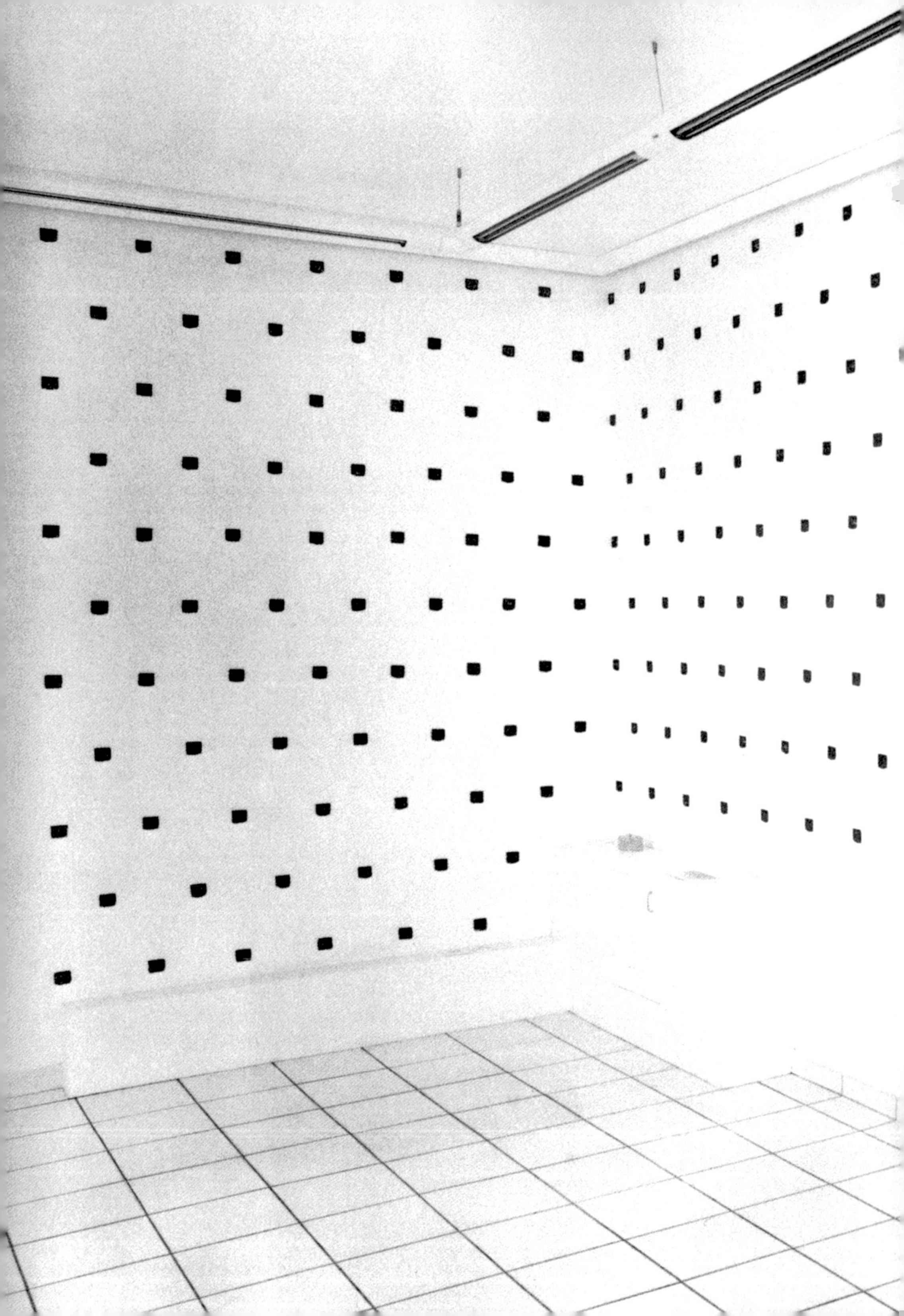

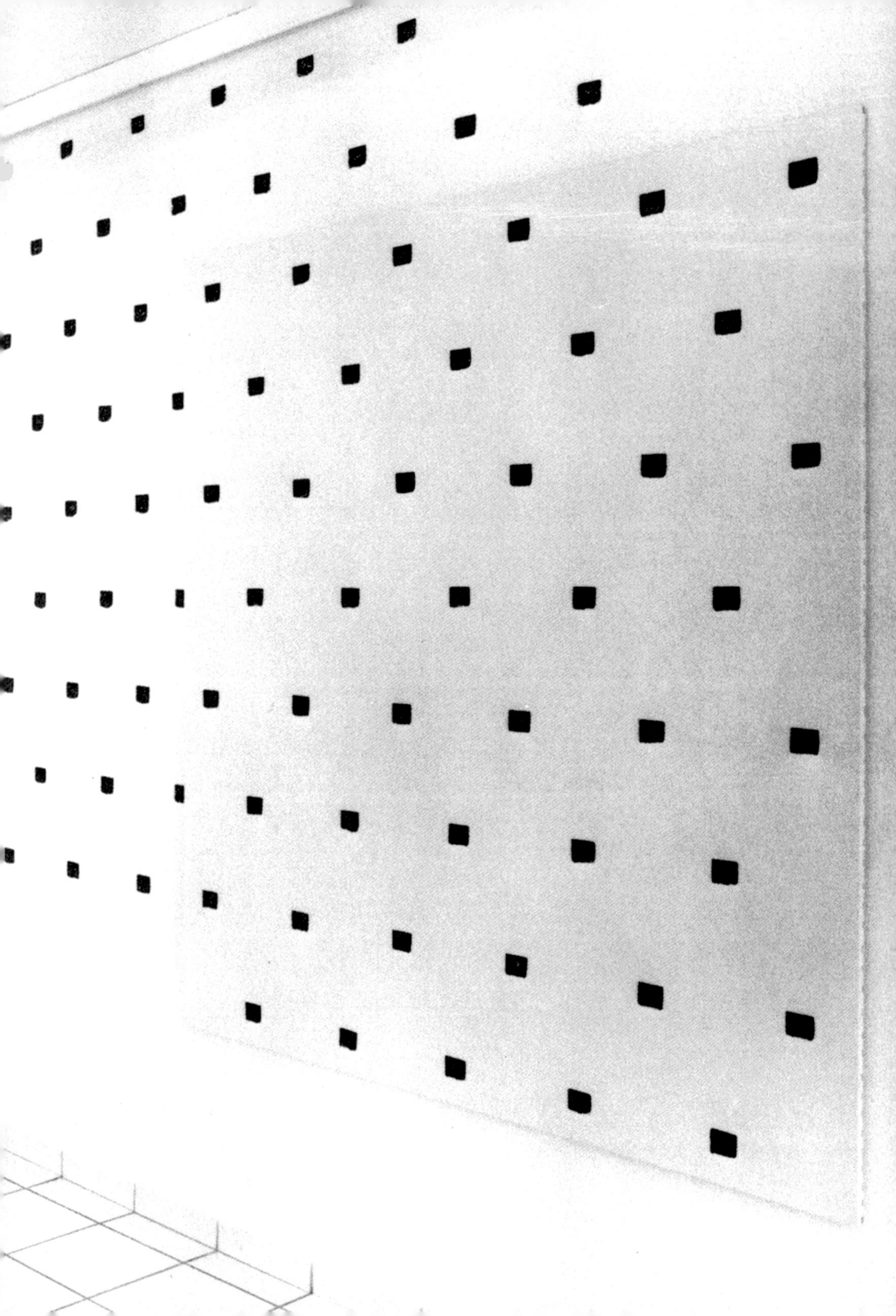

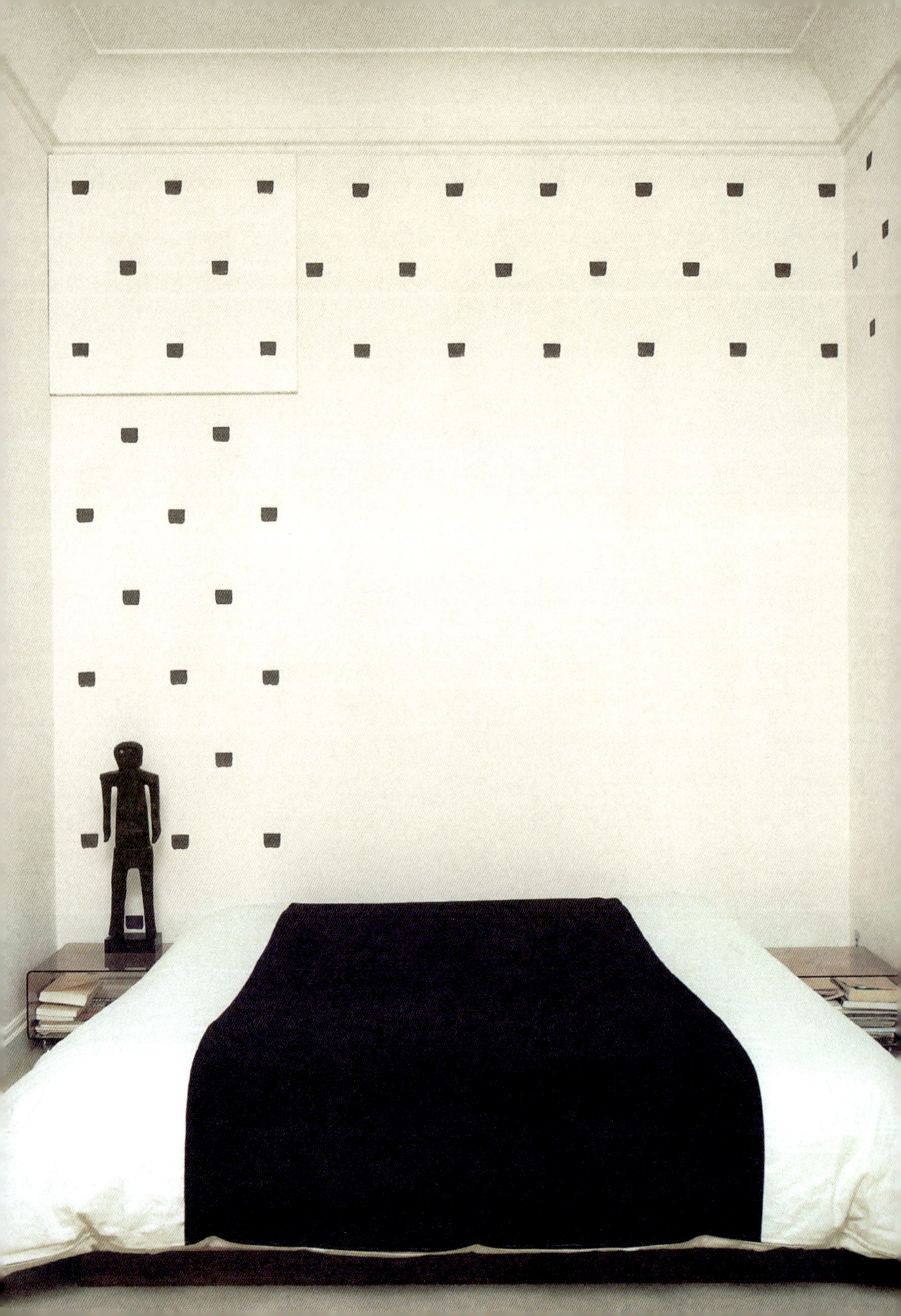

185

185

185

185

185

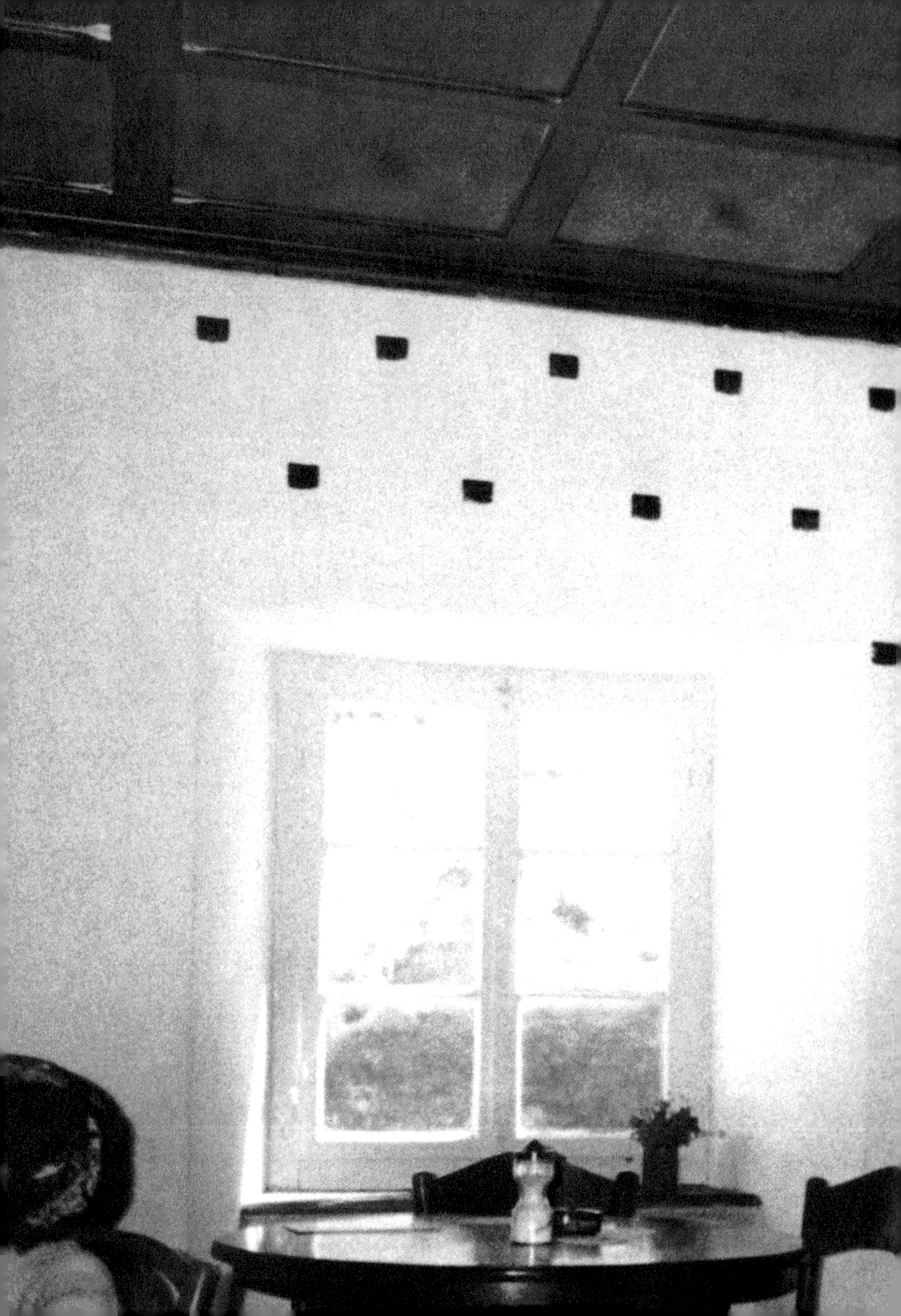

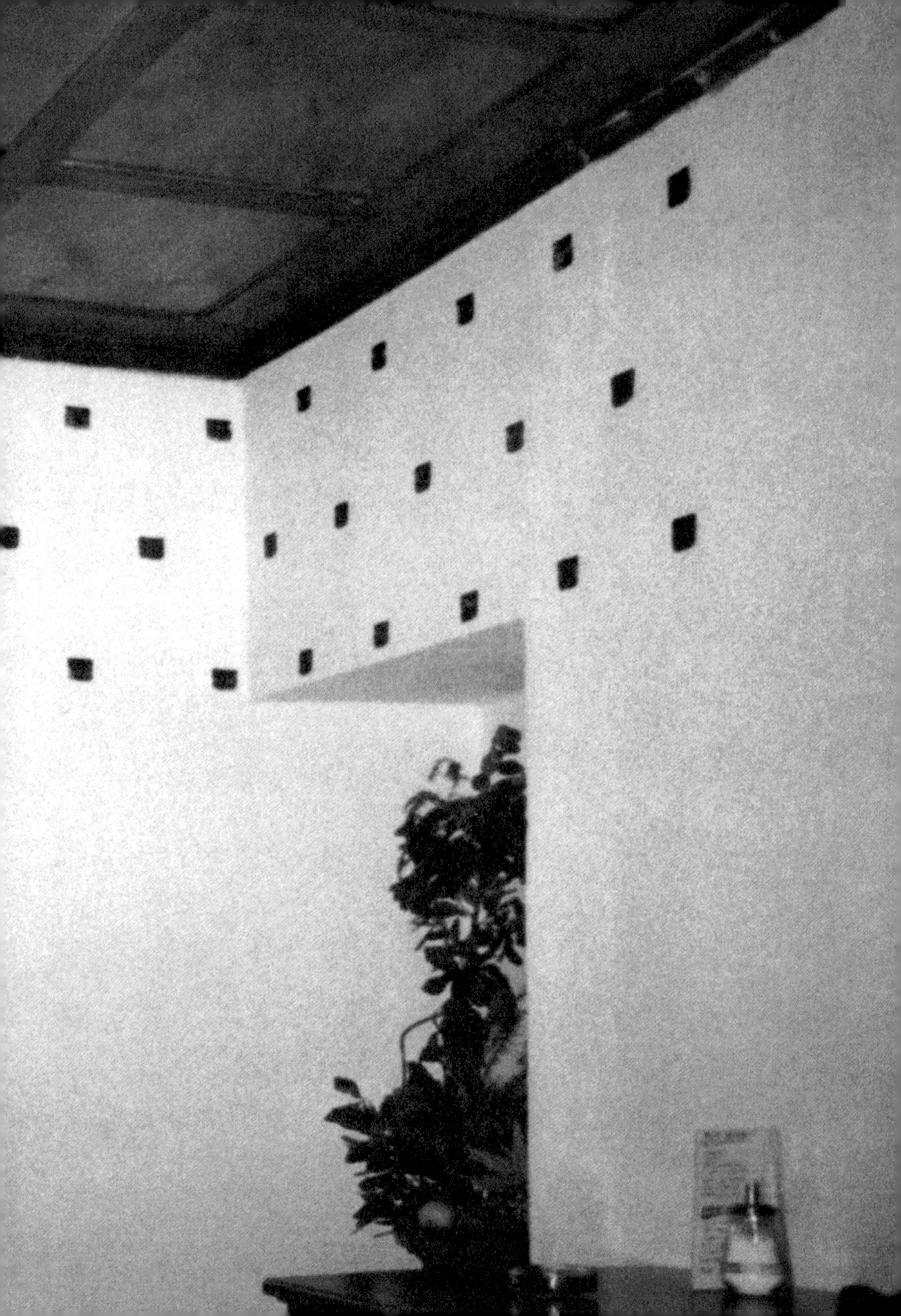

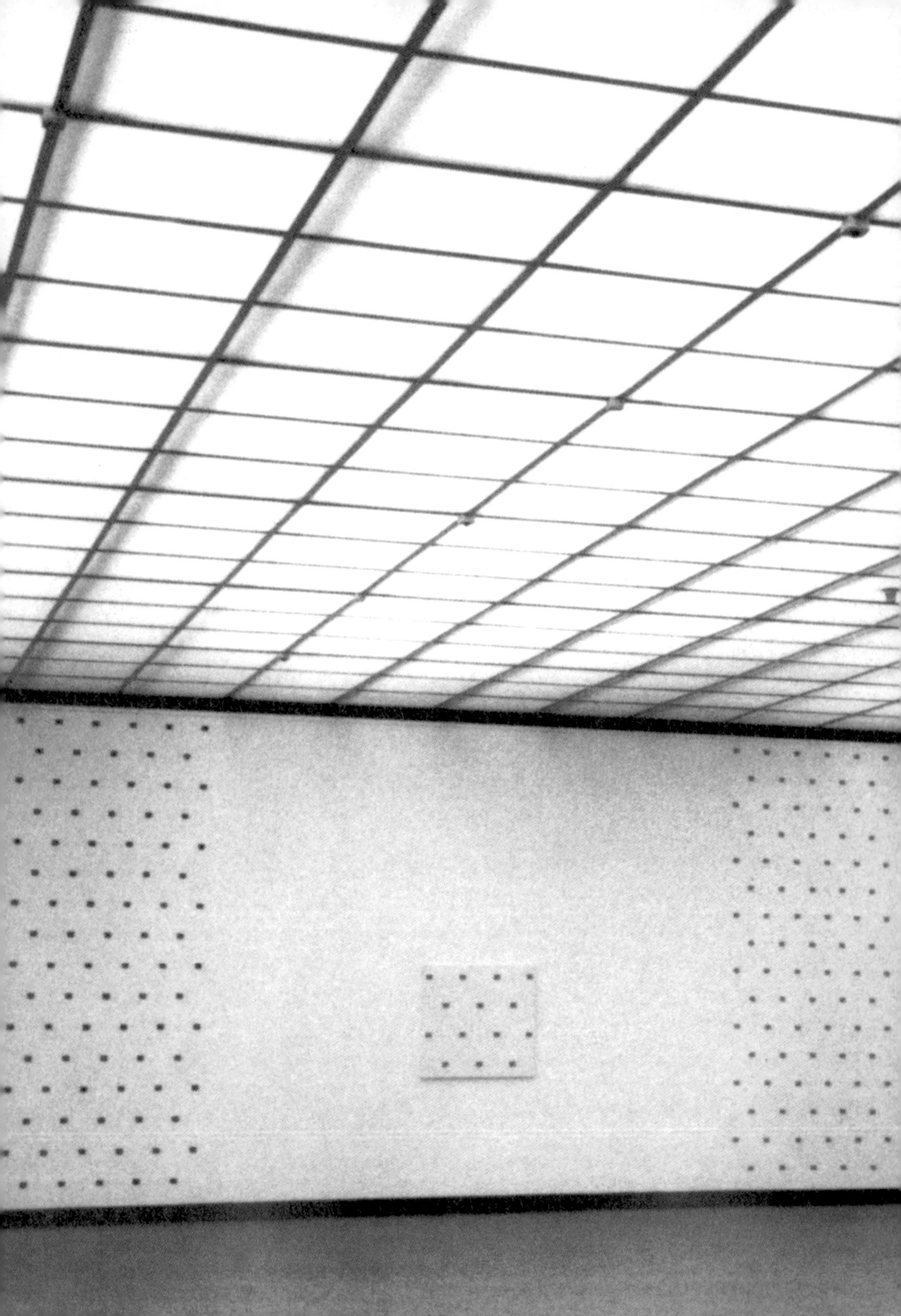

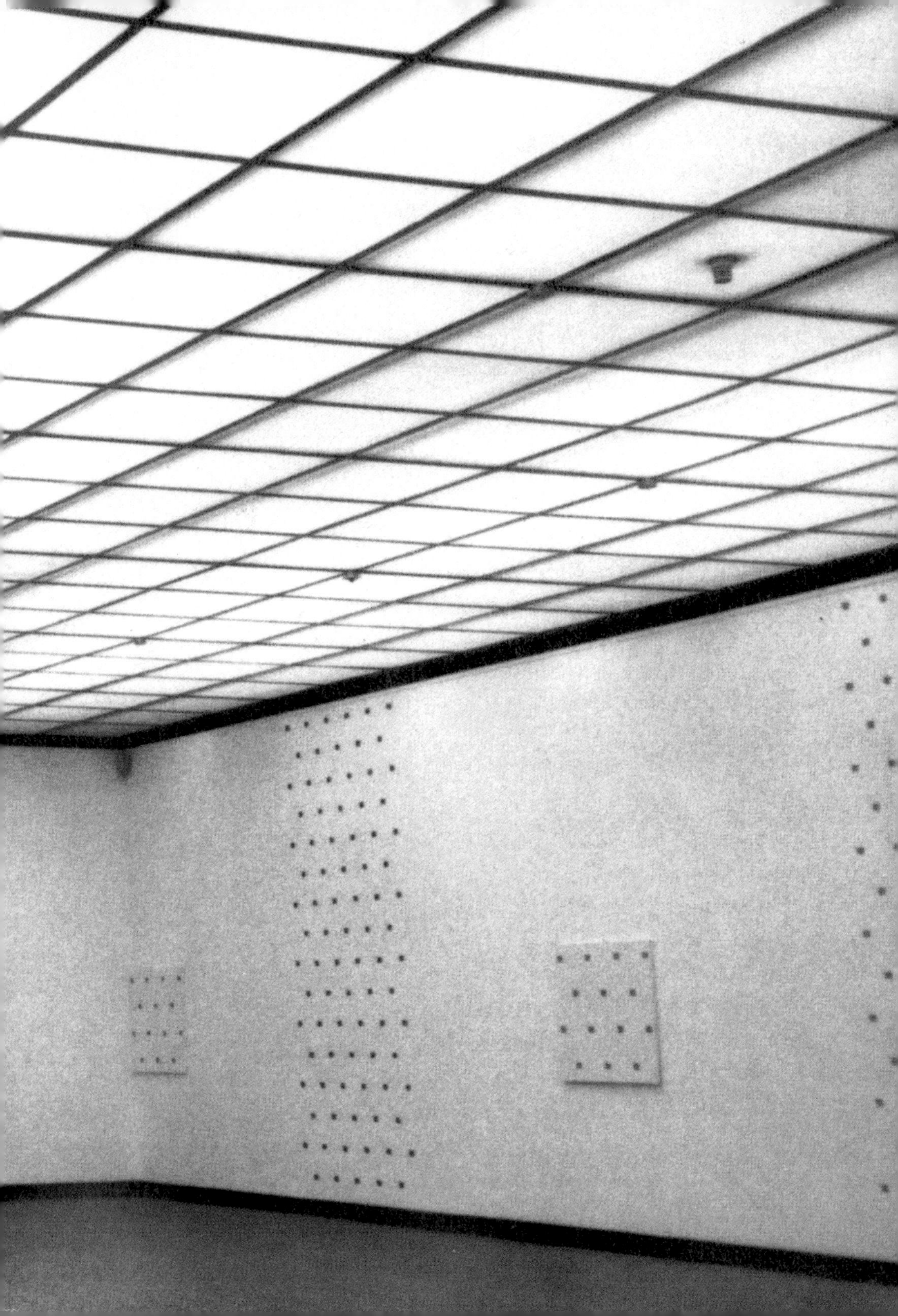

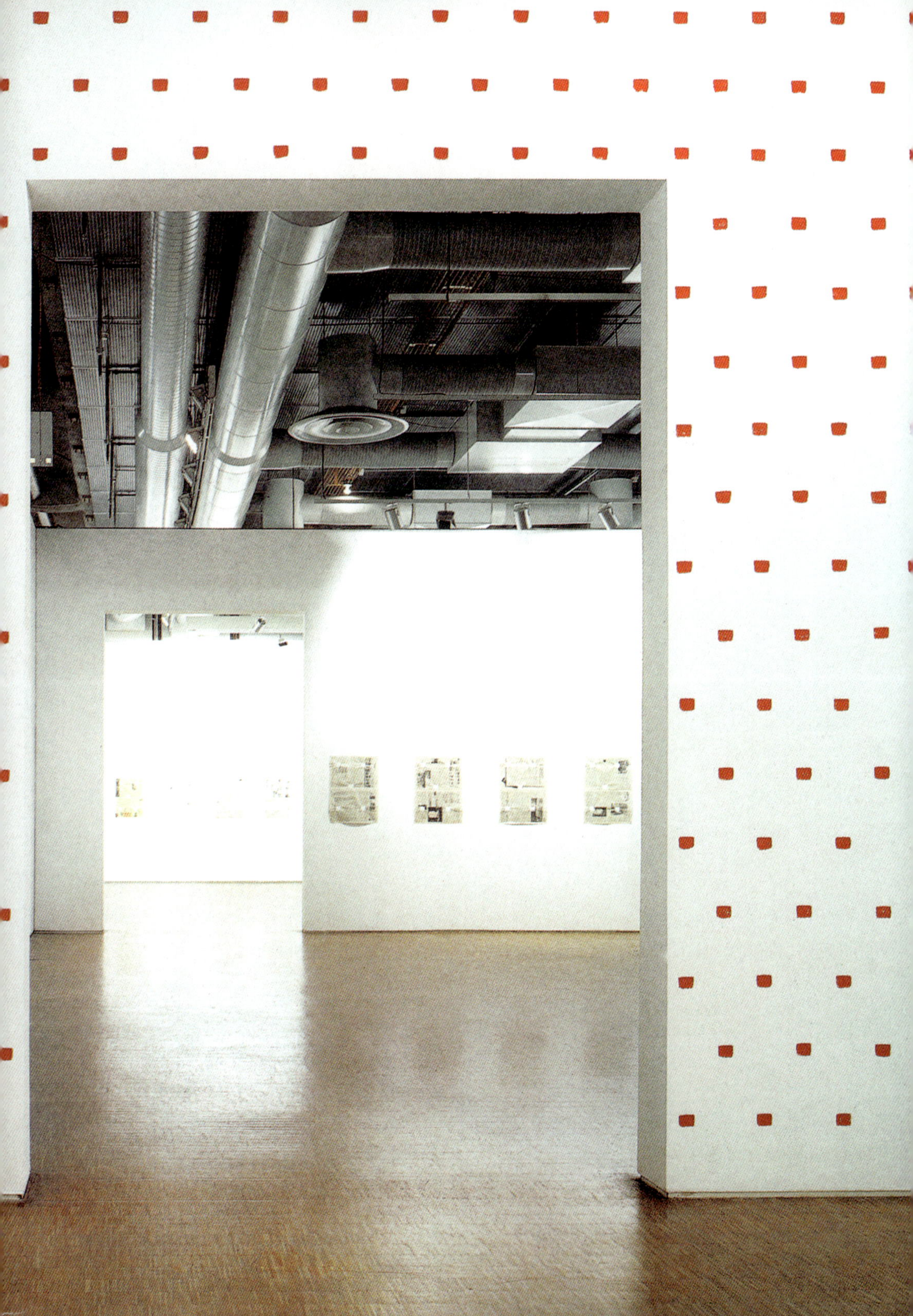

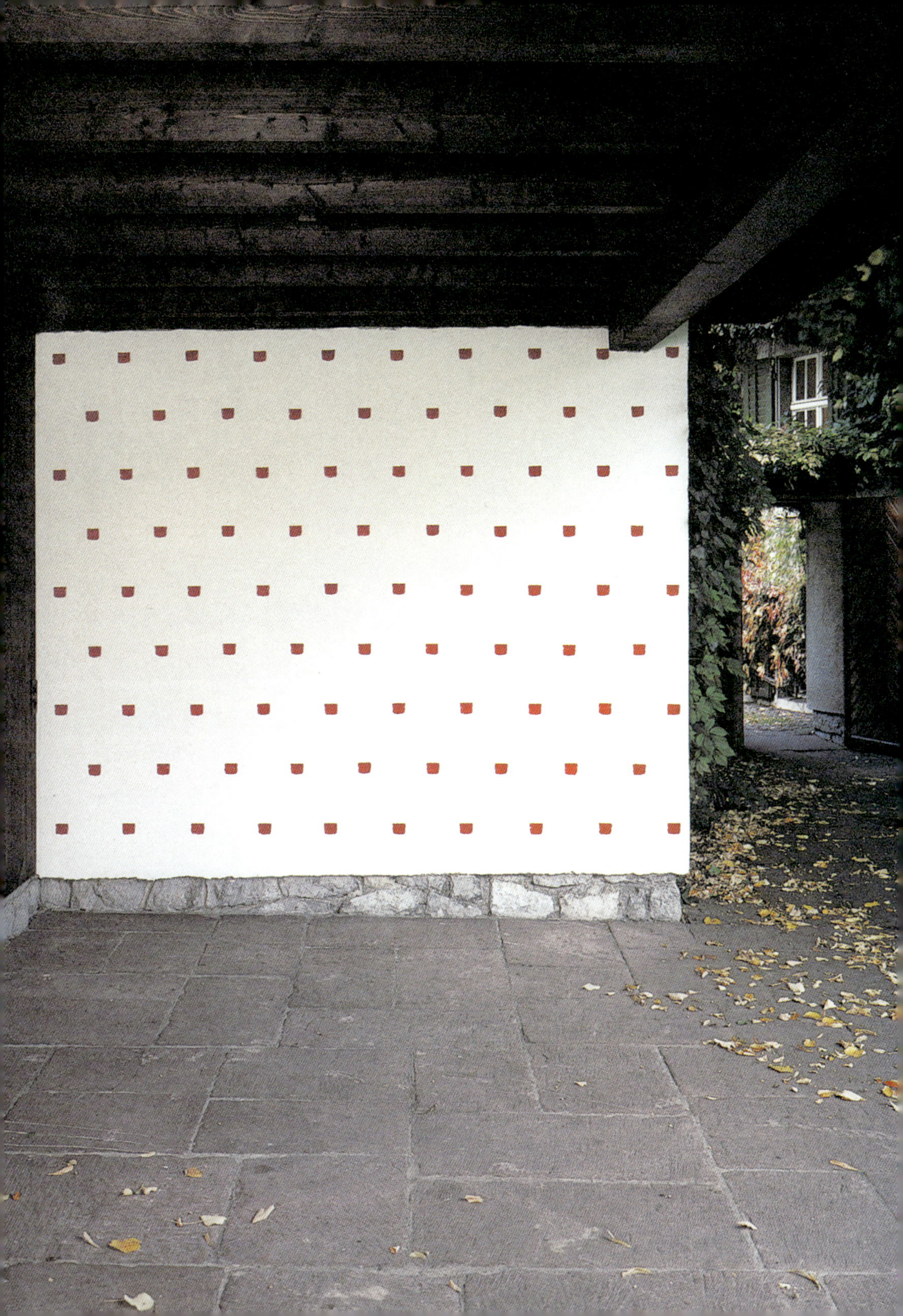

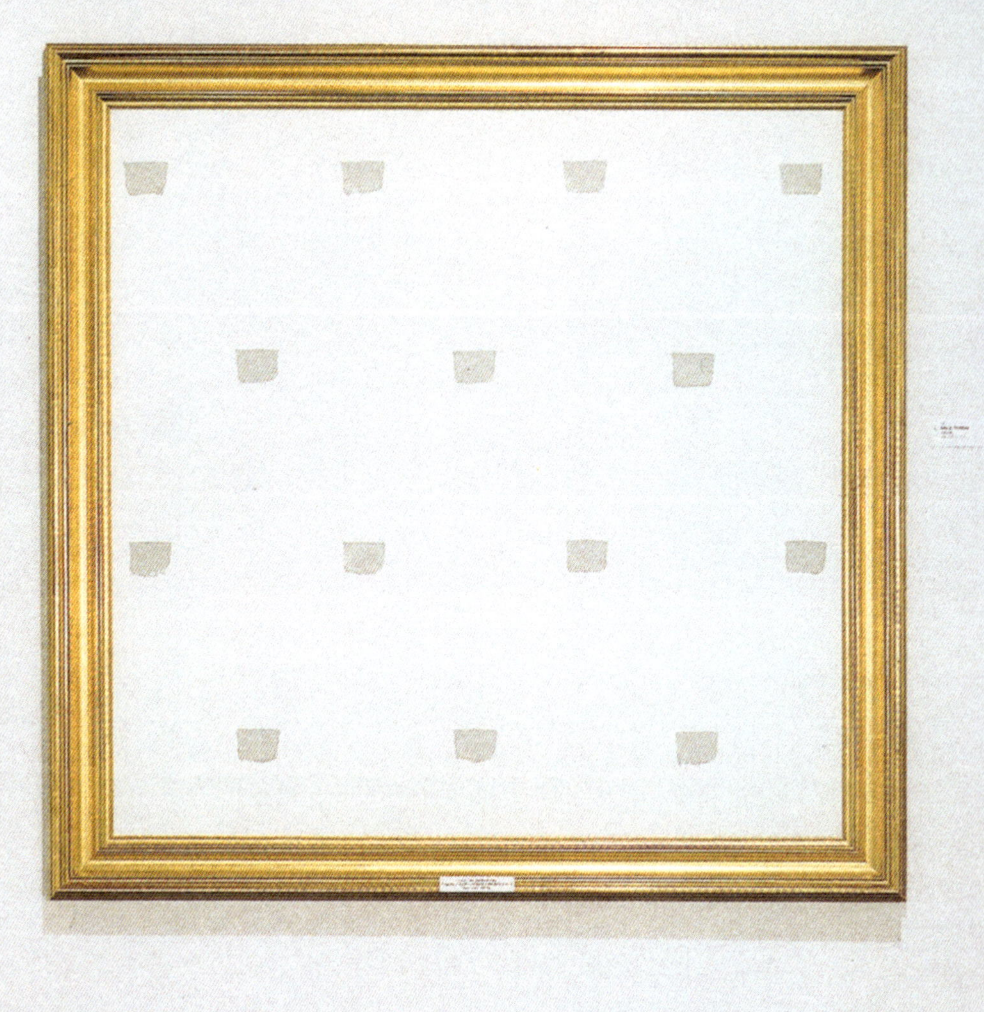

195 195

195

195 195

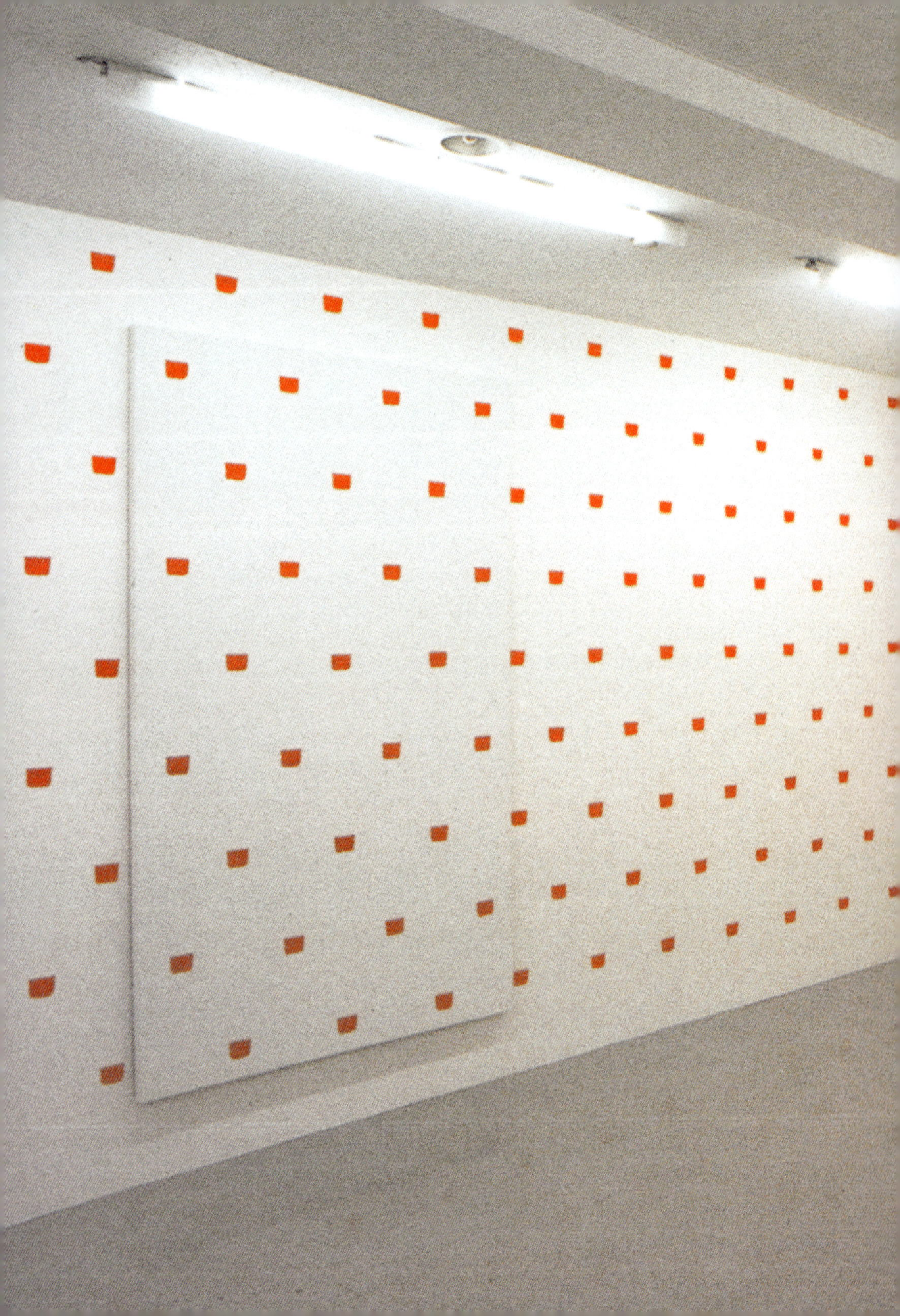

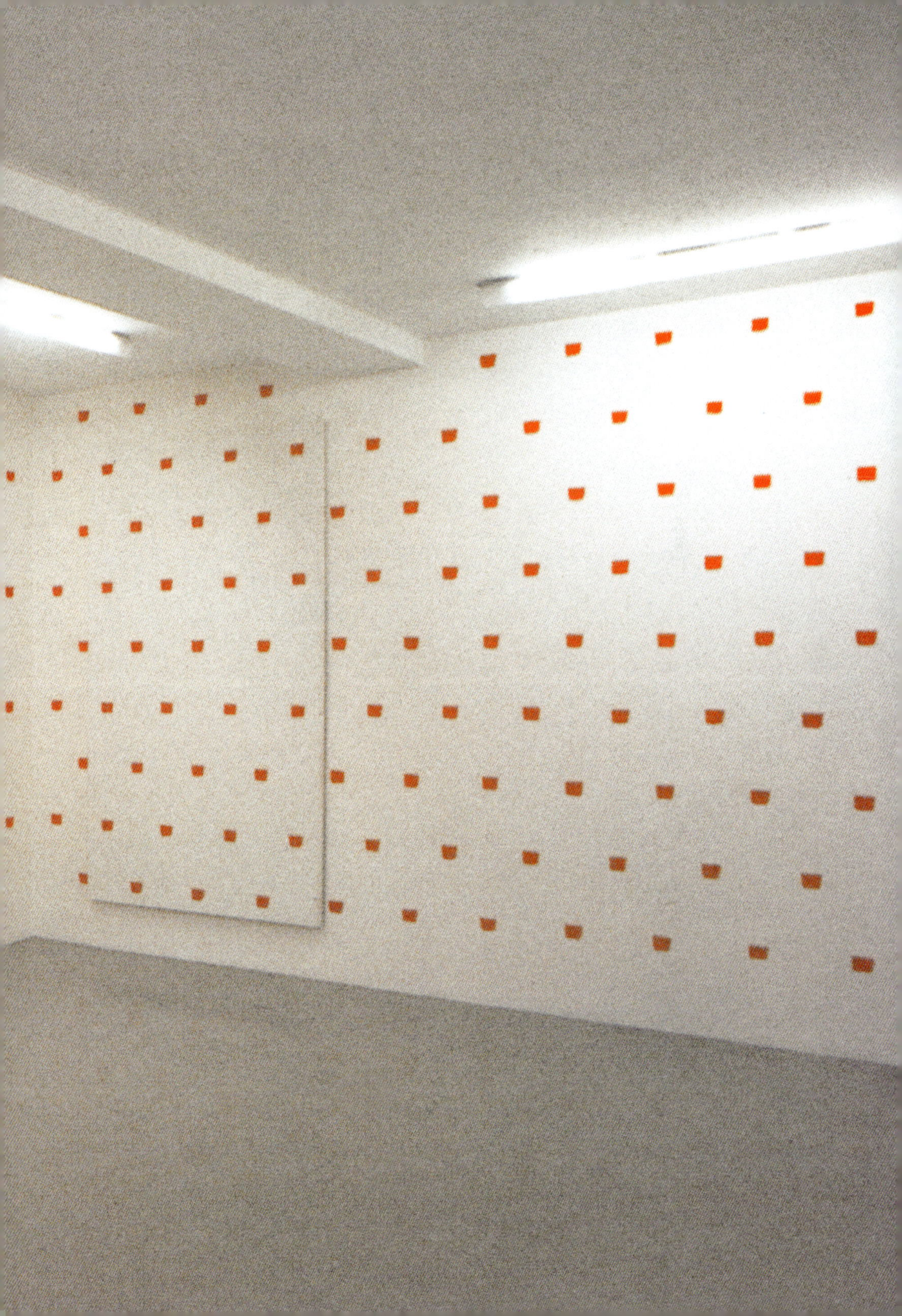

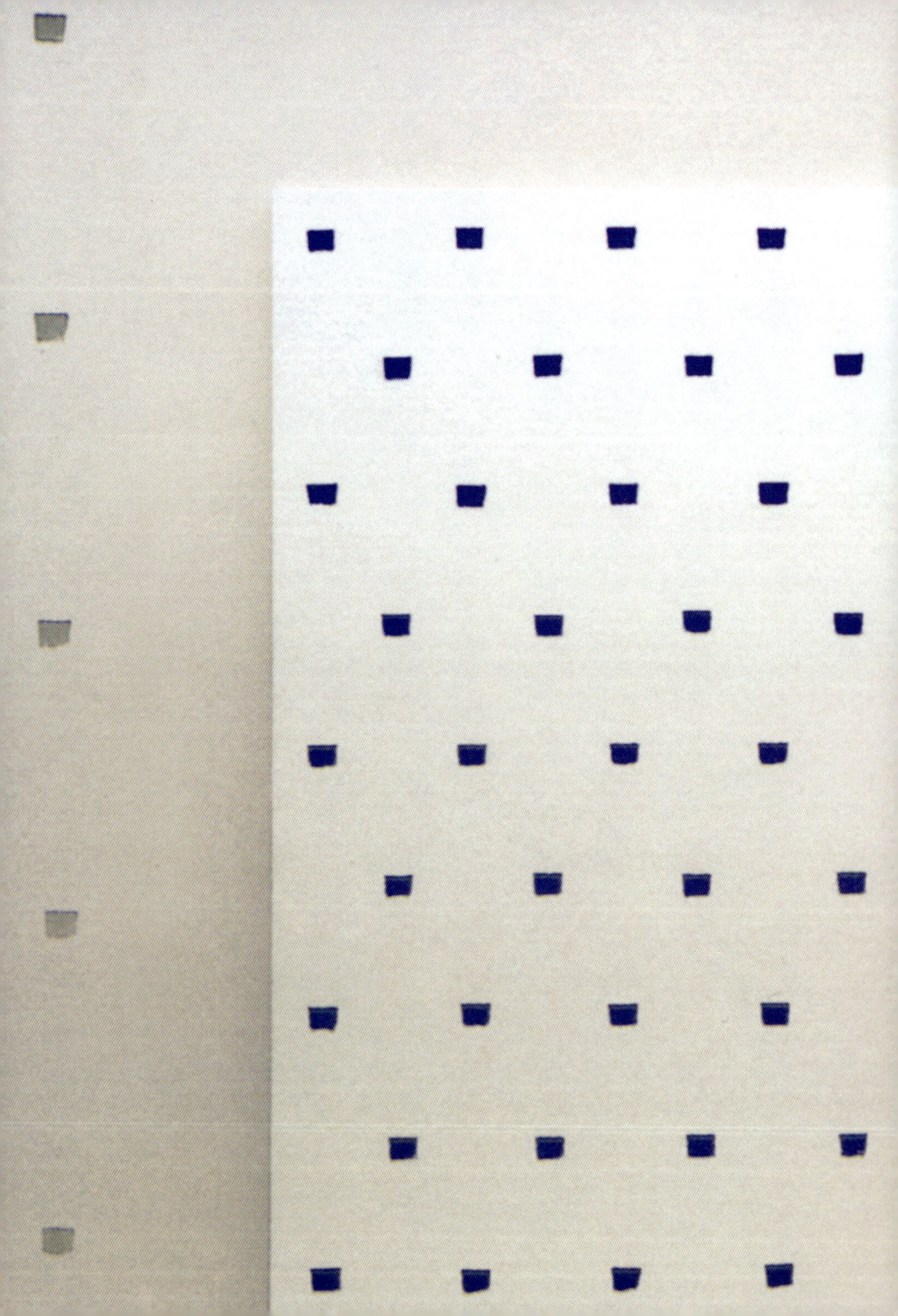

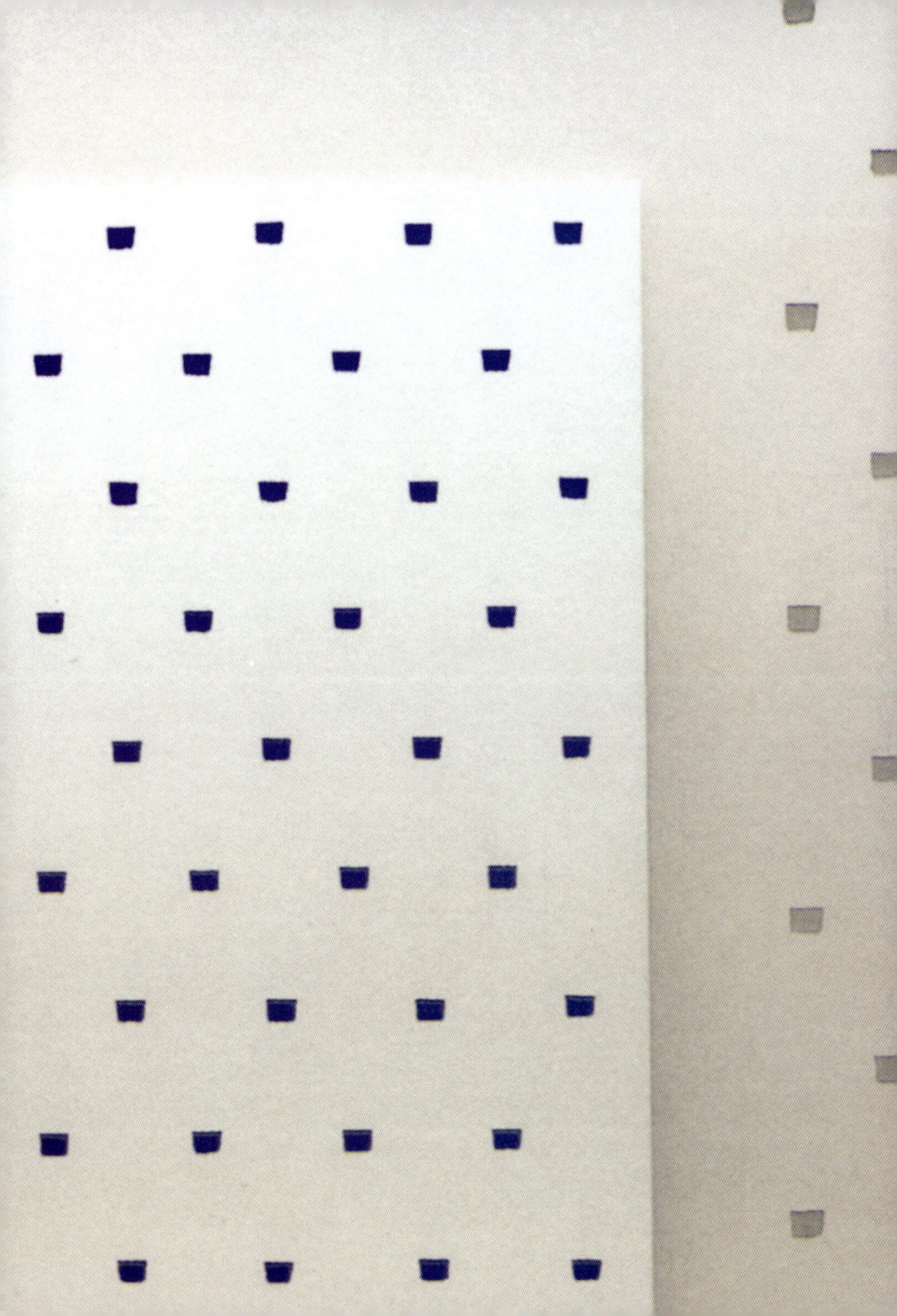

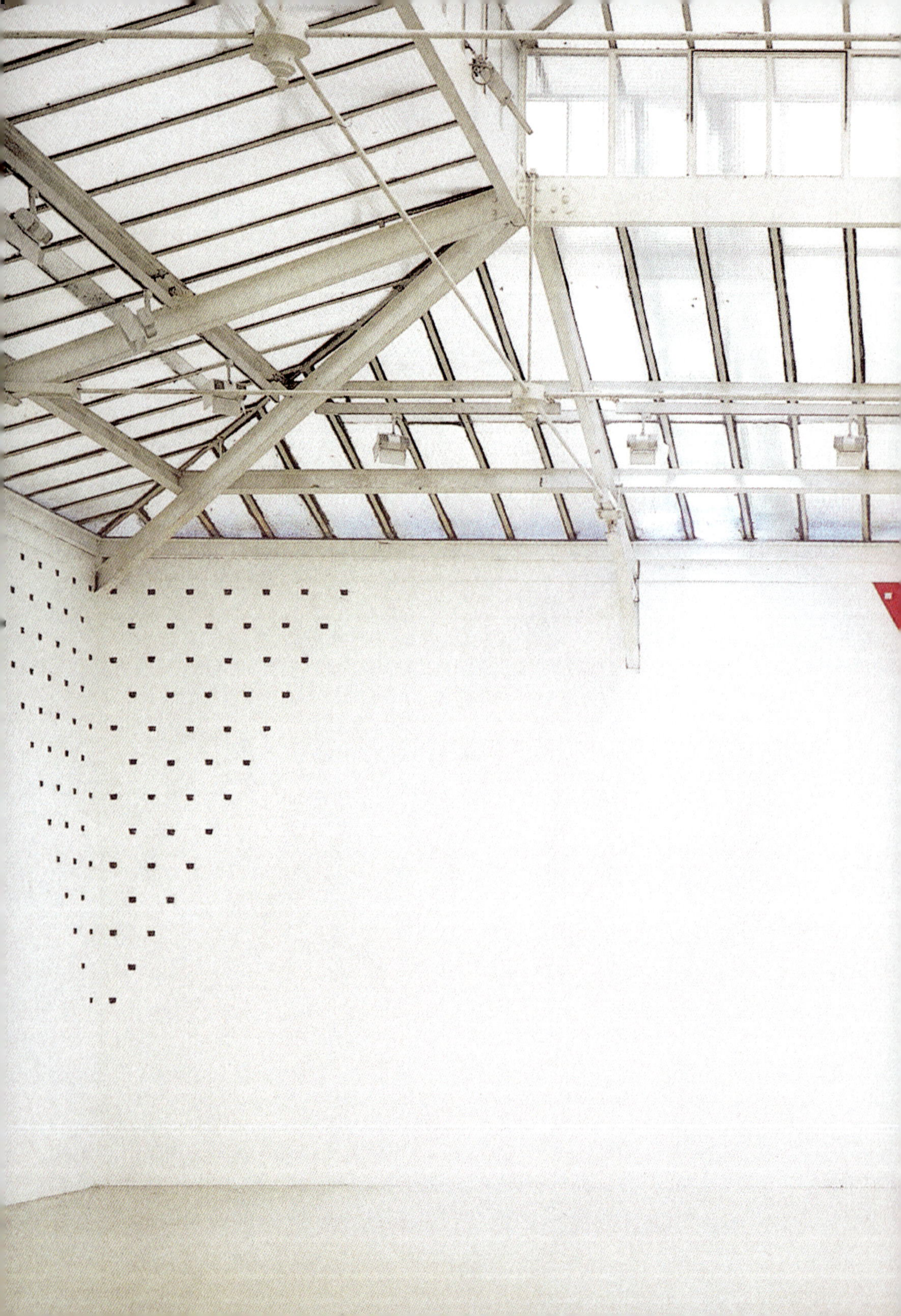

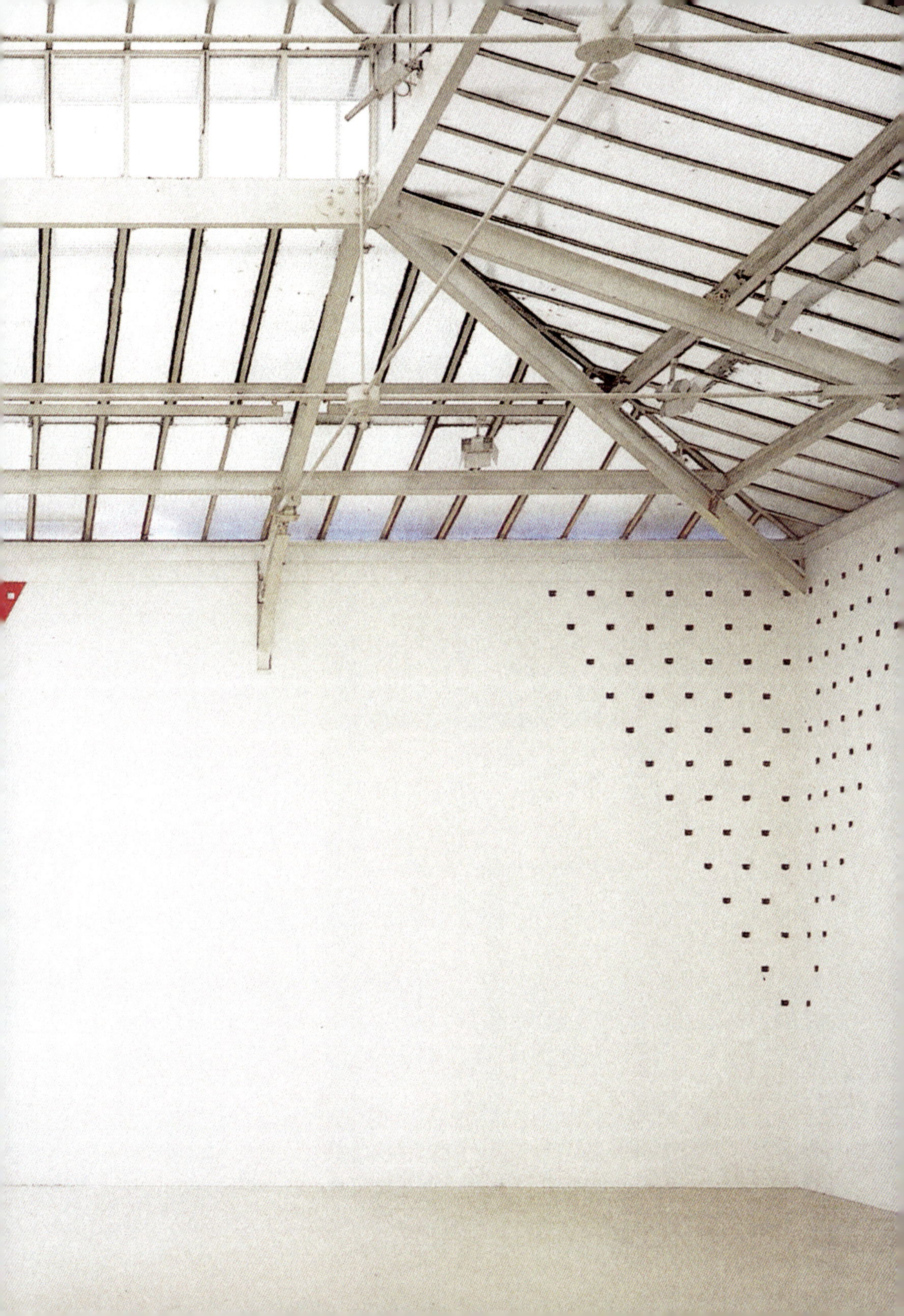

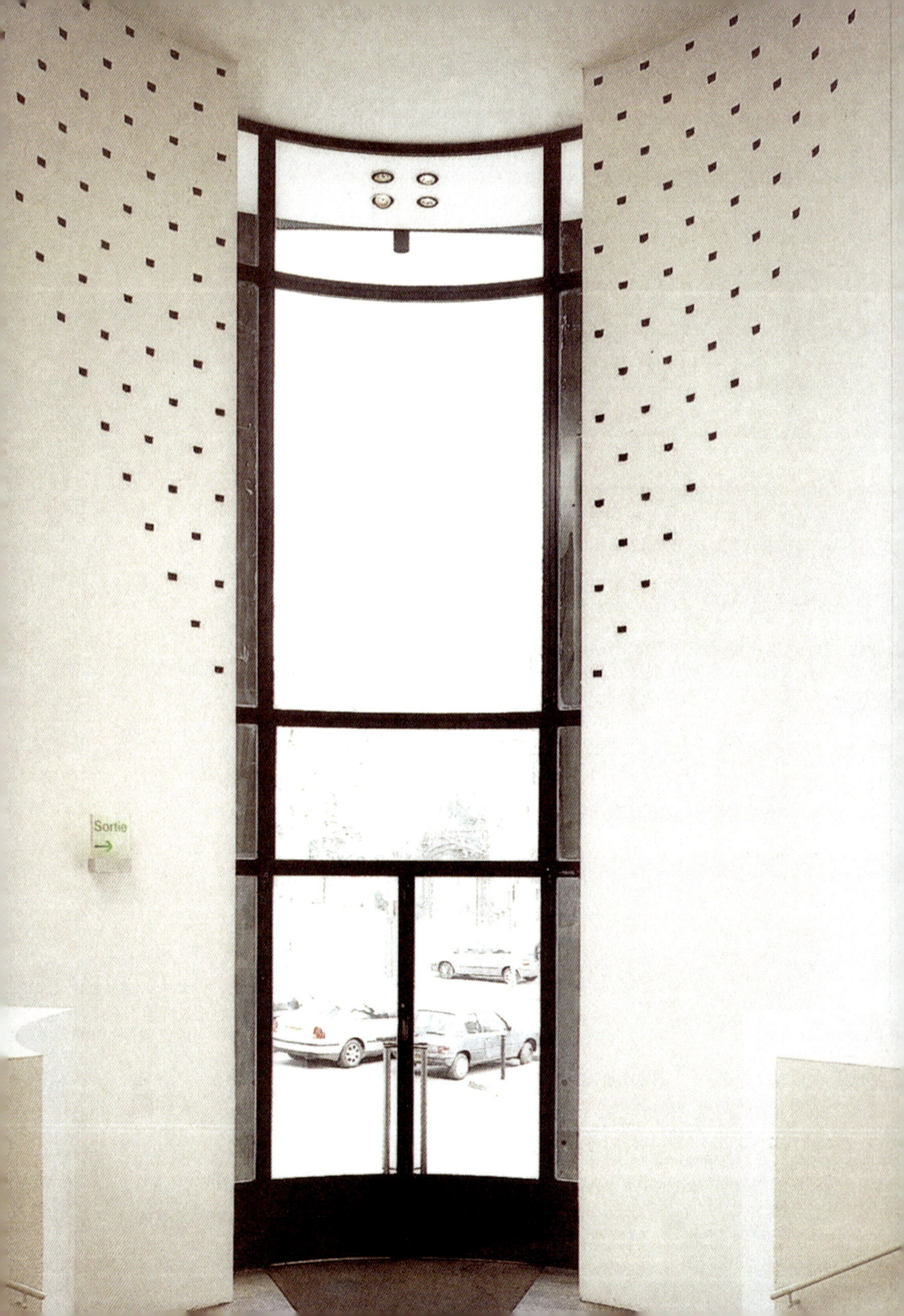
Sortie

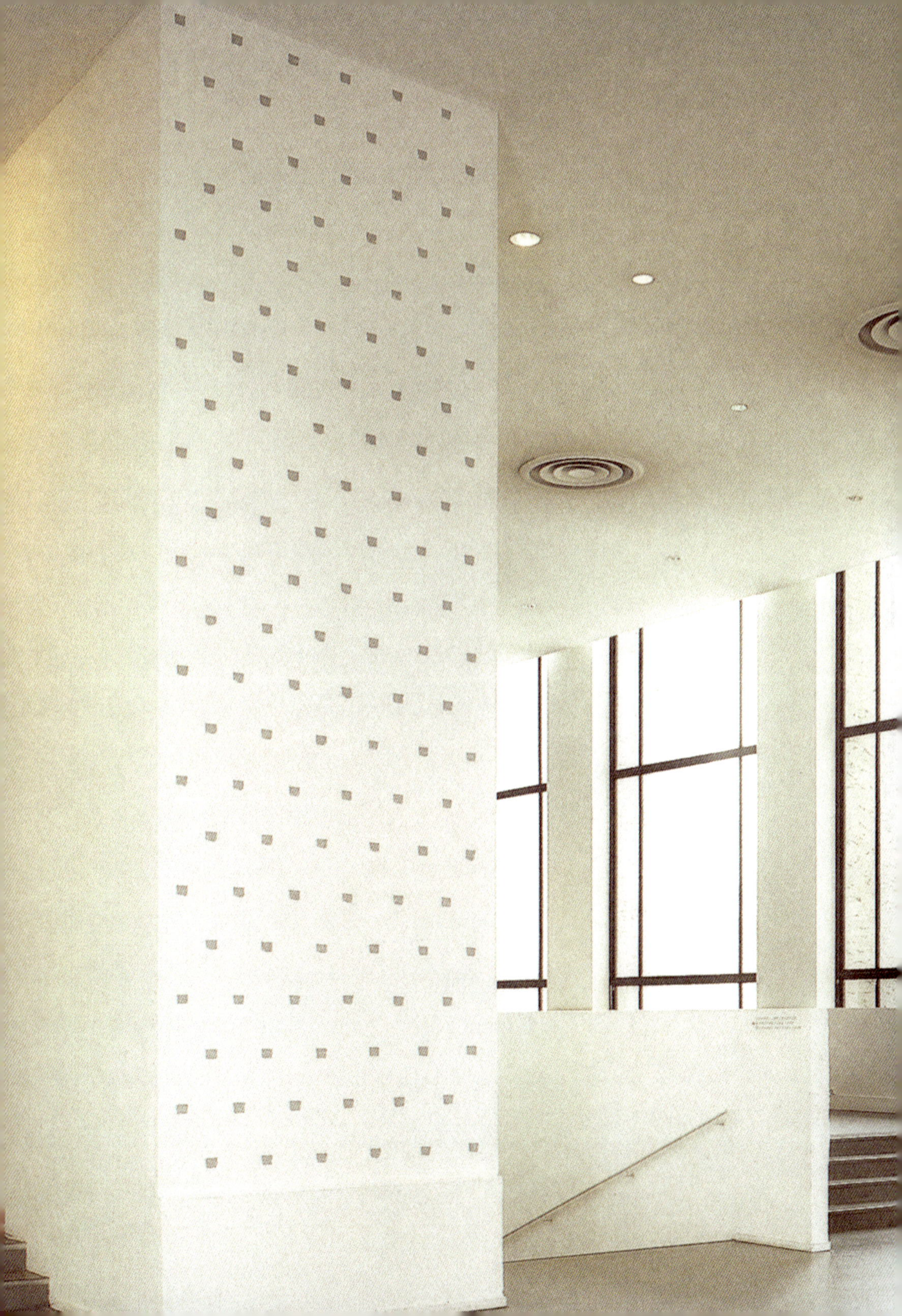

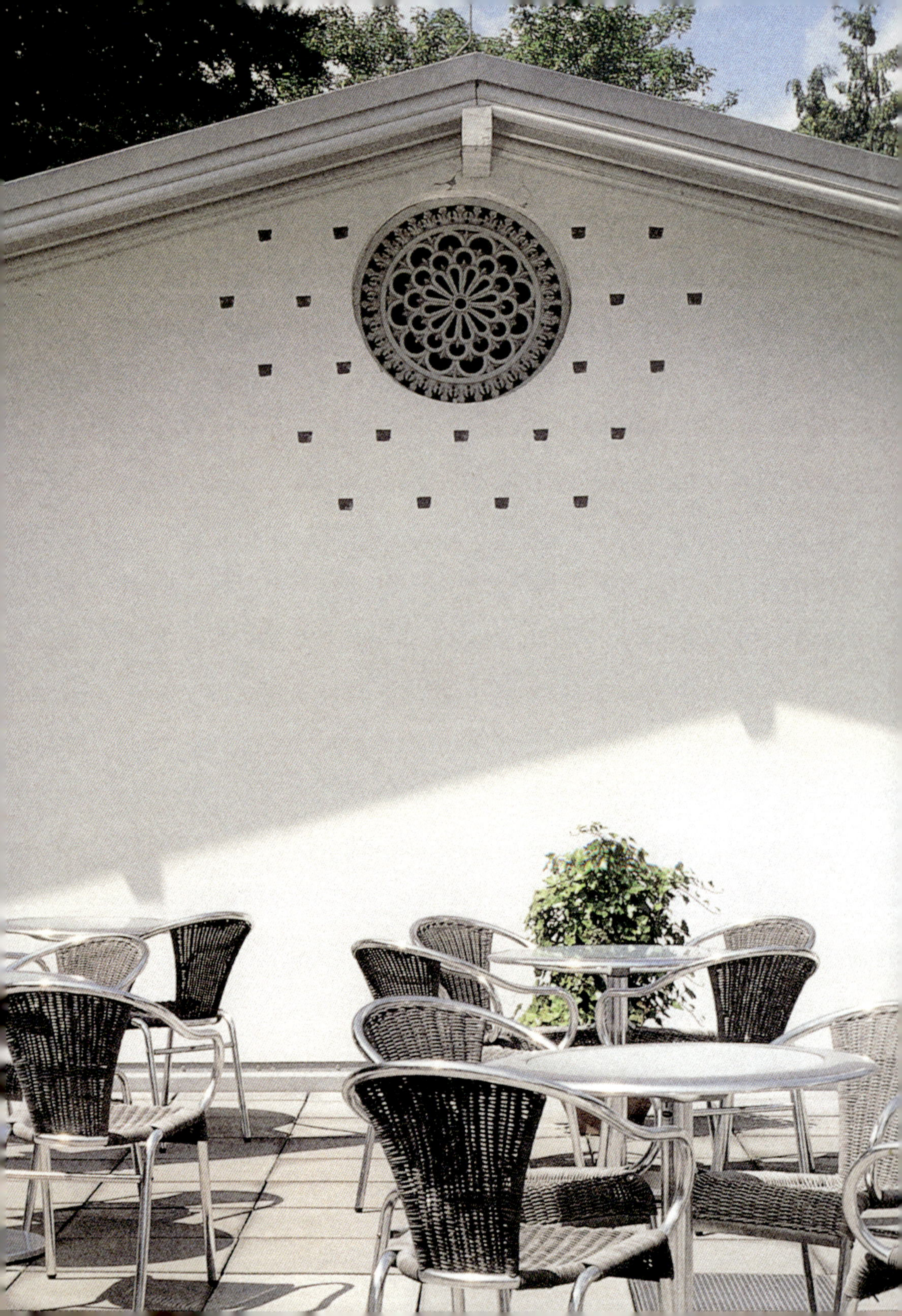

205

205

205

205

205

pp. 169-174: Portikus, Frankfurt, 1988
p. 177: Marian Goodman Gallery, New York, 1989
pp. 178-179: Collection F.E.B., Agra, 1989
pp. 180-181: Kunsthalle Lucerne, Lucerne, 1990
pp. 182-183: Galerie Pierre Huber, Geneva, 1990
p. 184: Collection Billarant, Paris, 1990
pp. 186-187: Hotel Furkablick, Furka Pass, 1990
pp. 188-189: Württembergischer Kunstverein, Stuttgart, 1991
p. 191: Musée National d'Art Moderne - Centre Georges Pompidou, Paris, 1991
p. 193: Galerie Tschudi, Glarus, 1993
p. 194: Private residence, Minusio, 1995-96
pp. 196-197: Gallery Shimada, Tokyo, 1995
pp. 198-199: Douglas Hyde Gallery, Dublin, 1995
pp. 200-201: Galerie Yvon Lambert, Paris, 1997
pp. 202-203: Musée d'Art Moderne de la Ville de Paris, Paris, 2001
p. 204: Museum Kurhaus Kleve, Kleve, 2002

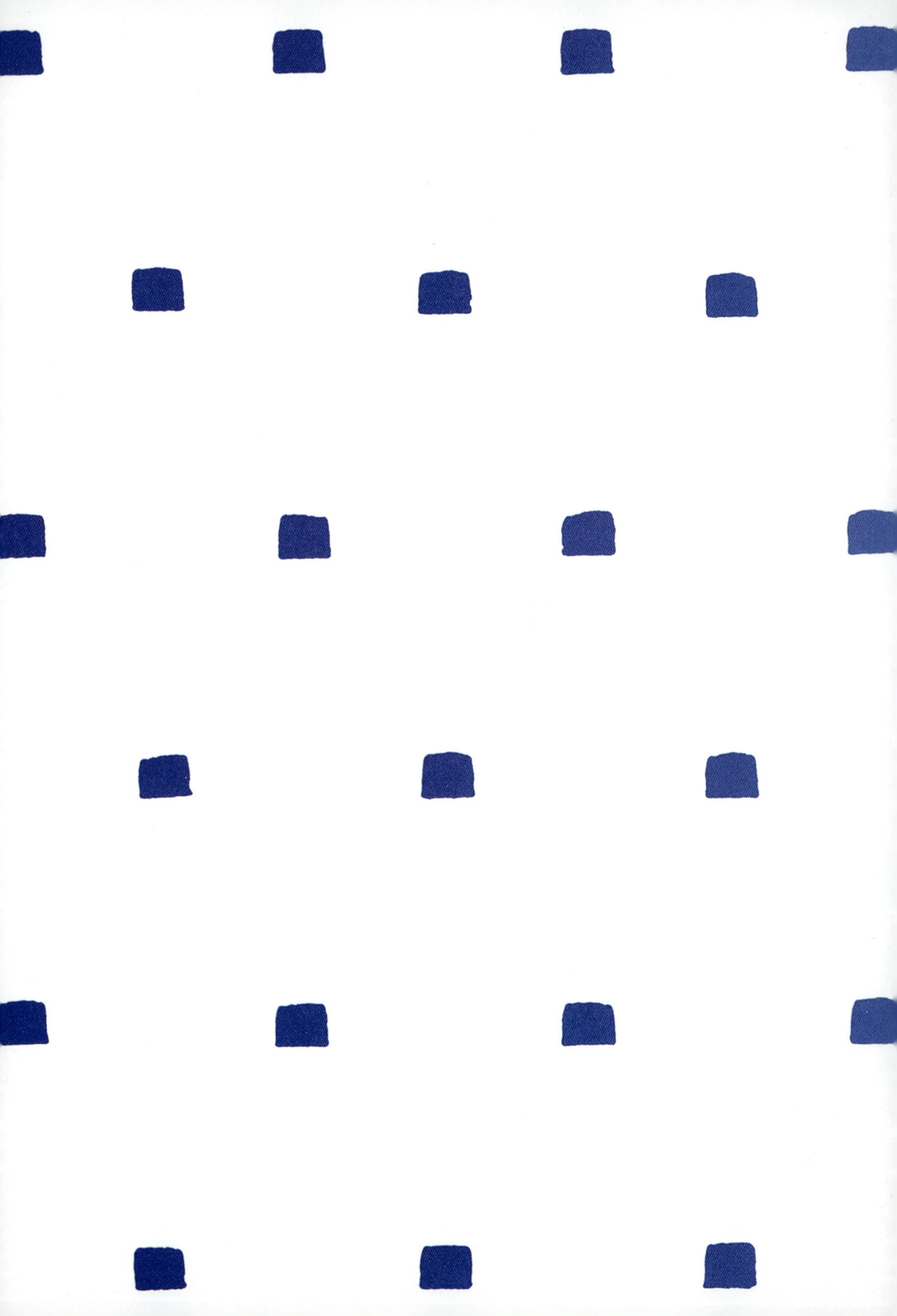

Niele Toroni's Extendability
Alex Bacon

Niele Toroni is one of a small and select group of artists—including Daniel Buren, On Kawara, Roman Opałka, Hanne Darboven, Ad Reinhardt, Bernd and Hilla Becher, and Alan Charlton—who have stuck most consistently, in terms of both duration and output, to a singular, regularized, nonobjective artistic practice. In Toroni's case, his continued vitality and stamina are likely due to how open and complex his painterly practice has been from the start. His marks may be uniform in dimension and spacing—the imprints of a no. 50 brush at regular intervals of 30 centimeters, as he has noted on innumerable occasions—but beyond this they are, by design, capable of being placed on any number of supports: from canvas to walls, tiles, ceilings, floors, windows, mirrors, and even kitchen cabinets and wine barrels. They are also not limited to any set dimensions. As long as they follow the simple dictates established by Toroni in 1967, they can migrate with ease across different surfaces.

Here—that is to say, in the spaces in which Toroni enacts his paintings—the politics of place become yoked to those of labor. He does this through the logic of extendibility that is essential to his work. By extendibility, I mean the sense in which Toroni's marks always have the potential, through the regularized logic of their dimensions and spacing, to extend through and across any number of spaces and supports, not obeying the unspoken rule of boundedness typical of art, and especially of painting. By drawing even more attention to space—and, by implication, to the architectural means by which it is shaped and controlled—than he does to his individual marks, he counters naive assumptions about the subject's effortless movement through space.

In a way, Toroni's intelligence is to stage our desire for that kind of interaction with public space. This desire is one that is simulated by architectural models of transparency that seem to assure us that we still have access, even as these very spaces are surveilled and privately owned and managed—to which Toroni implicitly draws attention by often presenting his work in private spaces, such as the commercial gallery, and through the vehicle of a painting, a privately held commodity. He allows us a sense of freedom and access which is yearned for but is not an actuality, in an increasingly privatized world with no clear boundaries between public and private. His imprints are thus ciphers for both the hopes and limitations of our moment—even in the way that his imprints take the form, in some cases, of both ephemeral, site-specific public works and atemporal, transactional, canvas objects. Essentially, the basic unit of Toroni's work, the imprint, is not indelibly tied to either, yet it has the ability to engage with both.

Toroni's gestures themselves are often understood as "mechanical," and indeed they are rendered matter-of-factly, without any specific pretensions toward facture, let alone any kind of expressive meaning we might attach to one or another kind of gesture. And yet, when confronted by an adequate amount of Toroni's work, we start to see distinctions and variations within what initially seemed to be inexpressive. In some imprints the traces of the brush are almost invisible, the paint sitting before us as an obdurate block of color, while in others, the puckering of the painted surface betrays the presence of a human hand, registering an index of the paint application. As such, the presence of the author persists, if at something approaching the lowest possible register. For however elegant Toroni's marks may be, they are produced via a means that requires, as well as betrays, the least amount of (conventional) painterly skill.

It is a gesture that can be executed by any number of people—theoretically, at least, since it is of course important that it is Toroni who does the painting, and not someone else who executes it for him. Yet it is he who has turned all this into a system and chosen to bring his imprint into any number of spaces. In line with this, his interventions do not have the sense of either of the two most common ways in which artists have intervened in architecture over the past hundred or so years: either forcing themselves into or on the space, or by producing a shift that is barely perceptible. Eschewing the ego that can be implied by either way of working, Toroni's interventions are clearly visible, referring to the space without either subverting it or taking it over. It is perhaps better said that Toroni's imprints cohabitate with the space, drawing our attention to it in new ways through our examination of the curious statement of presence that Toroni's painting amounts to.

It is a statement that is matter-of-fact in a way akin to that established by the rote insistency of On Kawara's *I Am Still Alive* telegrams or *I Got Up* postcards. Taken on their own, Kawara's messages, like one or even a few of Toroni's imprints, are simply declarative statements; however, taken together, they coalesce into the impression of a life lived. Even if we do not gain access to the psychology of the artist, we get a sense of his literal presence, his having been there—something that has taken on new meaning in our present age of social media. Both artists overlap in that they both make this impression in terms of an assertion of literal presence, rather than of a specific activity, movement, feeling, or achievement. They share this investigation of the instantiation of being, through the insistence of the regularized mark or gesture, with Roman Opałka and Hanne Darboven, whose practices also centered on the insistent marking of time and place. In marking up a certain space Toroni indicates, as one of the baselines of his practice, that he was there, and not too removed from someone scrawling graffiti in a bathroom stall. In line with this, he dates rather than signs his paintings, underscoring that a task—the results of which are clearly evident—was executed at a specific time, rather than making the atemporal claim to lasting and singular presence that the signature applies to whatever it is affixed to. Similarly, Kawara has a series dedicated to places he went, and specific times and places are often registered in his other bodies of work as well—including the Date Paintings, which mime the conventional typography and linguistic specificities of when and where they were made, underscored by the local newspaper clippings with which Kawara often lined the boxes that accompanied the paintings.

This resonates with Toroni's discussion of his painting as "work," since the marks he makes are not those conventionally associated with the art of painting. Toroni's marks do not even count as strokes, at least in the typical sense. Instead, they are closest, morphologically, to that initial moment of the act of painting: the laying down of the first mark. In this way Toroni underscores the labor of painting, its temporal quality, as the act of applying subsequent marks and coats of paint. In Toroni's case, the act of painting is thus forever frozen in the first instant, before the imprint turns into the application, let alone the image or the composition—that mythical moment wherein the white expanse of the canvas is broken by the originary mark, a moment of great existential and conceptual significance to the likes of Kandinsky, Malevich, and Greenberg, among others. Yet this instant is not isolated or spectacularized in Toroni's work; rather it is arrested, stopped cold in the water. Yet as soon as it is frozen in the form taken on by the fast-drying paint, it is born again in the next mark, and the next mark, and the next mark, and so forth. Thus Toroni's works are as laden with potential as they are a silencing or closure. He has isolated a mark and a way of working that begins and ends in the single act of making a single mark. It is endlessly repeatable, yet also complete and whole even in the isolated instance, and, further, contains within it no implicit or inevitable boundaries or limits.

At this stage, the painting of a wall by a house painter is indistinguishable from that of a canvas by a "fine art" painter. Toroni actively courts the potential for such a misreading when his marks march off the canvas and migrate onto doors, windows, building facades, etc. Toroni's work relies on his basic underlying organizational logic, by which one mark is typically (but certainly not always) joined by other marks—which, following the uniform spacing that Toroni established from the start, then become a pattern. This pattern is read as painterly primarily through, on the one hand, its placement in an art context—i.e., a gallery, museum, Kunsthalle, or collector's home—or else through the ways that it articulates (though likely not for every viewer) a painterly or artistic context for itself: for example, through an all-over mapping of a particular architectural detail. For it is equally a means of measurement, hence Toroni's insistence on the 30-centimeter separation between each of his marks. In this way, a work by Toroni is a reliable guarantee, much like the ruler or measuring tape that he uses to execute it, of a certain dimension, which is perhaps one reason why they are so well-suited to architectural sites, and why even a canvas or sheet of paper that has received the imprint of Toroni's brush feels as if it has been mapped like any other material might be.

What all this does is establish the basic affectual oscillation essential to the power and import of Toroni's rigorous and regimented practice: between the common, mechanical, everyday, workmanlike, and the matter-of-fact, and the ability for such a thing to be felt as aesthetic, playful, and even transformative. This is not to say that Toroni's practice is a spiritualized one of transcendence, for it is always rooted in the pragmatics of the here and now, but rather that it suggests how conventional readings of given structures and institutions might be subverted. Because of the variety of surfaces that have received Toroni's marks over the years, this is true even of canvas. While Toroni's peer Daniel Buren has imported the language of painting into a variety of contexts, working with a range of materials, Toroni has disengaged the painted mark from the province of being simply a self-reflexive component of painting and extended it even beyond the medium's own logic. When Toroni paints a kitchen cabinet or the facade of a building, for example, he does not turn it into a painting in extremis, since he works with a vernacular language of painting that carries none of the associations of the medium's history unless we, the viewers, bring them ourselves. Indeed, what parts of the surface Toroni leaves bare between the painted marks is as essential to the marks as the ground against which they become legible; but the unpainted parts are not relegated to background or mere support, since they are allowed to retain their material integrity, whether that is as canvas or plaster. This is because of the humbleness of Toroni's imprints, which exist at the same level of material specificity as the material on which they are made—something hard to achieve given the painted mark's proclivity for being legible as something other than what it is at a material level.

This is distant from the Greenbergian self-reflexivity of medium that painterly materiality was supposed to be in service of, and for this reason Toroni's practice has been inspirational for a younger generation of artists working today who are looking, consciously or not, for alternate models of artistic practice. They also embrace painting as a generalized field, rather than as a specific medium, because of the potential this way of working has for drawing attention to modalities of perception, materiality, and labor—often by addressing all three simultaneously. For example, take Oliver Laric's series of works involving the security stickers that often validate important documents such as credit cards and passports, which is to say documents that mediate financial and geographic access. Reducing the stickers to their straight-from-the-factory facticity, as sheets not yet located in any specific document, they amount not only to optically dazzling surfaces that suggest paintings, if more through morphological approximation than through a literal assumption of the conventional terms of the medium—i.e, the stickers are mounted on resin sheets rather than on canvas—but also to a malleable yet physical component for any number of installation contexts. Laric installed numerous panels propped against the walls of the Kunstverein München in 2012, and as components of a wall themselves, as part of Art Basel's Statements section that same year.

In the heated ferment around Paris in 1968, which gave birth to Toroni's particular brand of materialist practice, it made sense to pare down the painterly gesture to a point at which it was indistinguishable from any other kind of painted mark—labor laid bare. It also makes sense that, in an ever-more-mediated, digitized world, where we constantly look to screens to mirror our identities back to us and extend our senses in the process, artists have chosen not only the logic of malleability and extendibility established by Toroni, but also a formal problematic of frustrated opticality. If every gesture, to paraphrase and update Greenberg, is already mediated and made virtual at the moment of iteration, then why not stage this very transubstantiation in the work? For it is also an occlusion of labor that happens at a literal level, in terms of outsourcing, with all the geopolitical implications this has in our present state of globalization.

This is present in Laric's glittering fields, and also in Jacob Kassay's silver paintings, which are made through an

outsourced electroplating process and filter their surroundings into murky semireflections, in which it is impossible to get your full measure. If you move in, your reflection gets blurrier and harder to read, while, as you retreat, your image becomes clearer but harder to parse from such a distance.
Like Laric, Kassay has not limited himself to the individual canvas. Instead he has often installed his silver paintings in series and in relation to architecture. This was perhaps most evident in his installation at New York's the Kitchen in 2013, where Kassay had silver paintings installed in unconventional places in the institution: storage areas, stairwells, etc. They were taken off of the hallowed space of painting, the wall, and instead made to interact more directly with the exhibition space—while not totally losing their painterliness, as the canvas and stretcher were even more visible. Thus the objecthood of the work serves, as it does with Toroni, to underscore the oscillation that these artists share, between aesthetic transcendence and material facticity—this being perhaps the very oscillation that we all experience on a daily basis, as subjects in a digital age.

215 215

215

215 215

Exhibition: 2015

Swiss Institute, New York
June 3–September 6

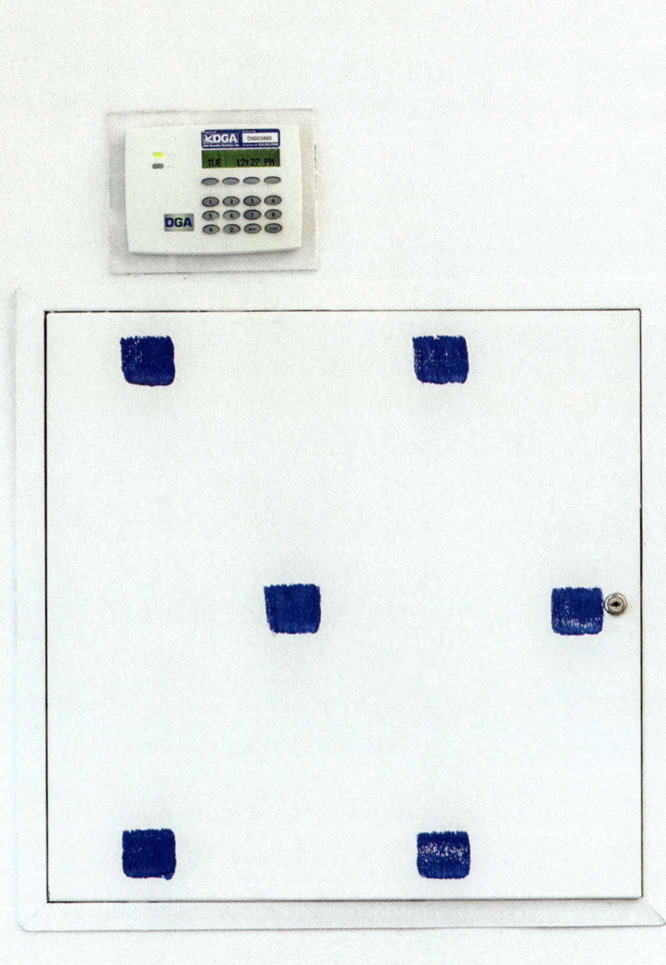
DGA
TUE 12:27 PM
DGA

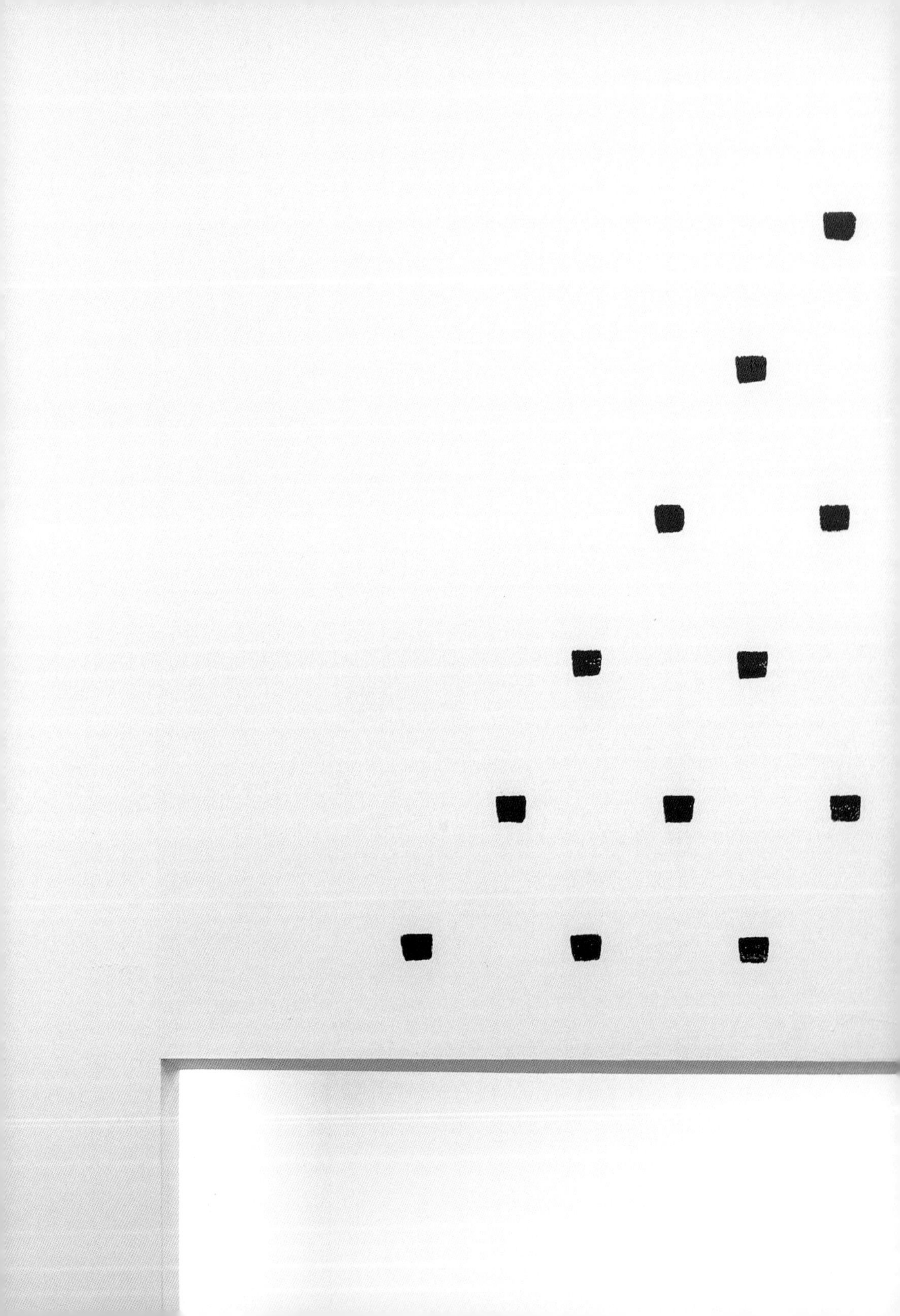

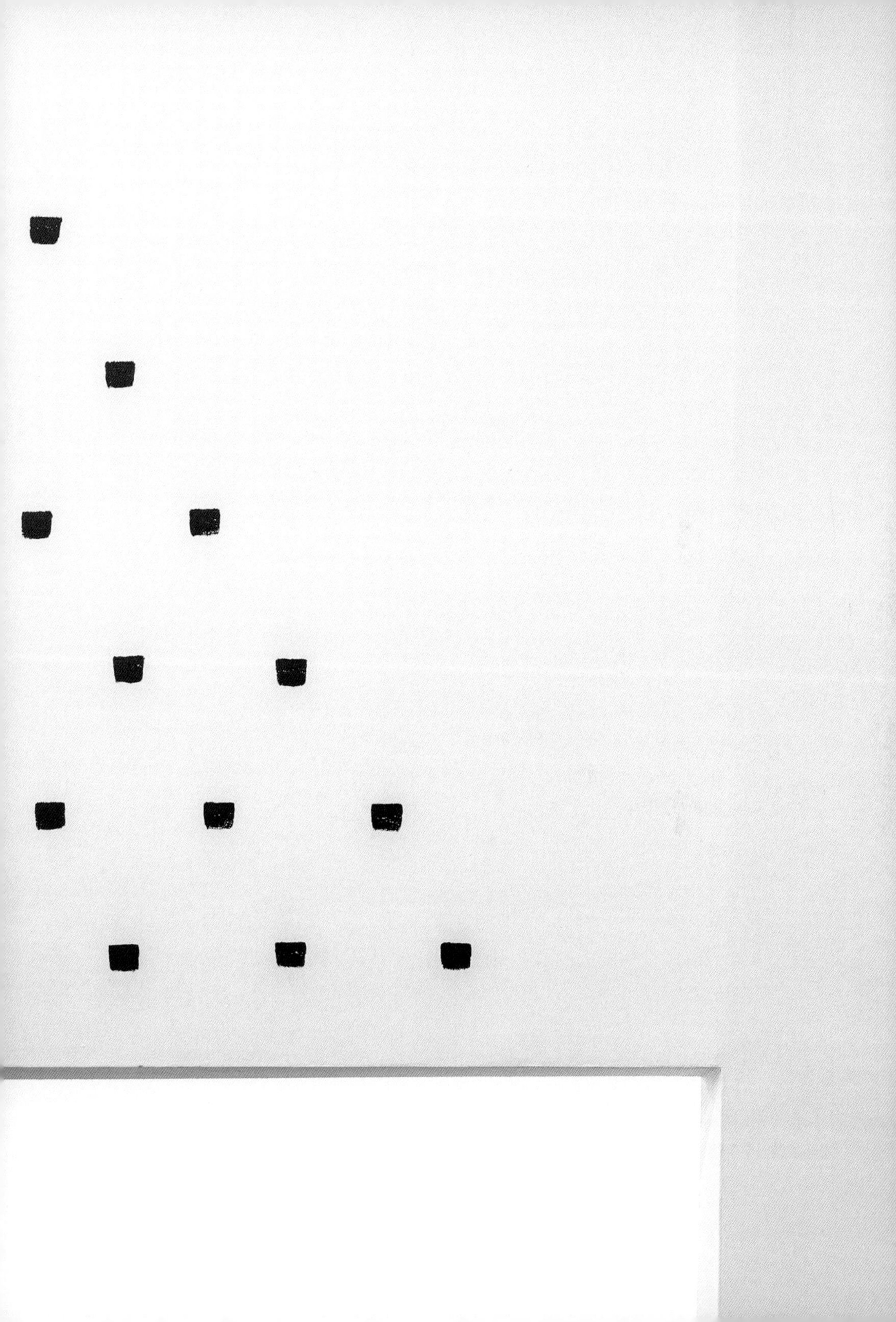

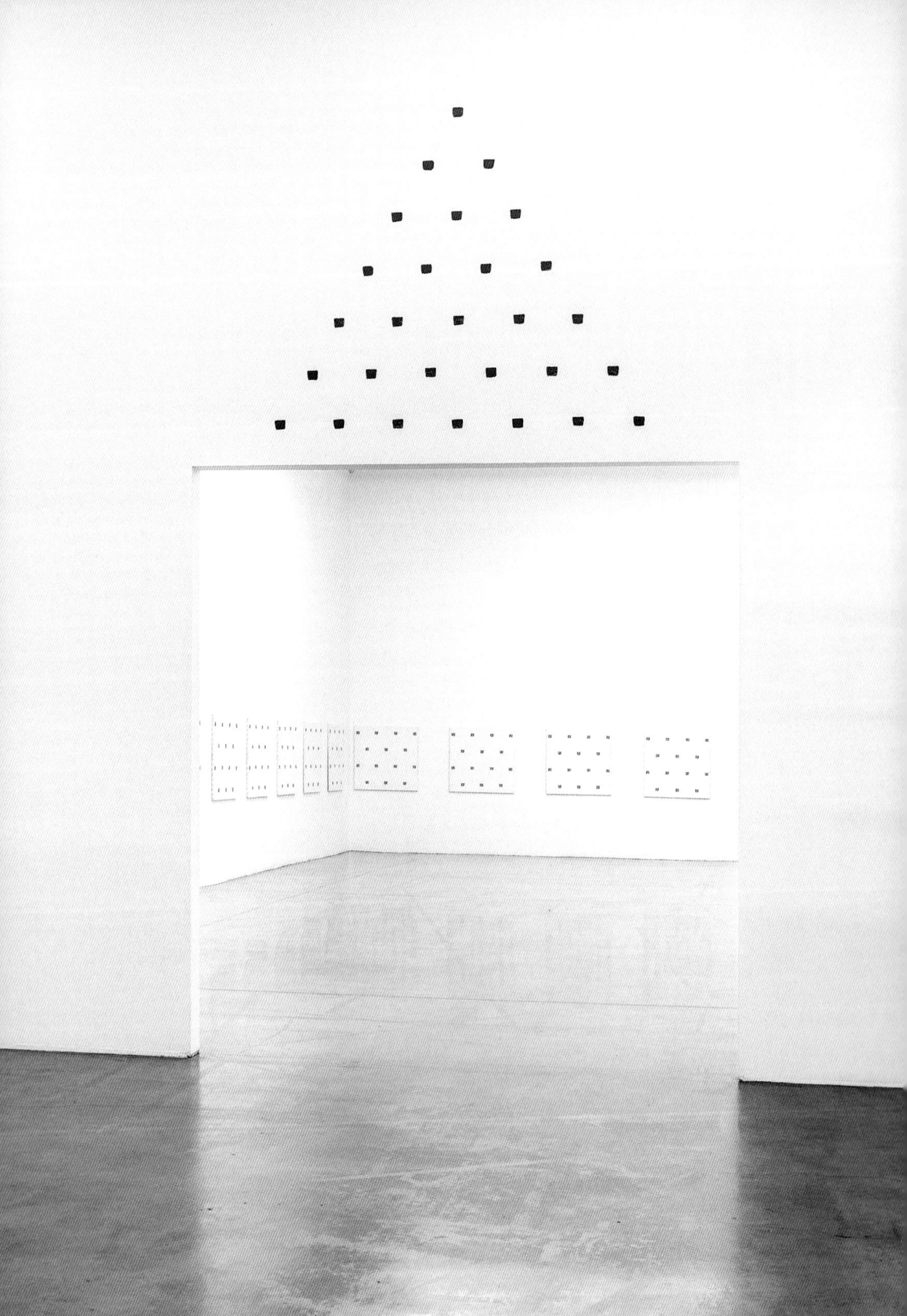

225 225

225

225 225

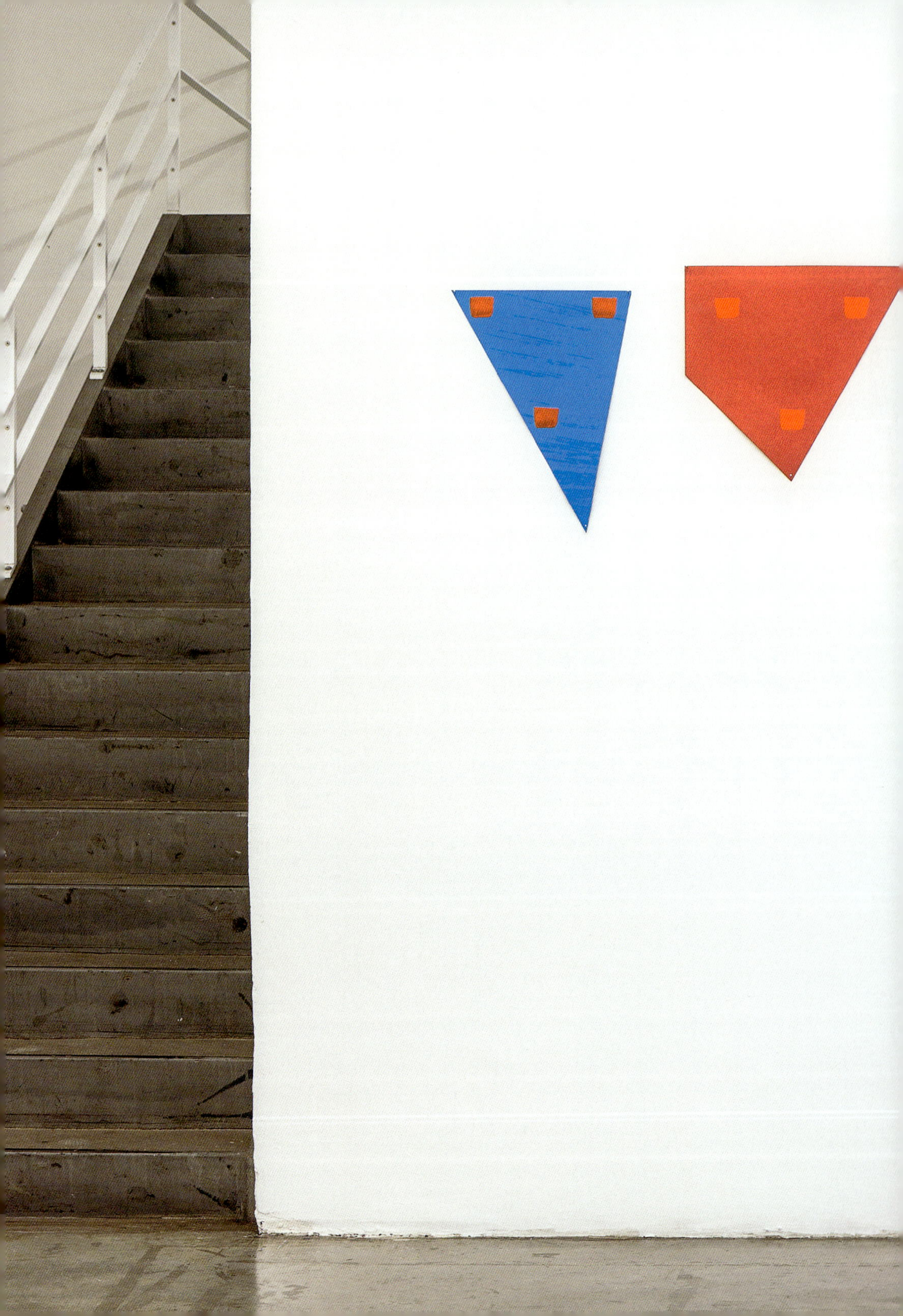

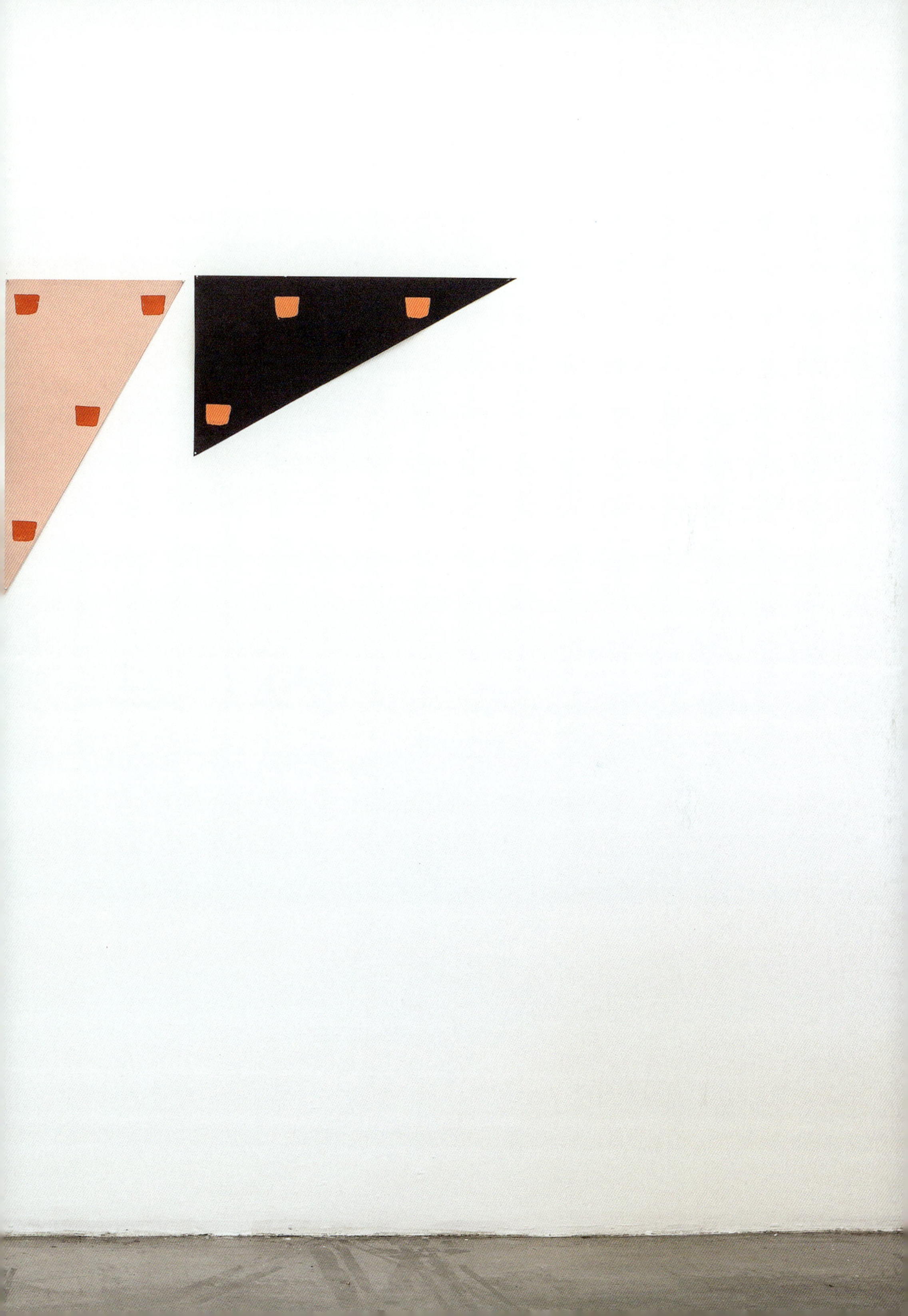

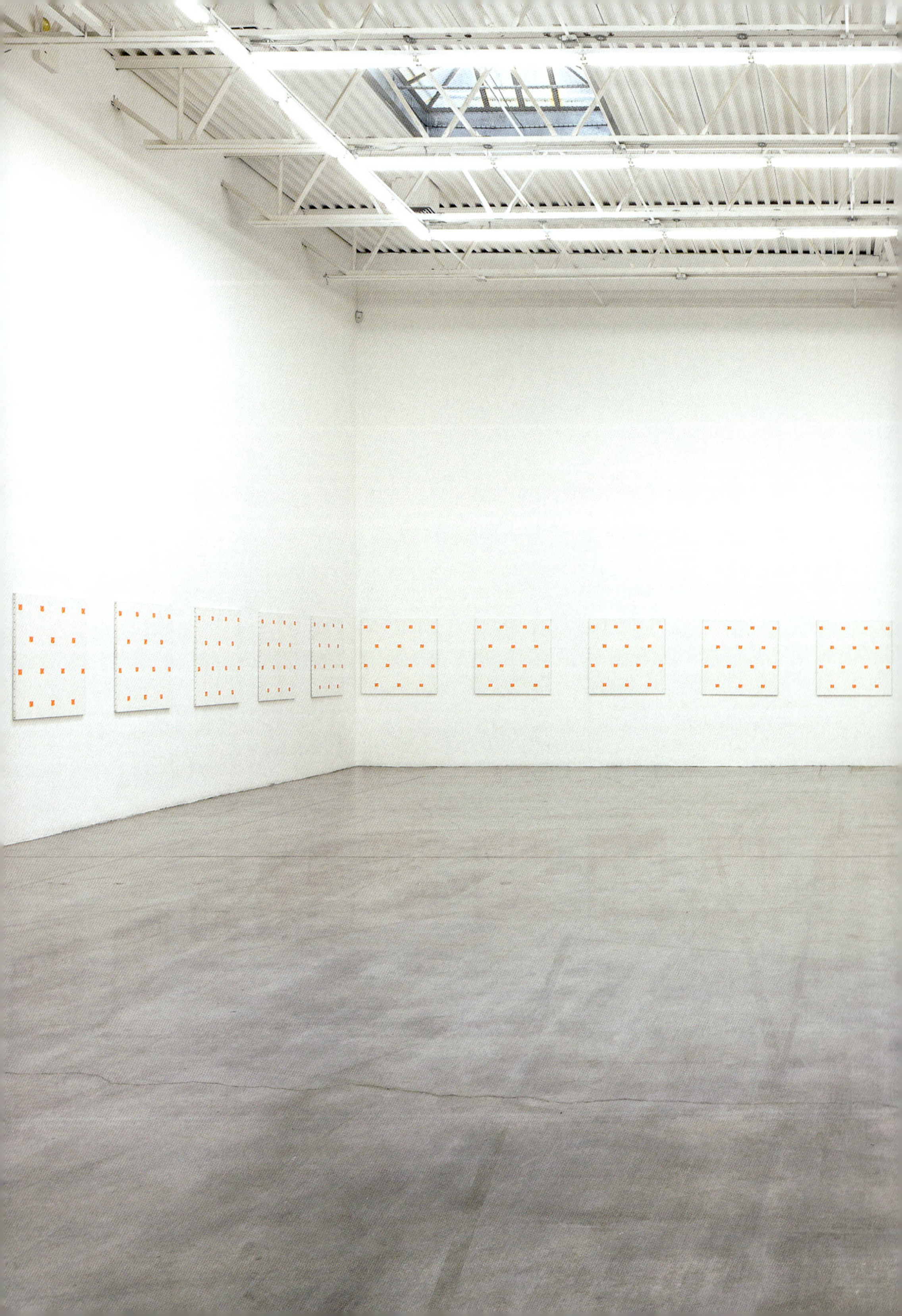

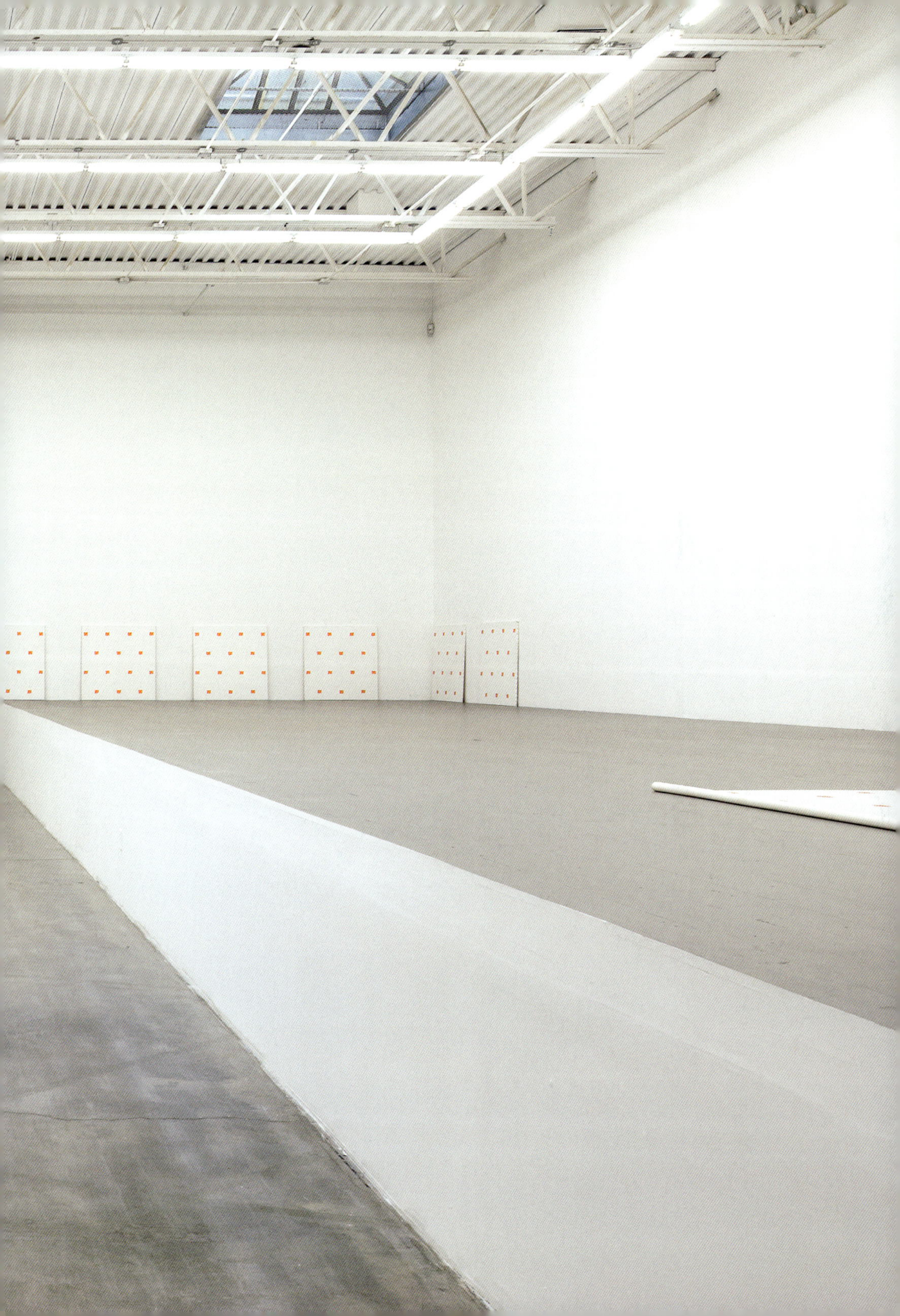

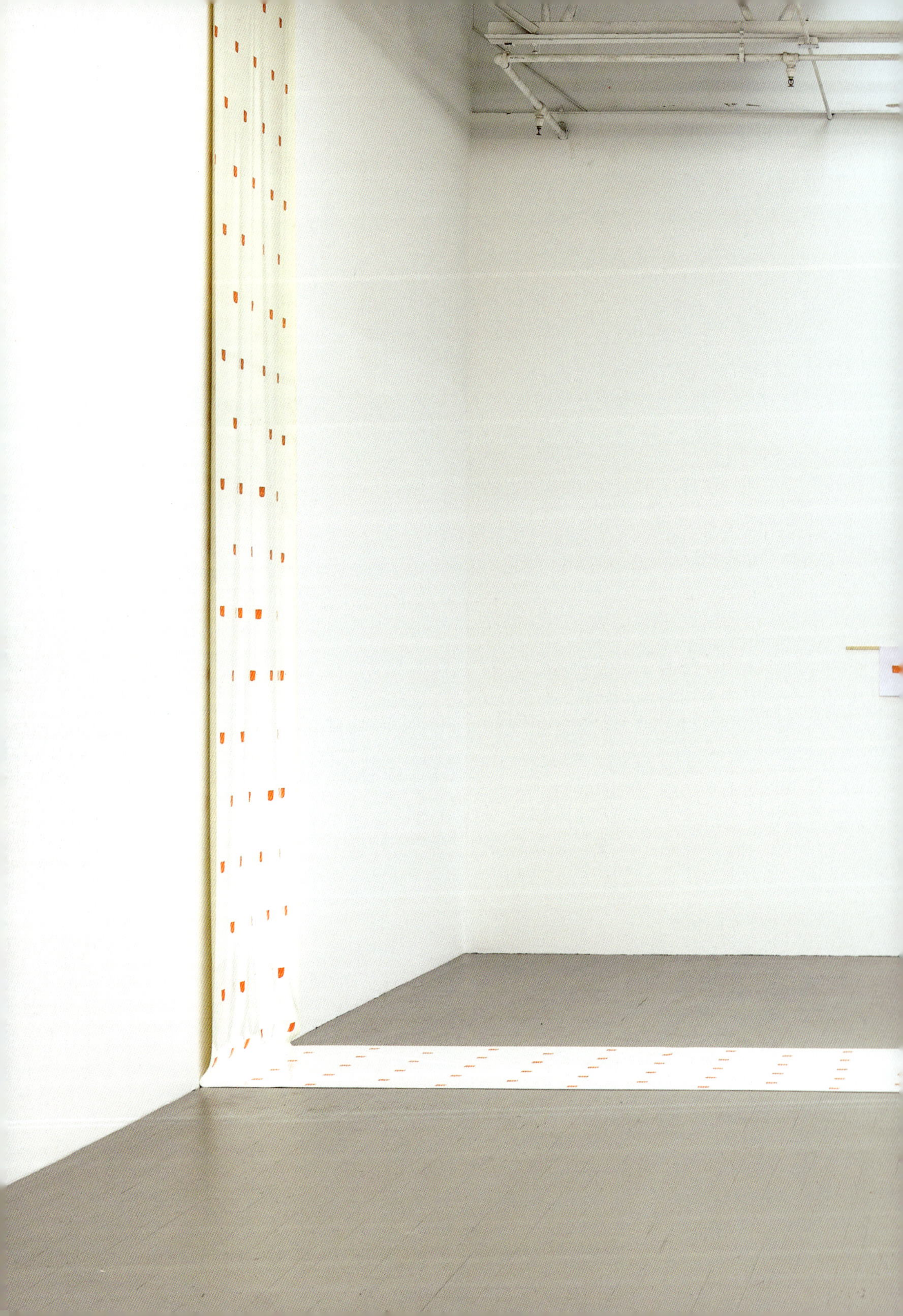

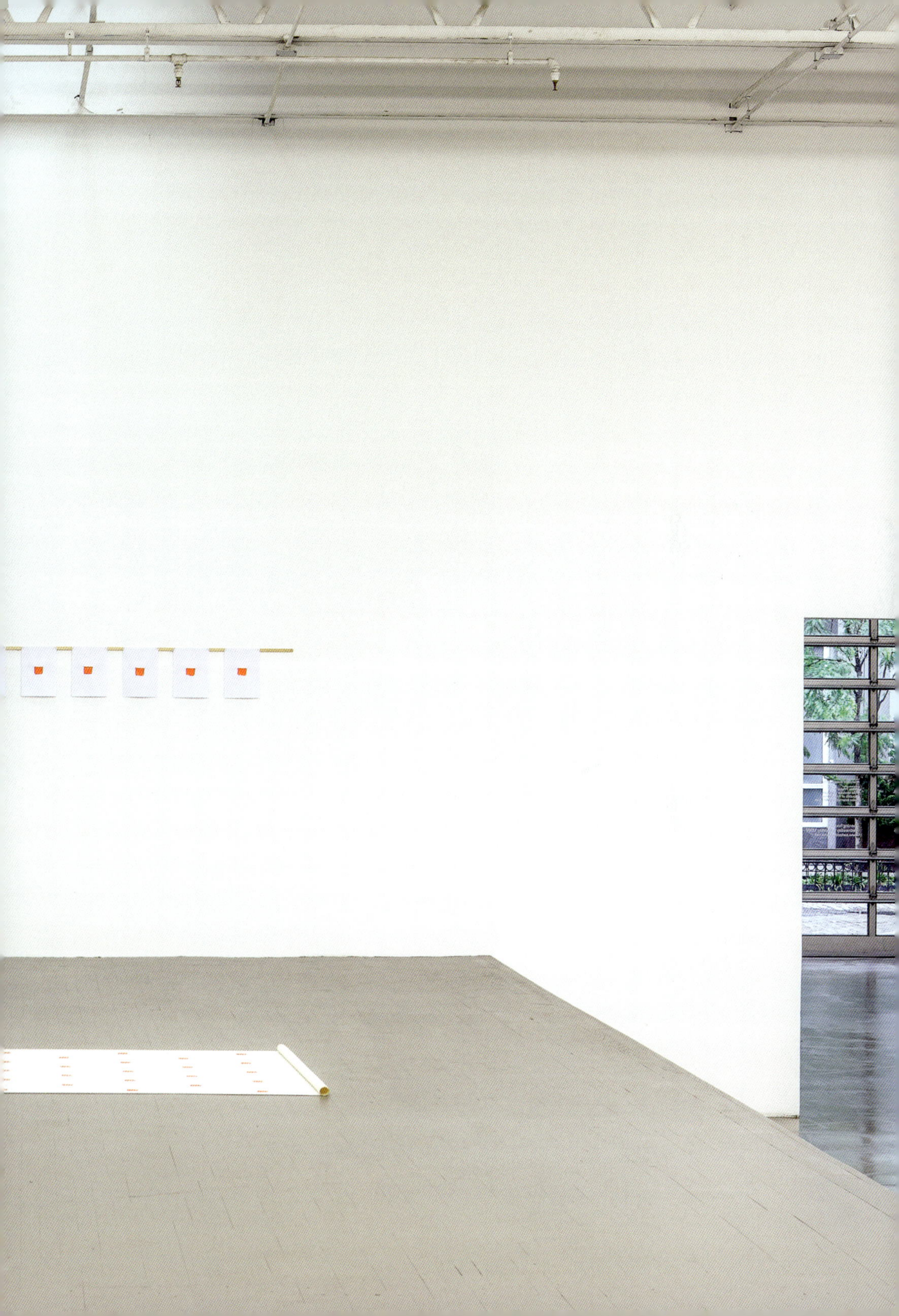

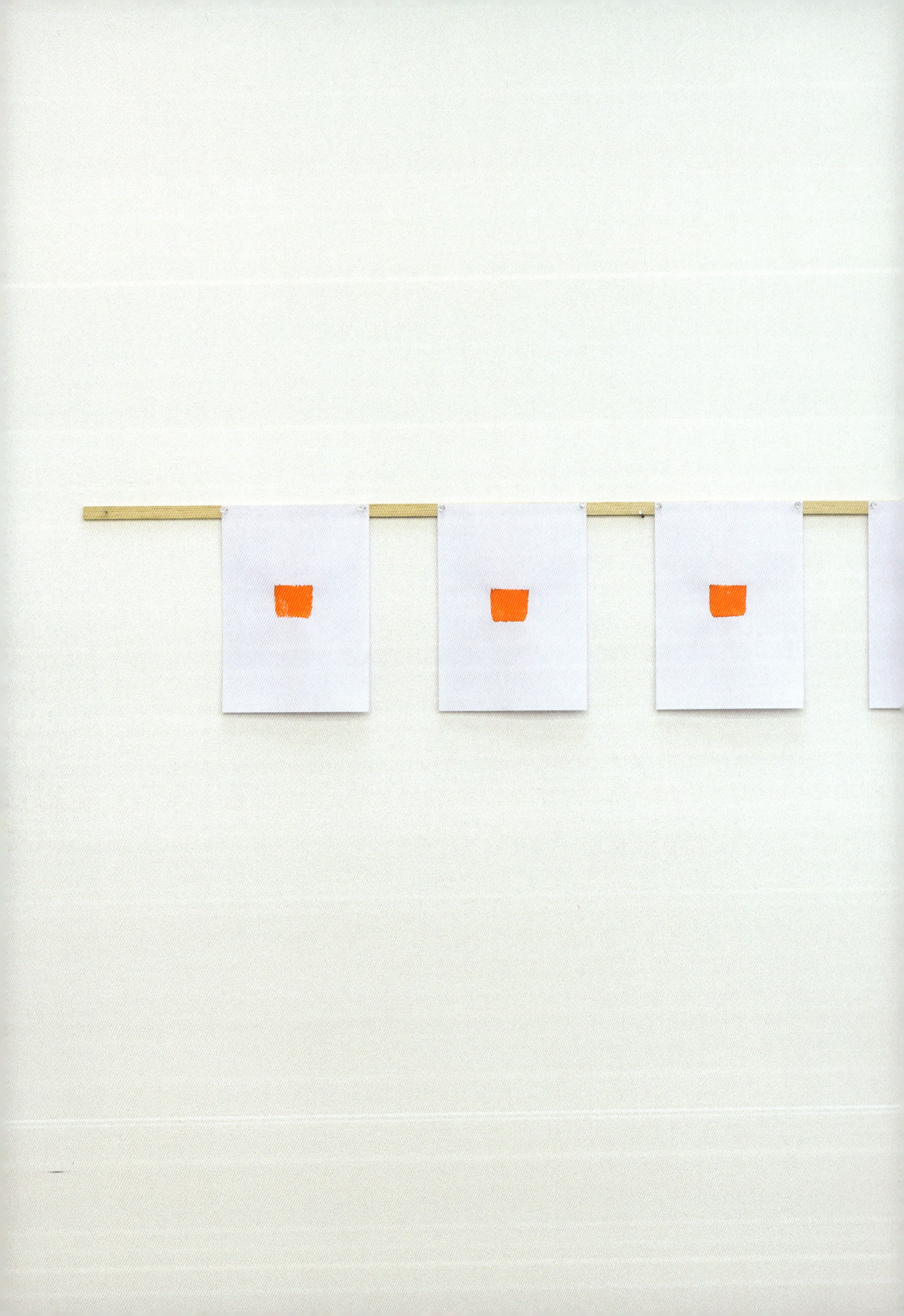

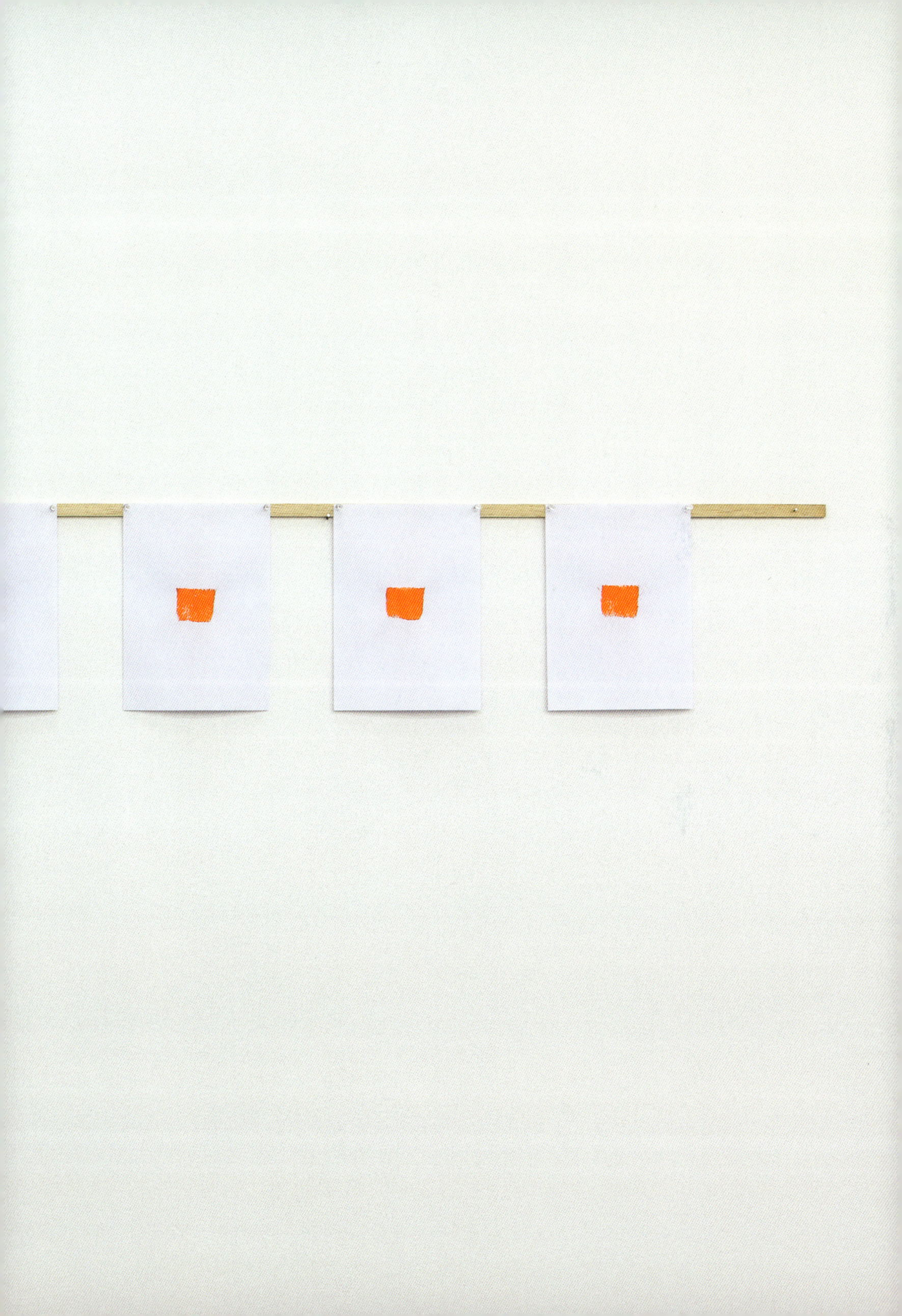

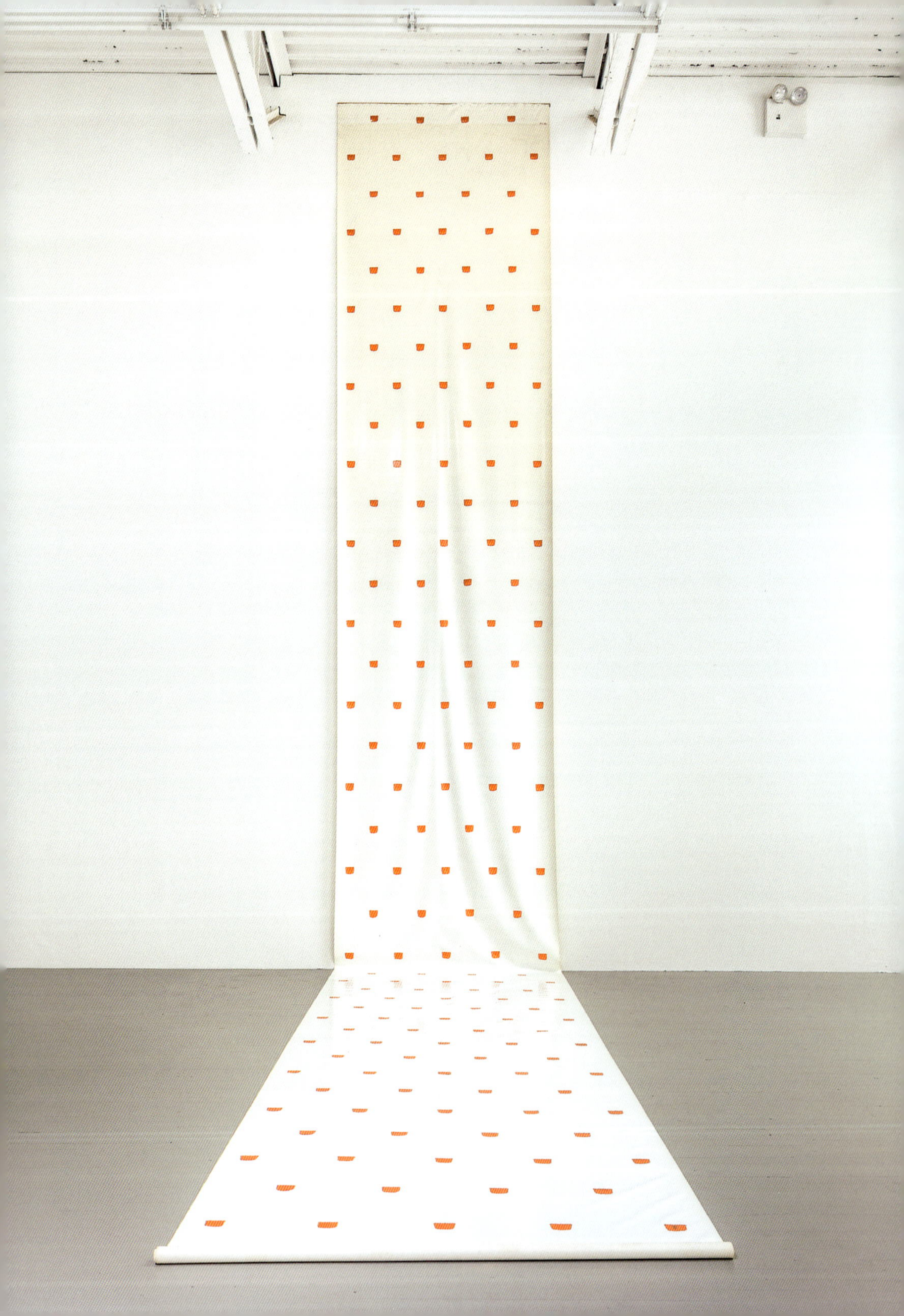

235

235

235

235

235

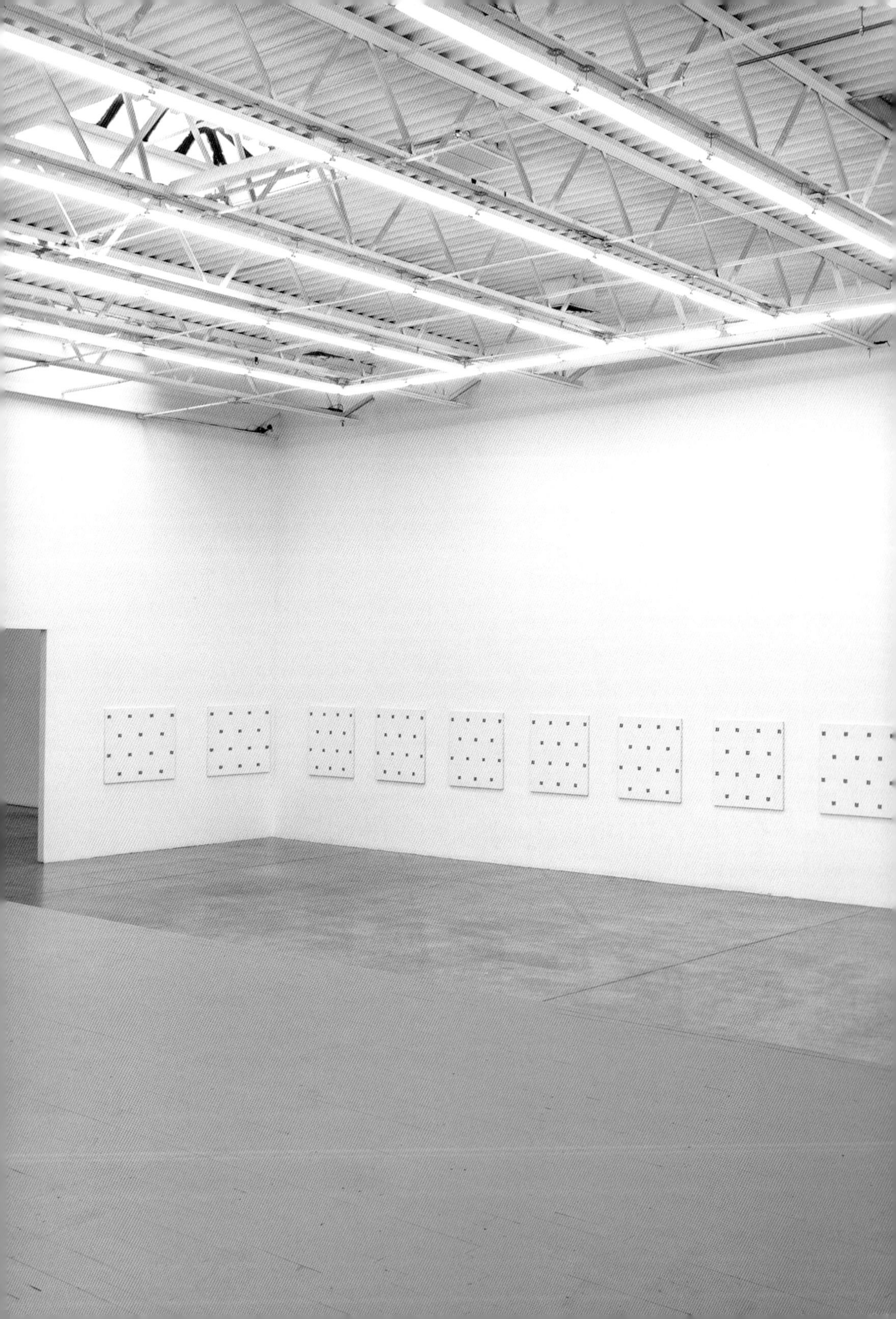

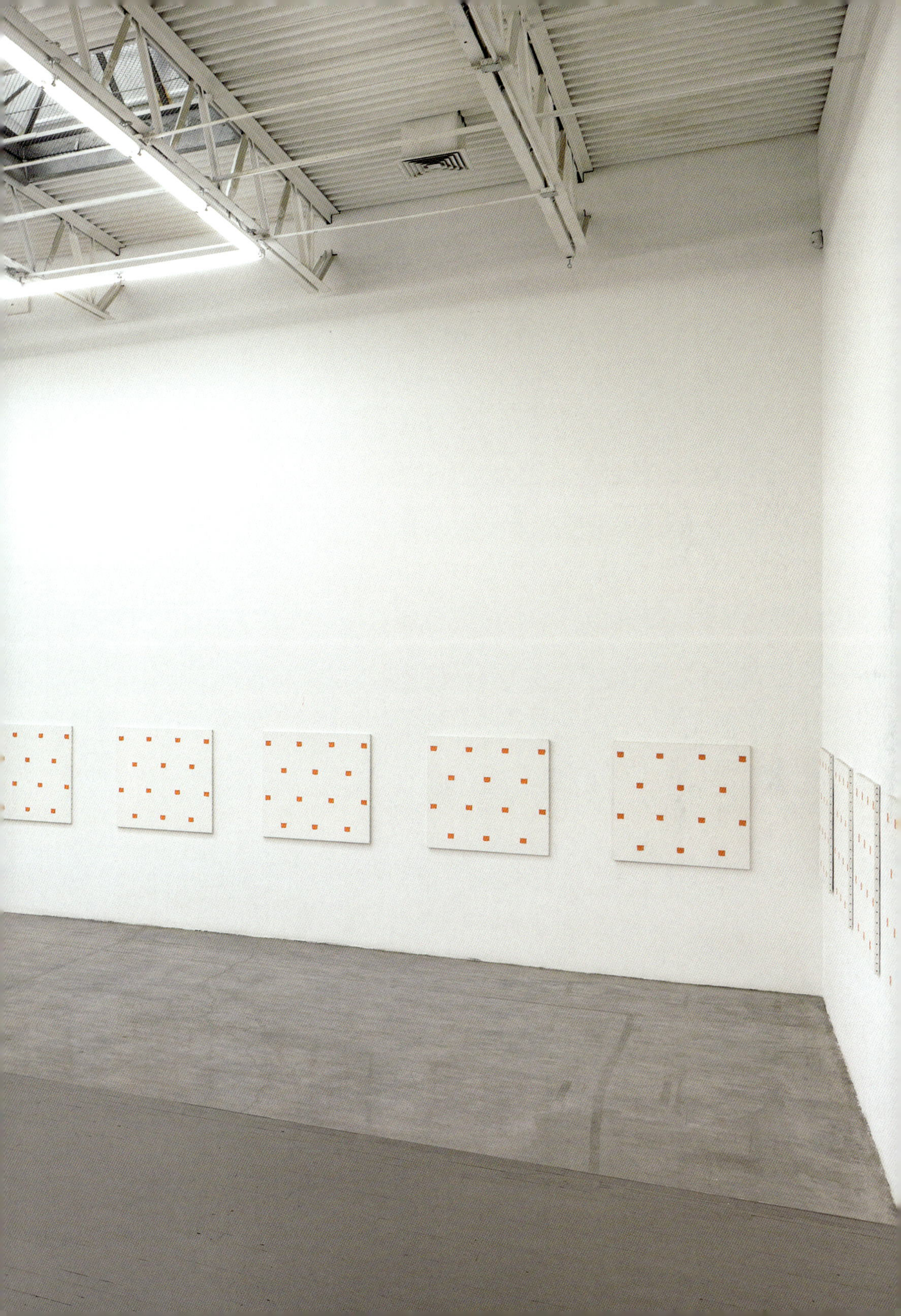

pp. 217-219: *Intervention*, 2015, white acrylic on window

p. 221: *Intervention*, 2015, blue acrylic intervention on electrical panel

pp. 222-224: *Intervention*, 2015, black acrylic intervention on wall

pp. 224, 228-229, 236-237: *25 paintings*, 1987, orange acrylic on twenty-five canvases, each 39 ¼ × 39 ¼ in (100 × 100 cm)

pp. 226-227: *Chutes (Scraps)*, 2000, orange acrylic on colored paper, 98 ½ × 28 ¼ in (250 × 72 cm)

pp. 230-231, 234: *Roll of waxed canvas*, 1968, synthetic polymer paint on coated fabric, 398 × 55 in (1011 × 140 cm)

pp. 230-233: *Seven imprints*, 2014, orange acrylic on seven pieces of A4 letter paper, each approximately 8 ¼ × 11 ¾ in (21 × 31 cm)

For the Swiss Institute exhibition image section, complete captions are included to catalogue this show. Because all of Toroni's works are entitled *Imprints of a no. 50 brush repeated at regular intervals of 30 cm (Empreintes de pinceau n°50 répétées à intervalles réguliers de 30 cm)*, these captions include descriptions that the artist gave to respective works, which are used as titles. In previous image sections, only the place and year of exhibitions are captioned, as other publications document these shows more extensively.

Letters

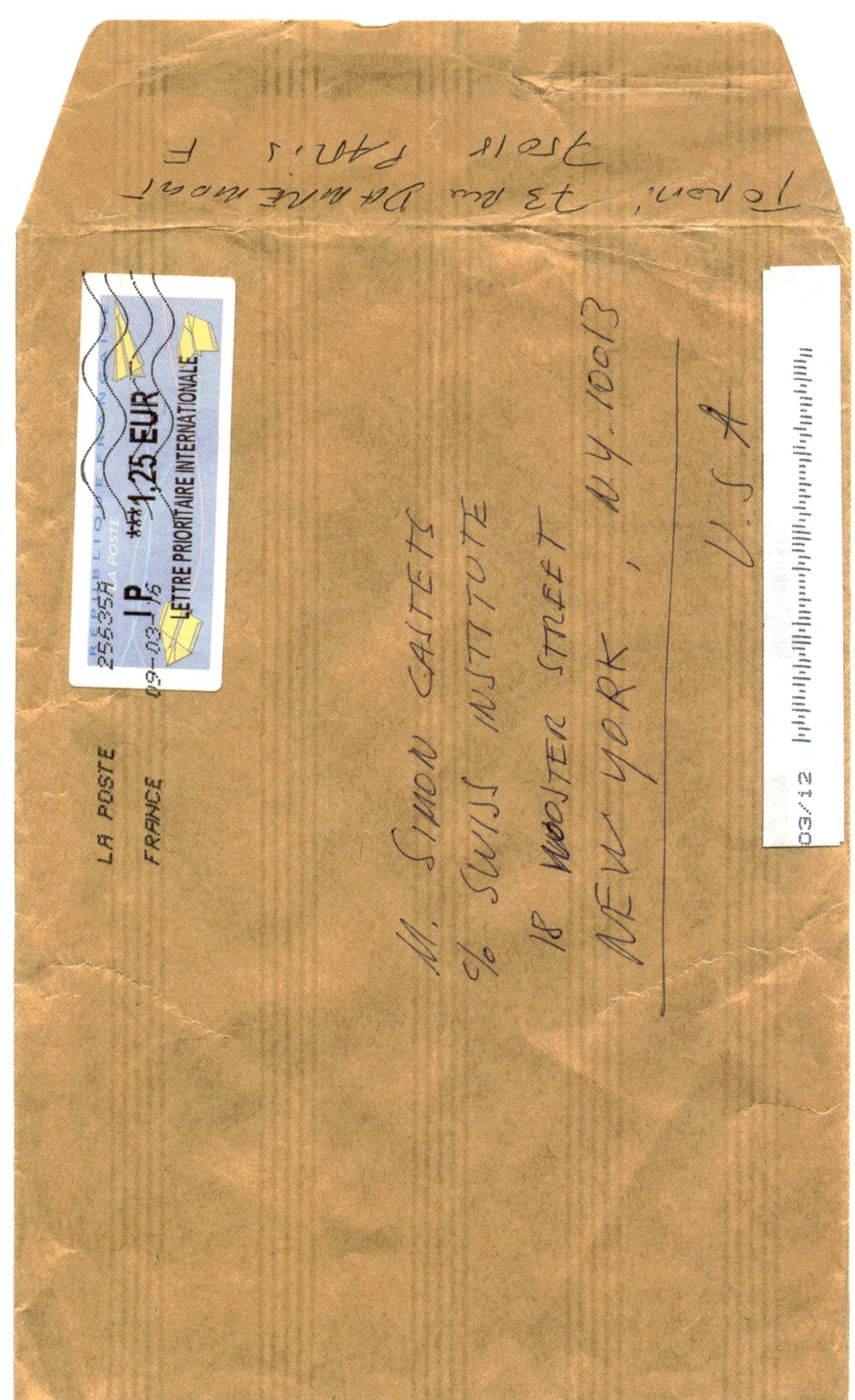

REPUBLIQUE FRANÇAISE
LA POSTE
1,25 EUR
LETTRE PRIORITAIRE INTERNATIONALE
LA POSTE
FRANCE
M. SIMON CASTETS
c/o SWISS INSTITUTE
18 WOOSTER STREET
NEW YORK, N.Y. 10013
U.S.A
03/12

Paris 8.3.16

My dear Simon
the Goodman expo is done (and well done!) So time now to think about the publication.
As I was saying to you, I tinkered a little with my old texts.
Here is one that seems to still be very current and corresponds, as I was saying in our conversation, to what I still think today.
Painting is painting, words, even written, are only words: . . . Even if the artists write them in neon!

Yours
Niele

PS: this text is included in the CAPC BORDEAU[X] catalogue.

The PS is referring to the letter to Johannes Gachnang found on pp. 246-248.

PARIS 8.3.16

Mon cher Simon,
l'expo chez Goodman est finie (et bien finie !) Alors voilà le temps de penser à la publication.
Comme je te disais j'ai tripouillé un peu dans mes anciens textes.
En voilà un qui me semble encore très actuel et correspond, comme je te le disais lors de notre conversation, à ce que je pense encore aujourd'hui.
La peinture c'est la peinture, les mots, même écrits, ne sont que des mots :..
Les artistes ont beau les écrire au néon !

Amicalement

Niele

P.S Ce texte figure dans le catalogue du CAPC BORDEAU

245

245

245

245

245

Dear Johannes, [— Dear Simon]

Why make a book? Or:

1) A book in which we would feel good, like in Rolando's boat, meandering in the sun and discovering plenty of things along the banks, the sky, the water. A book-boat, with neither message nor profession of popular faith, simply a little motor, the littlest, silent. To have the time, to be free, without being obsessed with the idea of rowing. Rowing, like artists, dealers, critics—in short, the organizers of the artistic regatta . . . A book-boat, the old fisherman's boat, large and flat, with hoops over which to spread the canvas in case of rain or strong sunshine, knowing its lake, its waves, its winds, not needing to be the strongest but stable, defiant of the storm despite its creaking. A book, thus, that would not please the socialites who love their museum cruises!

2) A book that we would desire, like the simple white wine Jean makes that we drink down in small glasses, bottle after bottle, taking our time. Without delirious enthusiasm at the beginning, but without nausea at the end. A book-wine. White wine made by the winemaker for his own consumption, that can't be bought in stores but is still there, from year to year, in his cellar. Wine without a label. You have to know a little bit about it in order to tell the slight difference from one time to the next. To have some palate. A book-wine you would have to soak in your mouth a bit, chew it up, spit . . . Vomit, if really you can't stand it. A book, thus, that would please neither the water drinkers nor the cold fish of self-control who hang around openings.

Cher Johannes, — Cher Simon

Pourquoi faire un livre ? Ou alors :

1) Un livre dans lequel on serait bien, comme dans la barque de Rolando, flânant au soleil en découvrant plein de choses au détour du rivage, du ciel, de l'eau. Un livre-barque, sans message ni profession de foi à la mode, simplement un petit moteur, le plus petit, silencieux. Pour avoir le temps, être disponible, sans être obsédé par l'idée de ramer. Ramer, comme les artistes, les marchands, les critiques, bref les organisateurs des régates artistiques... Un livre-barque, ancienne barque de pêcheur, large et plate, avec des arceaux pour y dérouler sa toile en cas de pluie ou de grand soleil, connaissant son lac, ses ondes, ses vents, ne se voulant pas la plus forte, mais stable et défiant l'orage malgré ses craquements. Un livre donc qui ne devrait pas plaire aux mondains amateurs de croisières muséales !

2) Un livre dont on aurait envie comme du petit vin blanc que fait Jean, qu'on descend à petits verres, bouteille après bouteille, prenant son temps. Sans enthousiasme délirant au début, mais sans écœurement à la fin. Un livre-vin. Vin blanc fait par le vigneron pour sa consommation, introuvable dans le commerce mais bien présent, d'année en année, dans sa cave. Vin sans étiquette. Il faut s'y connaître un peu pour trouver d'une fois à l'autre la petite différence. Avoir un peu de palais. Un livre-vin où il faudrait un peu se mouiller, sentir mâchonner, cracher... Vomir, si vraiment on ne supporte pas. Un livre donc, qui ne devrait pas plaire aux buveurs d'eau ni aux pisse-froid du self-control qui traînent dans les vernissages.

3) Un livre qu'on voudrait toucher, caresser comme le corps de J., avec ses coins secrets, humides, poilus, où les doigts s'enfoncent, affleurent, s'agrippent, pincent. Un livre-corps. Humain, animal, qui attire, répugne ; pleins, creux, trous, vides, à lécher, à remplir, à jouer, à jouir, à prendre, à peindre, à sentir ; à effeuiller, à s'effeuiller, feuille de rose, rosette, bouton. De nez à nez, de nez à cul, de nez à livre, y vivre, ivre. S'y endormir. Un livre-corps, gonflable comme une poupée qu'emporterait le marin dans son sac. Un livre donc, qui ne devrait pas plaire à tous ceux qui sur une île déserte emporteraient « l'histoire de l'art de Francastel ».

4) Un livre mallarméen où l'on verrait qu'un coup de/du hasard n'abolira jamais les dés. Deux petits livres-dés, qui permettraient de se détendre en passant, d'un petit coup de passe anglaise. Sept-onze-sept-sept-onze-sept-onze, je passe la main. Misez, misons, page sept, page onze, page onze mille, page vierge. Un livre où la chance aurait sa part et qui ne plairait pas aux malchanceux : aux sans soleil.

Eté 1983 – Hiver 2016

□ □
□

3) A book we would want to touch, to caress like J.'s body, with its secret corners, moist, hairy, where fingers sink in, come up, grip, pinch. A book-body. Human, animal, that attracts, that repels: full, hollow, holes, voids, to lick, to fill, to play, to come, to take, to paint, to sense: to pluck, to be plucked, "pink leaves," rosette, bud. Nose to nose, nose to ass, nose to book, to live, drunk. To sleep there. A book-body, inflatable like the doll the sailor takes into his sack. A book, thus, that would not please those who would bring *Art History* by Francastel to a desert island.

4) A Mallarméean [*sic*] book in which we would see that a throw of chance will never abolish the dice. Two little book-dice, which would allow the passing leisure of a little game of craps. Seven-eleven-seven-seven-eleven-seven-eleven, next. Put, let's put, page seven, page eleven, page eleven thousand, blank page. A book where chance would have its part and which would not please the unlucky, the sunless.

Summer 1983 [– Winter 2016]

250 250

250

250 250

251

251

251

251

251

252

252

252

252

252

253 253

253

253 253

254

254

254

254

254

255

255

255

255

255

256

256

256

256

256

257

257

257

257

257

258

258

258

258

258

259 259

259

259 259

19.4.16

My dear Simon

Here you go!

Your turn

I hope there will be some of your lines too

Ciao kisses

Niele

19 4 16

Mon cher Simon

voilà pour toi!

A toi de jouer

j'espère qu'il y aura
aussi quelques lignes de toi

Ciao Simon

[illegible]

NIELE TORONI

1937 Locarno-Muralto (Switzerland)
has lived in Paris since 1959

Method of work
To the surface at hand is applied a brush no. 50, at regular intervals of 30 cm.

Surface: canvas, cotton, paper, oilcloth, wall, ground . . . white, usually.

To apply: " . . . to put one thing on another in a manner that covers it and sticks, or leaves an imprint."

No. 50 brush: wide flat brush of 50 mm.

The work/painting presented
Imprints of a no. 50 brush repeated at regular intervals (30 cm).

NIELE TORONI

1937 Locarno-Muralto (SUISSE)
vit à Paris depuis 1959

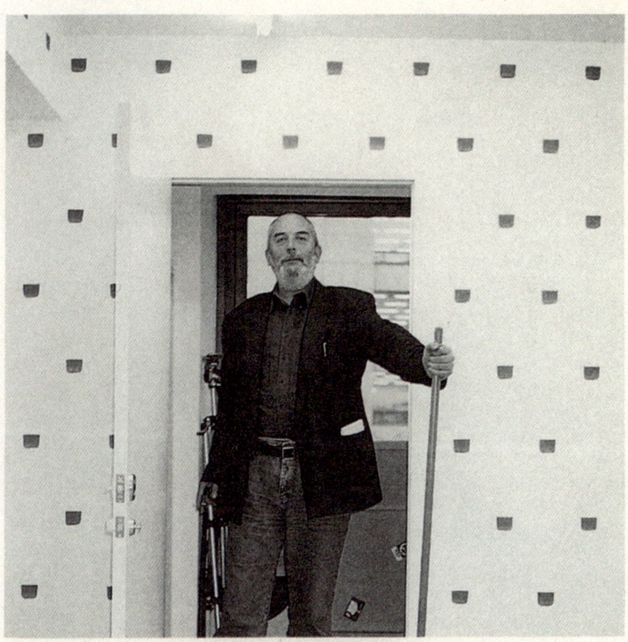

Méthode de travail
Sur le support donné est appliqué un pinceau n°50 à intervalles réguliers de 30cm.

Support: toile, coton, papier, toile cirée, mur, sol..., généralement des fonds blancs.

Appliquer: "...mettre une chose sur une autre de manière qu'elle la recouvre et y adhère, ou y laisse une empreinte."

Pinceau n°50: pinceau plat large de 50mm.

Travail/peinture presenté
Empreintes de pinceau n°50 répétées à intervalles réguliers (30cm).

14 mei – 2 juli 2000

NIELE TORONI

opening zondag 14 mei 11u

rondleiding:

Op zondag 28 mei om 11u geeft Edith Doove een gratis rondleiding in de tentoonstelling. Het aantal inschrijvingen hiervoor is beperkt tot 25 personen. Indien u interesse heeft kunt u zich uiterlijk vrijdag 26 mei schriftelijk of per fax aanmelden bij het museum.

lunch:

Na de opening van de tentoonstelling nodigen wij u graag uit voor een lunch in het Gasthof d'Ouwe Hoeve, Dorpsstraat 48 in Deurle. De kosten voor deelname zijn 750 BEF (inclusief wijnen en koffie). Gelieve uw deelname ten laatste dinsdag 9 mei te bevestigen op 09-282 32 52 onder vermelding 'Lunch Museum Dhondt-Dhaenens'.

sponsors:

Bank Degroof / CKA / Europabank / Hulp der Patroons / Ipsen / Nationale Loterij / UA Scania / Van de Walle-Lissnijder

met steun van:

Gemeentebestuur Sint-Martens-Latem, Provincie Oost-Vlaanderen, Vlaamse Gemeenschap, Pro Helvetia

De receptie wordt u aangeboden door Trappist Westmalle

openingsuren museum:

di-vr 13-17u / za, zo en feestdagen 11-17u / ma gesloten

museum Dhondt-Dhaenens

M DD

Museumlaan 14, B-9831 Deurle, België

tel. +32-9-282 51 23 – fax +32-9-281 08 53

info@museumdd.be – http://www.museumdd.be

265 265

265

265 265

T O

R

O N

I

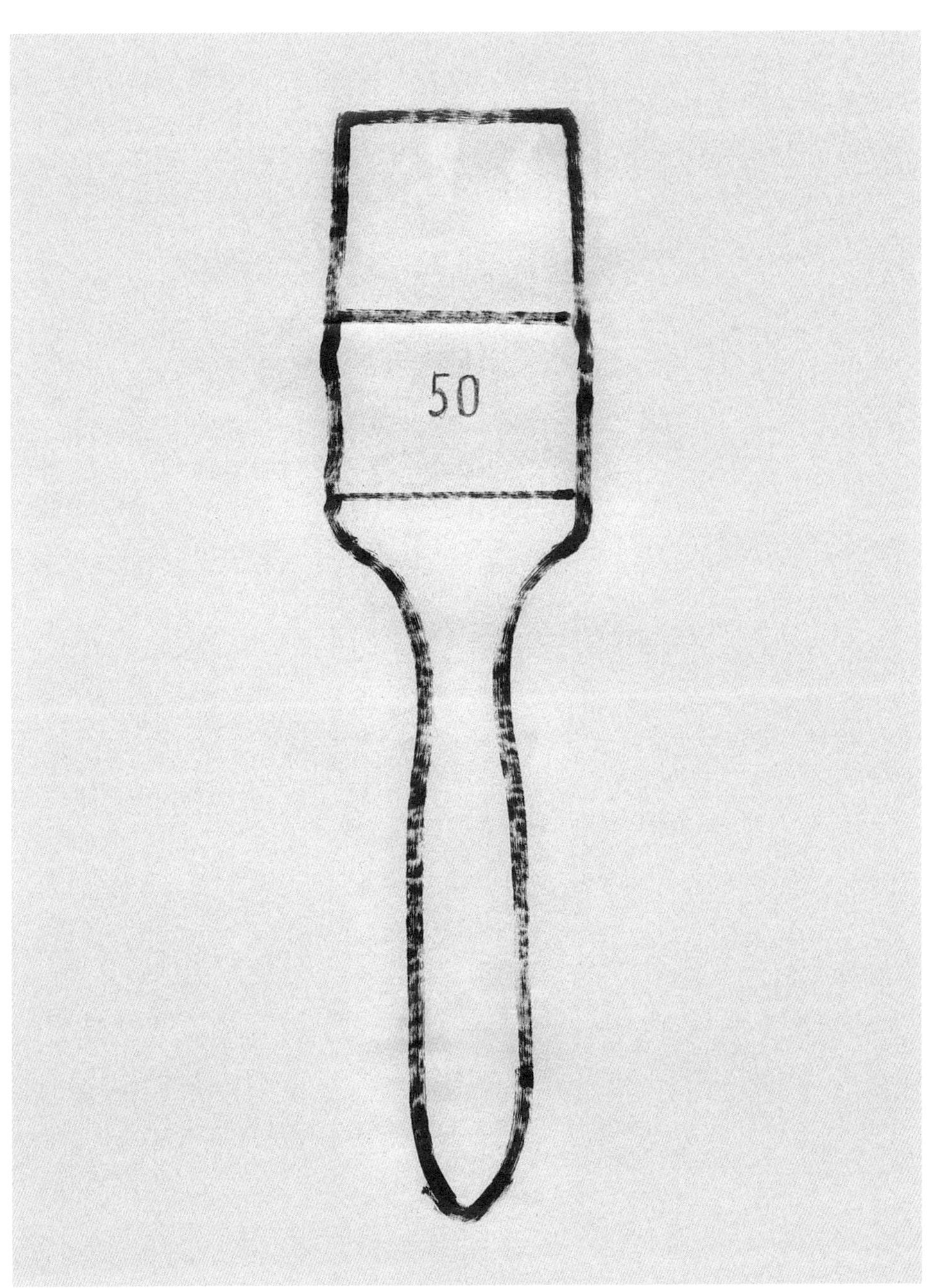
50

1. What is the AVANT-GARDE?
2. Do you consider yourself an avant-garde artist?
3. Is art in crisis today?
4. What do you think of the increasing responsibility of public institutions?
5. If art is in crisis, do you attribute this to the current economic situation?
6. Is there a general crisis?
7. Do you believe in progress?
8. How do you see the evolution of art tomorrow?
9. What question would you like to pose in return?

1. Given the context we would not speak, for example, of Gramsci.
Thus according to the *Petit Larousse* dictionary, if we forget about the military sense: "that which precedes its era by its audacities: avant-garde ideas."

2. No, truly, for according to the vocabulary, audacity (Latin *audacia*) = extraordinary hardness.
Since 1966, my activity as a painter has been limited to dipping a no. 50 brush into cans of different colors and applying it at regular intervals on the given surface to obtain imprints of a no. 50 brush repeated at regular intervals (30 cm).
Even if sometimes I climb a ladder to do this work/painting, we cannot speak seriously of audacity.

1 Qu'est-ce que l'AVANT--GARDE?
2 Vous considérez-vous comme un artiste d'avant-garde?
3 Y a-t-il une crise de l'art aujourd.hui?
4 Comment jugez-vous la responsabilité grandissante des institutions publiques?
5 Si crise il y a, l'attribuez-vous à la situation économique actuelle?
6 Y a-t-il une crise générale?
7 Croyez-vous au progrès?
8 Comment voyez-vous l'évolution de l'art demain?
9 Quelle question souhaiteriez-vous poser à votre tour?

1. Vu le contexte on ne parlera pas, par exemple, de Gramsci. Donc, d'après le petit Larousse, si on oublie le sens militaire, "ce qui précède son époque par ses audaces: idées d'avant-garde."

2. Non, vraiment, car toujours d'après le vocabulaire, audace (lat. audacia) = hardiesse extraordinaire.
Depuis 1966 mon activité de peintre se limite à tremper un pinceau n.50 dans des boites de couleurs variées et l'appliquer à intervalles réguliers sur les supports donnés en obtenant des empreintes de pinceau n.50 répétées à intervalles réguliers (30cm.).
Même si parfois je monte sur une échelle pour faire ce travail/peinture, on ne peut pas sérieusement parler d'audace.

3. Pour qui? Pour moi c'était avant. Depuis quelques années ça marche pas mal, merci.

4. Grandissante.

5,6. A propos de crise, ça revient régulièrement comme la Pologne: n'oublions pas les crises de fou rire ni le Père Ubu.
(Pour les chômeurs le problème est évidemment plus réel.)

7. Dans l'automobile il n'y a que ça de vrai. Dans le ski aussi.

8. Vu l'évolution de l'art aujourd'hui le demain sera hier.
"Viva il papa" et l'avant-garde.

9. Comment fait-on pour gagner au loto?

U. Toroni

vendredi 13 février 1981

Réponses au questionnaire dela revue +-0

3. For whom? For me it was, earlier. For several years now it's going well, thanks.

4. Increasing.

5, 6. About crisis, this occurs regularly as in Poland: let us forget neither those of hysterical laughter, nor Père Ubu.
(For the unemployed, this problem is of course more real.)

7. For cars, this is really all there is. For skiing, too.

8. Given the evolution of art today, tomorrow will be yesterday.
Viva il papa and the avant-garde.

9. How do you win the lottery?

N. Toroni
Friday, 13 February, 1981

Responses to the questionnaire from the review *+-0*

6 June 1982

Dear friend

You ask me if I have any “notes” on my work that could be published along with the exhibition to illuminate, you say, my process and my work itself. I am very sorry to disappoint you, but everything in my work seems simple and clear to me, that the only notes that I can send you

DO RE MI FA SOL LA SI

would only obscure the meaning.
If only we were singing it!

Kind regards

Niele Toroni

6 juin1982

Cher ami

vous me demandez si je n'ai pas des "notes" sur mon travail qui publiées lors de l'exposition pourraient eclairer,dites vous, ma démarche et mon travail lui même.

Navré de vous décevoir,mais tout me semble tellement simple et clair dans mon travail,que les seules notes que je pourrais vous transmettre

DO RE MI FA SOL LA SI

NEXFERAIENTXX ne feraient qu'en obscurcir le sens.

Si l'on chantait !

Bien à vous

Niele Toroni

TO LOOK UP

"This morning still very sunny.
I smoke my first cigarette on the balcony. The lake watches me.
I think of my father; today he would have been 91.
A swallow passes like an arrow, the first one I've seen this year.
This makes me happy." N.T., 1996

To modify the famous proposition about Sade's work, "written, shit does not smell," we might say: written, painting is not seen. Indeed, why beat around the bush any longer? Painting defies language. And this is singularly the case for Niele Toroni's painting. On the one hand there is a statement, unvarying since 1966: "On the given support a no. 50 brush is applied at regular intervals of 30 cm." On the other, there are the works (Toroni prefers to speak of work/painting), which are offered to the gaze and which, despite the identical method that presides over their execution, are all different. What is at play in the painting is precisely the gap that exists between what is said and what is given to be seen. If Toroni in fact always does what he says he does, and tirelessly says what he is going to do, each one of his works remains no less a visual event that is not interchangeable with any other. Toroni's works must be apprehended for what they are physically and not for what they represent conceptually. We must make ourselves available to Toroni's painting, receive its deployments, accept even its errors, and not approach it with the prejudices of formal thinking subjugated to language, even the language of art.

The gap between what is said and what is given to be seen contains, in this respect, no mystery, no transcendence. Before the imprints of a brush impregnated with color (depending on the circumstances) and applied on the most various of supports (paper, canvas, glass, walls . . .) we find ourselves confronted with a pictorial experience that summons no exteriority, that opens up to no other world. Toroni's paintings do not refer tautologically back to themselves, however. These imprints cannot be apprehended for themselves

275

275

275

275

275

outside of their strict relations with the context. In this sense each work only qualifies as monochrome insofar as each imprint only exists in relation to its background. In the same manner, an imprint only has meaning in relation to other imprints.

Yet it would seem inappropriate here to speak of contextual painting. Even if they are expressly destined for it, Niele Toroni's works take no added aesthetic value from the space that receives them. If this work/painting is always made to measure, it nevertheless remains the case that at the same time they defy the sacrosanct rules of the inscription of a work in its place. For the painter, it is rarely a matter of asserting space or asserting his work across it, but, more simply and more prosaically, of inscribing a work/painting in a precise situation ("I simply try to respect the places I am offered"). Just as the imprint is a manner of defiance to painting (because it is situated before the will to give sense and meaning to the act of painting), these works always free themselves from the spaces with which they are entangled, doubtless because Toroni never engages in games of strength with the context (material and ideological) that receives him. This painting is not the authoritarian imposition on a place; most often, it adapts itself to the circumstances, although without losing its irredentism (whose efficiency we can verify in the famous formula: "Toroni always does the same thing!"). Because it is not afraid of being generous with the spectator (by not obliging them to admire the spectacularization of artistic subjectivity), this non-imposing work, the polar opposite of expressive and decorative grandiloquence, nevertheless does not let itself be opposed by the contexts at the heart of which it is deployed ("I have often said that if my problem had been space, I would have been an architect").

Indeed, Toroni's work is neither reducible to the use of imprints nor to the inscription of imprints in a space. If there is an intention to the work, it is indeed that of "working to let painting work itself." To imprint is to remain in the act itself, beyond all formal or expressive prescription; it is to give body and place to painting in liberating it from its

REGARDER EN L'AIR

« Ce matin encore un grand soleil.
Je fume ma première cigarette sur le balcon. Le lac me regarde.
Je pense à mon père, il aurait aujourd'hui 91 ans.
Une hirondelle passe comme une flèche, c'est la première que je vois cette année.
Ça me fait plaisir. » N.T., 1996

Pour adapter une proposition célèbre concernant l'œuvre de Sade, « écrite, la merde ne sent pas », on pourrait dire : écrite, la peinture ne se voit pas. À quoi bon en effet tourner plus longtemps autour du pot ? La peinture met au défi le langage. Et singulièrement la peinture de Niele Toroni. D'un côté il existe un énoncé, invariable depuis 1966 : « Sur le support donné est appliqué un pinceau n°50 à intervalles réguliers de 30 cm ». De l'autre, il existe des œuvres (Toroni préfère parler de travail/peinture) qui sont offertes au regard et qui, en dépit de la même méthode qui préside à leur exécution, sont toutes différentes. Ce qui est en jeu dans cette peinture c'est précisément l'écart qui existe entre ce qui est dit et ce qui est donné à voir. Si Toroni fait en effet toujours ce qu'il dit et dit inlassablement ce qu'il va faire, il n'en demeure pas moins que chacune de ses œuvres reste un événement visuel qui n'est pas interchangeable avec un autre. Les œuvres de Toroni doivent être appréhendées pour ce qu'elles sont physiquement et non pour ce qu'elles représentent conceptuellement. Il faut se rendre disponible à la peinture de Toroni, accueillir ses déploiements, accepter même ses errements et ne pas l'aborder avec les préjugés d'une pensée formelle inféodée au langage, fût-il celui de l'art.

historical and ideological burdens (representation, imagination, inspiration, interior necessity). In 1997, Niele Toroni titled his exposition at the Yvon Lambert Gallery *Homage to Swallows* "simply because the works were developed in the corners." "This gallery," he remarked, "has many exposed beams, and because swallows have always made their nests in the corners, I wanted simply to underscore this double element. For once, for several minutes, spectators are not preoccupied with wondering whether they are walking in dog shit, a very Parisian worry but looking up." This homage has the value of an aesthetic and moral manifesto. Toroni's imprints make painting look up rather than complacently reinforcing the melancholic figure of the artist. Niele Toroni's favorite film is Pier Paolo Pasolini's *Uccellacci e uccellini* [*The Hawks and the Sparrows*], it is true.

Bernard Marcadé
2002

How it goes

How is your life?
-Full
You have the sun, you love the sea
-Full, full. Also I like oysters, full.
And women?
-Full
-I feel for you!
(from Plein pot, an unpublished text by the author)

Never, since the invention of home economics, has art entered so fully into banality. Art is full of the world; the world is full of artists. As if value were created in communicating vessels, as if filling and fullness were equal. Communication evacuates the dialectic. Between quality and quantity, it is massively obvious that only banality matters. If it's full, all is well.

For economics, growth requires belief. For religion, communication wants communion.

Art cannot please everyone. But plenty of art can satisfy plenty of people, especially if the world is full of artists. The stakes are clear; the extension of art occurs through the multiplication of artists.

In the time of cloning and of the web, the economy of art also globalizes exchange. It short-circuits the work. Supply and demand, connected to each other, are generated in continuous loop, like stock market speculation. The official work is the banal support for a commercial operation. To produce consumers who become producers of exchange value. Credo of art: "it's the viewer who makes the work."

Intermediaries or intercessors, art agents, collectors, gallerists, conservationists, curators, critics, academics, publics exchange in turn the role of the artist. This is the time not of the work, but of the onlookers. Role-play has replaced the play of the work. Generalized interactivity and household crafts, global art has taken the form of a giant karaoke. In Japanese,

Niele Toroni / Kleve

Ça gaze

Comment est votre vie ?
- Pleine
Vous avez le soleil, vous aimez la mer …
- Plein, pleine. J'aime aussi les huîtres, pleines
Et les femmes ?
- Pleines
Je vous plains !
(extrait de *Plein pot*, inédit de l'auteur)

Jamais, depuis l'invention des arts ménagers, l'art n'était entré aussi pleinement dans la banalité. L'art est plein du monde, le monde est plein d'artistes. Comme si les vases communicants créaient de la valeur, remplissage et plénitude s'équivalent. La communication évacue la dialectique. Entre qualité et quantité, seule importe la banalité d'une évidence massive. On fait le plein, tout va bien.

Economiquement, la croissance implique la croyance. Religieusement, la communication veut la communion.

L'art ne peut pas plaire à tout le monde. Mais plein d'art peut satisfaire plein de monde, surtout si le monde est plein d'artistes. L'enjeu est clair, l'extension du domaine de l'art passe par la multiplication des artistes.

A l'heure du clonage et du web, l'économie de l'art, aussi, mondialise les échanges. Elle court-circuite l'œuvre. L'offre et la demande, branchées l'une sur l'autre, se génèrent en boucle comme la spéculation boursière. L'œuvre en titre est le support banal d'une opération commerciale. Produire des consommateurs qui deviennent producteurs de valeur d'échange. Credo de l'art : « c'est le regardeur qui fait l'œuvre ».

Intermédiaires ou intercesseurs, agents d'art, les collectionneurs, les galeristes, les conservateurs, les curateurs, les critiques, les universitaires, les publiques s'échangent tour à tour le rôle de l'artiste. Le temps n'est plus à l'œuvre, mais aux figurants. Les jeux de rôle ont remplacé l'enjeu de l'œuvre.

Interactivité généralisée et art des familles, l'art mondial a pris la forme d'un karaoké géant. En japonais, *kara,* vide, et *oke*, orchestration. L'intérêt, c'est la banalité gérée comme un fourre-tout médiatique. On connaît la musique ! Mais c'est l'orchestration du vide.

kara, empty, and *oke*, orchestration. The appeal is banality managed, a mediated hodge-podge. We know the music! But it's the orchestration of emptiness.

How to situate the work of Niele Toroni under these conditions? The question today reflects a need for classification, which, by default, by banalizing the demand of the work, seeks to fill, to furnish a void and to create categories of artists, pre-identified in an aesthetic. Yet it is not a question of recognition or monopoly of situation, but of the situation of a work and its exposition. In the concert of art, it is a singular and disconcerting demand.

Toroni's work is not afraid of emptiness. It does not adorn itself with either an aesthetic foil or a social or technological alibi. Its only ornament is painting, the banality of painting, experienced on the spot, irrefutable and untimely in its obviousness, which breaks with the image of the artists as it has broken, for more than thirty years, with the banalization of historical representation. The work belongs to no "family" of art. The painting is not orphan; it is a flat-out break.

For Toroni, the banality of painting is not banal. It concedes nothing to the general banalization of works of art. On the contrary, it is the methodical condition of a singular work. It is, in the productive repetition of work, what makes way for the evident rupture of the unexpected work of painting.

Rupture of the work, rupture to the work, this rupture is in no way an aesthetic gesture that would be exhausted in the affirmation of a style. Against all stylistic devices, rupture crafts painting with the methodical necessity of an elementary and repetitive gesture, measured by the constraint of artifice.
The rupture is accustomed to the practice of painting. It is not decisive of an engagement in painting except to be the decision that in practice engages painting. The banality of method proceeds originally from painting, from its conditions of existence, of appearance or disappearance, of exposition. From the

outset, rupture is existential. It cuts to the heart of the division of the pictorial act. It locates, here and now, the coexistence of the conditions that it puts into play: functional conditions of instruments, material conditions of supports and colors, formal conditions of space and time. Concretely: to apply a brush imprinted with color on a given support, in such a way that it leaves an imprint.

The method describes the gesture of painting, but it inscribes it rigorously in the rupture of artifice. It is this rupture, material and symbolic, that engages the pictorial act and brings about the work of painting. It assigns a departure and a division to the work of painting. Rupture signals painting, beyond the gesture of the painter, beyond the imprint of the brush. This outside is exposition. It brings to light the spacing, which puts the work of painting into play.

Painting is not paint. It is not confined in an imprint, fixed in the frame of the picture, limited to the covering of a surface, no matter what the support. Each imprint is simultaneously the closing and the opening of the field of exposition of painting. Each imprint is a limit and a threshold. It locates and repeats the spacing that works painting. Painting does not hold still, in place. It runs away. So, too, is music evaded and explained. And, in the march, the imprint left on the ground is that which takes the leap.

The imprint is not a motif. Unlike other painters, Toroni does not paint imprints. He is the actor in a process, the cause of a function, of which painting is the vector, vehicle, and motor, but also the destination. There is no model, no obsessional image, no frame to fill, but a work to accomplish that only painting can produce. Work/painting, in proximity and rupture, difference and repetition where exposition plays out. To do the labor of painting insofar as the work of painting, the function of the work: to let painting make painting. When painting makes the work, it makes the leap into exposition. Painting "in person" shows the way of the work, says what belongs only to the work. The present of painting exhibits that which we cannot preempt. It exhibits us to the encounter with the work. It puts us to work. Poetics of painting, I have written, to indicate the irreducible parallel between painting and writing and, from work to work, the productive spacing that exhibits my texts with Toroni's pieces.

Exposition, always different, is the very difference that painting makes present. It is presented as the embodiment of time, giving place to the spacing where the signs that locate and reveal the work of painting meet, but leaving it in suspense. If painting is at work, it is never a finished thing.

Painting yields to the signs of the rupture of artifice that it puts into play here and now. What is signaled by rupture, cut by the color let by each imprint on the white of the support, is the seduction of an intimate sedition. Seduction puts painting outside itself, outside its artifice, outside of their conventions. There where it is left, each imprint lets appear, at the limit of artifice and the threshold of fiction, in the closing and opening of its own transgression, the field of exposition of which it here and now becomes the sign and the pictorial exhibitor.

An imprint is never alone. It conserves the trace, it liberates the sign of the field of appearance and disappearance. In this field, it locates a time of exposition. Occasionally, this is a time in the waiting, an exposition in suspense. Their realization as the present of painting does not happen through representation, but through the spacing and the representation, from each imprint, to the covering of paint that uncovers what makes it visible and that to which it gives vision: the fragmentary and multiple brilliance of appearance.

Literal definition of painting, to be read in the field of its inscription, seen in the time of its exposition: "imprints of a no. 50 brush repeated at regular intervals of 30 cm."

285

285

285

285

285

Painting is not a thing in itself. Work in infraction in the brilliance of being, it is the repeated test of the world that puts it into play. It remains, playing and replaying in the straight line of time. The painting of Niele Toroni is the contemporary of the banality of a world that has no era. It is a contemporaneity to be invented, a temporal marker, a present to be produced and repeated because there is no representation in unlimited banality.

It is not a question of painting the world, not least of representing clichés, repainting canonical images or canonizing artists. Traversed by the time of the world, the risk of painting is at play even with the world. The stakes are to signal, here and now, to make the work in a world that does not expect it, to make painting into the present of the world. This is not a banal present in the banality of the world. It is a present to elect and a radical engagement of painting, a choice without compensation: to live a world that is only the world and not the reverse of paradise.

Can we know what artists want? Only that the globalization of the world responds to it. It imposes the conditions that make little of want. Toroni's work shows what painting can do. Its plasticity, its coherence, its timing, its relevance measuring up to its power of exposition at play in the world. It is a power of play, not the illusory power of monopolizing the world in order to fill it with imprints. Work only plays when it is situated. It comes to accept places as they are. Imprints are not added; they are spaced. Their play situates the spacing of place. It empties place. At the site where it takes place, painting restarts, awakens what gives it place. It exposes the intimate exteriority of taking place to the play of the world. It is globalized.

René Denizot
June 2002

Notes

pp. 241-243: Niele Toroni, letter to Simon Castets, March 8, 2016.

pp. 246-248: Niele Toroni, letter to Johannes Gachnang, Summer 1983, originally published in *Niele Toroni* (Bordeaux: CAPC Musée d'Art Contemporain de Bordeaux, 1997), 104-105. Amended for Simon Castets, Winter 2016.

pp. 260-261: Niele Toroni, letter to Simon Castets, April 19, 2016.

pp. 262-263: Biography and method of work, originally published in *Niele Toroni* (Chiba: Chiba City Museum of Art, 1996), 3.

pp. 264, 266-267: Invitation to the exhibition *Niele Toroni*, Museum Dhondt-Dhaenens, Deurle, 2000.

pp. 268-270: Niele Toroni, responses to a questionnaire from the magazine *Plus Minus Zero: +-0*, no. 34 (1981), originally published in Niele Toroni (Bordeaux: CAPC Musée d'Art Contemporain de Bordeaux, 1997), 72, 74.

pp. 272-273: Niele Toroni, letter to a friend, June 6, 1982, originally published in *Niele Toroni* (Bordeaux: CAPC Musée d'Art Contemporain de Bordeaux, 1997), 101.

pp. 274, 276-278: Bernard Marcadé, "Regarder en l'air," *Niele Toroni* (Kleve: Museum Kurhaus Kleve, 2002), 28-29.

pp. 280-284, 286: René Denizot, "Ça gaze," ibid., 30-33.

All letters translated by Jocelyn Spaar.

Selected Writings

Bon appétit

The soup would soon be served. We were already all at the table, standing behind our chairs. We chanted: *We praise you Lord for this meal, for all joy . . ..*
The Lord must not have fancied being praised that evening, because at that exact moment the crucifix detached from the wall and plunged into the soup tureen. I had the unfortunate idea to chuckle, just a bit. At the stroke of Father K's large hand, I landed on the stove. The nail that had held the cross on the wall for years buckled in a corner.

1962

Monologue with you

It was still daytime and the red tree stood out amidst all this green foliage. Psssh, psssh went the iron. It was singing. All is well, like the well-folded handkerchief that you arrange on the pile. Tweet, tweet, tweet, your canary shirt. If you flew away I would catch you; the red parrot would twist your neck, wing, foot, only your eyes would he leave untouched. They are almond eyes and it's I who will eat them. Green olives, just fine. With or without spaghetti. Lord knows. You are a painter, so is he; but neither of you are paintbrushes. Nuance, no, difference. More paintbrushes, fewer painters and marines but also more seashores. Cliffs and bottomless seas, splash, everything out to float. Hello friends. Pass me the key. Yes, the one to the cage of sharks.

19 May 1963

Ah! These Artists

We were now tens of millions watching him.
He was gliding and clinging to his paintbrush.
He held himself up there for almost two hours. We were hoping we wouldn't have much longer to wait. His resistance was no longer humanly possible.
We were already shouting at him: go on, let go.
No, he was saying no with his head.
But look, don't be dumb, we can't lose our whole day, let go, let go.

No, he was shaking his tiny little head between his two outstretched arms up there.
He was holding onto his paintbrush!
Thus some of us became angry and climbed up to saw off the brush handle.

March 1964

Dear Family,

My models only have one chair.
It's toilsome
Could you send me a bit of money.
Your loving son

Christmas 1964

Face up to things.
Painting to blow off steam is everywhere, justifying the status of permanent painter artists.
These great souls: swooning to the right, the left, the middle, above, below, a little, a lot, passionately, have done us the honor of sharing a bit of their vision of the world.
What a delight!
Perhaps their games will continue.
For us, the games are over. We no longer confuse the dealer with the marble.
Long live the marbles! It's your move.

November 1966

Very often the major "artists" we learn about were not very interesting individuals on the human level.
And all their works are presented as being responsible for I don't know what forces, those that would bear witness to the greatness of man! But:
But the only great force is lucidity. Let's try to be a bit lucid. And to paint. Our paint trace may also take on an

ornamental burden.
We will take it on without a doubt; the eventual acceptance of the work will not happen right away. It will be a matter of setting things right.

December 1966

Works of art + works of charity = good works.
Artists and snails dribble, but only artists sell their dribble.

In every Norman village there are dozens of Modiglianis.

12 February 1967

It could be said of this painting:
how one makes it
it refers only to itself
it is (it says nothing and since the completed act of painting no longer has an affiliation with the performer, the possibility to change the performer therefore carries no "weight"):
it is by itself, hence the impossibility of linking it to an ethics.

February 1968

We could see the imprints of a no. 50 paintbrush repeated at regular intervals (30 cm) in January 1967 at the National Museum of Modern Art in Paris. Ever since, the work had been visible in locations, specialized or not, from the inside or outside. This does not make the work visible here and now more or less interesting or uninteresting.

We ascertain that this work has continued over a certain number of years. The work has not changed, only the mental laziness (dishonesty) permits certain people to regularly classify (to retract) it under the label of the avant-garde of the moment.

This work (imprints of a no. 50 brush repeated at regular intervals [30 cm]) being what it is (imprints of a no. 50 brush repeated at regular intervals [30 cm] is neither art nor its opposite.

It is currently visible in an art gallery because the problem with art must be posed: art being one of the superstructures upon which prevailing ideology rests.

September 1971

N.B. We do not want to impose convictions through our work: it would be sufficient to undermine these prejudices.

Banalities to repeat again and again in the art world

1st movement: Allegro ma non troppo
With or without a gallery, the dealer merely represents a cog in the system of art (a system arising and serving the system holding power) along with the critic and artist.
One generally forgets the artist and instead lashes out at the critic or the dealer. One always forgets to lash out at the collector-dealer.

2nd movement: Andantino
Tiziano Vecellio (Titian) 1477-1576
In 1557 Lodovico Dolce published *L'Aretino o dialogo della pittura*. He says in speaking about Titian: "He still was scarcely 20 years old when he collaborated with Giorgione"; yet this collaboration had taken place in 1508. Titian was therefore born around 1488 and not in 1477; but as a very practical man with business savvy (he also worked in the lumber trade, and let's not forget that Freud saw a symbol of the feminine-maternal in lumber), Titian arranged it so that he was born before Giorgione. But the fact remains that Charles V picked up the paintbrush of Titian and not that of Giorgione.
In this day and age certain people have not forgotten: it always pays to falsify dates.

3rd movement: Allegro vivace
Defenders of art
Defenders of lard
Dollar defenders

1972

Right, let's take the sea, for example. The sea, for many people, is blue, it always has been and always will be, even if they have never seen it. And so they look at the sea, but they no longer want to nor can they actually see it. These are people who, no matter the situation or seashore they find, will have the vision of this cliché "sea" and that's it; they wouldn't/couldn't even see a greenish sea: impossible, that couldn't be the *sea*. To respond to you, whenever people say "Toroni's work doesn't interest me because he always makes the same thing," I find that these tend not to be very interesting people, as they have already been completely conditioned by this "blue sea."

These are the people for whom it is impossible to see a precise work at a precise moment, in its continuity (the process of work that does not change) and in its diversity. Diversity linked to a physical reality of work of each manifestation (color of the imprints, materials used, dimensions) instead of atmosphere. Diversity performed by continuity, by repetition.

"It's always the same thing" has truly always seemed like the most stupid excuse to me; of someone who would say: walking is always the same thing, putting one foot in front of the other, so I won't walk anymore if I don't find any novelty, a new way of walking.

Generally, you might find that these are the people (it's evident in the art world) who, by way of newness, manage to forever stay in the same place and never move. One can find a whole category of these people anywhere, who really only enunciate change to be able to keep doing the same thing while keeping their privileges.

Since 1967, I have articulated work/painting with the same wording: it's the process of work that literally defines what is given to look at. One could say that the wording is the common denominator of all work/paintings that are shown; it says everything and nothing (means nothing) if one doesn't see the given work. One could also speak even of the diversity of each imprint at the interior of the work, due to the fact that each imprint is one "being," obtained each time by its specificity, not the ideal. But let's return to your question.

There is another example, that of medicines, of laundry detergents: one regularly one changes the packaging, more colorful, less colorful, fashionable . . .; inside there is always the same crap. Truly it's not my problem, to create new artistic packaging to pass along old ideology.

The formal pseudo-shift has become a formality. Good intentions, however artistic they might be, do not change anything. But enough already, would you waste your time discussing this with someone who would tell you "making love doesn't interest me, it's always the same thing"? That's their own business.

In 1972, at the time of my exhibition at Yvon Lambert, you asked me why the invite card specified:
"No text will be distributed to be attached as an explanatory label—to enforce the work/painting presented."

This seems pretty clear to me. I was evidently taking a polemical position at the moment when, in Paris at any rate, there was an inflation of "artists' texts."

But I'll confess that I still don't really believe in "artists' texts," especially when they are already established as such. Why? Because generally in reading them they seldom prove credible. Each time that you receive a text from an artist, you will notice what it wants to be, modestly theoretical; but if you take a good look you can see what the authors should have had the courage to call by name; a publicity text! And everyone knows, even if no one wants to admit it, that the goal of these theoretical-advertising texts is to be attached exactly like labels to the works of art produced at the same time as with their authors, to justify and promote them. You will also observe (with rare exception) that in the best cases possible, the writings of a certain relevance are unfortunately in the service of the artworks that stamp a date on them.

All that to repeat that my work/painting could not, should not be more or less interesting to you according to what I could tell you or what others might say about it.

It's a painting and that is all.

The imprints of a no. 50 brush (a typically pictorial work instrument) are visible, since to leave its imprint, the paintbrush is loaded with paint; paint is the color that one generally does not see because it is in the box and only the application of the brush will reveal it. Imprints of a no. 50 brush, "spots" of paint if you like (the surface covered in color being determined by the dimension of the bristle part of the brush, the part used to paint) repeating at regular intervals (30 cm), occupying the chosen surface while leaving it visible, legible.

Read a wall. Why not? It's up to you.

———

295

295

295

295

295

13 April 1977

Federal Office of Culture
Bern

Sirs,

I thank you for your invitation and must respond right away that I will not participate in the Bienal de São Paolo.

I always thought that under the guise of the magical word "art," one could neither make nor admit anything; and also that a work, despite the "artistic" alibi, couldn't be seen/read, if presented wherever, however, without taking into account the reality, the realities, of the particular location.

In this precise case, to participate under the conditions you propose to me for the Bienal de São Paolo would only condone a particular well-known system (with which, for my part, I share neither ideas nor methods) in participating with the adornment of walls that for three months will try to mask their miseries.

With my best regards.

N. TORONI

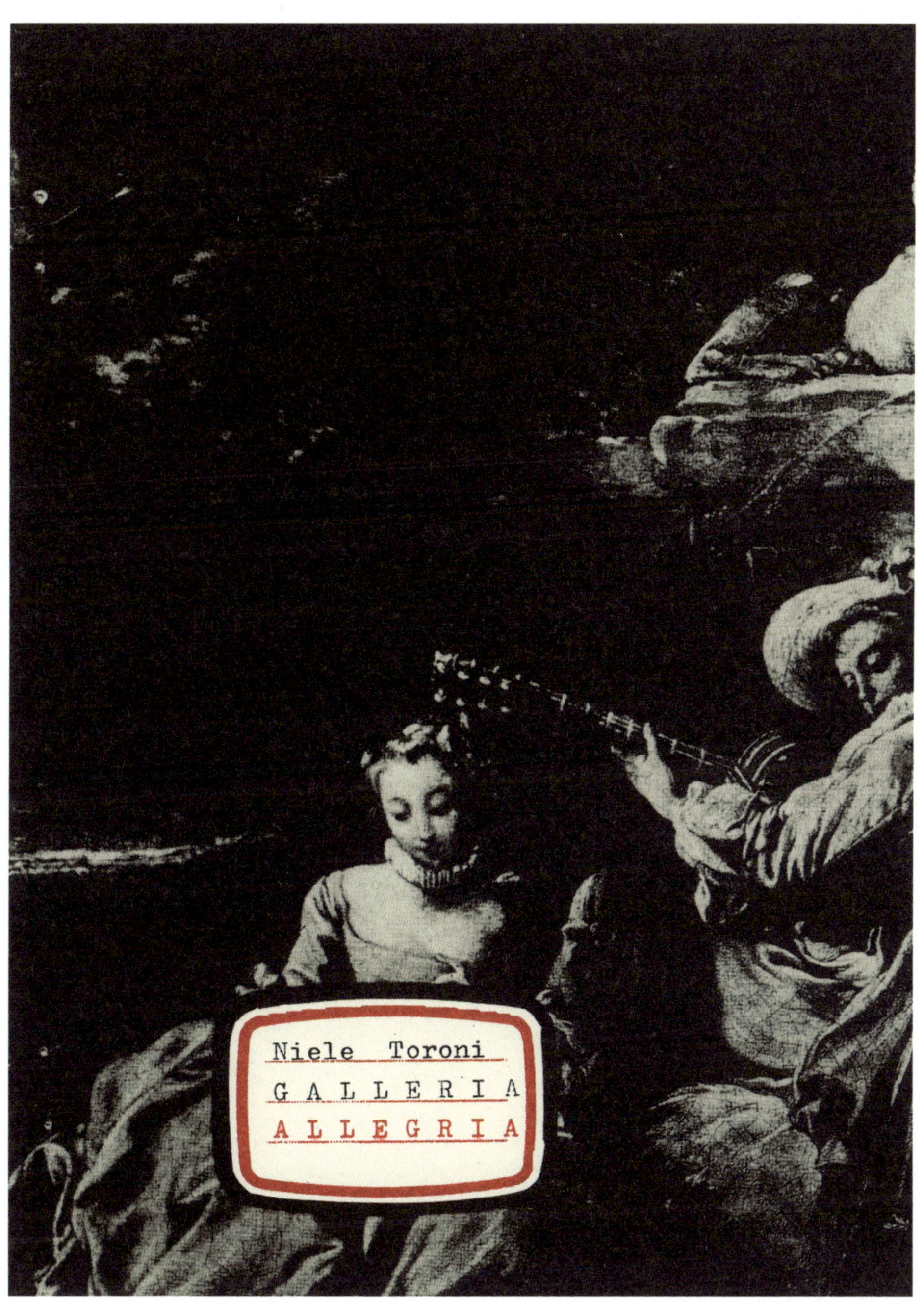
Niele Toroni
GALLERIA
ALLEGRIA

a quello che ha tradotto
stuzzicadenti con cure-dent

à celui qui traduit
cure-dent par stuzzicadenti

to the one who translated
toothpick with tooth-pick

to the one who translated
tooth-pick with toothpick

hommage n2

une empreinte de pinceau n.50

deux empreintes de pinceau n.50

trois empreintes de pinceau n.50

quatre empreintes de pinceau n.50

cinq empreintes de pinceau n.50

six empreintes de pinceau n.50

sept empreintes de pinceau n.50

huit empreintes de pinceau n.50

neuf empreintes de pinceau n.50

dix empreintes de pinceau n.50

onze empreintes de pinceau n.50

douze empreintes de pinceau n.50

treize empreintes de pinceau n.50

quatorze empreintes de pinceau n.50

quinze empreintes de pinceau n.50

seize empreintes de pinceau n.50

~~dix-sept empreintes de pinceau n.50~~

homage no. 2

one imprint of a no. 50 brush

two imprints of a no. 50 brush

three imprints of a no. 50 brush

four imprints of a no. 50 brush

five imprints of a no. 50 brush

six imprints of a no. 50 brush

seven imprints of a no. 50 brush

eight imprints of a no. 50 brush

nine imprints of a no. 50 brush

ten imprints of a no. 50 brush

eleven imprints of a no. 50 brush

twelve imprints of a no. 50 brush

thirteen imprints of a no. 50 brush

fourteen imprints of a no. 50 brush

fifteen imprints of a no. 50 brush

sixteen imprints of a no. 50 brush

~~seventeen imprints of a no. 50 brush~~

Why do rich people buy Arte Povera?
Why do the far right and the far left defend the same artistic pseudo-values?
Why is so-called new painting only a vehicle for outdated ideologies?
Why are they emptying churches, but filling museums?
Why is the Mona Lisa so sad?
Why is everyone upset when someone smashes a Michelangelo sculpture to bits, but could care less if someone destroys a Palestinian refugee camp?
Why don't those artists who are held captive by their illusions of freedom see (or wish to see) that they're jesters? Who are they performing for?
Why should painting ever be just an intellectual exercise?
Why if someone were to invent the steam engine today would everyone laugh, all the while the art world is pulled along by "steam engines" whenever it seems interesting?
Why is it that painted flowers rendered so beautifully, so realistically, never wilt?
Why aren't photographers considered the easel painters of our era?
Why are there more works of art in the safes of Swiss banks than there are in the museums? Is it for posterity's sake?
Why is it art's obligation to be enjoyable and reassuring?
Why should an artist's "sincerity" be enough to justify their output and activity? If a reactionary artist is "sincere," does that justify whatever they say or do?
Why are people who ride on the coattails of others called parasites, when those who do the same in the art world are respected as critics?
Why isn't painting just a job like any other?
Why let oneself always be duped by the dominant discourse that reduces problems of (figural) form to formalism, so that formality might better smother us all?

1978

Niele Toroni originally wrote this entry in Italian.

Interview (1982)

To me it always seemed essential that a work/painting might be seen at first glance. In my view, painting doesn't address the blind, which is perhaps sad, but there's nothing I can do about it. I don't believe at all in painting that can be be described, because it would only have to do with works illustrating a story, yet would have nothing to do with painting and would classify it as a comic strip. I have nothing against this, but it pertains to something else.

They say that I paint dots! I do not paint dots, not any more than squares or flowers (it's all the same). I do not paint any preestablished form. Since 1966, I have used flat brushes the width of 50 mm (no. 50), which I apply on the given surface at regular intervals of 30 cm. The more or less square "form" achieved is produced by the bristly part of the paintbrush saturated with color that, applied on a surface, leaves its imprint there. As the bristles are not rigid (fortunately!), each imprint is unique, different from its neighbor. It does not exist as an ideal form to reproduce.

Based on this methodology, I think it is fair to say that today there is already research into the possibility of a pictorial intervention that would let painting express itself, to work, from itself as such. To show a work/painting that is first and foremost itself and not an account of a state of the soul of the "creator."

Let's say that since 1965 I have been "working" with this pictorial issue. Before I could say that I did nothing or did everything, loved this or that. I think that this has no interest in regards to my actual work/painting and could only distort the concept (positively, negatively: which is the same).

For example, I hate exhibitions where in order to see the interesting works an artist made at a certain moment, one is obliged to pass through rooms full of works with no interest. Works from youth, from old age, that's not the issue. It's there to reassure, in quantity: so much work, what virtue . . .

Ah, virtue! One lugs around that good old Christian guilt.

I would say that my work/painting has nothing to do with works of the majority of artists. Those are artists (perhaps major); I am simply a painter! Banally a painter. I do not visualize ideas: I apply a paintbrush, imprints of the paintbrush become visible and this (work/painting) can give ideas.

And how each one illustrates its ideas.

———

The images that follow demonstrate and inform a part of the work/painting produced over the past 20 years.

Their point in common, the criteria for their selection, is that that they refer to works that are always inscribed on walls, floors, doors, places where they were visible.

These places can determine the different manner of each of these interventions, and often their duration as well. The majority of paintings exist only during their time in the exhibition. But in this case their precariousness makes up part of the game (my game your game his game our game their game) and can make for some risky bets. (Difficult to win every time! If art amateurs don't get it, too bad, the poker players will forgive me.)

In any case the frenzy of changing the site does not make any more work for managers than usual: one, two coats of white and voilà, no harm, no foul, so long imprint of a no. 50 brush. Only the images remain. After all, although one could never replace the work/painting itself, they have their right to make their merry way as images in a catalogue, which is always just a book of images. A beautiful catalogue, a beautiful wine list, but the essentials remain: to see, to drink. But this too is only an image, just like the "lively" wolf, turning round in his cage, in all the zoos of the world.

January 1985

It was suggested that I write several lines for the pamphlet published on the occasion of the exhibition. It seemed to me this time the reflections on art (evidently profound) abounded: its state, its life, its death, its resurrection, its workers, its dealers, its critics, its civil servants, its popular success, its avant-garde, its being modern. Postmodern, anti-postmodern, its fathers, its children . . .
Everything happens.

Well, while waiting for it to happen, I propose that on one hand you read my method of work, and on the other, an extract of a text from Tchang Yen Yuan [Zhang Yanyuan] which, although from the Tang dynasty, might reveal itself to be astonishingly contemporary.

Method of work: A no. 50 brush is applied to the surface at hand, at regular intervals of 30 cm.
Surface: canvas, cotton, paper, oilcloth, wall, ground . . . white, usually.
To apply: "to put one thing on another in a manner that covers it and sticks, or leaves an imprint" (Robert, French language dictionary).

305

305

305

305

305

No. 50 brush: wide flat brush of 50 mm.
Interval: " . . . distance from one point to another" (Robert, French language dictionary).

The work/painting presented: Imprints of a no. 50 brush repeated at regular intervals (30 cm). Imprints of a no. 50 brush repeated at regular intervals (30 cm) were visible for the first time in a public place in January 1967 (Paris, musée d'art moderne [*sic*], salon Jeune Peinture). Since then, the work has been visible in different specialized sites (galleries, museums . . .) or others, but the only enumeration of all these presentations of work that could have taken place since 1967 would not be in the least an indication concerning work/painting itself, thus it is useless.

. . .If the ideas of a painter are confused, he will become the slave of exterior conditions. In a true painting, each brushstroke reveals life. He who deliberates and moves the paintbrush intent on making a picture misses to a still greater extent the art of painting. On the contrary, he who reflects and moves the paintbrush without any intention of making a picture will reach the art of painting.

Tchang Yen Yuan [Zhang Yanyuan]
Historian of Chinese art, Tang dynasty (618-907)

Paris, 19 February 1986

"What are masterpieces?..."

As I do not believe in masters (horrible, the need of a master!), neither do I believe in masterpieces. There is a work made that produces a visible product: its product, known as the "work."

For me, the work is everything, produced by a certain labor (of painting, sculpting, writing...). That could concern a single period in the production of an artist: that which concerns and interests me; in any case it's never a lone object (canvas or sculpture or intervention) that as a "masterpiece" ought to be exhaustive. Therefore, I can tell you Pollock's works (his "drip" period) and Serra's works (only sculptures) are important to me. In searching more thoroughly I could find others, not many, but I don't like lists. I will add, modestly, that anyways, it is my own work/painting that interests me the most! Yet I'm convinced I have never produced a "masterpiece."

"The masterpiece"

The additional question disappears.
But in any case, if there were a masterpiece, it would be neither initiator nor symptom of a revolution, nor a marginal phenomenon, but a monument to the dead. One more headstone in the cemeteries of art, which generally provoke the same emotions as certain tombs in Père-Lachaise.
Can one carry out revolutions (even simply artistic ones) by waiting in line?

Paris, 10 March 1988

Extracts from interviews (1988-1990)

"Imprints of a no. 50 brush repeated at regular intervals of 30 cm" is the title of all my works and all my pieces. It's the literal statement as I have already written it; this wording is the common denominator of all work/paintings; it says everything and nothing (means nothing) if one doesn't see the given work.

It's neither the concept of imprint, nor whatever is imprinted that interests me. For instance, Yves Klein made gorgeous imprints with gorgeous ladies. At school, when we were small, we cut potatoes in half and made potato prints; this produced very pretty things. One foot in the snow, Robinson Crusoe who, thanks to the footprint he saw on the island, discovers Man Friday—yet this pursuit has nothing to do with my own concerns. My work does not consist of looking for forms that make beautiful imprints. Although, we could also talk about my dentist—he too makes imprints of teeth, very beautiful.

It's true that I do not sign my works, I date them. At my first solo exhibition at Yvon Lambert in 1970, my name did not appear on the invitation. People were invited to come see "imprints of a no. 50 brush repeated at regular intervals of 30 cm." Time passed and, today, by some sleight of hand, my work has been conflated as my signature. Apart from the fact that one could argue this for the work of any artist, regardless of whether or not his name appears at the bottom of the work (could one say that the baguette is the signature of the baker? Surely), I allow myself to repeat that I am not in agreement. Or else, going back to these remarks, I would say: my imprint of a no. 50 brush is made plainly, without lyricism. Application applied, an imprint of a no. 50 brush could also be made by someone else. But then this would be a way of returning to the simplicity and anonymity of the cross that served as a signature for people who did not know how to write. Let's not forget that this has already been done. Seeing a cross at the bottom of a page, one couldn't consequently attribute this as a signature always referring to the same person. The same thing happens when you see the imprint of a no. 50 paintbrush. What's important is what you see, its interest is not whether it was made by me or by someone else. It is no longer my image, just as the cross is the image of anyone not knowing how to write. Apart from this, I assert without shame the work/painting that I make, and I do not seek anonymity.

When someone tells me that I'm always making the same thing, this makes me laugh because it's false and foolish. I myself never know in advance what the reality of the paint will be. Anyone can say that work/painting is not of interest, but not that it is always the same. Each work is never the same thing, just as each imprint of a no. 50 brush is never the same. Hence the impossibility of reproducing it mechanically! One must go through it, one has to do it. I could stop tomorrow, in three days, in ten years. I don't know, but I do know that I should stop when I can no longer hold a paintbrush.

[. . .] I was working Friday night and Saturday in the hallways of a medical institute; Monday morning, the painting being dry, I rolled the waxed canvases and I carried 15 to 20 meters of paintings under my arms, so that I could next cut according to its needs. What already interested me at this time was to work in systematically "completing" the given surface, without looking, and refusing even the idea of the ideal format. I still think there is no ideal format except for the masterpiece: there is an "overall work," which one sees in parts, in clippings. Paintings on waxed canvas raise the question of visibility of the painting: the "piece" was visible according to where the roll was placed. If we had a picture rail of 4 meters, it would unroll and one would see 4 meters of painting, on a wall of 5 meters one would see 5 meters, on a balcony of the 3rd floor one would see 10 meters, etc. With waxed canvases, place has already physically circumscribed the given view.

When I make an exhibition, I work on site a lot, directly on the walls, according to the place that I find, considering the height of the walls, the type of architecture. Thus I rarely travel with canvases beneath my arms. Nevertheless, throughout the exhibition *Twenty Years of Imprints* at Villa Arson in Nice, and at the Museum of Painting and Sculpture in Grenoble, I showed several old works. Each time I have placed them with present-day interventions, for the purposes of disrupting the idea of the retrospective and revealing, in my case, its limitations.

[. . .] I often say, without coquetry, that I am not an artist but a painter. Banally a painter. Thus it is difficult for me to use other materials besides paint for paintings. Yes, it did occur to me to use Chinese ink. One summer I was on vacation, I didn't have much of a place to stay and I wanted to "explore" the possibilities offered by this ink. Very beautiful the effects that Chinese ink offers in drying! But, with my method of work, the chosen surface also determines and limits the choice of paint. For example, I cannot use glycerophthalic lacquer when I paint on the wall: it would drip, and I wouldn't want any dripping. To think that I went through a part of my life making drippy experiments, to come to doing something that doesn't drip at all! When I work, I also use acrylic paint, vinyl paint, that mixes with water.

I like to choose colors just as I find them, produced industrially. Unfortunately, the brands change, the styles, the acrylics become so glossy. As long as I won't be obliged to grind my colors myself one day! It came to me that I ought to propose to collectors who want a work/painting to choose the color that suits them. One that they ought to be able to endure. For my part, I can be guided by diverse motivations. In Grenoble, for example, my intervention in one of the rooms had one side red, the other black. For Stendhal. Why not? I could have done a green and yellow work, perhaps that wouldn't have been so interesting. Nor any better nor worse? I'll never know, not having been able to see this work.

My grand utopia, my grand stupidity, is to believe that there is yet something to do after Pollock, without using—either trivializing or rendering more precious—a preexisting form. What I call "imprint of a no. 50 brush" is a form that doesn't exist. I called it such, because it is the result of a work of painting: to apply the bristly part of the brush, the part used for painting, on a given surface, so that the color is deposited and becomes visible there. Well, one sees a spot of color, obtained in applying a brush on a surface. But in the *Petit Robert*, the French language dictionary, one reads: "To apply: to put one thing on another in a way that it covers and adheres to it, or leaves an imprint." Yet it's not I who leave an imprint, rather it's the no. 50 paintbrush!

Consequently, rather than talking about marks, of vaguely quadrangular forms, of brushstrokes, it seemed to me that the simplest thing to do was to name the "thing": the "imprint of a no. 50 brush." There it is. The imprint gives itself only to be seen. Its origin, a paintbrush of 50 mm long. The imprint is the form that this tool leaves, soaked in paint, on the "surface" where it is applied. This form exists thus because there is an act of painting and not because one fine day I woke up saying: "Ah! There it is, what a beautiful form!" It's for this reason that to cut a particular form, whether that be Matisse-like or geometric—as this comes back in style today—and to repeat it indefinitely doesn't interest me at all, be that by cutting, by imprint, or by collage.

[. . .] I do not refuse my subjectivity. Quite the opposite. But it must stay subjective.

I think that the things that have interested me in all realms are those that, by their force or their presence, go beyond the individual behind it, and become general.

Fundamentally, my aspiration is that one finds what I'm doing pictorially interesting without questioning who made it, as when one discovers anonymous frescos of the twelfth century.

[. . .] It happened to me long ago, that I started painting for entire days, during working hours, to paint as others work, with the same rhythm, 8 am-12 pm, 2 pm-6 pm. Methodically, I was collecting geometric bicolored painting motifs on the linoleum. This work, which could seem fastidious, already limits itself to holding a paintbrush and applying it to a painting; at the same time it allowed me to struggle against the image of the inspired artist, who could do whatever he wanted. Today, I think that the imprint of a no. 50 brush was born from gestures of markings on linoleum. I told myself: "I will put white here, blue there . . . " to "color" the preexisting geometric form seemed to suffice for a day, to be self-sufficient. There was the painted and not-painted. The painting no longer hid the surface, as it always had. Nor was the surface primed.

One could see that there was a pictorial intervention, played out by intervals. The equilibrium between the painted and not-painted seemed "right" to me when the intervals were 28, 30, 32 cm; let's say between 28 and 32 cm. These works drove me to push myself, to go even further in my discipline. For example, to mark in advance with a compass all the 30 cm, the points of intervention. All this is always done in a very pragmatic way. I could recount all this, but I am convinced that if I continue to paint today, it's because there are things happening there that escape any utterance. Irreducible to writing, to being photographed.

M.B. OF THE SACRED IN ART
TO FIGHT AGAINST SACRED ART*

M.B. died in 1976, without having been either an official artist or even professor at the Beaux-Arts Academy.
That's already not so bad.
During his life, his work, which never adhered to a

specific approach, disturbed, shook up quite a few common beliefs and, in the milieu of these "connoisseurs," though he was not known as one of the greatest artists of our century.
Too bad that he is no longer here to hear this. I see him laughing, a good laugh.

M.B. Clarity, irony, listening to the world (not only the art world).
Produced some good work and some less good work: currently the exhibitions devoted to him are no longer—could no longer—be his exhibitions (and we know what his presence was and his importance of "direction").
Sometimes one stumbles thus on exhibitions that are only suites of objects where the less appealing take precedence and it doesn't sit too well. From this comes what you might call a difficult reception for those who don't know M.B.
When M.B. was present in his installations, presentations, productions, there was always a "joy of learning" somewhere. His films and books remain (his catalogues are all little books) to watch in trying to see this.

M.B. was a great brewer of ideas, images, and words. That has always been clear to me: he, the Artist (with all dangers and deficiencies which this brings), me, simply trying to be a painter. Perhaps with *The Raven and the Fox*, one must now recall: *The Eagle, The Parrot and the Camel* or: the solitary M.B., the artistic milieu and his cacophony, the haughty visitor of exhibitions. Seated in the shade of palms, evidently.

But let's never confuse a palm tree with a urinal: this is not the same story.
Thank you Marcel Broodthaers.

Niele Toroni
Paris, 21 November 1994
(Response to Dorothea Zwirner)

**L'Angelus de Daumier*, exhibition by M.B. in Paris, 1975.

---

p. 289, "Bon appétit," 1962 and "Monologue with you," 1963: *Niele Toroni* (Bordeaux: CAPC Musée d'Art Contemporain de Bordeaux, 1997), 52. Originally published in Niele Toroni, *En roue libre*, ed. Alain Coulange (Saint-Julien-du-Sault: Éditions F.P. Lobies, 1984), hereafter cited as *En roue*.

pp. 289-290, "Ah! These Artists," 1964: Ibid., 52. Originally published in *En roue*.

p. 290, "Dear Family," 1964 and "Face up...," 1966: Ibid., 53. Originally published in *En roue*.

pp. 290-291, "Very often...," 1966: Ibid, 53. Originally published in *En roue*.

p. 291, "It could be...," 1968: Ibid, 55. Originally published in *En roue*.

p. 291, "Works of art...," 1967: Ibid., 55. Originally published in *En roue*.

p. 291, "We could see...," 1971: Ibid., 60. Originally published in *Niele Toroni* (Cologne: Galerie Michael Werner, 1971).

p. 292, "Banalities to repeat again and again in the art world," 1972: Ibid., 60. Originally published in *Actualité d'un bilan* (Paris: Galerie Yvon Lambert, 1972).

pp. 293-294, "Discussions with...," 1967-1977: Ibid., 63-66. Originally published in *En roue*.

p. 296, "Federal Office of Culture, Bern," 1977: Ibid., 66. Originally published in *Niele Toroni* (Bern: Kunsthalle Bern, 1978).

p. 297: Cover image of Niele Toroni, *Galleria Allegria* (n.p.: Printed by author, 1981), hereafter cited as *Galleria Allegria*.

pp. 298-299, "to the one...," 1981: *Niele Toroni* (Bordeaux: CAPC Musée d'Art Contemporain de Bordeaux, 1997), 77. Originally published in *Galleria Allegria*.

pp. 300-301, "homage no. 2," 1981: Ibid., 82. Originally published in *Galleria Allegria*.

p. 302, "Why do rich...," 1978: Ibid., 68-69. Originally published in *Niele Toroni* (Bern: Kunsthalle Bern, 1978).

pp. 302-303, "Interview," 1982: Ibid., 102. Originally published in *En roue*.

pp. 303-304, "The images...," 1985: Ibid., 105-106. Originally published in *Niele Toroni: Coup d'oeil* (Paris: Musée d'Art Moderne de la Ville de Paris, 1985).

pp. 304, 306, "It was suggested...," 1986: Ibid., 106-107. Originally published in an exhibition catalogue of unknown title (Coutances: Galerie L'Hermitte, 1986).

pp. 306-307, "What are masterpieces?," 1988: Ibid., 108-109. Niele Toroni's response to a questionnaire from Musée d'Art Moderne de la Ville de Paris, 1988.

pp. 307-310, "Extracts from interviews," 1988-1990: Ibid., 116-118, 120-121. Originally published in *Niele Toroni* (Stuttgart: Württembergischer Kunstverein, 1991).

pp. 310-311, "OF THE SACRED...," 1994: Ibid., 131-132.

All selected writings translated by Jocelyn Spaar.

Autobiography

My name is Niele Toroni. I was born on March 15, 1937, in Muralto, on Lake Maggiore. It is in Ticino, the Italian-speaking part of Switzerland, in the southern Alps, and in the spring the camellias and mimosas are in full bloom; there are also palm trees, banana trees whose fruit never ripens, and lemon trees, which do produce ripe fruit now and then. (Whenever this happens, it makes the press.) In the garden of my childhood, there were even gardenias. In Muralto, on June 29, 1940, Paul Klee died. I have been told that he did not live very far away from us, but quite honestly I don't recall him. Mikhail Bakunin had stayed in the same neighborhood—I think it was in the villa Baronata—but that was a long time ago. Four kilometers away, in Ascona, a number of unsuccessful artists and small-time philosophers had gathered, but I didn't experience those glorious times either. A pity; otherwise, I might never have gone to Paris.

When I was a little boy I used to accompany my father, a great trout angler. The mountain streams taught me a thousand and one of the tricks of good fishermen. In August I would catch grasshoppers—not the green sort, but brown ones with yellowish-orange bellies—which we had to attach to our hooks without damaging them too badly. You should have seen the trout leaping up to swallow the grasshoppers as they were borne along on the current!

When the water was muddy, during or after a storm, we would use worms for bait: beautiful, purplish-red worms that I dug up in the neighbor's garden, and which wriggled around in the can. It was important not to forget to pierce holes in the lid—otherwise, they would suffocate. It was quite an art to thread them onto the hook, making sure the metal was entirely covered and leaving only a wriggling tip free.

We used to make our own flies with feathers, threads of wool, threads of silk in every conceivable hue, variously sized hooks, and a little glue. Every stream had its favorite colors, for the trout were creatures of habit. Best of all, though, was fishing with live bait.

My mother had a beautiful voice. She often sang, accompanying herself on the piano; she knew a lot of French songs, from

315

315

315

315

315

"Roses blanches," which made me sob, to "Rikita," interspersed with "J'ai deux amours: mon pays et Paris."

Later came the time with my friends. In 1954, the brothels were still open in Italy. The ones in Intra and Como, just across the border, welcomed us with open arms. Even better, with the exchange rate in our favor, it was a gift! In Milan, the Chiaravalle really was a "clear valley" for us; on occasional Sunday afternoons we would go there on a pilgrimage, after the Milan-Inter game. It was there that I did my first nude studies. The blinds, always down to keep out the sun, accentuated the chiaroscuro.

In 1956, after indeterminate studies at the école normale, it was time for me to earn a living. I got a teaching post in Maroggia, Switzerland, on Lake Lugano. In the evenings I attempted to paint. Through my window I could see in the distance the lights of Bissone, the village from which Francesco Castelli, alias Borromini, had departed a few centuries earlier. Carlo Fontana and Carlo Maderno had set forth from the banks of the same lake before him.

In 1959 I decided to go to Paris "to paint." Today, December 6, 1986, I am still here and painting.

Paris, December 6, 1986

Let me update my biography by adding that on December 25, 1993, I played Father Christmas. Besides this, I keep trying to paint, despite a growing conviction that there's no gaining control over a painting.

Paris, January 30, 1994

Biography update

In 1997, the year of the buffalo, I celebrated (and celebrated well) my sixtieth birthday. I received a bottle of Armagnac as a gift, a vintage bottle that is supposed to be the same age as me. But the package, the bottle, the label, it's all so beautiful (a real work of art!) that I haven't dared have a go at it yet. So I still can't tell you if it is good, very good, very very very good . . .

Otherwise, I've noticed that, despite my sixty years, I still don't take myself too seriously. Luckily enough, I take the art world even less seriously, along with its regiments of arted forces, whose members I occasionally meet and sometimes read.

Probably this accounts for the fact that I still feel like doing my work/painting.

Everything is beginning. Look at this letter from Rainer Maria Rilke to Lou Andreas-Salomé:

Oberneuland near Bremen
August 11, 1903. Tuesday.

I don't want to separate art and life; I know that at all times and in all circumstances they have the same meaning. But in face of life I'm awkward, so it focuses all its efforts on me, stops me, holds me back, and makes me lose many opportunities—like in those familiar dreams when you just can't finish getting dressed, and because of the stubbornness of two shoe studs, you let an important occasion slip away. And it is true that life passes and that it doesn't allow for tarrying or wasting time, especially for anyone who wants to be an artist. Art is something that is much too big, too heavy, and too long for one lifetime, and old people have just barely started down the road. "I was about seventy-three when I understood more or less the real shape and nature of birds, fish, and plants," Hokusai wrote. Rodin has the same feeling, and so, no doubt, did Leonardo da Vinci, who died so old. And yet they lived out their lives in their art, focused on that single object and bringing all else back to it: how depressing then it must be for someone who seldom rises to his sanctuary because he lets himself get caught in all the snares that life sets to trap him, and helplessly collides against all the obstacles. If I seek with such anxiety and such impatience each day's work, each day's task, it is because life can only become art if it is at first labor . . . Please forgive me if I keep you waiting: like a guide you've started out on the journey, but I am still straying, straying like animals do when the hunting season is no longer closed . . .

Paris, July 1997

Translated by Gila Walker.

Niele Toroni includes an autobiography in all of his catalogues. He has chosen not to update his autobiography for this publication, but rather to publish the 1997 version, which originally appeared in *Niele Toroni* (Bordeaux: CAPC Musée d'Art Contemporain de Bordeaux, 1997), 151-152.

Biographies

ALEX BACON is a regular contributor to *The Brooklyn Rail*, has taught at the School of Visual Arts, and has served as a guest critic in the graduate painting departments of the Rhode Island School of Design and Academy of Art and Design St. Joost. He has curated several exhibitions, including *Morris Louis/Landon Metz* at Paul Kasmin Gallery, New York (2016), and is coeditor, with Hal Foster, of a collection of essays on Richard Hamilton (2010). Bacon has also written about artists including Francis Alÿs, Simon Hantaï, Frank Stella, and Ad Reinhardt, and is currently finishing his PhD in Art & Archeology at Princeton with a dissertation on the first decade of Frank Stella's career.

JOACHIM PISSARRO is the Bershad Professor of Art History at Hunter College and director of the Hunter College Art Galleries. He was formerly a curator in the Museum of Modern Art's Department of Painting and Sculpture. Pissarro received an MPhil in history of art from the Courtauld Institute of Art, London, and a PhD in art history from the University of Texas at Austin. In 2016 he curated, along with Annie Wischmeyer, *Buren, Mosset, Parmentier, Toroni* (Hunter College Art Galleries, New York). His most recent book, *Wild Art* (2013), and his forthcoming publication, *The Blind Spots of Art History*, were both coauthored with David Carrier.

HARALD SZEEMANN (1933-2005), one of the most influential curators of his generation, organized more than 150 exhibitions during a career that spanned almost five decades. Born in Bern, Switzerland, Szeemann studied art history, archaeology, and journalism in Bern and Paris. He organized his first exhibition in 1957 and, in 1961, became one of the youngest museum directors in the world when he was appointed to head the Kunsthalle Bern. From 1961 to 1966, Szeemann was also in charge of the exhibition program at the Städtische Galerie Biel. Szeemann gained prominence through a series of exhibitions that included early projects by Robert Rauschenberg, Andy Warhol, James Rosenquist, and Christo. In addition to showcasing developments such as kinetic art, op art, and happenings, Szeemann also examined areas of early twentieth-century modernism such as

Dada and surrealism, including work by artists such as Marcel Duchamp, Kazimir Malevich, and Vasily Kandinsky, as well as art brut, science fiction, and religious iconography.

ANNIE WISCHMEYER, while associate curator of Hunter College Art Galleries, together with Joachim Pissarro curated *Buren, Mosset, Parmentier, Toroni*, the first-ever exhibition on the BMPT group (Hunter College Art Galleries, New York, 2016). She has also organized numerous other exhibitions, publications, and events.

Acknowledgments

First, I would like to thank Niele Toroni for his invaluable contributions to this book. His willingness to provide readers with such a personal, candid glimpse into his interests and influences has imbued this publication with unprecedented insight into the artist's practice. I would also like to thank his longtime assistant Giovanni Varini, who played an essential role in bringing Toroni's exhibition at Swiss Institute to life.

I am deeply grateful to the exhibition's curator, former Swiss Institute assistant curator Clément Delépine. His sharp insights and encyclopedic knowledge of Toroni's oeuvre resulted in the artist's work being exposed to scores of new audiences, while simultaneously providing a long-overdue reexamination of his practice for those already familiar with it.

Distilling a career as expansive as Toroni's into just a few pieces requires the guidance of those who know the artist and his work exceptionally well. I wish to thank Marian Goodman and Nicolas Nahab for their support and wisdom every step of the way. I am also grateful for the sage advice offered by Yvon Lambert, Olivier Belot, and Alexa Brossard throughout the exhibition process, and would like to express my gratitude to the immensely generous Herman Daled, Sylvie Winckler, and Pietro Spartà for their contributions as well.

For their brilliant essays, I must thank Joachim Pissarro, Annie Wischmeyer, and Alex Bacon, who have managed to further historicize Toroni while simultaneously emphasizing his importance for the next generation of conceptual painters. I would also like to express my gratitude to Jocelyn Spaar, who provided translations throughout the book.

I would like to thank Karen Marta, along with Christopher Impiglia, Artrit Bytyçi, and Tommaso Speretta for their superior editorial guidance and ceaseless creativity. Without them, this book would not have been possible.

The brilliant team at Karma, Brendan Dugan, Sinisa Mackovic, Elizabeth Karp-Evans, David Schoerner, and Nicholas Weltyk, continues to impress with their talent and generosity. For that, I am immensely grateful.

I want to thank Walther and Franz Koenig, whose lasting commitment to Toroni is reflected in their dedication to this book. And I would be remiss if I did not thank D.A.P. as well, especially Emmy Catedral and Skúta Helgason.

The development of both Toroni's exhibition and this publication required the commitment and dedication of all involved. So, as always, I would like to express my utmost gratitude to our remarkable board of trustees and to the Swiss Institute staff and volunteers for their unyielding enthusiasm, particularly Alison Coplan, Laura McLean-Ferris, Elizabeth Baribeau, and Daniel Merritt.

Simon Castets

Swiss Institute

Founded in 1986, Swiss Institute is an independent, nonprofit contemporary art institution dedicated to promoting forward-thinking and experimental art making through innovative exhibitions and programs. Committed to the highest standards of curatorial and educational excellence, Swiss Institute serves as a platform for emerging artists, catalyzes new contexts for celebrated work, and fosters appreciation for underrecognized positions.

Swiss Institute programming is made possible in part with public funds from Swiss Arts Council Pro Helvetia; the New York State Council on the Arts, with the support of Governor Andrew Cuomo and the New York State Legislature; and the New York City Department of Cultural Affairs in partnership with the City Council. Main Sponsors include LUMA Foundation, the Andy Warhol Foundation for the Visual Arts, and Friends of Swiss Institute (FOSI). Leading Partners include UBS and Victorinox. Swiss Institute gratefully acknowledges Stella Artois as Benefactor, Swiss Re as Public Programs Sponsor, and SWISS as Travel Partner.

The SI Series

Embracing the conceptual framework of an exhibition at Swiss Institute and its related public programs, each book in the SI Series adds retrospective context through seminal essays, archival materials, event transcripts, artist portfolios, and exhibition documentation, as well as reprints and new translations of important texts.

OTHER TITLES IN THE SI SERIES

Allyson Vieira: The Plural Present
Heidi Bucher
The St. Petersburg Paradox
Fin de Siècle
David Weiss: Works, 1968-1979
Work Hard: Selections by Valentin Carron
PAVILLON DE L'ESPRIT NOUVEAU: A 21st Century Show Home
Hans Schärer: Madonnas and Erotic Watercolors
FADE IN: INT. ART GALLERY - DAY
Sam Lewitt: Less Light Warm Words

Published for the exhibition
Niele Toroni
at Swiss Institute, New York,
June 3-September 6, 2015

Editors:
Karen Marta, Simon Castets
Associate Editor:
Alison Coplan
Managing Editor:
Christopher Impiglia
Editorial Assistants:
Artrit Bytyçi, Daniel Merritt,
Tommaso Speretta, Drew Zeiba
Translators:
Jocelyn Spaar, Gila Walker
Copy Editors:
Madeline Coleman, Kyra Sutton
Proofreader:
Clare Fentress
Swiss Institute
Installation Photographer:
Daniel Pérez
Prepress: Ryszard Bienert
Production: Szaransky
Initial design concept by
Studio Marie Lusa

Swiss Institute Staff
for *Niele Toroni*:
Simon Castets, Elizabeth
Baribeau, Clément Delépine,
Alison Coplan, Alexandra
Zigrang, Daniel Merritt,
Scott Kiernan, Alex LoRe,
Lisa Hamilton
Volunteers:
Adriana Blidaru, Milena Buerge,
Oceane Francioli, Sarah Hibbs,
Gaëtane Perret, Kate Raber
Installers:
John McLaughlin, Donals
D'Aries, Victor De Matha,
Giles Hefferan

Niele Toroni wishes to thank
the entire Swiss Institute
team, past and present,
especially Simon Castets and
Clément Delépine, for the
realization of his exhibition
and this book.

This book was made possible in
part by generous support from
The Republic and Canton of
Ticino-Fondo Swisslos.

First published by:
Swiss Institute, New York;
Koenig Books, London;
Karma, New York

Swiss Institute
102 Franklin St.
New York, NY 10013
Tel: + 1 212 925 2035
www.swissinstitute.net

Koenig Books Ltd
At the Serpentine Gallery
Kensington Gardens
London W2 3XA
www.koenigbooks.co.uk

Karma
188 East 2nd St.
New York, NY 10009
Tel: +1 917 675 7508
www.karmakarma.org

325

325

325

325

325

pp. 230-231, 234: *Roll of waxed canvas*, 1968, synthetic polymer paint on coated fabric, 398 × 55 in (1011 × 140 cm). Courtesy The Museum of Modern Art, New York. Partial gift of the Daled Collection and partial purchase through the generosity of Maja Oeri and Hans Bodenmann, Sue and Edgar Wachenheim III, Marlene Hess and James D. Zirin, Agnes Gund, Marie-Josée and Henry R. Kravis, and Jerry I. Speyer and Katherine G. Farley.

Every effort has been made to contact copyright holders and to obtain their permission for the use of copyrighted material. Every effort has also been made to provide accurate information for all the documented exhibitions. The publishers apologize for any errors or omissions and would be grateful if notified of any corrections that should be incorporated in future reprints or editions of this publication.

Printed in Poland

Distribution

Germany & Europe
Buchhandlung Walther König
Ehrenstr. 4, 50672 Köln
Tel.: +49 (0) 221 / 20 59 6-53
Fax: +49 (0) 221 / 20 59 6-60
verlag@buchhandlung-walther-koenig.de

UK & Ireland
Cornerhouse Publications
HOME
2 Tony Wilson Place
Manchester M15 4FN
Tel.: +44 (0) 161 2123466
Fax: +44 (0) 1752 202 330
publications@cornerhouse.org

Outside Europe
D.A.P. | Distributed Art Publishers, Inc.
155 6th Avenue, 2nd Floor
New York, NY 10013
Tel.: +1 (0) 212 627 1999
Fax: +1 (0) 212 627 9484
eleshowitz@dapinc.com

ISBN:
978-1-942607-29-8
(Swiss Institute, New York)

978-3-96098-085-8
(Koenig Books, London)

With the exception of the Swiss Institute section, all exhibition images are from:

Niele Toroni (Kleve: Museum Kurhaus Kleve, 2002)
pp. 134, 144, 184, 191, 194, 200-204 © A. Abbot, J. Abbot, B. Burkhard, S. Crowe, Dalmaz, F. Delpech, M. Goodman, A. Gossens, R. Hofer, W. Kranl, N. Lanfranco, Mancia/Bodmer, A. Morin, A. de Roux, Y. Uchida, J. Ziehe

Niele Toroni: L'ALBUM
(Paris: Centre Georges Pompidou, 1991)
pp. 24, 26-27, 30-33, 34, 36-37, 38-39, 44, 46-47, 82-84, 86-89, 90-94, 96-104, 106-109, 119-124, 126-131, 132-133, 136-143, 148-149, 160-163, 177-183, 186-189 © H. Biezen, J. Brolly, D. Buren, B. Burkhard, M. Capone, G. Cima, S. Dabbeni, Dalmaz, J.F. Guerry, I. Kalkkinen, B. Katz, N. Lanfranco, B. L'Hermitte, A. Morain, A. Morin, A. Romimer, M. Schibig, C. Szwajcer, A.M.P. Toulouse, R. Truckenmüller

Eight people from Europe
(Gunma: Museum of Modern Art, Gunma, 1998)
pp. 193, 196-199 © Chiba City Museum of Art, Chiba; Gallery Shimada, Tokyo; Mancia/Bodmer

Niele Toroni (Frankfurt: Portikus, 1988)
pp. 146-147, 169, 170-174 © W. Kranl

Niele Toroni: 52 pages, 52 pagine, 52 Seiten
(Bern: Kunsthalle Bern, 1978)
cover, pp. 3-4, 6-14, 23, 28-29, 41, 43, 69-74, 76-81 © B. Burkhard

SI
SI
SI
SI
SI

SI

SI

SI

SI

SI